Before the Wind:

Charles K. Landis and Early Vineland

Vince Farinaccio

In memory of my parents

"…with the help of God, I hope to still keep the Vineland ship before the wind."

Charles K. Landis, 1868

"Human beings are imponderable, they can rarely be captured in words. If you open yourself up to all the different aspects of a person, you are usually left in a state of befuddlement."
Paul Auster, 2017

Contents

Acknowledgments

This book would never have been possible if not for the generosity and cooperation of the Vineland Historical and Antiquarian Society (VHAS). The support of its members over the last four years, including former president Ruth Shropshire and current president Sandra Hearing, and the invaluable material that comprises the Society's Charles K. Landis Archives have been vital assets for a book depicting the life of Charles K. Landis beyond the mythology that has defined him for over a century.

In particular, I owe a debt of gratitude to VHAS curator Patricia Martinelli, whose ceaseless efforts and dedication uncovered a wealth of source materials for *Before the Wind*. It was Patt who convinced me to undertake this project, and her belief that I could produce a worthy biography of Vineland's founding father remained the driving force behind my work in researching and writing this book. As a published author, Patt helped keep this project on track, and her encouragement and enthusiasm never failed to spur me on when the completion of this book seemed elusive.

I also want to thank Michael Epifanio and Deborah Ein. In establishing *The Grapevine* newspaper in 2008, Mike felt it was important to include a history column about Vineland and the region. Hiring me to write that column provided me with a welcomed return to the field of journalism, which I had placed on hold during my years as a teacher. From the first issue, Deb has overseen my articles, and there is no better editor with whom I've ever worked. It's not an exaggeration to say that Mike and Deb have provided me with one of the most rewarding experiences in my life, and that experience, in turn, afforded me the confidence to write *Before the Wind*.

My thanks also extend to John W. Carr, who worked his magic for the cover design of this book, Mark Demitroff, who offered information about Landis's early years, and Josephine Walker, who provided several newspaper articles that contributed insight into Landis's final years. This book benefitted significantly from their generosity.

I am grateful to my good friend John Kee for the loan of a multitude of historical materials over the years, including his *South Jersey Magazine* collection, and for his support in my various endeavors since our time together in high school. I consider John's feedback and article suggestions invaluable and his knowledge of local history impeccable.

My thanks also go to my friend and fellow musician Charlie Andaloro who, after reading one of the book's chapters as an early draft, allowed me to see those pages through his eyes and provided me with suggestions that helped strengthen the entire book.

I would also like to express my appreciation to the readers of my *Grapevine/SNJ Today* column. Because of their feedback, encouragement and support, the process of researching and writing each article has never felt like work.

And finally, I am forever grateful to my family – my daughter Jenn and her husband Lee, my daughter Alison and her husband Justin, my granddaughter Kaylee and my wife Kathy, who is my inspiration and my anchor. Together, they keep this ship that is my life before the wind.

Vince Farinaccio
June 2018

Introduction

History is a voyage of discovery. No matter how clear the coastline might appear to be when first glimpsed during the journey, the terrain can reveal some unexpected twists and turns upon closer inspection after you land. In that regard, South Jersey was a virtually uncharted region for many years. It wasn't until authors like John Cunningham and Henry C. Beck came along to share its stories that people began to appreciate its unique charm.

In recent years, Vincent Farinaccio has inspired new interest in the area's past with a weekly column titled "Vintage Vineland/Jersey Reflections" that he writes for *SNJ Today*, a popular weekly newspaper. When Vincent decided two years ago to write a biography about Charles K. Landis, a Philadelphia attorney who would make major contributions to the development of both the region and the state, he had a course already laid out before him. It was the story of a shrewd businessman who, at the same time, seemed genuinely concerned about the welfare of the immigrants who were flooding into the United States in the mid-19th century. It was also the story of a man who, despite all of his business success, suffered serious personal loss and unhappiness. Since the Vineland Historical and Antiquarian Society is the repository of most of Mr. Landis' personal and business papers, it was only logical that Vincent start his trip within the Society's archives.

Little did we realize where the journey would take him.

Wading through countless boxes of correspondence, personal journals and other records of Mr. Landis's life was no small task because the material had never been successfully organized -- until recently -- into a unified system. As a result, countless hours were spent scouring every piece of paper, every photograph for further evidence about the man who could not be stopped from achieving his dreams despite the advent of the Civil War.

Digging into the records of Mr. Landis's life revealed a profile of a complex individual -- a man who fought his business enemies fiercely and at the same time loved not wisely but too well. Intelligent and ambitious, he was a sophisticated world traveler who was not always comfortable around people. Far-sighted, he created a plan for the first Parkway in Philadelphia that would ease the flow of traffic between the downtown and the city's residential area. At the same time, Mr. Landis was sometimes extremely sensitive to what he perceived as a lack of respect toward himself and his goals and ultimately committed murder to avenge his personal honor. Shortly afterward, he wrote one of the first science fiction novels in America when the human race once more turned its collective gaze toward the stars, while revealing insight into the social order of his times.

Both Vincent and I little suspected that the details of Mr. Landis's story would reveal a new perspective not just into his private life but would tell the tale of a country in the midst of far-reaching social, political and economic upheaval. We sometimes tend to look back at the past through the proverbial rose-colored glasses but, the truth is, life in 19th century America was not so different from what we know now. The population was amazed by technological innovations, which at that time included the automobile, the railroad, the telegraph, moving pictures and the telephone.

Industry that formerly depended on the skill of the worker soon realized the advantage of the machine. Tensions ran high in the fledgling nation as some supported causes like abolition, women's suffrage and the end of child labor, while others wanted nothing more than to hold onto the status quo.

Mr. Landis's interest in these and other issues of the day are well-documented and his beliefs affected the course of Hammonton, Vineland, Sea Isle City, and a number of smaller communities that he founded between the 1850s and the 1880s. But while all of his real estate ventures were important to him, Vineland became his crowning glory and would also break his heart.

Charles Kline Landis had embraced the law at a young age, but real estate speculation soon became his passion. When the railroads successfully began to crisscross New Jersey, he -- like many other wealthy speculators -- began to focus serious attention on the region. Working with partners, he purchased land to create the town of Colville that is known today as Elwood. Later, he and a Philadelphia banker named Richard Byrnes re-defined Hammonton into a thriving community, but their partnership was soon marred by bitter disagreement over the town's future.

As a result, Mr. Landis decided to branch out on his own in a new direction. In 1861, he founded the "village of Vineland" on 20,000 acres purchased from Richard Wood of the neighboring town of Millville. Vineland would become his most significant project for a number of reasons. It was the first community that he planned completely on his own and, without partners to muddle his vision, became an internationally-known utopian community. Designed down to the smallest detail, Vineland was meant to be self-sufficient, with an industrial heart that provided what was needed to the farmers who settled on the surrounding acres that were devoted to agriculture. Before long, people, products and produce were shipped in and out by rail, attracting the attention of the nation.

Following the Civil War, Vineland experienced a population boom when thousands of Union Army veterans decided to relocate there to get a fresh start in life. Neither were they afraid to fight for the rights of others. From the start, Vineland was known as a cultural mecca, where speakers such as Victoria Woodhull, Frederick Douglass, and Elizabeth Cady Stanton addressed the crowds on the issues of the day. The women of Vineland are credited with reviving interest in the suffrage movement when they staged the largest public protest ever held in America during the 1868 president election. And, before long, the town welcomed a variety of ethnic groups who were not afraid to work hard to achieve the American Dream.

Although he never held public office, Mr. Landis was proud of this fledgling community and devoted the rest of his life to protecting its interests. Unfortunately, that dedication eventually took its toll. Although he and his wife, Clara Meade Landis, separated after only eight years of marriage, he was an adoring and adored father. Sadly, a rift eventually erupted between him and two of his three sons that was never healed in his lifetime. His personal difficulties soon alienated him from the townspeople, as well, including many who he had once called his friends. In response, he traveled to Europe and beyond but always kept a close eye on the place he once called home.

The Vineland Historical and Antiquarian Society is proud to have been part of this voyage of discovery, which literally has re-written the history of a man who played a significant role in the growth and development of New Jersey. Like many small American towns, Vineland has experienced both good times and bad in recent years -- often struggling to stay afloat in a difficult economy. Charles K. Landis would undoubtedly be proud to know that while the journey has not always been easy, it is far from over.

Patricia A. Martinelli

Curator

Vineland Historical and Antiquarian Society

Prologue

He lay unconscious since the previous evening in a bedroom of his residence on the southeast corner of the Boulevard and the street bearing his name. Outside, on this near-summer day of Tuesday June 12, the town he had established thirty-nine years earlier bustled with its daily business, its residents aware only through a brief newspaper notice that the founding father, who already had a liver condition, had suffered two strokes within a three-hour period and was not expected to recover.

It had been decades since his influence had been allowed to play any significant role in the town's development, but it never deterred him from persistently looking to improve his creation. Once, when his vision thrived, the town became a paragon of progressive thinking just as his design for the settlement foresaw an industrial center surrounded by a sea of agricultural opportunities. Business and farming remained bountiful even if the progressive traits had tapered off and disappeared into a conventional persona well-suited to the start of the 20th century.

A little over three months earlier, he had spent nearly thirty days on a trip to Jamaica, seeking relief from the influenza that had affected him for the past ten years and a change of environment from the one in which he had spent the last five years. Fog had delayed the departure of the steamship *Sampson*, a Quaker City Fruit Company vessel, for one day and foreshadowed the trip.

Forsaking a stop at Montigua, he had disembarked in Port Antonio, where he recalled the birthday of his mother, who had been dead for four years, on February 14. His father had been deceased even longer. At Kingston, he lived at a boarding house for a day, but couldn't bear the isolation of being the only tenant there. His next choice, the Willard Boarding House, provided the company he sought, his isolation again restricted to only his two younger sons who had been drifting out of his sphere of existence over the past year. His wife had drifted away twenty-five years earlier. He chose to write a letter only to his oldest surviving son.

Feeling better, he toured the plantations and took in Sunday services at the largest of Kingston's churches serving the Episcopal faith, of which he was a member. But the cold winds arrived, kicking up dust and dirt and resurrecting his cough, and now home looked like a better place to be. He returned to Port Antonio only to learn of the death of the daughter of a family he had met weeks earlier. The coughing continued. He had become worried about the business he had established decades earlier. And he was lonesome. In the final entry he would ever write in his journal, he reports on having "a very bad night coughing. Am getting anxious to start for home for fear that I shall not live to get there and suffer so much."

But he did live through the return journey, arriving in South Jersey where, despite his ailments, he resumed his preoccupation with running his real estate business with the help of a clerk and a secretary. Work continued throughout the spring. On June 4, he made the three-hour trip to New York on the rail line he had helped create some thirty years earlier but returned that evening, making his familiar trek from the railway station to his home across the street for the last time. The next night, he dined with one of the town's residents who had provided assistance in helping the Italian immigrants who had settled in the town to aid in its agricultural development. Afterward, he suffered a slight paralytic stroke that rendered him bed-ridden and under the care of a nurse.

Cautioned to avoid excitement in order to prevent an additional stroke, he stubbornly ignored the warning and continued to conduct his business interests for Vineland and Sea Isle City, the seaside resort he had also founded, from his bed, summoning his secretary, reviewing balance sheets and contacting his clerk about other work matters.

But at 4:30 a.m. on June 11 he suffered another slight stroke. At 7:20 a.m. a more severe stroke rendered him unable to speak. Later that morning, he wrote a message for only his sister to read and handed it to her. Despite his continued decline, he was able to recognize his eldest living son who visited at 4 p.m.

Sometime that night, he slipped into unconsciousness. When dawn arrived, the suffering was nearly over. As the clock ticked away the morning and afternoon, Charles Kline Landis spent the final hours of his life here on earth. We will never know what thoughts or regrets filled his mind before he sank into unconsciousness. Unlike Orson Welles's fictional Charles Foster Kane, there was no final utterance at the moment of death, no "Rosebud" left to decipher. Landis's life would never allow itself to be distilled into a single word or image and that is why, at 4:15 p.m. on June 12, 1900, he left behind a revealing archive and a town he once referred to as a ship that he pledged to keep before the wind. This is the story of that commitment.

Chapter 1
The Early Years
(1833-1860)

The history of the Landis family was researched and compiled by David Landis of Lancaster, Pennsylvania in 1888. His book, *Landis Family of Lancaster County, A Comprehensive History of the Landis Folk from the Martyr's Era to the Arrival of the First Swiss Settlers*, traces the legacy of his kin back to 16th century Switzerland, claiming "the Landises, among others…were noted for their piety, and were appropriately called Pietists," another term for Mennonites.

The first historical reference to an individual member of the Landis family was that of Hans, described by a contemporary as a "tall, stately person with a long black and gray beard and a manful voice." As "a pious witness of the

Divine truth," he had moved from an unnamed location to an undisclosed town along the Rhine River in the Swiss region and "lived there to feed and refresh others who were seeking after righteousness." The *Martyr's Mirror* reports that he was from Zurich, but this is not accurate since he was only associated with the city during the times of his arrests and death.

Although David Landis does not provide any further background, various other sources claim that Hans was not originally from Switzerland and refer to him as "a preacher from Wadenswil" and "the Anabaptist preacher from Hirzel, Switzerland," even reporting what is an unlikely account that he settled in Alsace. The name "Landis," according to some, is German in origin, but others contend that it is derived from Italian or Roman. The only thing certain is that Hans was the last Swiss Mennonite martyr, a victim of the Council of Zurich which, according to David Landis, consisted of the Reformed, "continuators of the cruel practices known to the martyrs' era" from the Catholic Inquisition that persecuted Protestants.

According to C. Henry Smith's *The Mennonites: A Brief History of Their Origin and Later Development in Both Europe and America,*

> Mandate after mandate was passed throughout the sixteenth century by the Councils of Bern, Zurich and several other neighboring Cantons, forbidding Mennonites under penalty of severe punishment to practise their own forms of worship, and demanding attendance at the state churches. They were ordered to recant and to have their children baptized. Rewards were offered for information leading to

their arrest. In case they refused to comply with the above orders they were fined, imprisoned, exiled and their property confiscated. In case exiles returned, as many of them did, they were tortured and executed, or sold to the French and Venetians as galley slaves…Anyone shielding Mennonites in any way or attending their meetings became subject to a heavy fine and temporary exile.

In an effort to halt his teachings, Hans was arrested by the Council of Zurich, but when the scare tactic didn't work, Hans was bound in irons and transported to Zolothurn, where he was imprisoned in the galleys that had once served Italian princes and were now penal facilities. Aided by a friend who smuggled in a file, Hans sawed through his chains and managed to escape, but he did not flee to South Germany, Alsace or Moravia, all of which "early had become an asylum for persecuted Anabaptists," according to Smith. Instead, he resumed his teachings and was re-arrested.

According to Henry Frank Eshleman, in his book *Historic Background and Annals of the Swiss and German Pioneer Settlers of Southeastern Pennsylvania*, Hans was ordered to leave the country immediately, but he adamantly refused, explaining, "God favored me with this land as well as all others and the earth is the Lord's." Eshleman reports that "he would remain in his native country, as he did not know where to go. Furthermore, he said he was now aged and did not fear death. And, indeed, he could verily say, he did not know where to go to, for in the adjacent Austrian countries the Baptist-minded or Mennonites were persecuted since 1601 unto death by Emperor Rudolph…"

Hans was condemned to death and beheaded in September 1614. Immediately prior to his execution, he encountered his family and an account reproduced by Eshleman reports that

> when the aforementioned Hans Landis was standing in the place of execution, to be put to death, his dear wife and children came to him in mournful crying and lamentation, to take a last and final adieu and leave from him. But when he saw them he requested them to go away from him, in order that his good resolution and tranquility of heart for the death awaiting him might not be disturbed or taken away by their weeping and grief; which having "been done, and he having commended his soul into the hands of God, the quickly descending stroke of the sword put an end to his life."

Eshleman also offers an account of an eye-witness to the execution who later wrote in a letter dated July 19-29, 1659,

> When [Hans], cheerful and of good courage, was led out by a rope, to the Wolfsstadt (being the place made ready for his execution), the executioner, Mr. Paull Volmar dropped the rope, and lifting up both of his hands to heaven, spoke these words: "O that God, to whom I make my complaint, might have compassion; that you, Hans, have come into my hands in this manner; forgive me, for God's sake, that which I must do to you." Hans Landis comforted the executioner, saying that he had already forgiven him:

God would forgive him, too; he well knew that he had to execute the order of the authorities; he should not be afraid, and see that there was no hindrance in his way. Thereupon he was beheaded. After his head had been struck off, the executioner asked: "Lord Bailiff of the Empire, have I executed this man rightly according to Imperial law and sentence?" as though he believed he died saved and rich.

David Landis reports that Hans was the last Swiss Mennonite martyr, but it did not signal the end of the persecution. As Smith explains,

persecution continued unabated for the next two hundred years. Especially severe were the measures passed by the Councils of Bern and Zurich during the middle of the seventeenth and the first part of the eighteenth centuries. Beginning with 1640, mandates were repeatedly renewed ordering the imprisonment of Mennonites. The prisoners were to be visited by the Reformed clergymen with a view to winning them back to the State Church. Failure to comply was punishable by exile. In case of return they were to be whipped, branded with a hot iron and again exiled. Prisoners were fed for months on a bread-and-water diet. Prison cells were usually damp and foul, and full of disease germs causing the premature death of many of the inmates. The property of those who were arrested and condemned was frequently confiscated and given to the nearest relative of the Reformed faith or turned over to the State Church itself.

In May 1637, two other members of the Landis family fell victim to persecution. Hans the Second, described by David Landis as "a steadfast minister of the church in Horgerberg," and his daughter Margaretha were imprisoned for sixty weeks while their property was confiscated and sold, the money pocketed by the authorities. Three years later, Oswald Landis, his wife and two daughters-in-law along with their infant children were incarcerated and Oswald's son Jacob was exiled. Eventually Oswald and his family were released, but they found themselves without property.

Hans the martyr's son, Felix, a member of the church of Horgerberg, was confined in Othenbach and deprived of food. According to David Landis, "his digestive organs became so impaired through protracted fasting, that his stomach refused to retain food, and he accordingly prepared himself for death. In this state he was carried by the persecutors to church during the sermon," and thrown under a bench where he expired. His wife was confined in Othenbach for four years where she endured a series of torments. Upon her escape, she discovered that her family had been scattered and her home and belongings sold. In 1643, the home of Verena Landis was attacked by religious officials. The assault rendered her sick and she was placed under house arrest. Harsh treatment and poor food supplies soon brought about her demise.

Around 1660, the Landises had been driven to the regions of Zweiburg and Alsace on the Rhine. Confiscation of their property became commonplace, but they persisted, becoming farmers for the German nobility. From 1643 until

1717, David Landis reports, there are no surviving records of individual Landises, but there is proof that Mennonites began an emigration to Chester County, Pennsylvania around 1683, taking advantage of William Penn's policy of religious freedom. In 1717, proof of the emigration of three Landis family members is recorded. Benjamin, Felix and John Landis purchased property from Penn and the Conestoga Indians and began to ply their farming trade in the New World.

David Landis writes that his ancestors, "like most of the pioneer settlers in the American wilds, these good people were comparatively poor in worldly possessions, and had their hands so full of work that they failed, it seems, to keep their family records. They became, however, instinctively American in their progress and proceeded at once to skillfully till the soil which has since made this county known the world over as a 'garden spot.' Here, also, these pioneer members of the family worshiped their God according to their desire, and in perfect peace."

David Landis's book offers a glimpse into a portion of his family's European history, but the tale seems to be more complicated than what is offered in this 1888 account. Eight years after the publication of *Landis Family of Lancaster County*, a Boston-published book, *Biographical Review*, asserts that the Landis legacy can be instead traced to Italy, where the family name was originally Landi. The *Casa Landi* website identifies Giovanni Landi, who was living in Florence in the 1590s, as an ancestor of Charles K. Landis. The online information, which differs from the events and dates contained in the David Landis book, reports that the family was distinguished, wealthy and not without influence,

Giovanni's cousins being the Princes of the Holy Roman Empire.

Disgusted with the corruption he saw in the Catholic Church, Giovanni became an early convert to Protestantism during the Reformation of the 1500s, a move which placed him in jeopardy of facing a Catholic Inquisition that could easily result in his death. *Casa Landi* cites Charles V Hapsburg as a friend and political protector of the family. However, after the death of Charles V, Giovanni found himself in a vulnerable position which led to political trouble. Neither the *Biographical Review* nor *Casa Landi* cites the specifics of the problem, but the online source does report that the matter occurred in Tuscany and that it was more than he could handle. Fearing that the Inquisition might be closing in, the Landi clan abandoned its native land for Switzerland, where property was purchased and the family name Germanized to a more acceptable "Landis."

In his new setting, Giovanni Landi became John Landis, but a change in name and location did not prevent the Inquisition from tracking him down. In 1600, John became a victim of the Catholic Church's attempt to counter the Protestant movement. Like all those who had converted to Protestantism, he was found guilty of heresy. He refused to recant and, according to *Casa Landi,* was beheaded.

The death of John Landis under the prevailing reign of persecution that confronted much of Europe left many with only one option if they were to live in peace with their beliefs. The Italian origin story of the Landis family omits details of the immediate aftermath of the beheading but soon merges with the Swiss account when discussing the emigration of Felix, Benjamin and John in their attempt to find religious freedom in the New World, their arrival in what would become Pennsylvania within the same time frame as William Penn and their settlement of what are today Bucks and Lancaster Counties. As of 1896, the descendants of the martyr John Landis, numbering in the thousands, owned much of those counties.

As to which historical account is accurate, David Landis's book, which was researched and documented by the author in Europe, seems more likely. It is possible the Italian origin story is derived from the many Italian immigrants who settled in Vineland during the 19th century and adopted the town's founder as part of their heritage. In his own writings, Landis never offered direct insight into his family's background, even in his journal entries while touring the Tyrol region during his 1874 trip to Europe. It is also conceivable that he was not aware of the details of his family's Old World history until the publication of his relative's book. It is only after the book appeared that he alludes to aspects of his legacy in several of his fictional stories.

As for the family's history in America, Landis's grandfather, John, was a resident of Lancaster, working as a merchant and farmer. He was a landowner, a magistrate, a high-ranking Free Mason and a member of the German Lutheran church. He married a woman identified only by the *Biographical Review* as "Miss Kline," whose Protestant family, originally from Wiirtemberg, Germany, emigrated to the New World around the same time as Landis's descendants and for similar reasons of religious freedom.

The Lancaster couple was blessed with an abundance of offspring. While Mary and Ann died in early and middle life, respectively, the rest of the siblings led successful or adventurous lives. Eliza and Matilda both married California men and settled on the West Coast. Amelia, betrothed to a local man, stayed in Lancaster as did Jesse who became solicitor for the city. Israel ran a saddle store in St. Joseph, Missouri and Edmund had a successful career as a physician in Chicago. John, the adventurer of the group, left to join the Texas Rangers and was never heard from again. It is believed that he met his end at the Battle of San Jacinto.

But Michael G. Landis had a different destiny from his siblings as time would reveal. Born in 1805, Michael began his career with a life of travel before settling down in relative proximity to his family but not in Lancaster County where he had been born. At the age of nineteen, he journeyed to China aboard the *Caledonia* under the command of Captain Bar. Upon his return to the U.S., he followed in his father's footsteps and worked as a merchant before becoming a railroad contractor.

Sometime in the late 1820s, while Michael was probably working in the Philadelphia area, he encountered Mary Lewis Quinn, a former Chester County resident with a background sporting a Quaker heritage and an impressive ancestry that had fought in the Revolutionary War. When exactly Michael met Mary Lewis Quinn is not recorded. Mary had been born June 14, 1808. The *Biographical Review* identifies her as a resident of Philadelphia at the time, her father William having moved the family from their Chester County home to the City of Brotherly Love where he worked as a merchant. His mother had two brothers and four sisters, of which she was the oldest.

Mary's paternal grandfather, William Sr., was a Chester County native whose parents combined a Quaker heritage and a military background. His mother was from the Coates line and owned a lot of property in Philadelphia. His father, an officer in the military, fought in the French and Indian War and lost his life in the Revolutionary War. Mary's maternal grandfather also served as an officer in the War of Independence and was wounded in the leg at the Battle of Brandywine. His wife was descended from the Vogdes family, landowners from the Willis Township region of Chester County.

On July 25, 1830, Michael and Mary married and, three years later, Charles Kline Landis was born in Philadelphia on March 16, 1833. Over the next decade-and-a-half, the couple would have three daughters. Mary, who eventually married John Davis Bishop and then Abbington Russell, died at an early age. Beulah was also married twice, first to James Whitney and then to Dr. Howard Campbell, both Philadelphia natives. Matilda Tyson, fifteen years younger than her brother, would never marry but would establish a close relationship with Charles, moving to Vineland and becoming a significant part of his life.

At the time of Charles's birth, Michael was probably still working as a merchant, but that would change. Over the next several years, he took a job as a railroad contractor with a line that was briefly referred to as the Macon Railroad and Banking Company in Georgia, uprooting his family and relocating to the South. A letter of recommendation from his Macon employer L.L. Griffin, dated March 27, 1838, reveals that Michael sought employment that year at the Western and Atlantic Railroad, a government-owned rail system founded in 1836 that operated from Atlanta, Georgia to Chattanooga, Tennessee. Sources identify that Michael worked for a time in Atlanta, having successfully secured a position with the rail line.

How long the Landises lived in Georgia is uncertain, but they had returned to Philadelphia by the 1840s. Once back in Pennsylvania, the family made regular visits to the Lancaster region to spend time with relatives. The location would leave Charles with vivid recollections of the architecture he encountered there and memories of a generous share of aunts and uncles.

Michael, however, seems to have drifted away from many of his siblings after this period. By 1865, in a surviving letter from his sister Matilda, who was living in San Francisco, he was informed, "I believe you are still in the land of the living tho I do not know where to find you." Matilda tells him, "I would like to see your handwriting once more, tho you did not answer my last letter. I thought I would make another effort…" She justifies her decision to relocate to California but demonstrates her estrangement with her brother by requesting that Michael send a photograph of Charles. "I want to see how he looks since he is grown to be a man."

The early years spent in the company of his parents and their siblings in Pennsylvania seems to have imbued Charles with respect for and devotion to his family. He would remain in contact with his parents throughout his early South Jersey endeavors and relocate them to Vineland once it had proven successful. Their support would prove significant. It was through his mother's efforts that Vineland's founder was able to make his initial payment for the land he purchased

15

from Richard Wood. "My available cash," Landis would later write in his account of the town's founding, "was about $500 in gold which my mother has saved up, and which she handed over to me cheerfully, without question or hesitation, with a mother's faith and devotion." Both Michael and Mary would eventually be buried in Vineland's Siloam Cemetery in the Landis plot that also includes their son and daughter Matilda.

Information about Landis's early years are limited. Since he forged much of his reputation in South Jersey, Landis left behind a lengthier trail of details from his Garden State endeavors. Still, the little that is known about his early life is enough to demonstrate that he was both precocious and ambitious and clearly displayed more than ample abilities in several areas.

Since he would not maintain a journal until the founding of Vineland, there are no records of his daily activities during his youth or adolescence. Neither is there any correspondence that exists from this period. What is known is that, while in Philadelphia, he studied law at the age of fifteen in the office of F. Carroll Brewster and, by October 1852 at the age of nineteen, had passed the bar and opened his law office in Philadelphia. He also established five or six successful building and loan associations, was a member of the Methodist church and a participant of the Democratic Club of the Third Ward, Spring Garden and was a subscriber in 1854 to the Apprentices' Library of Philadelphia, an organization founded in 1820 specifically to provide access to books for children employed as apprentices. Reports indicate that, as a young adult, Landis was around 5'8" with curly auburn hair, blue eyes and a smart, trimmed beard.

Photos of Michael and Mary Landis reveal that Charles closely resembled his father.

The earliest surviving evidence to provide insight into Landis is in the form of a fictional story he wrote in 1846 at the age of thirteen. It's clear that from an early age, Landis had developed a keen interest in literature and during his adolescence had begun to demonstrate an ability to pursue his own literary endeavors, devoting himself to his own writing exercises as time permitted. The extant tale, preserved in a re-copied manuscript which identifies it with the words "Rollin in Paris," was written in Philadelphia and dated September 15, 1846, probably its completion date. It is unlikely "Rollin in Paris was the intended title of the story as "Rollin" is the name of a Paris avenue and the narrative is set in ancient Egypt and focuses on the character of Lara and how her sixteenth birthday sets in motion the hands of fate.

Landis devotes the opening of the tale to a detailed description of his protagonist, "the beautiful Lara…with that excellent contour feature a fair and snowy complexion with dark hair and ardent eyes of the colour [sic] of jet and a form of that which your imagination would picture in some angel descending from heaven…" In Lara, he has created a character with whom he seems totally enamored, his depiction a rendering of the ideal qualities he would seek in a woman. He informs the reader that she "was the only daughter of Scambra the only child by a mother truly lovely who had been plucked from the earth in the first stages of her daughter's infancy…" whereupon she was placed into the care of a female attendant who raised her "in the suburb of the beautiful Palmyra." She was well-versed in the arts, developing "a temperament truly poetical" and "having a voice as choice as a nightingale, an ability on the Lyre chime she would transplant the soul to the spirit…"

Having introduced the reader to Lara, Landis wastes no time in establishing the conflict that will propel his narrative:

> When she had reached the period of 16 summers, when she was in the flower of her womanhood the youths of fortune from every different land hearing the fame of her accomplishments paid to her their vows, but she evinced not that giddiness usual to her sex[.S]he was dazzled by her admiration and indeed was so the point that Scambra began to fear that her affections would center on none of them[.H]is fears were right[;] she well understood their motives and entertained a high disgust for their profligacy[. H]er mind was far to [sic] virtuous and sensible to think of either wealth or rank in conjunction with her happiness and at length, disliking their importuning, she withdrew herself from company, sought relief in the wild scenery of the adjacent mountains where her father had a splendidly fitted palace[.A]t this her parent being not so magnanimous in his principles resolved to make choice of the suitors himself and choose the richest as her betrothed[.T]he person who he chose was one named Kalin, the son of the most wealthy and rich man besides himself in Palmyra…

Kalin travels with Scambra to the latter's palace and Lara catches sight of them arriving.

When she so unexpectedly seen [sic] her father she was much with delight, for nothing ever gave her more pleasure, and gently welcomed Kalin to their hospitalities; when they entered and the ruthless parent introduced the young man as the betrothed he had chose [sic] she was so struck with difficulty to...regain her senses but the half-idiot Kalin supposed that it was the emotions of love for himself and paid very little regard to it, but the father knew far better. He knew he had placed a sting of despair in his fair daughter's breast to pursue her unto death but with his relentless mind...

Interruptions postpone Lara's betrothal to Kalin, and she feels fortunate. But when she spies the character Hessian for the first time, she falls instantly in love with him, triggering a set of events. To prevent him from thwarting plans for a marriage with Kalin, Hessian is thrown into a dungeon carved into the rock of a cliff. To discover his whereabouts, Lara sends her servant Jenna, who talks to Mrs. Boolos. Returning home, Jenna relays the information and Mr. Boolos is enlisted to reach Hessian. The view from the dungeon through a small grated window overlooks the plains. Inside, Hessian is chained to the wall, filled with his love for Lara as the recopied manuscript concludes.

The cryptic title aside, the story bears evidence of the influence of several of Landis's early literary influences. The early descriptions of Lara emulate the love poetry of Byron and, like the poet, Landis may have modeled Lara on a real woman whose beauty was inspirational. The Middle East setting, also reminiscent of Byron, was a location Landis would eventually visit in the last decade of his life but, at this point, he was clearly inspired by his readings. By his teenage years, Landis was well-read in world cultures, especially the history, art and literature of Greece and Middle East.

The storyline reveals traces of the star-crossed lovers of Shakespeare's *Romeo and Juliet* and the protective father who contrives tests for the suitors of his daughter in the Bard's *Merchant of Venice*. Landis's early writing style is clearly in its formative stages. He can be forgiven for employing archaic terminology and favoring British spelling in imitation of his favorite writers, but the lengthy, exhaustive sentences winding from one page to the next, while largely indicative of 19th century prose fiction, reveal that his command of the language needed honing. Still, his style shows promise.

A second story written by Landis survives today in a copied version as well. The original manuscript had been preserved by Landis's clerk Marcus Fry after it had been given to him by the author's father, yet it appears to have been lost after it was copied. The manuscript apparently had been untitled and undated, but it may very well be traced to the early 1850s since, on the back of a page of the recopied version, in unknown handwriting, it is reported there was an inscription on the original that read "Charles Landis, Port Richmond, Philad. Co. Office Corner of 6th and Pine," and identifies Landis as "Attorney & Counsellor at Law," indicating that he had probably begun his legal practice at the time the tale was written. There are misspellings and inconsistencies, including variations in the spelling of several key characters' names throughout the copy, but there is no way to tell if these were the fault of the transcriber or if they existed in the original manuscript.

Landis exhibits a better command of the narrative here while more effectively establishing the exotic setting of the Middle East. His attention to detail when describing the décor of palaces and the ornamentation of cities demonstrates his development as a writer since his first story but is also an early example of the taste he would demonstrate throughout his life, most notably during his European travels.

The story opens with a semi-poetic description of the Egyptian desert where a caravan led by the Arab chief Heskel stops to face the East to worship. The leader, armed with pistols and a scimitar dangling from his belt, is accompanied by twenty warriors mounted on camels and horses. These include Heskel's son, Hespian, who displayed "the same broad forehead, the same decisiveness of countenance...and generosity of character" as Heskel. When the youth joins an Ethiopian warrior, Booloo, the reader learns that Heskel took refuge in the territory of "the wild and scorching hills" of Ethiopia in order to "escape degradation or what his noble soul conceived as such in the ranks of the Turk men."

During his time in exile, Heskel, while traveling with a small group of men including Booloo and his father, is attacked by one hundred warriors of an unknown savage tribe. In the ensuing battle, Heskel saves Booloo's life, but they are the only survivors of the encounter. The Ethiopian travels with Heskel and pledges his loyalty to him. It's revealed that Heskel's caravan is expecting to locate and battle the Egyptian forces in control, wrest power from them and free Booloo's captured son.

In the second chapter, Landis shifts the scene to Thebes, beginning with a detailed description of the scene that concludes with a prose-poem utilizing the archaic language of his models: "Oh Thebes that same moon seen all thy glories then – what ruins see she now, but still thou teachest a sound lesson for when we behold the ample preparations made for thy eternity in existence…" This territory contains an encampment of one hundred warriors, all asleep except for a lone sentry. When the soldiers are awakened, they mount their steeds and await orders from their chief, Scambra. He has "a curl upon his lip [that] told his pride and sarcasm," and shares the same name as the father in Landis's 1846 tale,

This group travels three days, eventually arriving in the proximity of Heskel's troops within the same timeframe as the start of the story. The organization Landis employs in the opening chapters works cinematically decades before the advent of film. Asking the reader to trust the narration, the author manipulates place and time, gradually unfolding the information and leading to the confrontation between the two caravans in a hail of arrows, musket fire and swordplay. In the course of the battle, Heskel is killed and his troops slaughtered. Hespian is wounded and taken prisoner just before a sandstorm obliterates all signs of the massacre. Tied to the back of a camel, he is brought to Cairo, where Scambra's military victory, the details of which are withheld, is celebrated.

In the midst of the rejoicing, Booloo suddenly appears, having survived the slaughter and escaping on a lame camel with Heskel's sword, and reveals to the governors the atrocities committed and the death of Heskel and capture of Hespian. The officials immediately take up arms and storm the prison to free Hespian. Confronting Scambra's forces, they are not successful at first, but redouble their efforts and gain access. They are unable to locate Hespian, but uncover a multitude of political prisoners, both dead and alive, that had been locked away for years, including a Christian knight who had starved to death in his armor. The insurrection then focuses on Scambra's palace, but the citizens find that he has already fled.

Some of the story points may not be properly explained and, along with character, could use more development but, as he would prove again later in his literary endeavors, Landis could successfully render an action sequence so that his readers remain riveted. These early attempts lack the precision he developed as his writing matured, but they are effective nonetheless and are arguably the strongest sections of the early stories.

When the narrative is resumed, Landis once again manipulates time to reveal what Scambra has been doing since the revolt began. Realizing that a revolution was underway, the chief and his guards fled the palace, taking Hespian with them and traveling for several days before reaching Palmyra. Hespian inquires as to his fate and does not receive an answer. Scambra is welcomed and taken to the palace, where his daughter is introduced. Hespian, bound by chains, is taken to this palace celebration, but the manuscript, certainly incomplete, concludes at this point.

However, it's obvious that Scambra's daughter is Lara of Landis's 1846 tale and the names "Hessian" and "Boolos" of the earlier story have been reworked as "Hespian" and "Booloo." Landis apparently meant for his 1846 story to follow his later narrative in what appears to be the beginnings of a novel that was never completed. If that is the case, then his later *A Trip to Mars* would serve as his second attempt at a longer work.

Landis's early aspirations as an author were not unrealistic, but certainly never seriously considered. With more focus on his characterizations and pacing, he could have pursued a literary career. Just how successful he may have been with the readership of his time is certainly open to conjecture, but it is likely that the trade of a writer, particularly one who dealt in fiction, was not seen as an assured or financially rewarding profession, a judgment which Landis would later reserve for the artistic proclivities of one of his sons. It must be remembered that, unlike music, theatre and art, the fictional genres of the American short story and novel were in their infancy in the 1840s, with Edgar Allen Poe, Nathaniel Hawthorne and Herman Melville not yet having published or been recognized for the masterworks for which they are known and Mark Twain still several decades away from defining the American novel. Landis's eventual decision to follow the calling of the legal world before assuming the duties of a businessman was a sound choice for someone as success-driven as he was. Yet, he never completely abandoned his creative abilities, occasionally resuming his fiction writing and using his artistic eye to help design the towns he would establish.

A literary accomplishment that has been attributed to Landis during this period is *Vanity or A Lord of Philadelphia*, a five-act play published by printers T.K. and

P.G. Collins in 1854 with corrections credited to J.B. Addis, a stage manager at the Arch Street Theater in Philadelphia. A copy of the fifty-four-page play is preserved in the Landis archives of the Vineland Historical and Antiquarian Society (VHAS), but there has never been any acknowledgement or existing records that prove Landis wrote the work. What also makes his proposed authorship of *Vanity* questionable is his newly established law practice and recent pursuit of other projects, which limited his writing to promotional pamphlets and advertisements. It seems doubtful he would have attempted to create a work for the stage that would have demanded considerably more attention than he could have provided during this time.

It is more likely that Landis attended a performance of the play and later purchased a published copy. The existence of a script of another play performed at the Arch Street Theater and preserved in the Landis archives at the VHAS seems to support this. Addis is probably the author of the work, and several sources, including the *American Drama Bibliography*, do list him as such. According to the 1870 *Story of the American Stage* by T. Allston Brown, Addis had been born in Kent, England, in 1804. By 1818 he was associated with a private theater on Catharine Street, Drury Lane, London and afterward began appearing at the East London Theater in plays that included a production of *Hamlet* in which he played Bernardo. He relocated to the U.S. in September 1833, and made his American stage debut as Scudio, in *The Mountaineers*, in a production at the Richmond Hill Theatre. For eleven years, he was engaged at New York City's Bowery Theatre, where he worked as a prompter and stage manager before becoming the Arch Street Theatre stage manager in 1855.

It was within two years of establishing his law practice that Landis turned his attention to real estate, setting the stage for his future accomplishments. He discovered he had an aptitude for it and began to favor it over his legal work. His first major real estate venture was as vice-president of a company that set its sights on establishing a town in South Jersey and Landis's involvement with this little-known project could very easily have ended his career as a land developer.

Eager to apply his land development skills in South Jersey, Landis realized that the key to any success he might have in this portion of the state was dependent upon transportation to carry products and passengers to and from locations like Philadelphia. Earlier in the 19th century, transportation of goods relied upon turnpikes, toll roads that used pikes to block passage until the required fee was paid. The surface of these roadways consisted of planks, which were discontinued prior to the Civil War when gravel was used. According to historian R. Craig Koedel, "toll gates were spaced at intervals of five to ten miles. On the average, fees were collected for carriages at the rate of one cent a mile for each horse, a half-cent per mile for a horse and rider, a half-cent for a dozen calves, sheep, or hogs, and a cent for a dozen cattle, mules, or horses."

At shore locations, however, turnpikes were in competition with steamboats, a cheaper method of transportation. And while they continued to be utilized until 1870, the toll roads suffered from inadequate revenue and were soon threatened by burgeoning advancements in other forms of transportation, particularly the railroad. By mid-century, South Jersey railroads were being established by entrepreneurs whose affiliation with glass factories required rail lines to transport their goods out and bring supplies in. Soon, the railroad would become as significant a boon for the farmer, transporting agricultural goods quicker and more efficiently while preserving the freshness of fruit and produce.

The first successful South Jersey rail system was the Camden and Atlantic Railroad Company. The idea for this rail line derived from two distinct business endeavors. The first was the proliferation of glass factories in Camden and Burlington Counties. According to Koedel, "at the southeastern end of Camden County, a cluster of glass furnaces was erected between 1822, when Jonathan Haines set up his Waterford Glass Works, and 1827, when a son of William Richards opened the Jackson Glass Works." Subsequently, a Winslow glass factory was founded in 1829 by William Coffin, Sr., and Jesse Richards opened his factory in 1846 at Batsto. Koedel reports that "by 1850, the owners of these companies were becoming enamored with the vision of financial gains that could be realized by a direct rail connection with Camden and its outlets to Philadelphia, New York, and beyond." This led Samuel Richards, son of the Jackson Glass Works founder, to look into the matter.

The second enterprise to influence a South Jersey rail system belonged to Jonathan Pitney, a physician, who saw the advantage of developing seaside resort towns. Koedel explains that "looking across the bay to Absecon Beach, [Pitney] envisioned a resort where crowds of people would come for ocean bathing, a pastime which he believed to be unsurpassed as an aid to good health." In conjunction with this, Pitney also began examining the possibility of a railroad. Together, Richards and Pitney would help create the first New Jersey rail line that reached across the state to the ocean, connecting the glass factories in the middle of South Jersey to Camden while transporting Philadelphians to a new seaside resort dubbed Atlantic City.

According to George Reeser Prowell's *The History of Camden County, New Jersey*, a charter for the new rail line was easily granted on March 19, 1852. As Prowell explains, "the applicants for the charter met with no opposition before the Legislature, for no one suspected the road would be built. There were no towns of any size on the proposed line, but few manufacturers, and absolutely nothing at the eastern terminus, save the broad expanse of the Atlantic Ocean."

Construction of the rail line began on November 19, 1852. Prowell reports that "the ferry property at Coopers Point, the western terminus of the projected road, was purchased of William Cooper for forty thousand dollars...In October 1853, the road was formally opened from Coopers Point through Haddonfield to Long-a-Coming (now Berlin), a distance of sixteen and a half miles... as any town was reached, a line of passenger cars would be put on, which produced some revenue and encouraged the stockholders. Occasionally rumors were afloat that the work would be abandoned and the slow manner in which the grading and track-laying east of Winslow was conducted seemed to confirm this story."

Koedel writes that "the ceremonial opening of the Camden and Atlantic was celebrated on July 1, 1854, when 600 invited guests climbed aboard nine railroad cars at

Camden and set out across the Pines to the seashore. Pulled by the engine *Atsion*, they traversed a distance in two and a half hours that, up to then, had taken two full days to cover by stagecoach...A year passed before tracks reached all the way to the island. Regular passenger service between Camden and the shore commenced on the Fourth of July 1854, three days after the formal opening of the railroad." Shortly thereafter, the rail system extended its telegraph line to cover the entire route.

The same year the Camden and Atlantic Railroad began service, Landis entered into business with land developers Clayton Allen and Ellwood Matlack that led to the development of the town of Colville, now Elwood, near the new railroad line. While it is generally believed that his first venture in New Jersey was the founding of Hammonton, Landis first became interested in a parcel of land further east known as the Wharton Tract that had housed the Wharton Furnace used during the Revolutionary War. The property was owned by Stephen Colwell, son-in-law of Samuel Richards, and Walter D. Bell, who began advertising its availability in 1851. According to newspaper reports, the land was being sold for $5 per acre and the owners offered any agent able to sell all of it a commission of $10,000 to $20,000. It wasn't until the opening of the Camden and Atlantic Railroad, which ran through the property, that they were approached by Landis, Allen and Matlack about purchasing a portion of the land closest to the new rail system.

The investor's interest in the property began in the autumn of 1854, but a newspaper account in the *American and Gazette* claims that Landis and his partners did not have "the means [and] it is charged that they entered into secret agreements with Colwell and Bell for the land at $7.50 per acre for that part fronting upon the railroad one mile deep and $5 per acre for the balance." A deed signed by all three confirms that what is variously reported as 24,000 or 25,100 acres of land from the north and northwest end of the tract was conveyed to Landis, Allen and Matlack on January 1, 1855. The following month, their business was incorporated as the Weymouth Farm and Agricultural Company, with Landis as vice-president, and work began. Emmett William Gans's biographical sketch of Bell, *A Pennsylvania Pioneer* reports that the property was divided into lots of twenty acres each near the Camden and Atlantic Railroad, creating around 1,200 lots that were soon sold to 600 to 800 interested buyers.

A certificate of indenture housed in the VHAS archives indicates that Landis borrowed from Colwell and Bell, on May 25, 1855, apparently in relation to Colville. The document describes the layout of the town and particularly addresses the Weymouth Hotel, a structure that filled a full block bordering Walnut, Front, and Elm Streets and Weymouth Avenue, a project that seems affiliated with Landis's company and that seems to relate to a $20,000 bond held by Colwell and reported in the later testimony of John W. Thackara who was told by Colwell that the money borrowed was to help the trustees "in building the Weymouth Hotel, paying for the survey of the tract, opening roads and meeting taxes as they came due."

As reported by *American and Gazette*, Landis, Allen and Matlack, "published a prospectus and invited the public to purchase shares, having, as is alleged, first appointed officers and chosen [sic] themselves as trustees. Meetings were subsequently held, a constitution adopted and a committee appointed to purchase the land." The committee was comprised of Landis, Allen and Matlack, who "reported that the land could be had for $10, which was the minimum figure. It was therefore purchased at $10 per acre and the deeds were made to them as trustees of the Weymouth Farm and Agricultural Society [sic]." The trustees repeatedly stated they had only the same interest as the other stockholders in the increased value of the land and pointed out that the property was purchased directly from Colwell with no intermediaries.

By this point, a pamphlet for the Weymouth stockholders, *Practical Hints at a Glance Upon Farming*, had been put together and in it Landis provides his first attempt at promotion. He says that farming is the intention of the stockholders,

> but there are advantages for all. As a residence, it is particularly healthy and agreeable – the water is of the purest kind, and such a thing as fever and ague is unknown. It is destined to prosper, owing to the excellent opening it presents to business. There are many occupations pursued in the city, where people labor under the most exorbitant rents, which could as well be carried on here where living would cost comparatively little. Weavers of fancy stuffs and mechanics of various kinds who send in their work once a week could as well and much better carry on their trades at Colville…it is one of the main stations for the cars and a junction of numerous stage

roads…Improvements are taking an active start, and a neat and commodious Presbyterian Church will soon be in course of construction. For public accommodation, a large hotel has been erected with every convenience. A very fine bowling saloon is within about fifty feet of the main building…a good livery stable will also be connected with the hotel.

If that wasn't enough, Landis appeals to readers by invoking the proximity of the town to the new seaside resort of Atlantic City: "Those who wish to build cottages for summer residences could not do better than by locating here. They would be but a short distance either from Philadelphia or the Sea Shore. They can go down to the beach and spend as much time as they desire and return the same afternoon – thus enjoying all the pleasures whilst they would avoid the dissipation and expense of a watering place."

And in a foreshadowing of his Vineland promotions, he offers, "the price of living is small, whilst such a fine opportunity is presented of laying out beautiful grounds and rural retreats that I think all who want to luxuriate in flowers, shrubbery and fruit should make this place, with ample grounds, capable of being beautifully adorned…at a trifling expense." Landis also anticipated his Vineland settlement by planting shade trees to provide Colville with an aesthetic quality in addition to protection from the sun. In 1880, while traveling on the Camden and Atlantic Railroad, he viewed his first South Jersey settlement, now rechristened Elwood, from the train window and "was pleased with the pleasant appearance." Witnessing the location a decade-and-a-half after its founding, he was particularly pleased with "the noble shade trees I set out."

Almost immediately upon its implementation, however, the paradise depicted by Landis began to show signs of corruption. Allen became secretary of the company with a reported salary of $1,500 a year. By October 1855, with suspicions aroused, the salary was lowered considerably to around $600 before William F. Johnson took over the role as secretary. But other matters contributed to a tainted image as well, particularly in the company's sale of farmland. The *American and Gazette* reports, "a committee [of the Weymouth Farm and Agricultural Company] appraised and fixed a value on each farm. The farms were then offered by outcry at a meeting and whoever offered the highest sum, by way of premium, had the choice of location."

The account also contends that the company "had reserved all the cedars upon a portion of the tract for the next five years." The charge was made that members were not informed of this until the reserved portion had been sold, "which had the effect of 'killing the premium' upon the part where good cedar was, which was not reserved, and it is alleged that all the good cedar land unreserved fell into their hands at little or no premium."

Things also looked grim in Colville itself, particularly when it came to the $20,000 borrowed from Colwell for the construction of the Weymouth Hotel, the payment of taxes related to it and the building of roads around it. The *American and Gazette* reports that John Thackara had informed Colwell that "the hotel was built by a private stock company" which had also paid the taxes, and that the trustees "had not opened any roads, that the [construction] company had done it and that the only money [the trustees] had spent had been upon their own property."

By the end of 1855, it was obvious the Weymouth Farming and Agricultural Company had a public relations problem. Landis was quick to bail out of the project to pursue real estate interests on the other side of the Delaware River. By 1858, the Weymouth Farming and Agricultural Company stockholders brought a lawsuit against Allen, Matlack and Johnson, claiming the defendants had attempted to defraud them. By then, the company had ceased to exist, the land had reverted back to Colwell and Bell, and Landis had already moved on to another land development project in South Jersey. How he avoided the lawsuit and the tainted reputation of fellow Weymouth compatriots remains a mystery.

A year after the Colville fiasco and his return to Philadelphia, Landis developed plans for a steam hydrant and published them in 1856 as *Description of a Steam Hydrant* through King and Baird Printers, a company located on Sansom Street. John W. Nystrom, a civil engineer, provided the formulas and examples on how to construct the invention.

But this new career possibility did not seem to hold Landis's interest very long. His pursuit of another land development opportunity was spurred when he chanced upon a like-minded individual by the name of Richard Byrnes, also a Philadelphia native. He was born in 1830 and, at the age of ten served an apprenticeship at the *Pennsylvania Freeman*, a publishing company, proofreading poems and newspaper articles, including some by renowned author John Greenleaf Whittier. He attended Catholic school and, at the age of sixteen, considered joining the priesthood, but was persuaded by his mother to reject the notion. Graduating from high school, he entered into the study of law but, unlike Landis, worked at a silk importing business before being hired by the Mechanics Bank of Philadelphia, where he was employed as bookkeeper and discount clerk and within six years secured a position as teller. In 1857, he left the bank, becoming a stock and note broker and forming a business partnership with Landis.

Landis and Byrne had both been involved in the Ridgeway Farm and Agricultural Company in Elk County, Pennsylvania in 1855. The company had purchased 27,000 acres of land and issued a promotional pamphlet, the title of which proclaimed *A Farm Within the Reach of Every Man: Pennsylvania Land*. The Ridgeway pamphlet lists Joseph Severns as the person in charge and his address as 43 South Third Street, Philadelphia.

What is most interesting is that the publication was actually put together by Landis's Real Estate Company of which Landis was president, R. Griffith Porter, a wholesale grocer, was vice-president, Franklin Butler, a wholesale jeweler, was treasurer and Samuel W. Catwell was secretary. The Board of Directors consisted of Edwin Jeffries, Abraham M. Brenneman, H.G.O. Ramborger, Charles C. Isling and Jesse Landis, Attorney at Law, Lancaster. The address given was Landis's law office located at 14 Sansom Street.

It's obvious this venture was not a long-term project for Landis. There were more opportunities opening up in South Jersey at the time and he seemed to have little interest in Pennsylvania real estate. By 1857, he would no longer be a part of Ridgeway, yet his commissions continued until at least the early months of that year since documents indicate that both Landis and Byrnes were still receiving payment from Ridgeway in 1857 for lands sold, with Landis earning $74.22 and Byrnes $55.66 on March 7. The partnership with Byrnes, who already had experience with land-warrants in states west of Pennsylvania, led Landis to an opportunity to once again deal with South Jersey property, with a choice of locations in Batsto, Atsion and Hammonton, and this time it would lead to success. Soon, the firm of Landis & Byrnes focused on Hammonton.

It should be noted that Landis and Byrnes did not actually establish Hammonton. Instead, they resurrected it from the ashes of an earlier incarnation. The origins of Hammonton can be traced back to two tracts of land that were combined to form the town in the early 19th century. One tract, a small portion of 13,821 acres owned by the West New Jersey Society and sold to William Richards, father of Samuel Richards, in 1805, was purchased by William Griffith in 1808. This land consisted of 654 acres. A year earlier, Griffith was deeded 944 acres that had originally belonged to the Kirkbride family. In 1808, both tracts became the property of John R. Coates.

Four years later, William Coffin, whose family hailed from Nantucket, Massachusetts, moved from Burlington County and entered into an agreement with Coates to establish and operate a sawmill on the land that became Hammonton. Plied by ambition, Coffin purchased both the mill and the land in 1814.

Illustrated History of the Town of Hammonton reports that "those were the days of small things, when a little money went a good ways, and trade was carried on by barter rather than bank checks. Still the industrious and economical prospered, and to this class Mr. Coffin belonged. The sawmill was his principal industry until 1817, when in company with Jonathan Haines, then in the business at Clementon, Burlington County, he commenced the erection of a glass factory. Haines and Coffin continued the business until 1821, when the firm dissolved, Haines moving to Waterford, and starting the glass business at that place."

Coffin continued to operate his sawmill and glass factory but, in 1836, he leased the works to his son Bodine and his son-in-law Andrew K. Hay. The new firm, Coffin and Hay, only lasted two years and the elder Coffin found himself back in charge.

Coffin's name was never applied to the new town, even though he had structured the settlement with his enterprises, a company store and houses for workers. Instead, just as his son Edward Winslow Coffin's middle name was used to christen a nearby township, Hammonton received its title from the middle name of John Hammond Coffin and, in its first true incarnation, was known as Hammondton, a variation of Hammondtown.

The town relied on other municipalities to provide necessary services. Through the efforts of Coffin, it had constructed a schoolhouse, which also served as a church, but it needed to recruit a preacher from another municipality whose schedule only allowed him to conduct services every two weeks. In the case of medical issues, a physician from Haddonfield was summoned.

Mail service in Hammonton began on December 18, 1827. A stage line that ran between Berlin and Leeds Point would pick up and drop off mail once a week at a station that was set up in the area of Hammonton Lake. Coffin served as postmaster many of the years before his death and was succeeded by several of his sons. But beginning in 1852, the town did not have postal service.

Prior to the arrival of railroads to transport products to Philadelphia and New York, stage lines operated in the area, but travel remained limited. There was a stage which ran from Camden to Leeds Point on Wednesdays and Saturdays, with return trips on Thursdays and Mondays. Businesses like the Coffin glass factory and other industries in the Batsto vicinity resorted to transporting their goods on flat barges by way of the nearby Mullica River.

In 1840, Coffin's glass factory burned down and arson was suspected. The owner wasted no time in rebuilding his facility but, suspicious that his workers had inflicted the damage on the original building, dismissed them outright. To replace them, he recruited workers from Massachusetts.

Coffin died in 1844, leaving his businesses in the hands of two other sons, John and Edward, who ran the mill and factory for two years before Edward decided to sell his share to John.   *Illustrated History of the Town of Hammonton* declares that the town's incarnation as "Old Hammonton" had existed as "a business and social oasis in the wilderness." Factory and mill workers in "Old Hammonton," subsisted on products from Coffin's company store, an arrangement that returned a portion of an employee's pay to the company. Coffin's death marked the end of "Old Hammonton," signaling a decline that, in six years, resulted in both the sawmill and glassworks closing, a consequence of the community's lack of self-sufficiency and its inability to expand and generate new businesses. With both factories gone, there was no security or anchor for the town and it was left staring at its own demise.

Illustrated History of the Town of Hammonton, in its appraisal of the legacy of the Coffin era, eulogizes Hammonton's first incarnation by claiming "while we may flatter ourselves that a decade of our time is worth a cycle of that of the older time, still an honorable fortune was made in those days, and happiness and good fellowship abounded 'at the lake' in those antebellum times."

Several factors, however, hinted at a rebirth for Hammonton in the 1850s, not least of which were the settlements of Egg Harbor City, Landis's first New Jersey real estate venture of Colville only a few miles from the floundering Hammonton and the arrival of the Camden and Atlantic Railroad that could facilitate the transportation of goods. Byrnes and Landis saw an opportunity in the struggling community of Hammonton. The closing of the town's two industries was indicative of the problems facing companies in eastern states in the wake of the movement westward to the new frontier. As William McMahon explains in his book *The Story of Hammonton*, "South Jersey, with the decline of the bog-iron empires and the closedown of many glass-making activities, was on the verge of turning back into a wilderness..." Ultimately, the two Philadelphia businessmen would formulate a plan to build a new community by luring new settlers and transforming the location into an agricultural center with the help of the Camden and Atlantic Railroad that bordered the town. With it, would come more autonomy than "Old Hammonton" afforded.

The pair probably began purchasing Hammonton land as early as 1856 with the intent to sell it in bulk to developers rather than to prospective settlers. According to *Illustrated History of the Town of Hammonton*, "several tracts of this wilderness, in and adjoining "Old Hammondton," were secured by Messrs. Byrnes and Landis to be disposed of as their judgments might dictate. These tracts of land were owned in part by Charlotte Cushman, the actress, by heirs of the Richards family, the Chew and Cooper families, and the Peterson family, of whom the Philadelphia publishing firm are members."

Landis and Byrnes entered their new enterprise with enthusiasm and optimism but immediately encountered a problem they had not foreseen. The sale of a large parcel of land fell through when the funds for its purchase could not be procured and the partners were forced to rethink their strategy of selling in bulk. They decided it would be best to sell smaller lots directly to settlers and began advertising their "Hammonton Lands" in various publications on the East Coast and the Midwest. Their advertisements reached some Northern states in an attempt to draw settlers to a more moderate climate away from the cold winters to which they were accustomed. Farmlands were part of their offerings along with tracts customized to meet the needs of the buyers. With the change in strategy, Landis and Byrnes moved their base of operations to Hammonton, establishing an office in the old Coffin residence on the Central Avenue side of Hammonton Lake and hiring Judge George A. Walker of Philadelphia as selling agent. The new office stood across from the ruins of the Coffin glass factory.

The fact that Hammonton was only a short distance west from Colville seems to have had no repercussions for Landis in his new endeavor. The town was right on the Camden and Atlantic Railroad line and afforded a direct route to Philadelphia for farm products and a direct line to the seaside resort of Atlantic City The railroad would also draw settlers closer to the tracks and away from what would become the White Horse Pike.

The *Genealogical and Memorial History of the State of New Jersey* credits Byrnes with christening the new town "Hammonton." It also reveals that some of the ideas Landis implemented in creating Vineland received a trial run when Hammonton was established. Faced with a territory that was largely undeveloped at the time, Byrnes chose to use some of the Hammonton land for farming to accompany the residential community he envisioned. Landis began marketing the town by placing ads in newspapers, targeting the New England states much as he would four years later when promoting Vineland.

The *Biographical Review* recounts an incident that resulted from Landis's marketing campaign. A newspaper in Augusta, Maine, which had carried an ad for Hammonton, saw fit to declare the South Jersey enterprise "a swindle." Landis immediately rented a hall in Augusta, advertising that he would personally appear there to speak about Hammonton. Facing a capacity crowd, he opened his lecture by inviting the person whose allegations had prompted this visit to take the stage and defend the accusations made against Hammonton. When no one accepted the challenge, Landis plunged into a sales pitch, refuting the "swindle" charges and illustrating the advantages of joining his new

South Jersey settlement. The lecture resulted in "a number of families" relocating to Hammonton. Emboldened by the outcome of his appearance, Landis booked other speaking engagements throughout Maine and Massachusetts to promote Hammonton.

Byrnes and Landis focused immediately on improving the roads in the town. *Illustrated History of the Town of Hammonton* acknowledges that roads "were surveyed in the Fall of '57 and Spring of '58 and opened up as fast as possible. The people came rapidly, and land was sold with a rush, faster in fact than the roads could be built to give the purchasers access to their possessions." Part of the road improvement project included the creation of a street in 1858 that ran from Main Road, the early name for what became the White Horse Pike, to the depot for the Camden and Atlantic Railroad. Upon completion, it was christened Bellevue Avenue.

Postal service was also restored to the town on June 19, 1857. George A. Walker, Landis and Byrnes's selling agent, was appointed postmaster and conducted his duties from his office at the old Coffin residence. Over the next few years, there would be several different postmasters and, most peculiarly, the designation of the Hammonton post office was changed to DaCosta before finally resuming its original designation.

The first land purchased in "New Hammonton" was by Philadelphian Matthew Seagrove on May 15, 1857. The transaction gave him four acres and a house that was a remnant from the property that once contained the Coffin glassworks. Several months later, Captain A. Somerby, who hailed from Newport, Massachusetts, bought property on what became Central Avenue. He constructed the first home of the new incarnation of the town. According to *Illustrated History of the Town of Hammonton*, "all of the first sales of land, and the early improvements, were made in the vicinity of the [Hammonton] [L]ake, and mostly on the Pleasant Mills road."

The appeal of the town even extended to Landis's father Michael who, according to two surviving deeds, purchased land in Hammonton. On November 24, 1860, he acquired a tract located on the Southwest side of Bellevue Avenue and, on February 8, 1861, he bought another tract near the first purchase.

Word of Landis's accomplishments had apparently spread to the Lancaster region. In August 1858, a letter arrived in Hammonton for Michael in care of Landis. In it, one of Michael's brothers notified him about the death of their mother, explaining that funeral arrangements would be held the following week "so that you and the rest of the family may have ample time to attend." The final statement in the correspondence seems to reference either Landis's busy schedule of late or a more aloof relationship he had been developing with his Pennsylvania relatives: "Tell Charles that I expect him present."

Landis and Byrnes had envisioned Hammonton, which was incorporated on March 5, 1866, as an agricultural community, and today it is recognized as the Blueberry Capital of the World, but that was not always the case. McMahon, in his book *The Story of Hammonton*, writes that the town was actually first referred to as "Peach City" because of its large peach orchards. The crops would dominate into the 20th century when, in 1951, a peach festival was organized, attracting thousands each year and sporting a selected Peach Queen, but over the next twelve years, blueberries would begin to dominate and put a quick end to the "Peach City" title that had been representative for nearly a century.

Landis remained in Philadelphia throughout his brief partnership with Byrnes, but by 1858, Byrnes had settled in Hammonton and would remain a resident there until his death in 1909. He continued to develop the town he co-founded, earning the respect of residents by serving as a community leader, as an official of various local boards and as a judge of the court in Atlantic County. According to the *Genealogical and Memorial History of the State of New Jersey*,

> he induced settlers to locate in his neighborhood, thus laying the foundation of his life's achievement— that of converting into profitable farms the wild and undeveloped land of Atlantic county, building up a neighborhood of honest and industrious people, and establishing what has become one of the most important towns in that part of the state. For this result he labored long and earnestly, and the residents of the section are reaping the reward of his labor. For many years he was the prime factor and leading spirit in every movement that tended to develop and improve the section in which he was interested.

In 1869, Byrnes married Fanny Gardner, a native of Boston, Massachusetts. Over the next several decades he served as president of the Hammonton Building and Loan

Association and of the People's Bank of Hammonton, which he helped organize, secretary of the Hammonton Cranberry and Improvement Association, a founder of the Hammonton Electric Light Company and master of Hammonton Grange, Patrons of Husbandry. His business interests were varied and extensive, yet under his control they were successfully carried forward. In 1879, he was appointed judge of the court of common pleas in Atlantic County, serving for twenty years. In 1901, his wife passed away and he married a second time the following year to Lily F. White of Washington, D.C.

The *Genealogical and Memorial History of the State of New Jersey* described Byrnes as

> tall and dignified in appearance, upright in character, of genial disposition, of unusual personality, loved and respected by all who knew him. He displayed keen discrimination in dealing with his fellow men, and for many years prior to his death occupied an eminent place as a leader of commercial interests. His reputation was unassailable, and in all his actions he ever manifested the most marked loyalty to the principles of justice and integrity. He was well known throughout the state of New Jersey, but more especially in the section which he developed and improved, and his death caused genuine grief among a wide circle of friends.

The town of Hammonton earned Byrnes's loyalty and his decision to serve it for the rest of his life was a benefit to the residents. But his former partner had grown restless in Hammonton and, as he had done with his previous projects, was ready to abandon it in pursuit of his next endeavor. In 1859, according to the *Genealogical and Memorial History of the State of New Jersey*, Landis "withdrew his interest" in the firm of Landis & Byrnes. An 1880 journal entry lamenting his current circumstances in Vineland reveals his primary reason for withdrawing from the Hammonton enterprise: "I find myself situated the same as I was in Hammonton, not enough land to advertise and unable to buy around me."

The appeal of establishing his own town, without partners or fellow investors appealed to him. Now it was a matter of finding the right location and his quest led him to temporarily consider Western territory. But that plan did not provide a proper location and Landis found himself looking at land he had already examined a few years earlier, before he had entered into a partnership with Byrnes and agreed to resurrect Hammonton. He now came full circle to the wilderness outside Millville that had first attracted his attention and lured him into a land purchase he seems to have forgotten during the Hammonton project. Slowly and methodically, he was starting to realize that he had already discovered the territory that would house his next endeavor and once his mind was set on it, it was a matter of working out the details to bring it into existence.

Chapter 2
The Birth of Vineland
(1861-1867)

Prior to the Hammonton project, Landis had purchased a tract of land in an undeveloped territory further south from the town he would create with Byrnes. An existing deed shows that he took ownership of the property on January 1, 1856, and that he remained in possession of this parcel until March 15, 1868. What makes this transaction so significant is that the property was in what would later become the Vineland location of Walnut and Orchard Roads, indicating that Landis had been eyeing this region for development well before his business venture with Byrnes. The only flaw with this territory in 1856 was that no railroad ran through it, thus making Hammonton a more desirable endeavor. By 1861, however, Millville had introduced the necessary transportation to build a successful new community and also provided another crucial connection for the young entrepreneur.

Millville's origins can be traced back to a set of log cabins reportedly near a sawmill in the Leamings Mill vicinity as early as 1720. There was one public road, a boat landing and a bridge. The seeds for the new municipality were sown when Joseph Buck was discharged from the Continental Army shortly after the 1781 surrender at Yorktown. Buck decided to settle in Cumberland County and soon became entrenched in area politics, even serving as sheriff from 1787 to 1790.

It was in Buck's final year as sheriff that two entrepreneurs, Henry Drinker and Joseph Smith, became involved in establishing a business in the area. Purchasing roughly 20,000 acres in the section known as Union Mill Tract, Drinker and Smith provided a dam to power the lumber mills that were developing along the Maurice River as part of their newly formed Union Estates Company. Union Lake was created in the process.

As Drinker and Smith's Union Company began to flourish, Buck began to evaluate the changes overtaking the location that once housed the log cabin settlement. By 1795, in the fashion of Charles K. Landis, he envisioned the area as a city comprised of mills lining the Maurice River with manor houses filling what would be the uptown region. In 1795, Buck acquired the mill belonging to the Union Company as well as a considerable amount of land in the vicinity. Delving into the real estate trade, he bought up acres of land, dividing the property into lots and selling them to those interested in settling in the area.

In the final decade of the 19th century, Millville, as Buck had christened the territory, faced a promising future in glass manufacturing, owing to the area's abundant fine white-grained silica sand. Additionally, the wooded area provided enough trees for the lumber necessary to fuel the mills.

In its original incarnation, Millville was incorporated as a township on February 24, 1801, formed from portions of Fairfield Township, but it was still in the early stages of its development. At the time of Buck's death in 1803, there were only twenty homes in the fledgling municipality.

In 1806, the arrival of James Lee, an Irish immigrant who had been living in Port Elizabeth, pointed the town in its new direction. He established a window-glass factory on the site of the future American Legion Hall and erected a dam to provide power for a new paper mill. Lee's glass factory eventually would be purchased by the Whitall Tatum Company.

Millville's identity as a glassworks city established the direction it would follow for over a century. Along with its industry came residents whose numbers, a meager several hundred in the 1820s, would grow significantly to 7,600 by 1880.

As Millville's glass industry blossomed in the mid-1800s, the arrival of an entrepreneur named Richard Wood helped to reshape the area. Wood was born in 1799 and raised in Greenwich, New Jersey. His family arrived with one of the first group of Quaker settlers to Philadelphia in the late seventeenth century. Wood eventually established a business in the City of Brotherly Love but returned to his home state

49

and took an interest in Millville, building an iron foundry and cotton mill there. By 1858, Wood had acquired from his half-brother, David, the New Jersey land that once belonged to Pennsylvania founder William Penn.

Penn owned close to 20,000 acres of what would become most of Cumberland County well after he had undertaken his "holy experiment" in Pennsylvania in 1681 and East and West Jersey had consolidated their governments in 1702. In fact, after his death in 1718, Penn's heirs continued ownership of much of Eastern Cumberland County, including the sections that would develop into Millville and Vineland. Penn had willed the land to his three sons, Richard, Thomas and John, and it was eventually bequeathed to Richard's son, Richard Jr., who, in 1776, sold the southern part that included Millville and possibly a portion of what became Landis Township to three businessmen. The remainder, including sections that would become Vineland and most of Landis Township, was sold in 1795 and parceled out to interested parties.

Between 1813 and 1816, Philadelphians David C. Wood and Edward Smith purchased the land that had once belonged to William Penn. By February 22, 1817, David Wood was the sole owner of the 19,962 acres. When he later encountered financial difficulties with his iron furnace and foundry, his half-brother Richard offered his help. The relationship between the two soon became fractious and, by 1850, Richard had acquired David's land in a sheriff's sale, giving him sole ownership of most of Cumberland County, including Millville and the stretch of land north of it. Wood, in partnership with William Wilson, also owned a lumber business in the northern portion known as Forest Grove, an area established by Wilson and his brother James. The business boasted a steam sawmill and housing for laborers. The remaining land, however, was not being groomed for development by its owner. Instead, selling it would offer more lucrative prospects.

Because of Millville's glass industry, Richard Wood was granted a charter in 1859 to construct a rail line that would connect his town with Glassboro, another glass manufacturing town. According to Don Wentzel's *South Jersey Magazine* railroad series, the Millville and Glassboro Railroad was incorporated on March 9, 1859 and organized on June 13th.

In fall 1859, construction of the twenty-two-mile rail system began. The rails for the line as well as the construction material were transported by boat. The railroad ties were made at Wood's sawmill at Forest Grove, which would be the only stop along the line associated with the Vineland area prior to its founding. The line would be completed by October 1860. The first engine used on the railroad was called "The Eagle," which had been shipped up the Maurice River by boat and then transported by men and mules up a hill and to High Street and the train station to the residents' amazement.

According to Wentzel, Millville's "original railroad yards occupied all of the land along Second Street between Broad and 'G' Streets, extending west to the passenger station at High and Broad. The station tracks were adjacent to High Street, as far as Powell Street, turning here slightly to the east. The freight station was opposite the passenger station with access from Broad Street. When originally built by the [Millville and Glassboro Railroad], the Millville yard contained an engine house and a turntable…Engines were then turned on a wye track which was located at the present-day McDonald's on North High Street. This track extended to the Millville manufacturing plant on Columbia Avenue just north of Sharp Street. Another extension of this branch line ran down the middle of Dock Street to the Whitall Tatum Glass plant at Buck Street and Columbia Avenue."

Passengers traveling on the Millville and Glassboro Railroad during the line's first year could reach Philadelphia in the early days of the rail line, but it was an involved three-hour process. Because no tracks connected Woodbury and Glassboro, travelers had to ride to Woodbury on a stage and then catch the West Jersey Railroad to Camden where they could take a West Jersey boat across the Delaware River to Philadelphia.

By the following year, however, changes began to reshape the line. As of October 1861, travelers could enjoy a two-hour trip, departing Millville on the rail line at either 6:30 a.m. or 1:10 p.m. and traveling to Glassboro where a recently completed West Jersey Railroad line would carry them to Woodbury and on to Camden and Philadelphia. Boats from Philadelphia left the City of Brotherly Love at the Walnut Street Wharf at 9 a.m. and 4 p.m. Passengers could then transfer to the West Jersey rail line and pick up a train from Glassboro at 10:15 a.m. or 5:15 p.m. The new route would better accommodate someone like Landis, who would continue to maintain a Philadelphia office for the rest of his life.

It was on the West Jersey and the Millville and Glassboro lines in spring 1861 that Landis toured the territory that would become Vineland and the surrounding territory of

Landis Township. Having explored possibilities in North Jersey and areas west of the state, Landis was again turning his attention toward South Jersey now that the Millville and Glassboro Railroad had been constructed. He had envisioned a city that would accommodate his idea of a settlement that could "afford the widest and most certain scope for individual success... on account of markets and of the opportunities for skilled labor in farming." His town would provide an aesthetic setting for its residents, who would transplant the progressive and free-thinking philosophies of New England into his settlement, whose center would focus on industry while its outlying territory would concentrate on farms and vineyards. Now that a rail line connected this area with Philadelphia, he was convinced this was the location for a planned community, writing, "the soil, climate and location were best adapted to my object. I wanted land more adapted to fruit than grain...it would give more opportunity for people of small means." He also noted that "the immense city of Philadelphia was at our door."

On April 1, 1861, Wood writes in his journal that "a person called Landis came to talk about the purchase of a large tract of land." Landis's account says the initial meeting occurred in Philadelphia and that Wood seemed to "appreciate the idea" for a planned city. Wood also saw in Landis's plan the advantage of a nearby source for Millville's agricultural and industrial needs. After touring the land, the prospective buyer found Wood "to be slow and cautious" and his price "exorbitant" at ten dollars per acre but Landis decided to "humor him in the negotiations" by visiting every day. After a week, Wood chose to visit Hammonton, where he dined with Landis and his parents, and was impressed to see how the town had grown in just a short period.

Landis was offered a second invitation to inspect the property he wished to purchase and visited Wood at his home the day before the tour. When Mrs. Wood asked Landis what he had in mind for the avenues in his new town, the Vineland founder gave a detailed description of how they would be 100 feet wide and "lined with a double row of shade trees." Landis writes that he had already been called "demented" when he explained that a swampy area of land could be drained and reclaimed "to make a good carriage road," and now his unorthodox view of Vineland's main streets would stir more controversy. The following day, Wood cautioned his interested buyer to refrain from discussing his plans since Mrs. Wood had awakened him during the night to warn him "against making any agreement with you, as she is afraid you are of unsound mind owing to your description of the avenue last night." Wood seemed convinced of what Landis could accomplish and suggested he not tell people "any more than their minds are prepared for."

Landis writes that Wood gave permission to commence operations on the land while negotiations continued, but that he insisted on having a deal before any work began. By May 8, 1861, the day after Landis was asked to write what he felt was an appropriate deal, Wood wrote in his journal that they had "agreed upon seven dollars per acre as the price he is to pay."

While Landis and Wood negotiated, however, the seeds of the Civil War, which had been planted over the past year, were now being cultivated in the Southern states. Following

Abraham Lincoln's election, South Carolina had seceded from the Union on December 20, 1860, and would soon be joined by six more Southern states, with eight additional slave-supporting states remaining a part of the Union at the time. Upon its secession, South Carolina began seizing federal facilities. One of its targets, Fort Sumter, strategically guarded the entrance to Charleston Harbor. Attempts by President James Buchanan and his successor, Abraham Lincoln, to re-supply the Union fortress failed, and the Confederate government commenced bombarding the fort on April 12, accepting its surrender two days later.

Concerned about the rumblings of war, Landis decided to visit Washington, D.C. According to his 1961 talk before the Vineland Historical and Antiquarian Society, J. Meade Landis, the founder's grandson, explained that his grandfather and Benjamin H. Brewster, a future U. S. Attorney General, traveled to the nation's capital to learn what they could and witness the concentration of troops. The founder's grandson explained that the two visitors "were assured by high ranking friends, including several members of Lincoln's cabinet that the attack on Sumter was of no great consequence." Lincoln, they were told, would be meeting with Southern representatives at a "high-level conference."

In an undated article titled "Washington in 1861," most likely written in the late 1880s or early 1890s since Brewster's role as U.S. Attorney General from 1881 to 1885 is acknowledged, Landis writes that "in the spring of 1861, after Sumpter [sic] had been fired upon, I happened to leave Hammonton on a visit to Philadelphia and called upon Benjamin H. Brewster...who for years had been my lawyer and personal friend." Landis mentions the negotiations that were underway with Wood to buy land for the founding of Vineland and writes that he was persuaded by Brewster's invitation to visit Washington to see the soldiers who had collected there.

Based on Landis's descriptions of Washington D.C., it is reasonable to place his arrival in the nation's capital around May 20, 1861. He mentions seeing a military man named Ellsworth and remarks that "he would be stretched out cold in death" in a few days. Colonel Elmer E. Ellsworth would die during the Union occupation of Alexandria, Virginia on May 24.

Adam Goodheart's book *1861: The Civil War Awakening* provides a wider view of the Washington Landis describes in his account as well as some insights into several of the events depicted. Goodheart's book devotes a chapter to a description of Washington in May 1861, the time frame of Landis's visit. Like many current historical studies, the emphasis has shifted to the view of the common person rather than the political and military leaders of the period. The author relies largely on reporters' first-hand accounts of events and conditions in the same way Vineland's founder rendered much of his own tale.

On their second day there, Landis and Brewster visited a number of military encampments where Landis found that amongst the soldiers "there was no belief in the probability of even the possibility of war..." Goodheart confirms the troops' presence while offering a vivid description of the scene: "The volunteers who had converged upon the capital sported scarlet plumes and gold lace, turbans and tyroleans...quite a few were in civilian garb. Some belonged to pre-war militias, but there were many newly formed regiments."

One of these regiments was made up of the one-thousand soldiers of the First New York Fire Zouaves, a group of firemen with shaved heads who were forced to bivouac in the Capitol building still under construction. Elmer E. Ellsworth was in command of this boisterous unit who quickly earned the respect of the Washingtonians.

On May 9, prior to Landis's arrival, a Pennsylvania Avenue liquor store caught fire, the flames spreading to a second building and threatening a third, the Willard Hotel. Goodheart reports that the Fire Zouaves were called upon and, commandeering a fire engine, arrived at the scene. Without ladders, the group formed a human pyramid to gain access to the roof. Armed with a hose and washbasins, tubs and pots secured from the hotel, they engaged in a war of a different sort, soaking the hotel roof and extinguishing the flames roaring from the other buildings. The actions of the regiment saved the hotel.

Landis and Brewster arrived at the Willard Hotel a week-and-a-half later, choosing this establishment since they were acquainted with owner Henry Willard who had converted the original Pennsylvania Avenue hotel into a four-story operation (it stands today as a 12-story structure still two blocks east of the White House). The influx of soldiers brought with them friends and family members, limiting the available accommodations and forcing Landis and Brewster to share a large room with two beds.

In a somewhat surreal segment of Landis's written account, the author is awakened by Brewster who announces his new title of brigadier general and Landis's appointment as a colonel. It turns out that the appointments were made by Simon Cameron, Lincoln's Secretary of War. Preferring to pursue his Vineland project over military duties, Landis agreed that they should visit Secretary of State William Henry Seward and then Cameron to question each about the increasing tensions between the North and the South. What they received was continued assurance there was no threat of war.

It's doubtful the military ranks conferred upon Landis and Brewster would have been awarded if officials believed a real war had been looming. Seward's reassurance that the aggression would not reach a critical level is unsurprising considering his background. Having lost the Republican Presidential nomination in 1860 to Lincoln, he was appointed Secretary of State by the new Commander-in-Chief, who some historians believe wished to keep his friends close and his enemies closer. According to Sean Wilentz in *The Rise of American Democracy*, during the Fort Sumter incident, Seward, "carrying over both his conciliatory strategy with the South and his ambition to undermine Lincoln's authority, secretly advised a group of Confederate commissioners that the government would indeed abandon Sumter...[which] would impress the Border South and impress the Unionists within the seceded states." It seemed, despite continued secessions and imminent battles, Seward continued to believe reconciliation was possible when he spoke with Landis.

Goodheart's book offers a somewhat reasonable, if not completely sound, explanation for the incredulous offer made by Cameron in granting Landis the rank of colonel. Desperation, it seems, may have provoked the gesture. since, according to Goodheart, "resignations still arrived daily at the War Department from many of the most seasoned officers of the regular army." Despite their new ranks, however, Landis and Brewster soon returned to New Jersey, confident that a Civil War would not evolve from the recent skirmishes. Landis would be back in Philadelphia by May 26, ready to complete negotiations with Wood.

A May 27, 1861 entry in Wood's journal reports that Landis was eager to finalize the deal, but by June 20, Wood writes that he had "read [a] letter from Landis, demanding a matter that I cannot comply with; I so informed him. It probably closes our negotiations." Landis makes no mention of this demand in his own account. Wood hints in his June 21 entry that the issue at hand seemed to involve "interferences in the survey I sold him." By July 4, at a meeting with his attorney and Landis, Wood "agreed to sign a paper of stipulations previous to the signing of the deed…" On July 22, 1861, one day after, as Woods notes in his journal, federal troops were defeated at Manassas, an agreement was finally signed with Landis, who, for his first payment on the land, had borrowed $500 from his mother, a sum that she had saved over time and gladly offered for this venture. In the same month, Congress authorized a volunteer army and approved Lincoln's May 3 call for 42,000 volunteers to supplement the regular army. The war that Landis had been guaranteed would never occur had begun.

Over the next few years, Wood and Landis would develop a successful working relationship, but initially Wood and his wife handled the deeds for the early lots Landis sold. Landis and Wood had also agreed that the former would sell the lots of land for a price that did not include the timber fees, a situation that could have recreated here the scandal that occurred in Colville. But settlers in Vineland did not challenge the stipulation. They purchased the land from Landis and were more than agreeable in paying the additional fee. For each plot Landis sold, he also received a commission from the timber fees, as evidenced in a letter and check he received from Wood on September 30, 1862. Wood identifies the enclosed payment, a total of $7.70, as his commission for a recent land sale.

The timber rights to the property sold in Vineland proved lucrative for Wood. In the September 2 entry of his journal, Wood writes that he had recently paid six thousand one hundred dollars in income tax. Eight days later, he reports that his son "Edward went up in the train, and I followed on horse, to Vineland, where we dined, and then, with crier and surveyor, began the sale of standing wood, and spent the remainder of the day…Sale amounted to over six thousand dollars, and was considered a good one." In one day, he had replenished the funds he had handed over for taxes.

As Landis was becoming accustomed to working with Wood, he received a letter, dated November 3, 1862, from his former partner Richard Byrnes about concerns over a matter of releasing Hammonton land still owned by Vineland's founder. Byrnes encourages his ex-partner to "attend to this at once" so Landis can use "the proceeds of some of them to pay your mortgage installment." Landis would continue to sell land he still owned in Hammonton over the remainder of the decade.

It's apparent from various correspondence that Wood was generous in business matters with Landis, offering to credit him in sales so that he could retain the amount he received from the buyers. For example, in an 1863 letter, he informs Vineland's founder that if there was a need for the money for a recent sale, he would accept his short note instead.

It's also evident that the Millville entrepreneur enjoyed his partnership with Landis, extending him the rare honor of naming a sloop Wood had just purchased. In a letter to Landis dated February 16, 1863, Wood writes, "We hear today from our partners at Millville that you desire the privilege of naming the steamer now building for the Millville and New York trade and that you would no doubt present her with a suit of colors. If agreeable to you to do this, we will be pleased to name her the 'Vineland' (the name we understand you have chosen) and would like your answer by return mail. The steamer is nearly completed and will probably be at Millville between the 1st and 10th March." Unfortunately, the steamer proved not to be as successful as its namesake and, in a journal entry a year-and-a-half later, Wood declares that he is "determined to sell the sloop *Vineland* unless something turns up to give us employment."

In June 1863, Landis would sign an in indenture with Wood for over $190,000 of land. The details of the deeds and mortgage and their repayment had been carefully worked out by Wood over the previous month. On May 4, 1863, he records in his journal, "After business at office, came home, at twelve, and began reading the deed to Landis with my son Edward, and read through the outside boundaries, which agree with the running, except a few small errors." On June 9, 1863, Wood rode his horse to Vineland after breakfast, but upon meeting Jones, his lawyer, he "returned with him, and spent most of the day in reading over the deed from myself and wife to C.K. Landis."

On June 13, 1863, Wood records that "Mr. Jones came, and Mr. Landis. The former worked at the completion of the deeds and the mortgage. B. came to take the acknowledgement; which he did and took the papers to put his seal upon them." Landis had signed the papers on June 13 but three days later, Wood writes, "At half-past twelve acknowledged deed and took mortgage from Landis. After dinner drove, with wife, over to Bridgeton. Left mortgage with recorder..." Wood's journal entry for July 1, 1863 reports that all had been finalized with Vineland's founder and that he "went to Vineland, and settled with Landis," who was to begin paying back the loan in July 1864 in semi-annual payments each January and July. The deadline for payment of both the principle and interest was 1869 and this arrangement would come to haunt Landis and compound the problems he would face in the early 1870s.

Once the deal with Wood had been finalized in July 1861, Landis wasted no time in delving into his new project. Still residing in Philadelphia, he began advertising for and soon hired a surveyor, who, before beginning his work, took the time to inform Landis that his enterprise was destined to fail. The new employee's attitude was conveyed in his "sarcastic questions and remarks" and "unfeigned astonishment." Landis was told that

> I had laid out the streets and roads uselessly wide, and upon such a scale that nobody could ever be made to believe that it could be carried out; and that the design was far too magnificent for the country, or the opportunity. He would advise doing away with the mile square for the town plot and make it much

smaller; and instead of ignoring the old wood roads of the country, he would utilize them by selling land upon them, and save the expense of opening new roads; also, that if anybody should be found willing to buy any of the land, he would advise the selling of it without any improvement stipulations. He would not exact them for fear it would prevent sales.

Landis argued that "a magnificent design would add value to the property and that the stipulation would give assurance that it would be carried out," but the surveyor remained skeptical and, according to Landis, saw the project "as the visionary scheme of a dreamer." Landis remarked in his account of founding Vineland, "I might expect a good deal of this for some time to come, and I hoped that as [the surveyor] saw people buying land and improving it after a while this would wear off."

Despite his misgivings, the surveyor boarded a Millville and Glassboro Railroad car on the evening of August 7 and traveled with his employer and several other passengers through South Jersey. Before reaching the Forest Grove station, Landis requested the conductor stop the train at an old dirt road that led to the farm of Andrew Sharp, one of Wood's agents, where Landis would soon take up living quarters. The conductor shook his head and walked away, leaving the pair of travelers no choice but to exit the locomotive at Forest Grove and walk the six-mile journey to Sharp's abode.

Sharp was originally from Burlington County where he earned his living as a farmer. In December 1858, he purchased 270 acres from Wood, who had partnered with

Sharp to develop farm land in this area before offering it to buyers. The Sharp farm was located approximately five miles north of Millville and about half a mile east of the railroad, where Park Avenue meets Main Road today. Wood could not have chosen a better man. By all accounts, Sharp was industrious and demonstrated an ability to direct others. By the time of Vineland's founding, he had cleared 231 acres and divided his land into several fields. He had also built a two-story home, a smaller house for farm hands, a stable and granary and several other out-buildings.

The day after Landis's arrival marked the birth of Vineland, simple, unadorned and preserved in the words of the founder. "On the morning of the 8th of August, we were up early," Landis wrote. "It was a beautiful clear day, but very warm. We breakfasted early and were taken to the railroad by Mr. Sharp within about three quarters of a mile from the point I wished to strike, which was the center of the tract. On reaching that point, I moved a little further south where the ground was higher, and then directed the stake to be driven for the center of Landis Avenue, and of Vineland." When the stake was driven at the center of town, Landis brought his city into existence with mythic grandeur.

It's significant to note that Isaiah Arthur, one of the African-American residents of the area that became Vineland, was the individual Landis supervised in driving the stake on that August day. In the next several years, black settlers such as Charles Gray, Solomon Royal, Steve Christdon, Retta Crawford, Etta Parker and Rev. Ellwood Hubbard arrived and made the area their home.

The most challenging of Landis's work lay ahead and, according to his account, the remainder of August and the months of September and October were spent on several crucial projects which filled this short frame of time with considerable work. The first was the completion of the mile-and-a-half stretch of Landis Avenue, from the very center of town to what was then known as Horse Bridge Road, today's Main Road. Landis saw this as vital in drawing prospective settlers and delayed the promotion of Vineland until the work was completed. Development of Landis Avenue would soon continue to Malaga Road, today's Delsea Drive and, as early as 1863, extend west toward Bridgeton and east toward Mays Landing.

Landis knew exactly what he wanted when it came to roadways for his town. His impressions of Millville are an indication of what he clearly wished to avoid in setting up his own city, writing, "the streets were not paved and had no sidewalks. They were deep in sand and the pigs were allowed to run at large. The houses were small framed buildings old and dilapidated." From the start, he had envisioned his new settlement having avenues one hundred feet in width and serving as the main thoroughfares running east-west and extending from the already existing Horse Bridge Road and Malaga Road.

These would become Landis, Chestnut and Park Avenues. Roads running north-south would be sixty-six feet wide with farm roads fifty-feet in width. "I rightly expected that this would make one of the most beautiful places in the country, and that the lack of natural scenery would be made up by the labor of art," Landis explains in his account of founding Vineland. "This result was to be reached after the planting of orchards and vineyards, shade trees and miles of hedges." Unfortunately, Landis's unorthodox width specifications for avenues and roads were seen by many as an unnecessary defiance of convention. According to A. G. Warner's *Vineland and the Vinelanders*, settlers who had already been living in the area were used to roads being only ten feet wide and thought Landis's idea of a more expansive roadway was a complete waste of land and manpower.

Landis secured several individuals from a group of "wood choppers and charcoal burners who lived around in log cabins with clay floors," to accompany him in the clearing of the land at the center of the Vineland tract. If the ideas he proposed about his town were considered radical, his beliefs about wages and workmanship were equally misunderstood and unpopular at the time. During this period, it was common for companies to set up stores for their workers and have the laborers' meager weekly salaries pay for what was purchased there, thus returning the money to the company. Landis paid his workers well and directly. He would pay each member of the team clearing the land one dollar per day in gold, double the wages they were used to earning in Millville.

> At the end of the week, instead of giving the men orders upon the stores at Millville, at the rate of fifty cents per day, as they expected, I paid them in gold at one dollar per day, at that time the current wages elsewhere in civilized places. They were much astonished, and two of them did not want to take it, saying the clerk at the store knew better what they wanted than they did themselves. This will scarcely be believed. It shows the depth of the ignorance that then existed in the wilderness. I had remarked that it

was time they had learned the use of money and paid them. Low wages are decidedly injurious to humanity. It degrades all, rich and poor, giving one class more than sufficient for their needs, encouraging luxury, selfishness and self-conceit, at the expense of the other class who are robbed and impoverished, and denied of all opportunity for self-improvement. My colony was not made for a class; but in all things I adopted a policy which would comprehend the whole.

Landis's views on this matter would be revisited in another essay entitled "How to Build Up a Town." This work, which exists as an undated manuscript, takes to task U.S. companies who exploit workers and places an emphasis on the importance of

> ...the earning of good wages by the working people. Without this they cannot buy lots and build houses even if they are aided by a Building Association...The most stupid of all men are employers who believe in lowering wages and degrading labor...without good wages, good work cannot be turned out. It is a notorious fact that the most successful manufacturers in the world are not those who have paid the lowest wages, but who have turned out the most works. This can be seen in America and Europe... [in the manufacture of] boots and shoes, clothes and other materials...The worst slavery on earth is when a working man is held down to low and unjust wages with a starving family

staring him in the face and he cannot help himself...America was settled...by the oppressed working people of Great Britain and the rest of Europe to get away from this so that they should be free and equal and have their just rights, the greatest of which was their honest earnings. This is what has made America great like a lighted torch in the eyes of nations and when these traditions are ignored and forgotten she will go down as quickly from her high position as a flaming torch thrown into the sea.

Before undertaking the daunting task of clearing the land, Landis had already determined that the town would be "free from taverns" and that temperance be observed by future residents. "I intended to fight this battle of the wilderness with sober men," Landis explains in his account. "I thought that this might be accomplished in the start, with an industrial population. In fact, I did not see how the people could success without temperance, as well as industry. The labor to be done in the clearing of the Vineland tract was something stupendous; and besides this, a living was to be made."

Work on Landis Avenue began immediately after the stake was driven. Landis was eager to begin shaping his settlement, but he remained patient in advertising his new town. "I made no attempt to advertise or sell land until my avenue should be opened to Main Road," Landis wrote. By October, the street extended past Main Road and all the way to Spring Road.

In order to secure ownership of all the land that would become Vineland as well as the township that would be named after him, Landis needed to buy the individually-owned property within the territory he had already purchased from Richard Wood. Prior to this, there was no interest in these properties except for their wood, and Landis now found these owners "anxious to sell." He hired a man who came highly recommended and who "was acquainted with property holders in South Jersey" and began inquiring after purchasing these "exceptions." The town founder soon increased his holdings, buying from such people as Fislerville (now Clayton) resident John M. Moore who provided 800 acres and became Landis's New York agent in the process. A related venture, the creation of a monthly publication called *Vineland Rural*, which would help market the town, was also organized in the three months after the stake had been driven.

For those purchasing land here, it was necessary for them to build a house within a year and clear two-and-a-half acres each year so that the development of the community would be guaranteed. Landis also stipulated that houses on the outskirts of town needed to be placed seventy-five feet from the road and those in town twenty feet from the road to provide space for flowers and trees. The purpose for this was to provide shade and to lure birds which would help control insects that could threaten the farm crops.

The attempt to establish a post office in an unpopulated town, however, was one obstacle Landis hadn't been prepared to encounter. His request was turned down because there were no residents to receive or send mail. Landis, however, felt that the post office would help draw settlers if it was already there waiting for them. He paid a visit to Washington, D.C. to speak with the Second Assistant

Postmaster who turned down the founder's pleas on economic grounds. A meeting with President John Tyler's son, Robert, whom Landis had met previously in Philadelphia, led to another confrontation with the Second Assistant Postmaster who still considered the proposal absurd. When it looked as if the request was about to be denied for a third time, Tyler addressed the official by stating that Vineland "is no wilderness, since Mr. Landis has resolved to build a city there, he has it in his head, and all he has to do is transfer it to the land..." Citing Landis's accomplishments with Hammonton and calling Vineland "a much greater affair," he helped secure Vineland's first post office. The approval was given, however, on the condition that Landis pay an annual fee of $20. On August 31, 1861, Vineland's town founder was appointed its first postmaster.

It was not until October that Landis finally settled in Vineland permanently. He took up residence at Andrew Sharp's house. Occupying a room in the northeast corner of the dwelling, Landis filled the rooms across from it with "my maps, and business table, and the draughting board of the surveyor." It was also in October that the first ads for the town were placed in the *New York Herald*, *The Public Ledger* and the *Boston Journal*. Landis later reported that letters soon began arriving and that he replied to each one he received, including a copy of the *Vineland Rural* with each response.

In November, the agricultural expert Solon Robinson visited the tract after an invitation from Landis. In only a few months it had grown to 30,000 acres or 50 square miles. Robinson was taken with the new settlement and wrote favorably about it in the *New York Tribune*. In the same way he had incorporated favorable articles about Ridgeway and Hammonton in earlier promotional material, Landis placed an excerpt of Robinson's review of Vineland into the town's first promotional pamphlet to help promote this latest experiment.

Landis's skills as a salesman, however, were not limited to print material. As he reveals in his account of the founding of Vineland,

> In selling land, I had a standard rule, which was to sell to a visitor the best location I had for the objects he had in view, and to make the sale and improvement of the good locations sell the less valuable. In this way property was certain to rise in value in the hands of the purchasers. They were sure to make good reports and that would bring a yet more rapid increase of population. I noticed however that many who bought land were not farmers, but I thought they might learn. Still, there were some that I should have refused to sell land to had I known them as well as I have since, by the light of subsequent experience. Yet even these did well. Their property increased in value greatly, and they could sell out to advantage, getting something over and above what they paid me. This was uniformly the case and there was no change until after the speculative rise in the value of improved places, years after. I now sought to make sales of the farm lands only, making no effort to sell town lots. I thought it advisable to turn the wild land into farms first, in order to give the town some support.

The initial advertising for Vineland drew an Englishman by the name of J.G. Colson, who arrived from New York and spent a day examining Landis's maps and discussing the area. By his second day in town, Colson bought some property, making him the first person to purchase land in the Vineland area from Landis. Vineland chronicler A.G. Warner reports that this transaction consisted of ten acres between Oak and Wheat Roads west of the Boulevard.

According to Landis, the sale occurred just as Richard Wood "had become quite impatient to see something done..." Since all deeds needed to be signed by Wood at the time, a trip to Millville was necessary, and Landis writes of Wood's astonishment: "...to think that a man would come down from New York and purchase a piece of this land for cash." Accompanying Landis and Colson back to Vineland, Wood took Andrew Sharp aside and discussed the first sale. Later the town founder learned that Wood had "charged [Sharp] to help and facilitate Mr. Landis in every possible way; for...he must be a great man."

Prospective buyers soon arrived at the Vineland tract, boarding at Sharp's farmhouse and affecting Landis's accommodations:

> I kept pressing on and pushing my business, and visitors increased in number. Sharp's farmhouse was crowded, much to his surprise. When there were more ladies than there were beds for, I always gave up my room and slept downstairs upon the floor, rolled up in a buffalo robe. I would have slept out of doors on the sharp edge of a plank if my success

required it. Moreover, the example enabled Sharp to fill his floors all over, with people with much less grumbling. My engineer, being of no use to me as a salesman, owing to his utter want of faith, I had to shoulder the spade myself, and attend to all the visitors. I think that for some time my daily walk might average twenty miles. I found that I could talk the obstinacy and opposition out of a visitor much more easily if I walked him down tired.

While many prospective settlers visited Vineland after Colson bought his property, it was difficult to sell more land because "there was such desolation in the appearance of the place that the idea of locating in such an unattractive locality sickened people." With the arrival of Captain Post, who purchased land across from the Sharp farm, Landis was able to apply his cash payment to an idea he felt would improve the lamentable condition of the town.

I had noted my best workmen and found out who of them understood farming and gardening, and proposed to them to buy ten acres each, offering at the same time to furnish them lumber and a carpenter to build for each a small house payable on long time. This proposal astonished them so much that at first they held back, but I had gained their confidence by paying cash and by the work they saw going on, and they soon fell in with it. This started a number of homes in different places, so that when I drove my visitors around the tract they would here and there see a new improvement going on, which gave the thing a look of reality and business.

By the end of 1861, it was estimated that Vineland's population numbered twenty-five.

Landis also established Vineland's first post office in Sharp's house. An article by Loren D. Flood in the *Vineland Historical Magazine*, describes the filing system used by Landis in Vineland's early days. "A nail driven through the letter into the north wall, kept the letter intact until it was claimed by the owner," writes Flood, who also recalls seeing the wall on which the mail was hung and reports that "it was covered with nail holes from just above the floor to near the ceiling."

Landis soon saw the advantage of headquartering the post office as well as his business and living quarters at the intersection of Landis Avenue and the Boulevard, in direct proximity to the incoming and outgoing trains. A suitable location in the center of town also offered constant access to businesses that would soon spring up. In the waning months of 1862, the Magnolia House, Vineland's first hotel, was constructed on the southeast corner. The structure, which was comprised of two stories and an attic, was described by A. G. Warner as having "a kitchen, a dining-room and small sitting room about 15 feet square, for both ladies and gentlemen." The second floor contained Landis's office and the apartment where he lodged.

A surviving 1862 letter from Russ Martin Builders contains the specifications for the second floor, which included the office/apartment. The facility was twelve feet wide by forty-eight feet long by seven-and-a-half feet high, with 5/8 of the wall covered by Jersey Pine board. The floor was of Jersey Pine lined with box boards and there was a well-nailed roof shingled with Jersey Pine shingles. The second-floor looks to have been originally divided into four rooms with the walls plastered with one coat. The builder noted the construction cost of $300.

Landis's room utilized slightly more than one-fourth of the floor, measuring 12 by 14 feet and overlooking the southwest corner of the building which offered a view of Landis Avenue and the railway. Also, part of the facility was the post office, now maintained by Wallace Holbrooke and later C.R. Morehouse. It remained in the hotel until summer 1863, when it was relocated to a store maintained by W.S. Basset, who acted as postal clerk.

Warner explains that Landis's office was where he "received and entertained the visitors to Vineland; often so many in number as to fill the apartment. Many times the bed, which occupied about one-fourth of the whole room, being occupied as a settee." Landis created a comfortable atmosphere for those interested in settling in his new town. He provided them with accommodations in the remaining five rooms on the second floor and, for those who chose to settle in Vineland, lodging was available in the hotel attic until a new home could be built. Warner reports that "most of the early settlers of that day will remember the comforts of that attic; but whatever of discomforts was found in the crowded state of lodgings was amply compensated for in the well-supplied table, the boarders being kept and slept for 3 ½ dollars per week."

As Vineland grew throughout the 1860s and sufficient housing and hotels materialized, the Magnolia House came to serve a different purpose for Landis. Separating his private life from a work schedule that incorporated weekends as well as weekdays, he set up a new office directly across the street on the northeast corner of Landis Avenue and the Boulevard and took ownership of the hotel, turning it into his domicile.

In 1962, former Landis employee George G. Walker recalled his employer's homestead, describing the property as 200 by 300 feet. The land included a backyard that allowed a horse, Polly, to graze and dogs to play and that housed a carriage, which Landis drove himself. The inside of the Landis home has been partially preserved on stereo-optic cards. A popular item at the time, stereo-optics employed a double image on a card that presented a 3-D effect when seen through a viewing unit. The Landis photos provide a glimpse into several rooms of the house, most likely on the second floor. While no first-floor photos of the kitchen or dining room are included, the existing stereo-optic cards convey a sense of the limited confines with which lodgers had to contend as hotel residents. However, as sitting rooms and studies of the Landis abode, they are transformed into mini-galleries that boast an assortment of artworks accumulated over the years. A variety of smaller statues, many classical in style, adorn the mantelpiece of several fireplaces, another of significant size rests on a larger piece of furniture, framed by stacked books on either side, and a bust is contained on a pedestal. A collection of books is displayed on a coffee table while others appear on a stand. Paintings and plates are mounted on the walls, an urn sits atop a piece of furniture, and a chandelier hangs above a room where a high-backed chair occupies a corner. Some of the art is religious in nature. The trappings are those of a person whose love of the arts is proudly displayed. No doubt they also filled the other rooms of the house not preserved in these cards.

It is likely that Landis's former office/apartment became the master bedroom and that the remaining five second-floor apartments were converted into studies and bedrooms for the children Landis would soon sire. This would remain Landis's Vineland home for the rest of his life, a choice location that put him in the center of town with direct access to the rail line.

At the close of 1862, Vineland's population had better than doubled from the preceding year, reaching eighty inhabitants. Most newcomers hailed from New England, a trend that would continue for the remainder of the decade, with occupations ranging from farmers to blacksmiths, carpenters, masons and a tinsmith.

From the outset, Landis had effectively planned his new creation down to the smallest detail, maneuvering the pieces methodically while maintaining an awareness of how each interlocking ingredient would shape the community. His account in the essay "The Social Science of Vineland," first published in the British periodical *Frazier's Magazine* in 1875 and later reprinted in the U.S. under the title "The Settlement of Vineland," is the most enlightening source of how and why he implemented each portion of his design.

The requirements that bound each resident of the settlement, including property frontage and the planting of trees and grass, were all part of a grand design to protect and enhance the community. According to Landis, the regulations "made each colonist labor personally to improve his lot and cooperate with his neighbor, and with myself, for our mutual benefit. It also kept the settlement continually growing, and made the outlands successively saleable," while also serving to remove "the greatest evil in new countries – speculation..." Landis asserted that he himself was not a speculator and admonished the practice of raising the price of lots and farmland "as the place improved and increased in population." He instead offered them at reasonable prices that would still provide "me a fair remuneration, and then I depended upon my profits in the rapid sales which would be produced by allowing the settlers to have the benefit in the rise in the value of land and their increased prosperity." Whenever it became necessary to repossess property "by reason of parties not complying with their improvement stipulations," he would resell it at market value rather than increasing the price.

The aesthetic stipulations were also seen as beneficial. Setting houses back from the roadway removed them from dust and "induced great attention to the ornamenting of front gardens with flowers and shrubbery." The insistence that trees be planted also increased the beauty of the town, but in ways that might not have been immediately obvious to residents. At his own cost, Landis had his engineer set the stakes for the lines of trees to be planted in order to "turn the uniformity of straight lines and right angles in the roads to a feature of beauty as well as utility" in addition to providing "a harbor for birds, which are necessary for a fruit country" and "a protection to roads, and affording a grateful shade in summer..."

In addition, the rule that "roadside should be seeded for grass within two years and kept seeded" was meant to

beautify the town but "also to prevent the spread of noxious weeds that had been usually allowed to grow up by the roadsides, from whence the seeds spread over
the adjacent fields." While residents were called upon to maintain their part in making Vineland and the surrounding township beautiful, Landis created "one-hundred-and-seventy-six miles of road" along with causeways and bridges at his own expense. In addition to draining marsh land "which re-claimed a good deal of the best land," he also "laid out squares in certain localities for public ornament and donated a park of forty-five acres adjoining the city plot for the same purpose. These were intended for fairs, festivals and public amusement."

One of the most innovative and farsighted tasks he undertook involved "the economizing of manures and sewerage." Landis introduced "earth-closets," what he described as "a sliding box under the seats, and a keg of dry earth, or generally a compost of muck and plaster, which was thrown into the box, and used with a little shovel, the whole of it to be emptied once a week.
This kept it thoroughly deodorized, and the manure was almost immediately suitable for use upon the land..." Such management gave farmers the advantage of then disposing of it "by running it in receptacles for liquid manure... through a box holding muck, sawdust and sand; the water would run out clear, the filtering matter would retain the fertilizing properties, and after a certain time would be emptied and replaced."

Landis noted that "at the end of the year, the sewage process amounted to considerable value. In the aggregate, in the whole settlement, its money value was very large." This attention to health factors proved a deterrent to diseases such as typhoid. His explanation claimed, "as you walk through the beautiful little town no noxious smells will ever assail you. The remarkable health of Vineland is no doubt greatly owing to this cause. Other towns in the neighborhood that live under the old system are greatly troubled with fevers and epidemics."

Landis soon turned the venture into a legal project when he "had a law passed making it finable in the sum of two hundred dollars to dig any cesspool that would possibly reach the water level of the wells." He concluded his evaluation of the process by stating that "Vineland is probably the only place in the world" in which all excrement and sewage "is economized; and the large crops raised are in great part owing to it," saving "many thousands per annum, and no difficulty has been found in carrying out the plan."

Just as he planned the waste control and layout of his town, Landis also looked after the success of the settlement's businesses. He persuaded the State of New Jersey to change the interest rate from six percent to seven percent to assist Vineland's manufacturers and provided an incentive for those same manufacturers by constructing "a large building, at the cost of some thirty thousand dollars, divided into different rooms. I introduced a steam engine of some fifty horse power into the building, and then necessary shafting through the rooms, and let out room and power to manufacturers for a very small sum— what was barely adequate to pay expenses. To some I gave room for nothing, or rather in consideration of their introducing their business." The result of this endeavor was the burgeoning of businesses that turned out "boots and shoes, buttons, straw hats, pocket-books, woodwork of different kinds, and various other things [that]are extensively manufactured in Vineland, constantly adding to its wealth and population, and always increasing and giving employment to men not naturally farmers and working girls and boys."

Learning that farmers were spending a considerable amount on flour and seed by buying them in shops, Landis "introduced a grist-mill in my steam factory building," and made the decision "to run the mill myself," providing residents with quality merchandise at fair prices. The mill was slow to attract buyers, but soon became successful enough to add more machinery and handle orders from Philadelphia.

Landis devoted further attention to the agricultural trade, explaining that, at first,

> it was necessary to introduce the cultivation of such products as were adapted to our soil and climate and markets. For the produce most sought after in the markets of Philadelphia, New York and Boston, our soil and climate were well adapted. These were fruits, such as grapes, pears, peaches, apples and berries of different varieties; also, vegetables, such as sweet potatoes, or yams, as they are called in England, early white potatoes, table and field beets, onions, lima beans, cabbage, turnips, cauliflowers, asparagus, pippins, and melons of different varieties. These all grow to perfection and ripen early. Our people also raised wheat, Indian corn, grass, millet, and stock for home consumption, but the other articles were raised to send away. I succeeded in

getting the settlers to plant extensive orchards and vineyards...Special attention was also paid to the introduction of the best stock of cattle, pigs and poultry...

During Vineland's early years, Landis hired, out of his own pocket, "an agent whose duty it was to take [the farmers'] produce to market, dispose of it, and return them the money, free of any charge for his services. In time, as the colonists became acquainted with business and the markets, this became unnecessary, and I withdrew this assistance."

Everything in Vineland at this time, however, did not revolve around work. Landis saw the importance in creating various organizations that would cultivate interests in areas such as literature and science. In the absence of taverns and saloons, he offered his residents opportunities to engage in astronomy, horticulture and other studies. He also promoted such things as music, writing, gymnastics and agriculture by offering awards ranging from twenty dollars to one hundred dollars in a variety of contests.

All the while he tended to business, Landis kept a close watch on the progression of the war and the decisions being made by the federal government. One of the issues that particularly caught his attention was Abraham Lincoln's 1863 Emancipation Proclamation and the corresponding attempt to expatriate or colonize freed slaves by relocating them outside the U.S. in areas like Haiti, British Honduras, Panama and Africa. A Bureau of Emigration had recently been established within the U.S. Department of the Interior to help with this plan.

In a July 7 letter to an unidentified newspaper, Landis responded to the expatriation plan by stating, "The natural right and title of the colored population to the soil of the United States is as clear and indefeasible as that of the whites. On an average they have been here as long, for as many generations and there are fewer foreigners amongst them…they may be considered purely a native population…who add vastly to the general health of the country. Their leaders have shown themselves good fighters and let them have the same educational advantages of the whites so that their labor can be as intelligently directed, and it will soon be as valuable."

Landis argued that the same reasoning for the colonization of former slaves can apply to the white race in America as well. "As to the plea that expatriation to Africa will be better for them," he writes, "we, with more reason, could expatriate a white American citizen whose grandfather was an Irishman back to the Emerald Isle with all their difference of institutions and customs, the German or Hollander back to his country…it is not supported in the name of Christianity and of citizens under a Republican form of government that we would rob them of their inheritance and cast them into the deserts of Africa." Unbeknownst to Landis at the time he wrote the letter, Congress had cut funding for colonization endeavors five days earlier.

Landis continued to advertise his new town in publications ranging from New England to the Midwest, but it would be another year before the large influx of settlers he had hoped for would arrive. In 1864, Vineland began to develop a solid population and, along with it, a variety of occupations that became the start of the town's business world.

Vineland's infrastructure was also growing at this time. Chestnut and Landis Avenues along with Walnut Road had been extended and West and Park Avenues, Vine, Oak, Brewster and Magnolia Roads and Elmer Street added.

Also, early in 1864, Landis became intent on creating Landis Township from the territory he had carved out in the wilderness, an area originally part of Millville Township, and he sought the proper legislation that could provide it. A firm belief in the approval of his township and in the success of his town is evidenced in what Landis inscribed on the elegant cane he purchased for his father in January 1864. The inscription at the top indicates that it was a gift from his son, and the panels of the gold handle are each inscribed with a location: "Vineland," "Landis Township," "Cumberland," "New Jersey."

But chronicler A.G. Warner reports that the birth of the new township was not as ensured as Landis thought, writing that "Landis Township nearly missed out on being born." The process to decide its fate in the State Legislature churned intensely with "the virulent opposition of such men as the narrow-headed poet, Thomas Dunn English" and other North Jersey delegates who saw to it that the bill awaiting approval on the township was, at one point, withdrawn.

English, a Democrat and author, had begun his career in literature and enjoyed a brief friendship with Edgar Allan Poe until falling out over a public scandal involving Poe. Afterward, English penned the novel *1844, or, The Power of the S.F.*, which reportedly contains attacks on his former friend's life and works. This literary assault apparently led to the inspiration for Poe's classic tale of the macabre "The Cask of Amontillado," a work purportedly seen as referencing and skewering English's novel. The two authors continued their feud into the pages of various publications, but the Philadelphia-born English entered the political arena after Poe's death in 1849 and eventually settled into Newark, New Jersey in 1858 and the State General Assembly by 1863.

If English had his way in the Landis Township decision, the history of Cumberland County would have been very different. However, English was opposed by one of the strongest State Senators at the time, Providence Ludlum, a former Assemblyman and leader of the Republican Party in Cumberland County who hailed from the Bridgeton area and championed the cause of South Jersey. His ascendency in the State Senate was quick and his influence seen as being more effective than any previous legislator from his county. Warner credits the work of Charles K. Landis in creating the township named after him but writes that it was Ludlum who "saw to it that the state legislature hatched the township into a separate entity." Ludlum was able to reintroduce the bill and ensure its passage, a feat Warner calls "one of the first important steps toward the building up of a great moral settlement." Unfortunately, Ludlum, who may well have become governor of New Jersey one day, died suddenly before the completion of his second term in the State Senate.

Landis Township was officially granted its independence on March 7, 1864, but its first order of business proved to be a trial by fire for the new municipality. Elections to establish a governing committee were scheduled for March 22, but opposition to the new township from neighboring towns had been festering for several weeks and threatened to infiltrate the voting in order to sabotage the process. According to Warner, "rowdies" from surrounding towns attempted to disrupt the elections and Landis spent the day "challenging those who were not entitled to vote and to help protect the inspectors of election."

A Township Committee of five members, consisting of Robert Brandiff, John Kandle, J.C. Parsons, James McMahan and C.P. Davis, was elected that day. Along with the political history of the township's early years, information about this group of municipal leaders is sorely lacking. It wouldn't be long, however, before the five-man committee would be replaced in 1873 with a three-man body. But the township's early financial state was precarious. In its first year, the township spent $500 on roads, $600 on schools and $600 on incidentals. The expenses whittled down the municipal budget to $84.50. In two years, when it became necessary to borrow $20,747.16, the available cash was identified as $39.69.

In the summer of 1864, an unidentified reporter for the *American Agriculturalist* visited the Vineland community to "examine its condition and surroundings," and his article, which appeared in April the following year, provides a helpful outsider's view of Landis's settlement at the age of three. The reporter admits that he had been to the area years earlier, "when it was a perfect solitude, with neither hut nor clearing," and he is pleasantly surprised at how the area has developed since then.

The forest had disappeared, and in its place was to be seen a settlement containing some six-hundred-

and-fifty houses and four thousand inhabitants. There was a rapidly growing town, having churches, schools, stores, mills and other conveniences. I conversed with numerous settlers as to whence they came and how they fared in their new location. As a body they belong to the better class of citizens, are educated, intelligent, moral and enterprising. The drones which infest other communities are never found in hives like this. Great numbers of them are from New England, while the neighboring states and even the West are largely represented in the common center. Many have built costly and elegant houses. Many are professional fruit growers and gardeners. Those who buy farms are practical farmers. There are wealthy families in Vineland who remain there because of the mildness of the climate and healthfulness of the place. Taken altogether, the settlement has an old and cultivated look already.

The reporter is impressed by the area's soil, which "varies from a sandy to clay loam, is retentive of manures and abundantly productive," and the abundance produced by the fruit trees and vines. He was particularly amazed by the winter weather, writing that "the winters are so mild as to allow out-of-door work nearly all through them. Mr. Landis told me that for seven years he had not known the ploughing to be interrupted by reason of frost for five days in any one winter."

Speaking with Vineland farmers, the reporter notes that no one wished to return to "the bleak climate he had left. I saw but one desirous of selling and removing, and but one house having on it a handbill as being in market."

The article's comparison of the older and newer farms in the town offers interesting insight into the development of Vineland over three years:

> Most of these farms were just carved out of the woods, showing piles of roots that had been grubbed up. They are, of course, rough looking, like all new clearings in a new country; but the hand of industry was rapidly taming their wilderness and bringing them into prime condition. The general testimony was that one day's labor on this soil would accomplish twice as much work as if expended on the heavy or strong soil from which they had migrated. Such was the condition of the farms bought within six months or a year. Those which had been taken up by the first settlers, those of two-and-a-half years ago, presented a very different appearance. The genial and tractable soil had enabled their owners to work a great transformation, even in that brief period. From most of these, the stumps had disappeared. Great fields of grain were whitening to the harvest; many acres of peach and apple orchards were to be seen, the former promising to yield a crop the coming season. Gardens were full of fine vegetables. The front upon the road had been trimmed up and seeded to grass, while shrubbery and flowers were visible on many of the lawns.

Writer Charles Nordhoff, the German-born journalist who had worked for *Harpers*, the *New York Evening Post* and the *New York Tribune* before becoming a book writer, purchased Vineland property for his wife's aunt and uncle later in 1868 and witnessed the continued development of the town on his occasional visits. His assessment of Vineland, published in his book *The Communistic Societies of the United States*, credits Vineland's success to Charles K. Landis's refusal to raise the price of land in the town. "One... part of his plan appears to me to have been of extraordinary importance," Nordhoff writes, "though usually it is not mentioned in descriptions of Vineland. Mr. Landis established the price of his own uncultivated lands at twenty-five dollars per acre. At that price he sold to the first settler; and that price he did not increase for many years. Anyone could, within two or three years, buy wild land on the Vineland tract at twenty-five dollars per acre. This means that he did not speculate upon the improvements of the settlers. He gave to them the advantage of their labors. It resulted that many poor men bought, cleared, and planted places in Vineland on purpose to sell them, certain that they could, [and] if they wished, buy more land at the same price of twenty-five dollars per acre which they originally paid."

Nordhoff contends this is what led to the town's longevity. "In my judgment," he writes, "this feature of the Vineland enterprise, more than any other, changed it from a merely selfish speculation to one of a higher order, in which the settlers, to a large extent, have a common interest with the proprietor of the land. He might have done all the rest— might have laid out roads, proclaimed a 'no fence' law, prevented the establishment of dram-shops, helped on educational and other enterprises — and still, had he raised the price of his wild lands as the settlers increased, he would have been a mere land speculator, and I doubt if his scheme would have obtained more than a very moderate and short-lived success."

Having become familiar with the people who inhabited Vineland during its first dozen years as well as the town's farming and industry, Nordhoff was able to evaluate the effects of Landis's early endeavors, concluding that "in twelve years, the founder of Vineland was able to collect upon his tract — which had not a single inhabitant in 1861— about eleven thousand people. Most of these have improved their condition in life materially by settling there. Many of them came without sufficient capital, and no doubt suffered from want in the early days of their Vineland life. But if they persevered, two or three years of effort made them comfortable. Meantime they had, what our American farmers have not in general, easy access to good schools for their children, to churches and an intelligent society, and the possibility of good laws regarding the sale of liquor."

Landis continued to provide his residents with the best means of success during the town's first decade. To counter any problems with settlers who were not paying what they owed on their land, Landis decided at one point to offer a deal. According to a printed announcement that was circulated among those to whom it applied, the founder encouraged payment on purchased land by allowing what he called "one all payments…at the rate of 8 percent discount. As all unpaid sums bear 7 percent interest, this allowance is equivalent to 15 percent per annum, clear of taxes. Under these circumstances, it is more profitable to pay up for your land than to hold Government Bonds or any other security. This is open only for a limited period."

Despite Landis's early apprehension of establishing a new town as the Civil War was beginning, he wound up benefitting from the nation's conflict. With the South temporarily separated from the Union and the need for able bodies in the battlefields, prices of farm products rose significantly. Since Vineland would be as much an agricultural center as a manufacturing hub, the war provided guaranteed success for agrarian endeavors. Geologist Mark Demitroff believes that "Vineland's success was in part due to high value farm commodities during the Civil War."

John L. Burk arrived in Vineland in 1865, having already been hired by Landis as his bookkeeper, clerk and cashier. Burk had served in the Civil War, rising to the rank of Lieutenant Colonel in the 13th Pennsylvania Cavalry by the end of 1864. He would serve his new employer into the early 1880s, assisting him considerably over the years. At the time of Burk's arrival, the Landis tract contained 28,501 acres. By now, Landis employed twelve men to promote interest in his property and fifty to sixty employees to conduct real estate transactions, a situation that lasted until 1874-75, when the force was downsized because, as Burk later testified, "business was not so brisk…" From 1865 to 1875, Burk said, 17,196 letters had been received, 39,490 were sent and 89,934 circulars were mailed. There were 1,801 newspapers in which Landis placed ads which cost a total of $66,000. There were 1,507 individuals who purchased land and Landis sold 13,210 acres of his own land and 4,507 acres belonging to others.

Unlike his promotion of Hammonton, which included appearances before crowds in New England, Landis now relied exclusively on mailings and ads to do the marketing for him. An example of his promotional technique from this time can be seen in an Albany, New York newspaper titled *The Country Gentleman, A Journal for the Farm, the Garden and the Fireside Devoted to the Practice and Science of Agriculture and Horticulture at Large*, edited by Luther Tucker and Son and John J. Thomas. In the September 28, 1865 issue, a classified ad for Vineland can be found. Landis's promotion, under the title "Vineland, Fruit and Farm Lands," begins with a description of the location and informs farmers that they can expect

> a mild and healthful climate thirty miles south of Philadelphia by Railroad, in New Jersey on the same line of latitude as Baltimore, MD. The soil is rich and productive, varying from a clay to a sandy foam, suitable for wheat, grass, corn, tobacco, fruits and vegetables. This is a great fruit country. Five hundred vineyards and orchards have been planted out by experienced fruit-growers. Grapes, peaches, pears, etc., produce immense profits.

Landis follows his introduction with an explanation of how Vineland is rapidly growing. He cites the requirements of residents to discourage land speculation and lists the variety of items that would appeal to his readers while fudging the number of years the town has existed:

Vineland is already one of the most beautiful places in the United States. The entire territory, consisting of forty-five square miles of land, is laid out upon a general system of improvements. The land is only sold to settlers, with provision for public adornment. The place, on account of its great beauty, as well as other advantages, has become the resort of people of taste. It has increased five thousand people within the last ten years. Churches, stores, schools, academies, societies of art and learning, and other elements of refinement and culture have been introduced. Hundreds of people are constantly settling. Several hundred houses are now being constructed, and it has been estimated that five hundred will be built during the summer.

In the following section, Landis gets down to business, describing what is available for an interested farmer and what they can expect to pay:

Price of Farm lands, twenty acre lots and upwards, $25 per acre. Five and ten acre and village lots for sale. Fruits and vegetables ripen early in this district than of any other locality north of Norfolk, VA. Improved places for sale.

Landis is also quick not to discourage any other professions who might be reading his ad:

Openings for all kinds of businesses – Lumber Yards, Manufatories [sic], Foundries, Stores, and the like.

His sales pitch ends with a summary of appealing details as well as a guarantee that he will respond to inquiries and provide further information and an assessment by one of the leading agriculturalists of the day before signing off with his contact information.

For persons who desire mild winters, a healthful climate and a good soil, in a country beautifully improved, abounding in fruit and possessing all other social privilege, in the heart of civilization, it is worthy of a visit. Letters answered, and the *Vineland Rural*, a paper giving full information and reports of Solon Robinson, sent to applicants.

To ensure that farmers took his ad seriously and considered relocating to this newly established South Jersey community, Landis concludes his promotion with a portion of the report that Robinson had completed. Robinson was highly regarded in the farming world at the time and Vineland's founder, flaunting the evaluation like an A+ paper in an English class, provided his most convincing argument.

From the report of Solon Robinson, Agricultural Editor of the *Tribune*: It is one of the most extensive fertile tracts, in an almost level position, and suitable condition for pleasant farming that we know of this side of the Western prairies.

Following the first major influx of settlers to Vineland, Landis seemed to realize that he couldn't handle the task of land sales on his own. In order to maintain control over his operation and keep it out of the hands of land speculators, he approached his friend William A. House with an offer. On August 21, 1865, a deal was struck between Landis and House in which the former would provide a team of sales representatives for the latter to exhibit land for sale in Vineland. According to the agreement, Landis would be paid "two-and-a-half percent on all sales made of lands not belonging to said Landis by said House or any person employed by him to make such sales." House was furnished with a map of the Vineland settlement and would be paid two-and-a-half percent for the sale of any lands belonging to Landis. One of House's hired assistants had to be approved by both parties, but House was prohibited by the contract from interfering with any other agents "on business of said Landis."

House would be the first of Landis's land agents. By 1866, an advertisement for sales of property identifies John Gage as another salesman. A Midwestern industrialist and progressive, Gage and his wife Portia had settled in Vineland and would become two of its prominent early citizens.

Back in 1864, the *American Agricultural* reporter had noted the advantage of the rail line that connected the town with other South Jersey locations as well as Philadelphia. In fact, Vineland businesses enjoyed a prime location for access to metropolitan markets. For all residents, a simple visit to the big city could be easily accomplished. From the start, rail transportation to Philadelphia via Camden had been provided by the Millville & Glassboro Railroad, but, for seven years, Vinelanders traveling on this line usually met with the same ridicule and resentment that befell Landis at the hands of the railway crew who thought that founding a settlement in the middle of nowhere was pure folly.

Initially, two planks served as Vineland's train station, and Landis requested that a station be built by the rail company in Vineland. He recounted the response in his essay on the founding of the town:

> I now asked the lessees of the railroad to build a platform station at the Landis Avenue crossing, to land my passengers. The lessees refused, as they had no confidence in the enterprise – did not believe that a station would ever do business to get their money back. Finally, I had to furnish the few dollars' worth of rough lumber to have the platform built. I think I also built it.

What Landis constructed was an uncovered thirty-foot long wooden platform that replaced the original two planks but that was still lacking as a proper station.

Evidence of Vineland's growth failed to sway the rail line's opinion. Landis lamented that even though "lumber and goods began to come in by railroad," he continued to be "greatly embarrassed for the want of a station. The railroad lessees still pretended a lack of faith."

Before it was completed, the Millville and Glassboro Railroad had sought a franchise to build a rail line from

Millville to Cape May, at the time known as Cape Island. The franchise was granted on March 15, 1860, but it wasn't until April 1862 that construction began. However, after ten miles of track were completed, the company ceased work in the town of Manumuskin and the project was halted for a year until the Cape May and Millville Railroad acquired the franchise and completed the line. During the interim, the Millville and Glassboro system turned over its operations to a company headed by George Thomas and S. A. Garrison. Thomas took control in August 1861 around the same time Landis drove his stake at roughly the same point as the rail line's tracks at Landis Avenue and the Boulevard. But within two years, the railroad was leased to a new group comprised of Thomas, Alfred Porter and Nathaniel Chew.

In the summer of 1863, Vineland residents continued to ride the Millville and Glassboro rail system and were among the many that graced the railway cars on the Cape May extension. But A.G. Warner notes that the railroad's management continually inconvenienced Vineland inhabitants, branded as "Winelanders", by dropping them off in the woods, at the Forest Grove stop or at the Millville station.

"There was never so illy (sic) conducted a [railroad] before," Warner writes, "there never will be again. Even the [train] engineers and firemen had as loud a voice of command as the Directors themselves and were always sure to pass the Vineland platform at full speed."

By 1864, that platform was part of a two-story stone building called Union Hall that served as a train station on the north side of Landis Avenue, east of the tracks. In order to ensure that the railroad company would build it, Landis promised to lease the second floor as a meeting room for five years. At the same time, a South Vineland Station was added on Sherman Avenue and the Forest Grove site was renamed the North Vineland Station.

The residents of Vineland were forced to tolerate the prejudice and inconveniences of the rail line, but in 1867, the West Jersey Railroad exerted its power and threatened to build a rail system that would run parallel to the Millville and Glassboro track if it was not allowed to purchase or lease the smaller line. According to the book *Railroads of New Jersey: Fragments of the Past in the Garden State Landscape* by Lorett Treese, "In 1868, the New Jersey legislature permitted the Millville and Glassboro Railroad Company to be merged with the West Jersey, which leased the Cape May and Millville the same year. The West Jersey also leased four other South Jersey short lines, thus gaining control of most of the railroad mileage in that part of the state. The resulting West Jersey rail system made Cape May even more popular and allowed South Jersey farmers to ship produce to Philadelphia more quickly."

Landis may have foreseen the inevitable monopoly the West Jersey Railroad envisioned for itself even before the Millville and Glassboro line was approached but, according to what he recorded in "The Social Science of Vineland," what proved the least tolerable circumstances were the "high charges for freight upon our single railroad. I remonstrated with the company and received from its general manager fair promises about reduction, but these were not fulfilled." His solution was to organize a group of investors to create a Vineland rail system that would offer a competitive transport of Vineland goods that would also provide access to new markets. He writes that he, "with much difficulty, obtained a charter from the State Legislature for a new railroad leading direct to New York and Baltimore."

In early 1866, Landis and his investors filed with the State of New Jersey an application for a new rail line that would connect Vineland with these locations by way of the Raritan and Delaware Bay Railroad. The coming of Vineland's second railroad was proudly announced a few months later in the *Vineland Weekly*. The newspaper published a March 7, 1867 telegram from Landis who had traveled to Trenton to witness the approval of the railroad bill that allowed for a new line running from Atsion to the Delaware Bay. Both Vineland and Bridgeton were planned stops.

At the time, the standard route to New York by rail from South Jersey consisted of a line running from Camden to Atco aboard the Camden and Atlantic Railroad, which then switched to a branch of the same line in order to reach Atsion. Another transfer in Atsion placed passengers on the Raritan and Delaware Railroad which would drop them off in Sandy Hook where they could take a boat to Manhattan. The new railway would put Vineland on a direct path to New York.

An organizational meeting of the newly-created Vineland Railway Company was held July 27, 1867. The election of officers resulted in Landis as president, Hiram Bostwick as vice-president, William A. House as secretary and Marcius Wilson as treasurer. Before surveys could begin, however, the Vineland Railway Company encountered a setback that would cost the project five months. A.G. Warner writes that because of an injunction imposed by the Camden and Amboy Railroad, the Raritan and Delaware Bay Railroad discontinued its run to New York. Faced with this dilemma, the company sought and was granted approval by the State Legislature to use the Camden and Amboy line which was considered a more direct route.

In a letter from September 1867, Landis addressed investors in the railroad project, writing of the necessity of the new railway for his town and explaining that "the people of Vineland are extremely anxious on this point and the aid received here is given as such for the purpose of obtaining relief…in making the connection to New York." But Landis also conveys his reluctance in allowing the new rail system to run through his earlier settlement of Hammonton. Expressing "my sympathy in running the line of our road through Hammonton," he adds that his reservations stem from "consequences of early associations."

When the town of Hammonton discovered five years later that it was being ignored by the new rail system, the *Hammonton Item* ran the following editorial comment on February 3, 1872:

> Either the officers or employees of the Vineland R.R. or both seem disposed to ignore the existence of Hammonton. Such ignorance as the employees profess to entertain is unpardonable. Several cases have come to our notice where the conductors and ticket agents were with difficulty made to understand that there was such a place as Hammonton, although given upon the time-table and there being a very neat station building at that point. There seems to be an understanding between the employees that they are to use every effort to keep people away from

Hammonton. If Mr. Landis or anyone else expects to push Vineland ahead by any such underhand means, they will some fine day find themselves "hoist of their own petard."

By December 28, 1867, surveys for the railroad from Vineland to the Delaware Bay were concluded. In the fall of 1868, surveys from Atsion to Vineland were completed and work began shortly afterward.

After several years of continued growth and success, Landis was about to face a number of challenges. The first was a rumbling of discontent among some of the residents. According to later testimony by Hosea Allen, "Mr. Landis asked me about people who had bought land making complaints; in 1866 it took place; he sent a messenger to me stating that he wished to see me; he asked me how the people were feeling, whether they were satisfied or dissatisfied; I told him some were satisfied and some uneasy and dissatisfied…he did not ask who the individuals were who were dissatisfied; told him many felt discouraged and many did not; did not tell him what they were dissatisfied with; I mentioned to him at an interview, held sometime during the summer of 1866, that people claimed that they had been deceived and were here and spent their all and did not know what to do; they said they were deceived by the advertisements; the statement I made to Mr. Landis was true."

If Landis felt threatened, it wouldn't have been the first time. Allen would later reveal that he "acted as a guard to his house, I think in the summer of 1864, at night; George W. Pryor was with me; we sat up during the night and occasionally walked about the streets; there was a rumor that Landis's property might be burned; I watched no other property but his."

Still, the dissatisfaction expressed by certain Vinelanders had already become an invitation for land speculators to set up operations in the town a full year before Landis questioned Allen. A new land office by the firm Hall and Branch opened on Landis Avenue on February 23, 1865. Run by Richard Hall, already a resident of the town, and John L. Branch, the real estate agency, according to Branch in his pamphlet *Vineland: An Expose and History*, catered to the sale of "improved lands," property owned by disenchanted early Vineland settlers looking to sell.

Landis considered the enterprise detrimental to Vineland and, according to later testimony by Frank Bingham, the founder gave a speech at a mass meeting called by the residents and held at Plum Street Hall: "Landis made a speech and said in substance that he had been at quite an expense in advertising and he considered it unfair for any persons to come there and hang out their signs and take advantage of the people he had attracted by his advertising; he desired no land office established for a period of two years; a resolution was introduced which passed by an almost unanimous vote sustaining Mr. Landis's wishes…"

Bingham offers a condensed version of the situation, but Branch provides a more detailed, albeit self-serving, account of how the course of events played out. "We employed a man to distribute our cards upon the [railroad] cars between Vineland and Philadelphia," writes Branch. "Not a week elapsed after we opened our office before we had over $15,000 worth of improved lands for sale, which had been put into our hands by residents of Vineland who were anxious to leave the place. As our cards fell into the hands of every passenger going to Vineland, and there are many every week, we soon began to trench upon the business of Mr. Landis."

Hall and Branch may have accumulated $15,000 worth of improved lands within a week, but Landis did not wait that long to act. The meeting discussed by Bingham, what Branch termed as "secret," occurred on Saturday February 25, a mere two days after the firm opened its office. On Monday February 27, Branch was approached by a committee assembled to request that the firm end its business practices in Vineland. With Hall away in Philadelphia, the committee extended Branch an invitation to attend a meeting addressing the issue, which he did, listening to the proposed resolution that denied another land agency in town for a two-year period. When asked to explain the firm's views, he requested and was granted an adjournment until the next day when Hall would return. However, when the committee met with the partners on Tuesday, it was informed that all further discourse on the matter would be conducted only in writing.

Branch claims that the committee left the office, deliberated and returned soon with a written statement that proclaimed that it believed the firm's presence in town was "against the policy – the best interests, present and future, of Vineland, contrary to and against public opinion, and doing an injustice to the founder of the place" and requested that Hall and Branch "close your office and remove your sign." The partners declined. In response, cards were then apparently printed at the *Vineland Weekly* and distributed among residents warning of the danger posed by the new real estate firm. A March 5 meeting, preceded by a procession of citizens past closed storefronts of Landis Avenue to Plum Street Hall, addressed the issue publicly for the final time. Hall and Branch, fending off hisses, offered their defense, but the resolution to prevent any new land offices in Vineland for the next two years passed.

Later, at the Hall and Branch office, the partners were confronted as to their intentions. They said only mob violence would force them to comply. No such violence erupted. "We continued our business some days after, but the men who gave us Powers of Attorney to sell their property, revoked our authority, and we did not deem it advisable, under those circumstances, to continue," writes Branch in his pamphlet, which variously serves as an account of his experiences while plying his trade in town, a refutation of Vineland's advertised features and an indictment of Landis's practices.

The pamphlet may simply be retaliation against Vineland and its founder for shutting down his business, despite the inclusion of such disclaimers as, "we don't wish to disparage the great work that Mr. Landis has accomplished in settling up that great wilderness with an industrious and thrifty people, yet we believe the future success of the place is being seriously impaired by abuses in the management that ought to be corrected." Relying on what he calls "facts" that "were furnished us by resident citizens of Vineland," Branch admits that "some errors may have inadvertently crept into these pages but we have aimed to make it reliable." He does not identify if those who provided "facts" included any landowners dissatisfied with Vineland and looking to sell.

Branch dismisses much of Landis's advertising, remarking that Vineland's "manufacturing, agricultural or mineral resources make no promise of reward," calling its taxes "very high, often oppressive" and a cause of "great complaint and disaffection among the people," noting that the winds of the previous winter were "unusually severe" in contrast to the mild climate Landis promoted, arguing that Millville is a better manufacturing center than Vineland and debating the advertised healthy climate by stating that one local physician treated "over twenty cases of fever" the previous year. He rejects the property of Vineland at one point as having "always been regarded as poor and unprofitable land." It's curious, then, why he would choose Vineland as a location in which to sell property.

Branch's own prejudices can also be witnessed in the pamphlet and might reveal why he did not command more support from the populace. In discussing his attempts to maintain his Vineland office, he refers to "a stuttering secretary" at one meeting, describes a committee member as "a simple-minded creature," concludes that the resolution against him was "drawn by a conceited, vollute [sic] fellow, with more ear-wax than brains" and describes the end of the Landis Avenue procession as "'brought up' by a few of the enthusiastic bloomerhood, which abound in Vineland."

Yet Branch's publication also contains certain statements and accusations that cannot be ignored or dismissed as easily as others. In a long series of questions, he charges Landis and his real estate agents with unbecoming actions: "Have you not confiscated the lands of your neighbors, together with all improvements, and forfeited the money paid, to gratify your inordinate desire for gain, upon the pretense that they were acting against the wonderful 'Vineland Policy?' Is there scarcely a house and lot or a farm upon the 'Tract' but that is for sale and do you not object to having a man disposing of his own property?"

While it was in Branch's best interest to paint an unflattering portrait of Landis, the founder's own actions, regardless of his reasons, demonstrated his unwillingness in 1865 to allow competition from other realtors in Vineland. But Branch's specific allegations, if true, are more alarming. He queries of Landis, "Didn't one of your agents assault an old gentleman, lame and unable to defend himself, for attempting to sell his own land?" and then asks, "When citizens have advertised their lands for sale, haven't your agents torn down their advertisements, or caused them to be torn down?" His next question may very well apply to himself: "Has not one man been drummed out of town for attempting to engage in the sale of real estate in Vineland?"

Branch then questions Landis's use of pending legislation in the State of New Jersey to "authorize the sale of lands in Vineland for the non-payment of taxes within four months after the same become due and are unpaid." The introduction of a state law to protect his investments was not unprecedented for Landis, as evidenced by his actions over the next decade. Branch also mentions another pending law to "regulate the school system of Vineland, and making certain gentlemen a body corporate, three of whom are your agents, and with full power and authority to assess and collect taxes for schools and school house purposes, at the discretion of the board."

What Landis accomplished by suppressing the firm of Hall and Branch and providing a two-year window in which his sales continued to be the only ones allowed in Vineland only delayed the town's inevitable paradigm shift. Staving off land speculators proved impossible to avoid forever and, when the resolution expired in 1867, outside realtors once again looked to residents who were dissatisfied or who hadn't achieved the success they envisioned in their business ventures in Vineland. To be fair, the failure of some, particularly those in agriculture, may have been due in part to the post-war era itself. Several years after the close of the Civil War, the country had returned to its pre-war conditions and farmers began to face lower prices for goods.

Looking back in 1880, Landis summed up in a journal entry the change that he and Vineland were about to experience: "The first settlers ushered in bought their land of me at a low price and improved; the result of this improvement and advertising was that these lands went up enormously. Then came the speculative time and the speculators bought the people out who had bought their lands of me at fabulous prices...The first settlers were all my friends, but the speculators with whom I had nothing to do, were acrimonious enemies, and no doubt remain so to this day."

If the true vision of Vineland is to be witnessed, however, it requires a look at town life in the 1860s when the dreams and ideas Landis envisioned and implemented not only flourished untainted, but also defined the town and earned it its most honorable coverage in the national press.

Chapter 3
Early Vineland

Vineland would prove to be rather progressive in its formative years by drawing settlers from an area Landis targeted early on. When he began placing his advertisements in New England publications in 1861, he sought an audience familiar with the types of businesses and farming he wished to establish in Vineland and the region was also a hotbed of philosophical thought and reformist causes. The notions of "self-reliance" and "civil disobedience," from the works of Ralph Waldo Emerson and Henry David Thoreau respectively, echoed loudly from the northeast corner of the country, feeding the imagination of writers as diverse as Nathaniel Hawthorne and Walt Whitman and provoking puzzled responses from guardians of the conventional.

At a gathering of some seven hundred Vinelanders on Christmas evening in 1863 at the Landis residence of the Magnolia House, a husband and wife offered an unaccompanied performance of original lyrics set to the tune of "Hurrah for Old New England." The dinner, organized and implemented by a committee of six women whose work included preparing mince and plum puddings, writing invitations and creating the decorative wreaths and stars that would adorn the hall, was hosted by Landis and featured members of the Vineland Brass Band providing musical entertainment. The evening was filled with food, song, dance and conversation and offered a view of the close-knit community Vineland had become in two years. And its New England contingent had a hand in creating the town's early identity.

Many of Vineland's New England settlers transferred their lifestyles to Landis's utopian experiment of a planned community and, by July 1864, a group of fifty-two men and women became the first to plant a progressive flag in Vineland by organizing themselves separately from the religions first established in the town during its early years. This group of free thinkers called itself The Friends of Progress because of its belief in every individual's right to think as he or she pleased and to express those thoughts openly. According to the *Vineland Historical Magazine*, this society, which included Quakers, atheists, skeptics, deists and free love advocates, consisted mostly of Spiritualists who, following the philosopher Emanuel Swedenborg, believed in a deity and communed with the dead.

The society's constitution stated its purpose was to "promote the interests of mankind...by holding ...meetings for free discussion, lectures and sermons as will tend to…promote progress and development." Because of its position outside the established churches of the time, the group wasn't allowed to use any of the city's religious facilities for meetings. Landis offered three lots on Plum Street to the Friends of Progress. The society additionally purchased three lots on Pear Street and lost no time in constructing a meeting house of its own, Plum Street Hall, which soon became a popular gathering spot for all of Vineland.

The structure was described in Thelma H. Taylor's *Vineland Historical Magazine* article on the history of the hall as being 60' by 70' with a flat roof. It was lit by oil lamps and heated by four iron stoves. Settees which seated up to six individuals were not cushioned but were movable so that audiences could enjoy dancing. The motto of the Friends of Progress, "Liberty, Equality and Fraternity," was emblazoned in bold letters above the stage which was located on the north side of the building. Three large entryways were at the south end of the structure.

Early on, the venue also served as a gathering point for residents on New Year's Day when they would be greeted by Landis. Taylor's account reports that, throughout the year, debates were common at the hall. On many occasions, a speaker presented one viewpoint on one evening and the opposing view was discussed by another resident the following night. Each speaker was then given another evening for rebuttal. Such events would provide the townspeople with a full weeknight schedule.

Plum Street Hall also played host to various distinguished figures who visited Vineland at the behest of Friends of

Progress members like Cornelius B. Campbell, who was known prior to his arrival in Vineland for his anti-slavery efforts. In 1868, African-American author and orator Frederick Douglass delivered his lecture on "Self-Made Men" at Vineland's Unitarian Church on April 10. The next evening, he spoke at Plum Street Hall and returned there the following afternoon for another appearance. During his stay in Vineland, he also visited with Campbell at the latter's home on Park Avenue.

At a time when women dared not test the resolve of election officials, Portia Gage attempted to vote in Vineland as early as 1868. When a temperance vote was placed before residents on March 1, she secured a ballot and proceeded to cast her vote in the decision. When informed that her vote could not be accepted for reasons she knew quite well, she yielded but, before withdrawing, explained that her effort was made simply to put the principle of women's suffrage to a test.

The first American Equal Rights Association (AERA) member to visit Vineland was Lucy Stone, who arrived in in the town ahead of her compatriots Susan B. Anthony and Elizabeth Cady Stanton by nearly a year. She, along with other suffrage advocates, appeared at a women's rights convention at Plum Street Hall on November 29 and 30, 1867. Stone was one of the key speakers, and the convention would certainly prove an influence on the women in Vineland the following year.

Anthony's visit occurred September 5, 1868, and the information handed down over the years has her traveling to Vineland alone. However, according to *The History of Woman Suffrage, Volume 3*, edited by Stanton and Anthony, that was not the case. The text reports that in "1868, Mrs. Stanton and Miss Anthony attended a two days' convention in Vineland and helped to rouse the enthusiasm of the people."

The two women put in an appearance at Plum Street Hall and attended a meeting of the Woman Suffrage Association of Vineland, but during their spare time, the two activists made it a point to acquaint themselves with the town. A letter from an unidentified woman included in *The History of Woman Suffrage* reveals that the two visitors discovered that Vineland had a perfect model for the activists' cause at one of the town's churches.

> The Unitarian church in this town is highly favored in having for its pastor a young man of progressive and thoroughly liberal ideas. Rev. Oscar Clute is well known as an earnest advocate in the cause of woman. Last Sunday the communion or Lord's Supper was administered in his church. One of the laymen who usually assists in the distribution of the bread and wine was absent, and Mr. Clute invited one of the women to officiate in his stead. She did so in such a sweet and hospitable manner that it gave new interest to the occasion. Even those who do not like innovations could not find fault. And why should anyone be displeased? The Christ of the sacrament was the emancipator of women. In olden time they had deaconesses, and in most of our churches women constitute a majority of the communicants, so it seems particularly appropriate that they should be served by women. Women vote on all matters

connected with this church, they are on all "standing committees," and sometimes are chosen to act as trustees.

The impression Anthony and Stanton left on the town's female population would be put into practice that autumn. By the end of October, 172 women residents decided they would cast votes in the presidential election in early November. Elizabeth A. Kingsbury's account of Election Day in Vineland on November 3, written two days later and published in the November 19, 1868 edition of Anthony and Stanton's newspaper, *The Revolution*, offers an intriguing view of the event:

> At a meeting of women, held the week before election, a unanimous vote was taken that we would go to the polls. John Gage, chairman of the Woman Suffrage Association of Vineland, called a meeting, and though the day was an inclement one, there was a good attendance. A number of earnest men as well as women addressed the audience...At 7:30 A.M., November 3, John and Portia Gage and myself entered Union Hall, where the judges of election had already established themselves for the day...We seated ourselves in the chairs brought for the occasion, when one gentleman placed a small table for our use. Another inquired if we were comfortable and the room sufficiently warm. "Truly,' we thought, 'this does not look like a terrible opposition."

Kingsbury notes what transpired next:

As time passed, there came more men and women into the hall. Quite a number of the latter presented their notes at the table where those of men were received, where they were rejected with politeness, and then taken to the other side of the platform and deposited in our box. Shall I describe this box, twelve inches long and six wide, and originally a grape-box? Very significant of Vineland. Soon there came to the aid of Mrs. Gage and myself a blooming and beautiful young lady, Estelle Thomson, who, with much grace and dignity, sat there throughout the day, recording the names of the voters. It would have done you good to have witnessed the scene. Margaret Pryor…sat there in her nice Quaker bonnet by the side of Miss Thomson a great part of the day.

While the women's votes in Vineland that day weren't included in the final count, the results indicate that Ulysses S. Grant received 164 votes, his Democratic opponent, Horatio Seymour, received only 4 votes, Elizabeth Cady Stanton 2 votes, and candidates identified as Fremont and Mrs. Governor Harvey of Wisconsin 1 vote apiece. Anthony acknowledged the event in a letter to Campbell ten days later: "Vineland women did splendidly on Election Day and will no doubt continue to do the same."

The first convention of the New Jersey State Woman's Suffrage Association was held in Vineland at Plum Street Hall on Wednesday December 2, 1868. The convention served as a reflection of the free-thinking movement that defined Vineland's earliest decade. It was also a noteworthy achievement that earned the attention of the national press. The invitation to the event read: "All representatives who are opposed to the existing aristocracy, and who desire to establish a republican form of government in New Jersey, based upon the consent of the governed, are respectfully invited to attend. This is woman's hour." The convention established a platform for the movement in New Jersey and the 150 women in attendance witnessed Lucy Stone's second appearance in town.

For the next two years, Vineland women continued to vote. In the March local election of 1869, 182 women cast votes. The November 1869 county election witnessed 214 women voting, but one year later only 130 showed up to cast ballots. At all three elections, the votes were collected in a separate box and ignored. In December 1871, about a dozen women led by Portia Gage attempted to vote in Landis Township. But Gage explained that it wasn't until 1873, a time when the free-thinking progressive movement that had earned Vineland so much attention had lost its local appeal and newsworthiness, that "our claim to vote seemed to most of the voters to be a just one."

Victoria Woodhull, a Spiritualist and champion of free love, visited Vineland before joining the Equal Rights Party and, in 1872, became the first woman to run for U.S. President. She selected as her running mate Frederick Douglass, the first African-American nominee for Vice-President.

The grandest task undertaken by The Friends of Progress was an attempt to establish an Industrial School in Vineland for males and females. Co-educational institutions were relatively new in the U.S. at the time. The first was Ohio's

Oberlin College, having admitted women in 1837. Very few documents about this Friends of Progress project survive, but several articles that appeared in a Boston Spiritualist weekly and which were excerpted in the *Vineland Historical Magazine* indicate that plans for the college were launched in March 1865 by the Gages, Campbell, Warren Chase and George Haskell. Land was purchased at what today is the area of Chestnut Avenue and Delsea Drive. The time and place were certainly right for such an institution in Vineland. The Morrill Act of 1862 gave each state federally owned lands to sell for the purpose of instituting colleges for agriculture and industry. Vineland, as its history has proven, was suited for both, but this apparently was the one failed project for The Friends of Progress.

The bond that existed among Vineland's earliest residents is perhaps best reflected by how the town reacted to a crisis that threatened its existence within the first few years. The Civil War was fought nowhere near South Jersey, but the state would send more than 88,000 soldiers into battle for the Union over the course of the war. Better than 6,000 soldiers from New Jersey lost their lives in battle. Vineland would have its share of Civil War veterans, a few who were residents here when they volunteered in the early years of the war and many who settled in the town in the aftermath, but Landis's settlement was faced with a difficult decision when draft options were eventually offered.

President Abraham Lincoln's first call to arms occurred in May 1861, three months prior to Landis's founding of Vineland. By March 1863, with casualties and desertions rampant, a draft was established. Along with it, however, were provisions whereby an individual could buy his way out of serving or find a substitute to take his place in the military. The draft and its alternatives soon proved controversial in many of the northern states. Riots broke out in various cities and the perception among the lower and middle classes was that the option of buying one's way out of military duty favored only the rich. One of the most famous insurrections, the July 1863 New York Draft Riots, provoked several days of violence on the streets of Manhattan during which time several police stations, the mayor's home and a hotel were attacked and set on fire and several African-Americans were lynched in the streets.

While Vineland may not have welcomed conscription, it did not resort to violence in order to express its disapproval. Additionally, the town welcomed the alternatives, seeing them as a practical advantage for the community rather than evidence of an ideological "rich man's war and poor man's fight," as some called it. A.G. Warner, in his *Vineland and Vinelanders*, states that there were no problems securing volunteers to fill the town's quota of twenty-one required recruits in the 1863 draft. These individuals were offered a "substantial bounty" as incentive and fulfilled the requirement.

In 1864, however, a second draft determined that seventy-two men were needed from Vineland and Landis Township. "The citizens of that day were mostly men of families," writes Warner, "and with but small means or being engaged in opening new farms, felt it almost like ruin to be compelled to leave their work and families to go to the field of war." A meeting of township citizens resulted in a unanimous decision "to buy the quota, at any price." That price, it was reported, totaled $50,400 in addition to $10,500 in costs apparently connected with the bounties promised to those serving in the first draft. A committee consisting of John Kandle, William A. House, Henry E. Thayer and W.O.H. Gwynneth was given the power to borrow money on the credit of the town. For those who believed that only the rich could buy their way out of service, Vineland sent a different message about the use of the option, one that demonstrated how its solidarity guaranteed the survival of the town during a time when failure in businesses meant failure of the community.

There were some individuals in Vineland who privately chose to hire someone to substitute for them on the battlefield. The process was to have included full reimbursement from the town. However, the *Vineland Historical Magazine* reported in 1922 that a Pardon Gifford paid $150 to hire an agent to procure and compensate an Englishman to serve as a replacement. Gifford complained in 1911 that the deal cost him a total of $800, yet claimed he was only reimbursed half the amount by the town. What became of the Englishman is still a mystery.

"Not a single man was drafted from Landis Township, "J. Meade Landis, the grandson of Vineland's founder, reported in 1961 and military records for those who registered in Cumberland County in that 1864 draft support his statement. While all other townships at the time are represented, Landis Township is conspicuously missing.

In explaining his vision for Vineland, Landis was very clear about what would constitute a successful municipality. "In order to secure its success," he wrote, "establish therein the best of schools, and different industries, and the churches of different denominations." He referred to these necessities as "essential to the prosperity of mankind."

The education of the children was of utmost importance for Landis. The town's first school began classes on July 28, 1862, less than a year after the stake was driven at the Boulevard. It was a private institution whose little yellow building and lone teacher, Luella S. Richardson, were financed by Landis. The twelve-week session was attended by eleven students who, according to the *Vineland Historical Magazine*, were "nearly if not quite all the children of a suitable age to attend school on the Vineland tract." Vineland's first group of students consisted of Alexander Bachelder, Martha Bachelder, Moses Bachelder, Fannie M. Cotton, Carrie Davis, Ansel Faunce, Frank Fish, George Fish, Hattie Perry, Katie R. Richardson and William Willis.

The school building was utilized by the community in its early days as a meeting hall for organizations in the evening, a place of worship for various religions on Sunday and an entertainment hall at other times. By 1863, however, the population of Vineland had grown, and fifty-five students needed to be educated. The town organized a school district and made arrangements for the use of the original school building as the first public school in Vineland. It opened May 4, 1863, offering another twelve-week session that concluded July 24. Richardson was the teacher. Only four of the students from the previous year, George and Frank Fish, Richardson and Davis, returned for the 1863 session.

In 1864, when Vineland witnessed a major influx of settlers, the growth of the community from a one-school town to a school system occurred. By 1869, sixteen public schools and a series of private institutions were in place. The

Vineland Historical Magazine, in the article "Early Educational Developments in Vineland," identifies some examples of the rates advertised by the Vineland Academy, one of the private schools. The institution's quarterly charge for higher English and vocal music was $8, while French or German cost $5 and Greek and Latin only $3. Drawing was $4. Common English cost $7. For students under twelve years of age, English and vocal music were $5 each, while the study of piano and guitar were priced at $12.50 each. Private vocal lessons cost $7. The Academy, also known as Morton's Academy, conducted its classes in the old yellow schoolhouse after a new two-story structure was built in 1868 for public school use.

Tuition fees were not favored by everyone in the community and public sentiment soon demanded a free high school. Districts 5, 6 and 8 were consolidated to make way for the opening of Vineland High School, with Charles H. Wright as principal, on January 24, 1870. Because no official building existed yet to house faculty and students, Plum Street Hall became the temporary home of the high school.

The aesthetics of Plum Street Hall did not offer the best educational environment. The large structure was barewalled. In lieu of desks, students were seated on benches at tables. Eight students were arranged on each side of the table. The seating formed two long rows in the center of the room, with the boys in one row and the girls in the other. The teacher sat on a platform where only half of the students could see him/her. Initially, the curriculum was limited. Algebra was the extent of high mathematics and rhetoric and grammar represented the English requirements, with spelling bees promoting healthy competition with an educational agenda.

Prior to the Civil War, public education in the U.S. was confined to elementary school. Secondary education was college preparatory in nature and was conducted in private or parochial institutions. It was only in the 1870s that the concept of public high schools was looked at favorably. R. Craig Koedel in his study *South Jersey Heritage*, reports that "proponents of public high schools first made their voices heard in Trenton in 1871." It wasn't until the 1890s, however, that the state required all first and second-class cities to establish high schools. Vineland apparently was a year ahead of the Trenton discussions and twenty years in front of state legislation on public high schools. Koedel points out that, while it seemed as if Camden was on its way toward fashioning a public high school in South Jersey in 1865, "Vineland led the way by opening a high school in 1870." The City of Salem followed in 1875 with Camden, Gloucester City, Atlantic City and Egg Harbor City all establishing theirs in the 1890s.

An official high school facility for Vineland was on the horizon, however. On September 26, 1873, according to B. F. Ladd's *History of Vineland*, a ceremony was held for the laying of the cornerstone of the new Vineland High School building, located across from Plum Street Hall. The ceremony featured speeches by Rev. J. L. Beman, Rev. N. B. Randall and Rev. William Pittenger. On August 22, 1874, the city was flooded with dignitaries who assembled for the dedication ceremony. New Jersey Governor Joel Parker, former Senator A. G. Cattell and General Orville Babcock joined President Ulysses S. Grant in Vineland for this momentous occasion. Ladd reports that "Company D, 4th Battalion, and the Vineland Cornet Band met the distinguished party at the depot and escorted them to the residence of Mr. Henry Hartson, where they partook of light refreshments and then proceeded to Plum Street Hall...where the exercises were to take place." Speeches by Grant, Parker, Cattell and others filled the ceremony for the new $25,000 three-story façade that was Vineland's first high school.

Even after the building was constructed, commencement exercises continued to be held in the former Plum Street Hall, newly rechristened Cosmopolitan Hall, for another thirty years. The hall received a $2,500 facelift in 1875. The stage was expanded, the roof replaced and intrusive center posts removed. The following year, gas lights were added. The new name signaled a change from the meeting place that once served as a forum for free thinkers, debaters and activists visiting the town. The suffrage conventions were no longer part of the hall's schedule, with interest turning to local and touring musical acts and dramatic performances and local commencement exercises.

Vineland's early recognition of the importance of providing a high school education, however, did not guarantee a large student body during the 1870s. Ladd records that the May 1877 graduation was held in Cosmopolitan Hall where C.F. Scofield, John Wells, Phebe Wilbur, Lizzie Vanderburg and valedictorian Stella Ingram received diplomas from school board president H. N. Greene. In 1878, over 1,000 people turned out at Cosmopolitan Hall to witness the graduation of "a large class" which consisted of ten students. The 1879 commencement had H. M. Pratt, the principal of the high school, conferring diplomas to a class of fourteen. Thelma H. Taylor points out that it was common to sell tickets, take up collections or charge admission to graduation ceremonies. A ten-cent admission fee was part of the 1887 commencement, and the money collected was used for the library fund.

When it came to businesses, Vineland was filled with a plethora of entrepreneurs and merchants who relocated their shops and enterprises to South Jersey. Many were farmers plucked from other states who wished to take advantage of Vineland's climate and soil conditions, but there was also a burgeoning newspaper trade with several publications at a time serving up local and national news any given year.

Shortly after its 1861 founding, Vineland nurtured the business of pearl button manufacturing as one of its earliest enterprises. While specialized buttons of gold and ivory were around since the 14th century, pearl buttons were a relatively new and popular commodity of the 19th century, initially produced in bulk in London, England and Vienna, Austria. Button manufacturing in the United States didn't begin until 1826 when Samuel Williston started a modest business which soon led to the construction of a factory and world distribution.

While the pearl button boom occurred in the 1880s and 1890s, Vineland was well ahead of most of the country. By August 1, 1868, Captain S.F. Hanson and a Mr. Bryant, established a factory on the northeast corner of Sixth and Quince Streets and began production of pearl buttons using imported shells from China, Panama and the Red Sea.

Hanson and Bryant had hired as superintendent a Newark, New Jersey resident, David James, whose reputation was one of the best in the field of pearl button manufacturing. Within a year of working for Hanson and Bryant, James established his own business, and within two years, had the sole pearl button factory in Vineland from 1871 to 1872. In 1875, the business was placed in the hands of a relative while James opened yet another button factory in Landis Township.

In March 1876, another pearl button manufacturer opened its doors and three years later, E.O. Mills & Company was established, led by Thomas Jones, an entrepreneur whose previous experience in the Philadelphia pearl button business guided the Vineland enterprise to a production schedule of 1200 gross of buttons weekly and a staff of 50 workers. Housed in John Gage's machine shop at the Boulevard and Pear Street, the company was considered one of the biggest pearl button manufacturers in the United States.

As the town further industrialized, the manufacture of shoes became a lucrative if short-lived operation. The first mention of a shoe manufacturer in A. G. Warner's *Vineland and Vinelanders,* appears in the account of the town's eighth year, 1868. Warner writes of J.M. Wiswell & Co., a shoe factory located in a three-story brick building at Landis Avenue and Sixth Street, as "one of the most important manufacturers in Vineland." At the time, Wiswell had forty employees. Warner's history also mentions a factory owned by a Mr. Demmon who produced children's shoes. The location of his facility was Landis Avenue, east of Fourth

Street, but Mr. Demmon's employees worked largely from their homes.

B.F. Ladd identifies Thomas H. Proctor's shoe factory as opening in 1872. Proctor employed between fifty and one hundred hands and produced between 1,000 and 1,600 pairs of shoes weekly. J.H. Hunt's shoe factory began operation in 1874, employing over fifty workers and turning out over a thousand pairs of shoes per week. Like most of his Vineland competitors, Hunt's business was equipped with the most recent machinery and sold its goods in New Jersey and Pennsylvania.

In 1875, Charles Keighley opened his shoe manufacturing business on Sixth Street with only ten workers and little capital. Within a short time, Keighley moved his operation to the corner of Sixth Street and Landis Avenue for three months before his business's success required a larger facility and additional workers. Relocating to Montrose Street and East Boulevard, the proprietor enlarged his new building and staff so that he had, according to Ladd, "the largest shop in Vineland" and a workforce of one hundred. Keighley's weekly production averaged two thousand pairs of shoes in 1880. The company was included in *Vineland. Its Products, Soil, Manufacturing Industries and Commercial Interests*, a report published in 1888. Its findings reveal that over eight years, employment had risen to 130 workers and production increased to 3000 pairs of shoes per week. Keighley was also credited in the report with the invention of the heel burnisher, a machine not only used in Vineland's shoe manufacturing plants, but in factories around the country.

Thomas M. Hawkins started his factory in 1876 with only ten employees and minimal machinery. Within three years, he moved to Sixth Street, updated and expanded his equipment and increased his staff to over one hundred. Hawkins sold his products throughout the country.

Chandler's Shoe Factory, founded by D. Harry Chandler in 1885, grew rapidly so that by 1888, what was once a workforce of a dozen grew to seventy that could turn out up to 2,000 pairs of shoes per week.

As Vineland's businesses increased, a Board of Trade was established in 1888, but it wasn't until the 20th century that Leo L. Reading, a former newspaperman, convinced others that there was a need to a Chamber of Commerce in the town. He helped organize the first meeting in 1919 and served as the organization's first secretary while Eugene M. Kimball, who would serve as president until 1923, chaired the event.

Landis gave equal attention to education and businesses, establishing both within the first twelve months of Vineland's existence. But his desire to achieve a municipality filled with an abundance of religions and places of worship may have received most of his generosity.

It would take a bit of time before more churches were added to the area. Initially, the school house served as the location for religious services of Presbyterian, Episcopal and Methodist congregations on Sundays. The day was divided among the three groups and also accommodated their meetings throughout the week until each was able to settle into a building of its own.

In 1863, Landis began filling his town with churches by providing free land to the various denominations and promising a bell to the first building to be constructed with a steeple. On August 8, 1863, the Episcopal Society, which had been founded and organized here as a mission, held an organizational meeting. By August 19, it was decided Trinity Church would be the name of the parish.

Trinity Episcopal Church was deeded land at Fourth and Elmer Streets in September 1863. The cornerstone was laid November 4 and when construction was completed shortly afterward, Vineland had its first official place of worship. When the structure was enlarged in 1865, a steeple was added, and the church received the bell Landis had promised. On July 16, 1871, according to Ladd, one of the worst storms ever witnessed in South Jersey struck this area that Sunday afternoon. The tempest caused the collapse of the church's steeple, which fell onto the roof, destroying the entire building. A new home in the form of a stone structure at Eighth and Wood Streets replaced it in 1873.

The Presbyterian Church, first formed on June 14, 1863, was officially organized July 7, 1863. There were twenty-nine members in the initial congregation when it was given the lot on Landis Avenue near Eighth Street that later became the site of the Post Office. A frame for the church was completed before the conclusion of 1864 and the construction of the wood building was finished the following year. The church seated a total of 300 people, which is what the Presbyterian congregation numbered by 1869.

Warner reports that, on April 12, 1863, twelve men and women met in order to "further the Methodist movement in Vineland." On June 2, 1863, they voted to construct their own church. By June 26, 1864, the cornerstone was laid for a building at Landis Avenue and Seventh Street. The structure was completed before the end of 1864 and was used for approximately three years. It was destroyed by a fire and was replaced by a new facility which seated 500 people.

By 1868, South Vineland Methodists did not attend services at Landis Avenue and Seventh Street. Instead, they chose to meet "in a one-room frame building" located on Sherman Avenue near the Boulevard. This facility, in somewhat modified form, became, in the 20th century, the Little Theatre/ Cumberland Players Theatre. The First Baptists formally organized June 15, 1865, and they soon began holding services at Union Hall. Two years later, they broke ground for their own building on Landis Avenue near East Avenue.

On November 26, 1865, the first meeting of what became the First Congregational Unitarian Society was held. Warner describes this group's goal as providing its members with "a church organization that shall conduce to their spiritual growth and that shall be in harmony with their views of the principle taught by Christ, to provide a Sunday School…and to promote among men the growth of that practical Christianity taught in the Old and New Testaments." On the last day of 1865, a Sunday School and Bible class were established and, by April 5, 1866, services were conducted in Mechanics Hall. By 1869, work began on a 400-capacity stone structure that was designated as the denomination's new home.

In 1868, the Christ Episcopal Church took up residence at the South Vineland Railroad depot. Two years later, they occupied their own building on the Boulevard.

Prior to Landis's founding of Vineland, Lewis Collins and Zachariah Murray established a church that became the basis for the African-American sects of Mount Pisgah U.A.M.E and the New Bethel A.M E. According to the Vineland 1961 *Centennial Program*, services were initially conducted in a Buena Vista Township log cabin. The Mount Pisgah Church received a home in Vineland when it was deeded land on Plum Street in 1880. The New Bethel Church was constructed on Seventh Street in 1874. According to Ladd, that structure was destroyed by a fire in April 1878. The facility was insured for $1,150 and the money was immediately applied to rebuilding the church.

The origins of the area's Pilgrim Congregational Church date back to 1871 when a group of twenty-four gathered at Temperance Hall for the purpose of organizing. By 1874, the denomination was soon housed in what Ladd calls "a neat well finished building" at Seventh and Elmer Streets.

Italian immigrants mostly settled in the eastern portion of Landis Township known as New Italy and continued the farming that they left behind in their native country. Religious services for this predominantly Catholic group were held in the rail station in the center of Vineland and were conducted by a priest from Millville's Fathers of Mercy. By 1874, however, a Catholic church was warranted, and construction began on a stone structure on Eighth Street. On Christmas Day of that year, Sacred Heart Church officially opened its doors. Twelve years later, a second Catholic parish, St. Mary's, was established with a church in the center of the New Italy colony.

The Wesley Methodist Society was established in Vineland in the early 1880s, and according to Ladd, was originally housed at Seventh and Grape Streets in a brick church that was dedicated on January 23, 1881. The group moved to a new building on Elmer Street ten years later. A German Methodist Church also existed at one time on Grape Street. The German Methodists rented their facilities to the West Baptists, a group organized in 1895 and comprised of members of the First Baptists from the west side of town who wanted a church closer to their area. The West Baptists eventually established a home of their own on Landis Avenue.

Founded in 1897 on Plum Street, Ahavath Achim was the first orthodox synagogue in South Jersey. With the addition of Ahavath Achim, Vineland closed out the 19th century with a wide range of faiths represented and an abundance of places of worship, a situation that would continue to grow throughout the next one hundred years.

While the industrial and cultural life of Vineland existed in the heart of the town, another crucial facet of Landis's vision, the agricultural agenda, could be found in the surrounding township. Landis envisioned his town surrounded by vineyards and farmlands in contrast to the residential and business districts that would serve as the hub of his community. But when Landis purchased the territory he would establish as Vineland, a number of outlying farms, including Andrew Sharp's, were already part of the area that became Landis Township, so that the founding father's vision had a head start.

William A. Wolcott's 33 acres of farmland was located on Main Road just north of Grant Avenue. Further down Main Road, near Clayville Switch, stood Robert Brandriff's farm, reported to be the best in Landis Township. Before the wave of Italian immigration transformed East Vineland into an agricultural center, Peter Vanaman owned a farm located on a now defunct road that ran from Buena Vista to Millville. Vanaman's property was south of Genoa Avenue and west of Union Road.

While these properties bordered the east and the south of Vineland proper, many of the farms occupied a stretch of land on what is now known as Delsea Drive. As far north as Garden Road and as far south as Sherman Avenue, farmlands of various acreage abounded.

The Gillett property consisted of 106 acres which filled all four corners at Garden Road. The Coney farm could be found on 150 acres just south of Oak Road. William Garrison owned and, along with his son, farmed 150 acres of land south of Walnut Road. The property stood on both sides of Delsea Drive, with Garrison setting up residence on the east side and his son building his home on the west side. A barn was built near each of the homes.

Fifty acres of farmland was owned by John Riddle on the southwest corner of Sherman Avenue and 123 acres south of Parvin's Branch belonged to Joel Davis who also owned 108 acres that filled both sides of the Boulevard north of Park Avenue. The "Burnt Mill" farm was located on Delsea Drive as well. Its twenty acres were owned by Furman L. Mullford, a Millville resident. The land had, at one time, housed a mill which burned down, hence the title of the farm.

Mills were also a part of the outlying area when Landis purchased his property. Souders' Mill stood on the south side of Lincoln Avenue near Menantico Stream. Panther Branch Mill, a sawmill belonging to Joseph Cooper, also existed in the early days. Landis would purchase 5,620 acres of land from Cooper's heirs in March 1864, but not the mill property. The largest of the mills in the immediate area was the Forest Grove steam sawmill near the railway line.

Farmers and mill owners weren't the only individuals in the area prior to Landis's purchase. Other residents as far east as Lincoln Avenue resided here on land that ranged from 30 to 100 acres. But it would take considerable time before anyone residing in these outlying areas would be called Vinelanders.

While the outlying farms were important to the fledgling town, some of the livestock became a source of contention during the early days and resulted in an unfortunate series of events that earned the title of "Bovine War." Warner reports that before Landis founded Vineland and the township named after him, it was customary for the farmers in the outlying areas to let their cattle, hogs and sheep graze in the area. When the land began to slowly fill with settlers, the farmers continued to let the cows graze within the township. The result apparently called for drastic action on the part of the town and a sort of clandestine war was soon declared on the unsuspecting marauders and their owners.

The new settlers first approached the original farmers with demands that the roaming cattle be confined to the land on which they belonged. Warner reports that the new settlers' ultimatum was met with "sneers and boasts" from the farmers who were aware they didn't have the necessary acreage to accommodate grazing. Warner reports that an association known as the Cattle League was formed on May 15, 1863, consisting of sixty-three men including Landis, whose signature is the first on the group's declaration which states that the members are bound "in honor and secrecy to assist each other…"

The newly formed association immediately appointed committees to once again petition the various cattle owners. When their pleas were disregarded, the Cattle League presumably undertook covert operations which they apparently had anticipated would be necessary and which would require illegal measures. The pledge of secrecy and assistance ensured that anyone apprehended for a crime would have the monetary support of the others in the event of a trial.

Shortly, the bodies of dead cows were discovered strewn throughout the woods and swamps of the township. There is no indication that any member of the Cattle League was ever arrested or brought to trial, but Warner seems to imply that more than a few in the group didn't agree with the League's course of action. It's very likely that Landis stood among those who found the carnage distasteful. The farmers, faced with the possible loss of their herds, soon retreated and surrendered to the settlers, confining their livestock to the farms outside the township. Ironically, the fences used to contain the cattle were exactly what could have averted any Bovine War had Landis not been opposed to their use other than as ornamentation in Landis Township.

According to William Paul Dillingham's 1911 *Reports of the Immigration Commission*, "Mr. Landis felt that the building of fences in a fruit region was a waste of land and an unnecessary expense, and that stock should be kept in rather than fenced out. This was a new, strange and unwelcome doctrine to the native Jerseyman, whose wild cattle had been allowed to roam the woods at will."

Landis explained his reasoning in "The Social Science of Vineland," writing:

133

By the laws of the State of New Jersey cattle were allowed to run at large, and all persons who improved land were compelled to fence their grounds to keep out their neighbors' cattle. This was a wasteful habit. It involved an immense outlay to begin with; also the cost of keeping the fences in repair and the loss of the manure of the cattle. Upon an estimate, I found it would cost over a million dollars to the settlers to fence the Vineland tract. To keep the fences in repair would cost ten per cent, per annum, which would be 100,000 dollars, and the loss of interest at six per cent, would be 60,000 dollars per annum.

To combat the situation, Landis successfully had a law passed "prohibiting all cattle from running at large, and repealing the Act requiring fences to be built, so far as it related to my district. People then kept their cattle in enclosures, and soiled them, as the farmers term it; much to the good of the cattle, the saving of manure, and the saving of capital." The law also induced farmers to grow root crops "which added to their wealth and benefited the land." The law nearly produced another war, this time against Landis, but farmers eventually acquiesced.

Vineland's early years of farming allowed the town to live up to its name through its grape production, the most abundant and profitable of its crops. But it wasn't long before the town faced its first agricultural crisis when a threat appeared in 1869 in the form of a fungus known as black rot. At the start, the extent of damage was slight and, even by 1873, grapes were still Vineland's staple crop, but the disease continued to spread over the years, decimating local grape crops, diminishing the amount that could be sold each year and affecting most of the crops by 1876.

It was primarily the Concord grape that was affected in Vineland, but such a blight brought with it the hope for a remedy or a means of preserving crops. Even Landis, writing in a September 14, 1878 journal entry, reported that he "went up to the vineyard and tied the Red Muscadine Grape with white rags, that I may know them when the leaves are off and save the cuttings for distribution among the people, as this is a grape that has withstood the rot.

Vineland, however, was not the only location in the country suffering from the effects of grape rot. According to a special report at the time by Frank Lamson-Scribner of the Agricultural Department, "black rot occurs throughout the States east of the Rocky Mountains on all wild and cultivated vines. It is especially frequent and destructive in the States bordering the Atlantic, the Great Lakes, the Gulf of Mexico and along the banks of large rivers, notably in the states of Missouri and Ohio. Its virulence lessens as the humidity diminishes. Thus… in western Texas where it is very dry, the disease has not been observed."

By 1879, measures were in place to curb the disease in Vineland and national attention was focused on the results. The source of the rot had been identified as a fungal infection, and experiments were underway. After nearly a decade of watching this area's grape crops slowly destroyed, several methods were soon adapted from Ohio farmers. Once these methods were employed, time and patience were required. By August, the rot had appeared, and the favorable outlook promised in the spring was replaced by despair.

Interestingly, in the absence of its defining crop, Vineland found that its blackberry production had become an unexpected replacement. One million quarts of blackberries had been marketed by the town in 1879, making it the most profitable industry in Vineland's fruit farming. The success of this crop could have significantly altered how Vineland was viewed, and the familiar grape image might have been discarded in favor of the blackberry. But farmers refused to forsake what was once their number one crop, and further solutions were sought to end grape rot.

On June 7, 1880, Landis was awake by 6:30 a.m. He had an appointment later that morning with a Philadelphia man interested in purchasing some town lots, and afterwards visited New Italy, the Italian farming colony he created for immigrants. While there, he couldn't help noticing that the grapevines "never looked better than this spring." By July 11, the city was experiencing a heat wave, but Landis noted that "vegetation is growing and there is little or no grape rot." Despite the founder's optimism during spring 1880, the crops would again yield only a fraction of what was produced during the town's first decade of existence.

But 1880 would prove a somewhat significant year in the battle against grape rot. Edwin Curtis Bidwell, a physician who had settled in Vineland in 1866, became interested in the cause of the disease. While in Ohio, he had made a name for himself in his studies of how cholera was transmitted and, although he had turned his attention to operating a drug store in Vineland, he began studying the grape disease in the late 1870s.

Bidwell is credited with discovering the fungus that caused the black rot and it would eventually be called Lae stadia Bidwellii. But several French scientists, most notably Pierre Marie Alexis Millardet, had begun research into the cause of the disease around the same time as Bidwell. The French had been battling black rot and other diseases associated with grapes longer than the U.S. and, in the 1840s, had dusted grapes with sulfur in order to treat powdery mildew. The sulfur, however, had less effect on grape rot and downy mildew, the two forms destroying Vineland's and other U.S. crops.

Concurrent with Bidwell's discovery of the grape rot fungus's highest form, Millardet's detection of spores in the fungus explained how it spread. Millardet's 1882 studies of grapevines dusted with copper sulfate and lime revealed they remained free of downy mildew unlike vines that were untreated. The French scientist spent the next two years searching for the best mixture of ingredients to combat downy mildew. The Bordeaux mixture, as Millardet's treatment was called, was tentatively endorsed in the U.S. by Scribner, the Agricultural Department scientist who was conducting his own work on solving the grape rot problem. But Scribner realized there was still much to learn from the European work that had been accomplished in this area. Scribner felt the U.S. government needed to elevate the work being accomplished in this area of science in order to quicken the pace and increase the efficiency.

In 1886, the United States declared war on black rot. With Scribner as the head of the new governmental section, the search for a solution to grape rot took a significant turn. Scribner chose vineyards in four U.S. locations, including Vineland. The 1887 testing affirmed the Bordeaux mixture and another combination, Eau Celeste, as effective in the treatment of down mildew, but the overall results were mixed. During the tests, however, farmers and the special agents began treating the grapes only after the first sign of infection appeared.

The arrival of Pierre Viala of the Ecole Nationale D'Agriculture at Monpellier, France to the United States in the summer of 1887 marked a turning point in the battle against grape rot.

Viala's work with plant fungus had followed the discoveries of Vineland's Bidwell. The visit to Vineland proved fruitful and Viala, who had already suggested that the rot and leaf spots originated from the same fungus, proved beneficial. Lab work convinced Scribner that Viala's theory was correct and a more controlled test for the 1888 growing season was prepared. Instead of working from a number of stations throughout the country, only one site was selected for the experiment. The location chosen was Vineland, where the Bordeaux mixture proved successful.

During the time of Vineland's grape rot epidemic, residents were able to retreat from the agricultural problems to Cosmopolitan Hall, which by now offered an extensive array of entertainment. An examination of the venue's 1886 itinerary, as preserved by Vineland Historical and Antiquarian Society member Frank D. Andrews in the pages of the *Vineland Evening Journal*, reveals a productive, albeit conventional, agenda when compared to those of two decades earlier. The series of dramatic performances, concerts and conventions identify a largely local flavor and a more conformist taste.

The hall's first offering in January 1886, the closest to the bookings that once graced the Plum Street Hall stage, was a free lecture by Mr. I. Loewendhal who discussed what Andrews cites as "incontrovertible proof of immortality" he wished to share with others. The talk was followed thirteen days later by a performance of the play *Our Jonathan*.

On February 2, the operetta *The Mikado* opened before an audience that fell below attendance expectations for opening night. Following a lecture by a New York reverend on the 6th, a melodrama entitled *The Capture of Major Andre* was presented on the 9th by the Seminary of the Sacred Heart. The play was accompanied by a small orchestra comprised of violins, flute, cornet, cello and piano. On February 11, the Children's Progressive Lyceum offered a literary program. The month concluded with a temperance lecture.

The hall's schedule for March included the Republican caucus, a Pawnee Indian Medicine Company exhibition, a St. Patrick's Day dinner and the Edwin Forest Dramatic Association's performance of the drama *The Colleen Bawn*. During the spring and summer, the programs included a concert by the blind African-American pianist Blind Tom, productions of the plays *Past Redemption* and *Charlotte's Maid*, the Vineland High School commencement ceremonies, a Trinity Parish performance of *The New Flower Queen Cantata*, the return of *The Mikado* and the operetta *Lily Bell, the Culprit Fay*. The autumn months featured Pat Rooney's New York Star Comedy Company, which provided a "Whirlwind of Fun, a Cyclone of Merriment and a Typhoon of Laughter," Saturday night dances, and productions of the plays *A Box of Cash* and *Fashion and Folly*.

Cosmopolitan Hall would undergo one more transformation and change of name. In 1907, after years of complaints about the deteriorating conditions of the building, plans were made to construct a new building and sites were explored. At the time, however, the Friends of Progress, whose popularity had long since waned and its numbers had considerably diminished, were willing to sell the hall and the additional lots for $4,000, so the decision was made to remodel Cosmopolitan Hall once again, renaming it the Auditorium in the process.

From its beginnings, Vineland was a town comprised of readers, and it wasn't long before the need for a library was recognized. Ladd cites the date the first Library Association was established as January 15, 1867. However, he points out that "it did not prove a permanent success." Ladd reports that on May 24, 1876, another meeting was conducted for the purpose of organizing a Library Association, the purpose of which would be "to encourage the study of art, science and literature by the establishment of a library and reading rooms, courses and lectures..." The Association's library, backed by several prominent local businessmen who were part of the group, officially opened May 27, 1876. According to Phyllis Zislin's study, *A History of the Vineland Free Public Library*, while research and browsing were allowed, only dues-paying members were permitted to borrow books.

Prior to the Association's establishment, another group of residents who felt that the town required a public library, began meeting March 28, 1876. What they established was another system that required a membership. Zislin's study reports that a yearly membership of two dollars required for borrowing books from this public library succeeded in discouraging patrons. There were other problems as well. The library had built its collection from donations but was lacking in new publications. When it became difficult to pay the librarian's salary, a new arrangement was sought. The solution involved John and Eliza Duffy, the husband-and-wife team behind the *Daily Times* newspaper. In return for the use of the library's back rooms for their printing operations, the Duffys would oversee the front room, which served as the library. Eliza Duffy soon put together a catalogue of the facility's collection and published it in the *Daily Times*.

Despite the new arrangement, the public library's demise was inevitable due to lack of support. Zislin dates its closing as January 1879 during which time its books were donated to the Vineland Historical and Antiquarian Society (VHAS) and to Vineland High School. In 1892, Zislin reports, the Library Association also turned its collection over to the VHAS and talk of a school library "that would merge into a public library" began to circulate before dissolving into rumor.

Seven years later, the Vineland Women's Club was formed and within its first month began the task of establishing a public library in town. Zislin's study reports that the group had already received a donation of 1,275 books from Professor W. B. Webster and was raising money for the purchase of additional reading material.

On June 8, 1900, Women's Club President Dr. Mary J. Dunlap presided over a meeting about the library at Temperance Hall. The next day's *Evening Journal* article indicated that another library group existed at the time and that residents involved in the cause openly declared their allegiance. Some citizens voiced opposition to a public library loaning books for free. Dunlap confirmed that thirty people had already expressed a willingness to pay a $5 membership fee. Zislin's research reveals that the Women's Club, which hoped to establish the facility and then turn it over to the municipality, was already charging a $2 annual fee or 25 cents monthly for borrowing books from its collection. The meeting concluded with Dunlap appointed chairman of a committee to explore options in establishing Vineland's library.

While the birth of the Vineland Public Library can be traced back to the 1899 efforts of the newly formed Women's Club, its first home was provided by a resolution of the Borough of Vineland Council on November 13, 1900. According to the *Evening Journal*, the resolution allowed for rooms in Town Hall to be used as the library, which was officially turned over to the municipal government on this night. It was also determined, despite some public sentiment to the contrary, that there would be no membership fee for borrowing books. The dedication of the Vineland Free Public Library occurred on the evening of October 1, 1901.

Landis viewed the establishment of churches, schools and a library as paramount to a new town. He also felt the preservation of that town's history was of equal importance. And so, on January 6, 1864 a group of Vineland residents convened in the confines of a school house, to conduct the first meeting of what they would call The Vineland Historical and Antiquarian Society (VHAS).

According to Theresa Winslow's Master's thesis on the history of the VHAS, that first meeting wasted no time in assigning members research papers on such topics as biographies of Landis and the first Vineland settlers, records of first births, marriages and deaths, and the history of the first house constructed within the city proper, which was built in 1862 by Chester P. Davis, a Vermont native and one of the first township committeemen elected here in 1864, and Lester Richardson and occupied a spot on the northern corner of East Boulevard and Landis Avenue before being moved across the railroad tracks to the north side of Landis Avenue.

The VHAS also organized a presentation on the history and settlement of South Jersey by Millville resident Dr. Richmond to christen a proposed monthly lecture series. The bylaws and constitution of the society, established during the second meeting, identify the group's purpose as preserving biographies, materials and accounts of events "interesting and instructive to those who come after us."

VHAS members at the time consisted of several free thinkers from The Friends of Progress, including Cornelius B. Campbell and his wife Phoebe. When elections were held at the third gathering, Joseph Morton, the first president of Siloam Cemetery, was selected to lead the VHAS through its formative stage.

In its second year, the VHAS brought Horace Greeley to Vineland and conferred upon Landis honorary membership in the society. It also sought a permanent home for the organization, something that was destined to elude its grasp for another several decades and confine its members to school rooms, homes and meeting halls.

Winslow's research indicates that a period of inactivity for the VHAS, from 1870 to 1875, was caused by an inability to secure a meeting place and a storage facility for the society's accumulated records and artifacts. This was solved when, in 1876, the town's Library Association agreed to house both groups in its Landis Avenue facility in return for $84 and the right to circulate the VHAS book collection. The collaboration was yet another short-lived endeavor, however, when limited finances shut down the Library Association. While the VHAS did inherit the Association's books, it once again found itself without an official headquarters in which to house its growing collection.

The situation seems to have brought about the second period of inactivity from 1877 to 1888, although a reorganization meeting was held in 1884 during which Thomas B. Welch, Vineland resident and the inventor of grape juice, was elected to the board of trustees. In 1888, trustee Cornelius Campbell allowed the use of his home for meetings and storage of the society's collection. After Campbell's death in 1890, the organization's materials were moved to a building located on the corner of East Avenue and Peach Street known as "The Studio." The owner, Daniel F. Morrill, served as the group's fourth president and eventually donated the building to the VHAS, which decided to transport it to its Peach Street lot between Sixth and Seventh Streets.

Frank DeWette Andrews, originally a Hartford, Connecticut resident, settled in Vineland in 1869 and joined the VHAS as librarian. He first appears unassumingly in 1888 in the society's records and would become secretary and treasurer of the organization in two years and the driving force who would carry the organization into the 20th century with a renewed sense of purpose, directing its activities for the next five decades.

Andrews immediately saw the advantages of having a headquarters to house the society's meetings and collections.

It was decided that the VHAS needed to be more centrally located. The group waited patiently for three years for an opportunity to relocate. In 1893, John S. Shepard purchased and donated a lot on Seventh Street between Grape and Elmer Streets, and the Morrill house was soon transported to this site.

Winslow reports that Shepard stipulated in the deed to the lot that the land must be used for the purposes of the VHAS and cannot be disposed of at any time. He also specified that the lot should accommodate a library and reading room. In 1897, a 16' x 37' addition, which would serve as a reading room, was completed at a cost of $400, half of which was paid for by Shepard.

By this time, Andrews had opened the facility to the public. Beginning July 7, 1894, Vineland residents could visit the VHAS collection on Seventh Street on Saturdays from 2 to 5 p.m. Andrews had publicized the opening in newspapers and his efforts garnered a fair amount of favorable editorial recognition in those same publications. Andrews understood the power of print and the historical value of publishing and appealed to residents for contributions of archival material through newspaper articles while arranging for the society's annual reports to be printed. He learned the printing process at the *Evening Journal* and purchased a small hand press to produce his own works. Additionally, he established, edited and wrote for the *Vineland Historical Magazine*, which began its existence January 1, 1916. His work fulfilled Landis's vision of preserving the history of Vineland.

Chapter 4
Controversy, Clara and Carruth
(1868-1874)

In 1868, Landis began writing the first of a series of journals. He would diligently record each day's activities and then suddenly suspend his writing for weeks, months or even years, only to resume on a random date. His 1868 journal captures his everyday existence in the town he founded seven years earlier and it is far from a complete account of the calendar year, beginning in late January and ending less than two weeks into June. Yet, in just over five months of entries, he manages to convey his daily routine and note an inauspicious moment that would serve as a portent for his immediate future.

In a February 6 entry, Landis comments that he has discovered "a mean and abusive attack has been made upon me in a paper published in this place, called *The Independent*. It was evidently written by Earle, who wants the public to imagine that he has a quarrel with me, and the editor of this sheet thinks it will make his paper sell by creating curiosity. This paper has been opposing me from the start. It has done much damage, but with the help of God, I hope to still keep the Vineland ship before the wind."

The Vineland Independent had been established the previous year and edited by Earle H. Hale and William Taylor. It was begun as an extension of the political Independent Party, which had committed to supporting it financially. When the group reneged on its promise, the editors decided to serve their own interests and those of the public instead of an overt political platform and developed into what has been called in early Vineland histories, a "well-supported and good family newspaper." It seems doubtful either of those attributes is accurate.

The residents who conceived *The Independent* felt they had been shortchanged in some way on the opportunity Landis promised to all those who moved here. In his series "History of Vineland Newspapers," former *Vineland Historical Magazine* editor Frank D. Andrews explains that those who harbored resentment over their lack of success here were quick to point a finger, "blaming their failure upon the promoter of the enterprise."

Because the town's first newspaper, the *Vineland Rural*, had been created by Landis and the second, *The Vineland Weekly*, had been influenced by Landis, who even contributed letters and articles, it was felt that an opposition publication was necessary. Andrews writes that those disenchanted by Vineland's founder "formed a party whose leaders furnished the financial backing, in part, toward the establishment of *The Vineland Independent...*" The new publication debuted on March 2, 1867, one-and-a-half years after *The Weekly* first appeared. While *The Independent's* title professed a neutral political stance, Andrews identifies its politics as a "less pronounced" version of *The Weekly's* Republicanism.

With Taylor as proprietor and Hale as editor, *The Independent* was launched as a weekly publication, its opening editorial proclaiming it would support the side its editor deemed correct and basing its stance on the line, "be just and fear not," from William Shakespeare's *Henry VIII*, according to Andrews. But, just as the Bard of Avon's authorship of that particular play would be challenged, *The Independent's* adherence to its principles to "be just" would soon be open to question.

Unlike *The Weekly*, which would exist twelve years under its original ownership, *The Independent* would be plagued with an abundance of management changes. Six months after the appearance of its first issue, Hale relinquished his share of the ownership and Charles W. Blew became Taylor's partner in the business a month later. In less than a year, Blew sold his interest in the newspaper to Taylor, who became sole proprietor and editor for the next two years. On August 5, 1870, Taylor sold the operation to William H. Gill, Jr. and T. F. Mackenzie whose ownership lasted less than a year.

The Independent, however, wasn't the only newspaper in town that had become critical of Vineland's founder. In a

June 30, 1868 journal entry, Landis decries the actions of "the atrocious sheet called the *Vineland Democrat*" which had recently printed "several slurs against my business."

The *Democrat*, originally called the *Vineland Advertiser*, boasted as editor A.G. Warner and was published by his brother. The newspaper, unlike its rivals, which either promoted the town or supported, in varying degrees, Republican politics, initially favored the Democratic Party's outlook, which may explain why it attacked the Republican Landis's business in June 1868.

When the publication commenced on December 13, 1867, it was an 11" x 15" eight-page bimonthly distributed in Cumberland County as well as throughout the country. It became the *Vineland Democrat* the following year when it assumed a four-page 19" x 32" format and the annual subscription price, originally set at twenty-five cents, was raised to one dollar. By autumn 1868, Warner switched allegiance to the Republican Party, endorsing Ulysses S. Grant and earning the wrath of fellow Democratic newspaper editors. The publication was later renamed the *Vineland True Democrat*, assuming a more independent stance, but the changes proved ineffective. Warner faced a dwindling patronage that soon left him no choice but to close his business and the paper ceased operation shortly before Warner's death on December 15, 1871.

While *The Independent* and *Vineland Democrat* merited mention in Landis's first journal, there is no reference in these early entries about a young lady Landis had met at the start of the year. Clara Forsyth Meade apparently made Landis's acquaintance through her brother Richard at the family's home at 167 F. Street in Washington D.C. in

January 1868. By early March, Clara, along with her mother and four siblings, moved back into the family's home in Brooklyn, and Landis became a regular visitor to the New York residence. By the time he ends his first journal with the June 11 entry, the relationship had become serious despite Clara's father's opposition to the thirty-four-year-old Vinelander courting his nineteen-year-old daughter, allegedly threatening physical harm if Landis continued to show up at the family's doorstep. Before long, however, the couple's plans to marry would succeed in unhinging Landis's future father-in-law.

Clara's family background has been well-documented due to the prestigious military careers of her father, uncle and brothers. Clara's father, Richard Worsam Meade II, was born in Spain where his father worked as a commercial agent for the U. S. Government. When he was ten, the young Meade and his mother settled at the family home in Pennsylvania. Educated at private Catholic schools and Baltimore's St. Mary's College, Meade entered the Navy in 1826, serving as a junior lieutenant and conducting survey work on the *Washington*. Eventually, both Meade and his ship would become part of a high-profile situation.

In 1839, a Spanish vessel named *Amistad*, illegally carrying slaves from Africa, was headed to the U.S. when the passengers freed themselves and overpowered the small crew, killing the captain and a crew member in the process. Believing that one of the sailors could return them to their homeland, they entrusted him with the task only to soon discover that they had been piloted to Long Island. The boat and all aboard were taken to New Haven, Connecticut where a famous trial was conducted to determine the fate of the passengers.

The story of *Amistad* was turned into a feature film of the same name by Steven Spielberg in 1997, a far cry from the suspenseful and morally ambiguous rendering it was given in Herman Melville's novella *Benito Cereno*. But to its credit, the film version includes Darren E. Burrows in the role of Lieutenant Richard Meade, the officer who led the boarding party when the U. S. seized control of *Amistad*.

Meade continued to serve aboard various vessels for the next several decades, resigning his commission several times but soon returning to duty. He served as commander of the Receiving Ship in New York during the Civil War and retired in 1867, the year before Landis met his daughter.

Clara's Uncle George made even more of a mark in history books than her father. George Gordon Meade spent most of his life in the army, establishing his reputation in the Second Seminole War and the Mexican-American War. During the Civil War, he served as a general and earned his place in history.

It was at the Battle of Gettysburg, considered by many historians to be a turning point in the war, that General Meade faced General Robert E. Lee's Confederate forces in what turned out to be a three-day battle. With Union troops nearly decimated after the first day, Meade positioned his remaining soldiers defensively and called for the remainder of his Army as reinforcements. By the end of the third day, Lee's troops were in retreat. Although Abraham Lincoln was critical of the Union's failure to pursue the Confederates, Meade was promoted to brigadier general. Reputedly a short-tempered man, Meade closed out the war without any further significant accomplishments.

Clara's brother, Richard Worsam Meade III, entered the Navy in 1850, serving in both the Mediterranean and Pacific Squadrons until 1861 when he provided gunnery instruction before becoming Executive Officer of a steamship and gunboat at the start of the Civil War. In 1862, he earned the rank of Lieutenant Commander and was involved in suppressing the New York Draft Riots and commanding gunboats in South Carolina and the Gulf of Mexico.

During the post-war years, Meade would rise in rank, achieving the title of Rear Admiral in 1894. He served both on land and at sea and ended his career as commander of the North Atlantic Squadron. He would die in 1897 and be buried at Arlington National Cemetery alongside his brother, another military man, Lieutenant Commander Henry Meigs Meade, whose Navy career was limited and undistinguished. Another brother, Brigadier General Robert Leamy Meade, a part of the U.S. Marine Corps, served in the Civil War, the Spanish-American War and the Boxer Rebellion. One of Charles and Clara's children would be named after Henry Meigs, and a second child, Richard Worsam, after Clara's father and brother.

An 1885 article in the *St. Louis Globe-Democrat* indicates that when Landis met Clara in 1868, she had been "quite a belle" in Brooklyn's aristocratic society. Landis attests to this in a letter published later that year in a Vineland newspaper. According to a 1961 speech given by her grandson, J. Meade Landis, Clara had been educated abroad and was fluent in French and German. She was adept at horse riding and her skills in photography and golfing made her one of the first women to pursue these activities.

Because Clara had been born January 6, 1849, she was under the legal age to marry in 1868, so parental consent was necessary for the wedding to take place. Landis met with a "stern and positive refusal" from Commodore Meade, who was asked to explain his reasons for denying approval. Meade is reported to have said that his objection was over the Vinelander's age. Landis felt that "such an excuse was a mere subterfuge, given for want of more valid reasons" and that there was justification in "resorting to extreme measures in getting [Meade's] objections out of the way."

While Landis's age may have contributed to Meade's reaction to the proposed marriage, another factor seems to have been involved as well. In a letter to the *New York Times*, physician William T. Nealis reported that his first encounter with Meade later that year included

> a violent ranting tirade against the several members of his family, who had, he declared, utterly disgraced themselves by apostatizing from the Roman Catholic religion. His son had become a Protestant, and now his daughter had disgraced him and her whole family by marrying a Protestant. He then fell upon his knees and began to pray with great vehemence, invoking God to curse them, and immediately following his petitions by execrations.

Later testimony by Meade's wife, also named Clara, suggested that her husband's vehement reaction to Landis, the marriage and other issues stemmed from a traumatizing incident that had occurred three years earlier when he was in command of the *USS San Jacinto*. On New Year's Day 1865, the ship struck a reef in the Bahamas. While some of its equipment was salvaged, the ship itself was beyond saving. An investigation into the incident failed to exonerate Meade, who had been suspended from duty for a period. His wife claimed this "agitated the mind of her husband to an intense degree" and eventually led to a stroke which left the naval officer partially paralyzed.

During his recovery, Meade was tended to by his daughter Mary but, following his recuperation, he became paranoid, fearing she would poison him. Meade's wife reported that she began to lock the doors to the children's room as well as hers to protect everyone from what she called "his extreme irascibility and violence toward the members of his own family." Shortly thereafter, she testified, he made threats against his brother-in-law Charles A. Meigs, his friend B.F. Corliss and Landis.

Meade's wife explained that the idea of Clara marrying Landis "excited the mind of her father to an unusual degree" and he sought to prevent the wedding from occurring. In August 1868, Meade purportedly scoured the New York area from Brooklyn to Staten Island in search of Clara, who was presumably hiding from him. He planned on forcefully removing her from the area and relocating her to Washington, D.C. His alternate plan was reported to have been "destroying the life of Mr. Landis," and later testimony by B.F. Bache, a Navy doctor who encountered Meade on a Brooklyn streetcar, claims the commodore made the statement, "I have come on to wash my hands in the blood of this scoundrel Landis." And the *New York Times* reported that, at one point, Commodore Meade had chased Vineland's founder "with a shotgun and for years after threatened to shoot him on sight."

Meade's wife claimed that in December 1867, a diagnosis had concluded that "a clot or fatty substance formed" on Meade's brain and needed to be "absorbed." Meade destroyed the written evaluation.

Somewhere around October 10, 1868, Meade's family seemed to agree with Landis that "extreme measures in getting [Meade's] objections out of the way" were necessary, but those measures do not paint a flattering portrait of Vineland's founder. Newspaper reports during Landis's lifetime claim that he approached Clara's eldest brother Richard and secured his help in portraying the commodore as "the possessor of a diseased mind." Citing the commodore's current rants and previous episodes, the family succeeded in securing the arrest of the elder Meade.

Physician William T. Nealis, in a letter to the *New York Times*, recounted his evaluation of Meade:

> On the 13th of October, Richard W. Meade was brought to the "Tombs" by officer Croker, charged with being insane. He was accompanied by several naval gentlemen, who were not known to me. One of them, I think, was his son. A gentleman of the party had a letter from Dr, Bache, a surgeon of the navy, which stated that Dr. Bache had known Commodore Meade for many years, and believed him to be insane, further recommending that he should be conveyed to some proper place for safe keeping...

155

Meade's tirade about his children turning their backs on Roman Catholicism decided the matter for Nealis:

> He acted like a maniac. I then made my affidavit that he was insane. Dr. Anderson, my assistant, also took part in the examination and joined me in the affidavit. The Justice at the Tombs then committed him to the Lunatic Asylum at Bloomingdale.

During his incarceration, Meade maintained a team of attorneys who ordered a writ of habeas corpus, attempting to bring the commodore into a courtroom to prove his sanity. The writ was granted on October 23 but, according to one counsel, A. H. Sidell, had not been obeyed as of December 8. He and his co-counselors, Waring and DeWitt, would soon achieve their goal but, in the meantime, they offered their arguments in the pages of the *New York Times*, declaring in one letter that there is no blame placed on Nealis for committing Meade since

> [he] saw Commodore Meade, for the first time, under a high state of mental excitement, growing out of what he conceived to be a family disgrace, coupled with an utter disregard for his parental authority, such as any father might feel who saw his favorite daughter about to marry a man who incurred his deadliest hate. The Commodore had declared his intention to prevent their marriage, by force if necessary; and on finding himself arrested and bound over to keep the peace, it was natural that, being a man of violent temper, he should give vent to his

feelings…The persons who procured his arrest were present, armed with a certificate, obtained by what we claim to be false statements, from a naval surgeon, who had not seen Commodore Meade for weeks previous. These persons informed the physician at the Tombs that the Commodore's family desired that he should be sent to the Asylum, in order that he might find that rest necessary to restore his shattered mind; and believing this statement, he gave the necessary certificate. Nothing was told him then of the cause of the Commodore's excitement or of his having made a will disinheriting certain members of his family…

The letter also addressed the matter of the writ of habeas corpus by claiming that Meade's family "succeeded by various tricks in evading the order of the Court to produce his body in Court, on a writ of habeas corpus issued some five weeks ago[and] are permitted free access to the Asylum at all times, while those friends who are endeavoring to procure his release are prevented from seeing him, and his counsel are not permitted even to communicate with him by letter, so that he is at this moment ignorant of the efforts being made in his behalf, and is probably suffering from fear that he is deserted and condemned to perpetual confinement...all the above statements are fully substantiated by affidavits now before the Court."

In her father's absence, Clara was left, in the words of the *Globe-Democrat's* report two decades later, "without any responsible guardian." Her older brother Richard assumed control of all family matters that now included his sister's wedding to Landis. Over the past century, rumors persisted that the couple had eloped due to the elder Meade's disapproval, but a public ceremony had been organized in advance of Meade's incarceration. In fact, the ceremony occurred the day after Nealis's evaluation had committed Meade to Bloomingdale.

The wedding was held on October 14, 1868. The location was St. Peter's Catholic Church, New Brighton, Staten Island, Richmond County, New York. The Reverend J. Sloman, pastor of St. Peter's Church, presided over the ceremony and signed the marriage certificate, which was copied for the parish register on January 29, 1869. Witnesses were R. W. Meade and C.F. Meade.

Two days before the wedding, Landis's mother Mary had been informed by a letter from attorney James Nixon that her son had agreed to pay her an annuity for the remainder of her life. The payment may have been a display of appreciation for the money she had lent Landis to purchase land for the Vineland venture or a promise on the eve of his marriage that he would continue to care for her financially. The October 12, 1868 letter informs her that payment of the annuity of $1,500 in monthly sums of $125 would be made by Landis and that "arrangements made thereon will be made directly to you by your son and will not pass through my hands."

On November 9, 1868, Landis and Clara held a public reception in Vineland at Plum Street Hall. From 7:30 to 9 p.m., many residents showed up to congratulate the newlyweds. The evening concluded with dancing.

Meanwhile, enough noise was being made by Meade's friends and attorneys to secure the release of the one relative missing from this occasion. A letter printed in the *New York*

Times provides a summary of events over the month of November and, like the previous letter by Meade's attorneys, mentions the notion of Meade disinheriting members of his family:

> Physicians and others who have seen Commodore Meade, since his confinement in the Asylum, are ready to make oath as to his sanity. And every diligence is being used by his friends to obtain his release; believing as they do that a desire to break his will, by which it is said he had disinherited certain members of his family, has [led] to this persecution. Indeed, so positive have been the assertions of all who have seen him, other than those interested in his confinement, as to his perfect sanity that his family have ordered that no one, not even his legal advisers, be allowed to see him, which instructions the officers of the Asylum have carried out to the letter. There is a great danger that the treatment to which he is subjected may bring about the result which seems to be desired – namely, his actual insanity.

The disinheritance mentioned in the letter pertains to Richard, the son who bore the brunt of Meade's anger in having brought Landis into the commodore's home. The fact that the letter indicates more than one family member means that Clara also may have been disinherited.

Whatever animosity existed between Landis and his father-in-law seems to have blinded them both to the traits and tendencies they shared. In a way, the obsession that consumed Meade at this time eerily foreshadows a number of deeds and decisions, both actual and alleged, in Landis's later life. From rumors of insanity, bouts of anxiety and eruptions of violence to parental obsessions and acts of disinheritance, the remainder of Landis's life would contain more than a few parallels with those of his wife's father.

It would be one month from the Landises' public reception that the writ of habeas corpus was honored so that Meade could have his day in court. Judge Sutherland presided. Meade's physician, Dr. Halstead, testified that his client was not insane and Bloomingdale physician Dr. Brown stated that his patient had improved during the previous two weeks but still exhibited traces of insanity in that "he imagined things that didn't exist." Meade responded to several points he found erroneous. Ultimately, however, Sutherland's conclusion that the defendant was not insane prevailed, and Meade found himself free to once again pursue the matter of his daughter's marriage, but this time without any threats of violence.

Since the newlyweds were residing in Vineland, Meade was quick to invoke New Jersey law which, according to the *Globe-Democrat*, stated that "if any woman not full of age shall marry without the permission or consent of her parents or guardians, the person officiating at such marriage shall be liable to a fine of $300, and such marriage shall be null and void." The commodore knew Landis would pay the minister's fine, but dissolving the union was all that mattered.

Meade then "notified all the parties concerned" that his daughter had married "without his parental consent and against his will" and that he intended to "commence proceedings in the courts to have set marriage set aside and should also make use of the agency of the law to recover damages for loss of the services and society of his daughter."

The maneuver succeeded in getting Landis's attention, but the Vinelander was aware that this was merely a warning shot and that the second barrel could be more serious. With the law on his side and a solid case against the marriage, Meade meant to use the courts to inflict damage by not only annulling the union but humiliating Landis in the process.

Landis, a lawyer himself, examined his options and consulted with others before strategizing his next move. Ultimately, his legal background played less of a role in the events than his reputation as an entrepreneur with the right political connections. Landis approached the New Jersey legislature, something he had already done on previous occasions in the development of Vineland, and before long, a bill had passed through both houses that legalized the Landis marriage.

The action Landis undertook was enough to protect the couple from the impending threat by Meade. Any court case using the existing law about minors needing the consent of a parent or guardian would not hold up if brought against Landis and his bride and the commodore found himself flummoxed once again by his son-in-law. He continued to rant and complain, particularly about his treatment at the hands of his son and Landis, but remained powerless to dissolve the marriage into which his daughter had entered. But this wasn't the only legal matter dealt with in this period.

Because Landis undoubtedly valued what he had achieved in Vineland, he apparently felt it necessary to protect himself, even within the bond of marriage. An entry in the book *Acts of the Legislature of the State of New Jersey* reveals that eight days prior to the wedding, Landis filed a pre-nuptial agreement. The document identified that Clara agreed to the stipulations that presented a "valid and effectual bar to any claim of dower…in the real estate of the said Charles K. Landis," made it lawful for Landis to "to make and execute deeds of conveyance for all lands and real estate held by him during said coverture (sic) without the said Clara joining in said deeds and all" and guaranteed his land holdings at the time of marriage and any "he may hereafter acquire shall be held by him and the respective purchasers of the same, or any parcel thereof, free and discharged of and from all claim and dower therein by the said Clara F. Landis." Regardless of the legal agreement, Landis would allow Clara to participate in the sales of land and in the signing of deeds over the next six years.

By December, word had reached newspapers that Landis had been involved in the confinement of Commodore Meade to an asylum, and the town founder felt the need to address the issue. The December 12 edition of *The Vineland Weekly* contained a letter written by Landis two days earlier. In it, he attempted to defend himself from the accusations recently printed:

> As numerous reports have been published in the papers giving an incorrect statement in the case of Commodore Meade, and as my own name has been made more prominent in the truth as the circumstances fairly admit, in short, "that I had Commodore Meade arrested on a criminal charge and that, when he could not be held upon that charge, I had him incarcerated in a lunatic asylum upon the

certificates of two Tombs physicians," I beg the liberty of setting myself right before the public... I never heard before or in fiction of a man first confining his intended father-in-law in a lunatic asylum and then immediately marrying his daughter, and I am not ambitious to be the one to start such a precedent.

His letter recounts meeting Clara earlier in the year, explaining,

I first met my wife at the Commodore's own house in Washington last January. I was then told it was worth as much as a man's life to pay any attention to [Commodore Meade's] daughter. Of the number of suitors who had actually been driven away by force of arms, upon further inquiry, I ascertained this to be a fact. When I decided to propose to my wife I sent a formal notice to him and a request for his consent. His answer to this was a peremptory order to desist from all attentions to his daughter, reiterated by another letter threatening serious consequences in case I continued these attentions, and placing the grounds of his objections as follows: -- 1st, my age, -- 2nd, my religion, -- and 3rd, being an utter stranger. Being at the time thirty-four years old, I was at a loss whether he meant that I was too young or too old. I did not care about adopting any new religion; and being fully his equal in both birth and education, and having lived for eleven years upon my own estates in New Jersey…I could not possibly sympathize with the last objection.

Landis reports that he then sought advice on the matter from some of Meade's friends and family members: "Lt. Commander R. W. Meade, Father Francioli of Brooklyn, formerly his priest, Admiral Hiram Paulding, the father-in-law of two of his sons, Chas. A. Meigs of New York, his brother-in-law and other members of his family." Landis claims that

> they all advised me to pay no attention to it, "that the Commodore was suffering under aberration of mind and had been in this state for some time." This I fully believe as I knew the Commodore had suffered great injustice from the Government in being unjustly kept out of a claim, amounting, I believe, to millions of dollars even after the legality and injustice of the claim had been fully established. And also that from some personal jealousies, he had suffered from the court martial for the loss of [his ship] *San Jacinto* and had not been awarded the rank and promotion which he deserved, which, to an officer, is worse than death.

After this, Landis writes, he had been "informed that the Commodore was watching around the Staten Island ferries that he might shoot me at the first opportunity. I continued my attentions the same and would have blushed at the thought of anything like personal danger influencing my conduct. For some time previously, my marriage was appointed to that place on the 14th of October, at the residence of my wife's uncle, Chas. A. Meigs, Esq., of Staten Island. A few days before, I received a warning that the mind of the Commodore was disturbed and that he would shoot me for certain in case he saw me. I decided, however, that upon the 14th of October I would cross the ferry in open daylight, and in an open carriage, and stand any amount of shooting that was necessary."

Landis, accompanied by his father, his sister Matilda and his clerk John Burk, arrived at the Meigs residence. He claims in his letter to *The Weekly* that

> Lt. Commander R. W. Meade immediately informed me that they had performed a melancholy task the preceding day – that of placing the Commodore in the Bloomingdale Asylum; that for months past he had been threatening different people" including Mr. Meigs and Secretary Welles of the Navy. Also, when they searched the Commodore, several revolvers were found on him and four more in his valise. It was also discovered that he had hired a gang of ruffians to attack Landis upon his arrival, in the hopes that it would provoke him to postpone or cancel his wedding plans.

But, as Landis points out, the wedding ceremony was uninterrupted:

> I married her, thank God! and with [H]is help, I hope to stay married and shield her all her life from every evil that may threaten. My marriage has received the approbation of every member of my wife's family,

165

excepting the Commodore. Relative to the Commodore's confinement, I had no hand in it; nor had my wife; nor did I know of it before the morning of my marriage. But I have seen letters from Secretary Welles of the Navy and from General Geo. G. Meade and others, approving of the confining of the Commodore upon the ground of humanity, and expressing surprise that it had not been done long before.

As if to remove any remaining doubt in the reader's mind, Landis singles out his brother-in-law as the person solely responsible for the fate of the elder Meade. "The Commodore was placed in confinement by his son Lt. Commander R. W. Meade, who is now in the Pacific Ocean in command of the U.S. Steamer *Saginaw*…" he writes.

While the letter does not necessarily exonerate Landis in the decision to confine Meade, it does foreshadow his upcoming journal entries. It would soon be common for Landis to minimize his family's appearances in his entries, mentioning them only briefly and without much detail. The letter is the first indication of the impersonal terms Landis will use in referencing his wife in later journal entries. In the letter she is referred to only as "my wife" or "my affianced," never by name or a romantic or endearing term. She will remain "wife" and "Mrs. Landis" throughout the entries in which she is mentioned.

Despite his claims of innocence in the matter concerning the elder Meade's commitment to an asylum, Landis began to exhibit signs of a growing paranoia over his unresolved grievance with the commodore, fearing a violent retribution from his father-in-law. Deputy Sheriff Thomas Cortis discussed the earliest indication of Landis's paranoia in later testimony, revealing that "in December 1868, I received a letter through the post office asking me to call at his residence. I did so and Landis said to me, 'I am going to be assassinated... The parties were coming from the direction of New York.' He called his wife to fetch him various pictures of person(s) that he said had been servant(s) in [Commodore] Meade's family... so that in the case I saw them I would know who they were and that he expected that they would come on the train and approach his house and wished me to have 4 or 5 men at the station at the arrival of every train armed with pistols and Bowie Knives." Cortis said Landis suggested several Vinelanders who were either good with a pistol or Bowie Knife. Cortis did go to the train station several times, unarmed, to observe in order to placate Landis, but he thought Vineland's founder was insane.

This would not be the only instance in which Landis shared his anxiety over the arrival of his in-laws who, he imagined, would, in the style of a 20th century Western, disembark from a mid-day train ready for a showdown. Landis's fears were not hidden from Clara, who was aware of these anxieties and seemed to tolerate them. On an occasion when Alexander Pearson dropped off a pair of pistols Landis had requested, he did not find the founder home. When he handed them to Clara, she explained that Landis didn't need the pistols for himself but for some friends since he was going to give a talk at Plum Street Hall that evening and feared he would be assassinated and wanted friends to be around to defend him.

Despite Landis's growing paranoia, the newlyweds settled into Vineland and managed to enjoy several years of, if not complete marital bliss, a comfortable bond of love and trust. In an 1877 account, Clara admitted that "up to 1872 our marriage was comparatively happy." On September 1, 1869, Landis and Clara celebrated the birth of a son, Henry "Harry" Meigs Landis, but tragedy struck the following year when the infant died of cholera in Lenox, Massachusetts on August 15, 1870.

Henry seems to have been a victim of what is referred to as cholera infantum, a form of the disease that affects infants. While it reached epidemic proportions on more than a few occasions in U.S. urban areas during the second half of the 19th century, the disease claimed 1,914 lives in Massachusetts in 1870, according to records. It seems likely that Henry contracted the illness in New England, possibly during a vacation to visit Clara's relatives in the summer of 1870.

The Vineland Historical and Antiquarian Society's (VHAS) archives contain a surviving photograph, from the collection of Landis's sister Matilda, of baby Henry laid out for his funeral, a common practice at the time. The photo, taken by a Pittsfield, Massachusetts photographer, is made even more tragic by the inscription on the back by Matilda, who identifies the subject as "my darling nephew Harry" with the dates of his birth and death. He would be the first to be buried in the Landis plot at Siloam Cemetery in Vineland.

The loss of their first child was devastating for the parents, particularly Clara, but less than a year later, on March 28, 1871, Charles K. Landis Jr. was born, and would soon become his father's favorite. By the time the couple's third son, Richard Worsam Meade Landis, destined to be his mother's favorite, entered the world on March 22, 1873, the lines had already been drawn between the parents.

As early as January 1867, Landis had begun meeting with state legislators to expand Landis Township, already comprised of parts of Franklin and Buena Vista Townships. Dr. Harry Gershenowitz's insightful research, published in a 1984 *South Jersey Magazine* article, reveals that the plan was to secure additional sections of Franklin Township. In four years, the scope of this project became clear when Landis convinced his friend, Assemblyman William A. House, to introduce a bill that would establish Landis County.

On January 16, 1871, Assembly Bill No. 31 was recorded. It stated that its purpose was to "erect part of the counties of Salem, Cumberland and Atlantic into a new county to be called the county of Landis." The details of the bill identify that the projected Landis County would consist of all of Pittsgrove, Landis and Buena Vista Townships and a portion of Maurice River Township.

Resistance to the plan began gathering force even before the bill was introduced. Gershenowitz writes that "flurried responses from the opponents of this bill" enumerated the detrimental effects a new county would offer, most notably an increase in taxes to account for building a new courthouse, clerk's office and jail. Meetings to fight the proposal quickly sprung up in Malaga, Mays Landing and Newfield.

Gershenowitz notes that none of these gatherings were reported in the Vineland newspapers, which is not surprising considering the strong support that still existed for Landis's endeavors in 1871. A *Salem Sunbeam* article, however, reveals that the opposition to the plan was a surprise to its supporters who then offered to call the new county "Fruitland" instead of "Landis."

But it was a *Bridgeton Chronicle* article, published January 21, that made clear the reasons for the opposition. Addressing Vinelanders directly, the article declared that the bill "will be fought to the bitter end," and that its opponents would not be "swallowed up by Vineland." As Gershenowitz puts it, the bill was seen as "the aggrandizement of a greater Vineland" and Landis's bid "to become emperor of South Jersey." The bid for a new county failed, but the image it had painted of Landis endured. It wasn't long before residents of his city nicknamed him "King" and began to challenge the founder's authority.

Encountering such opposition would not have been met favorably by Landis. He must have realized that the response of the outlying municipalities would slowly creep into Vineland and begin to challenge his authority. *The Independent* had already begun its volley of criticism and those whose financial gamble in Vineland property had ended in failure were already casting aspersions and threats against the founder. Those in opposition to Landis would soon recast Vineland in their image, but for the moment, the town celebrated the start of its second decade in style, with the founder's accomplishments still recognized.

Bouts of paranoia and attacks by *The Independent* and other municipalities wouldn't be the only issues Landis faced at the time. Financial problems with the newly established Vineland Railway had delayed the laying of the tracks. It wasn't until June 1871 that the rails extended from

Atsion to Dutch Mill Road before moving into Vineland over the next month. By August 9, 1871, a Vineland resident was able to pay $3.25 for a ticket at either the Main Road or Wheat Road stop and at the end of a five-hour-and-thirty-five-minute journey, arrive in New York City.

The rail line also extended into Bridgeton during 1871, but problems continued. A telegram, which was sent by Landis to an official on November 1, 1871, indicates that the rail workers were not being paid and that he "will not feel justified after today in keeping men at work" unless money is provided to pay them. Landis was also anxious about completing the line to the Delaware Bay to afford faster transportation for the fishermen in the area. In a letter dated November 8, 1871, he was finally notified that the time it would take to have the tracks in shape for trains to run from Greenwich to the Delaware Bay would take two to three weeks. It wasn't until the following year that the line reached the Delaware Bay.

The completion of the tracks to Greenwich signaled a connection with the state of Delaware and other states south. But in May 1873, Jay Gould, head of the New Jersey Southern Railroad, told the *New York Times* that his system was planning on extending its line beyond the Long Branch cranberry region. He announced that his railway would extend into Delaware and Maryland and connect with the Baltimore and Ohio Railroad. How he planned to accomplish this was not stated at the time, but a little over a month later the answer was provided when the Vineland Railway Company failed to meet its expenses. The line was sold to Gould for $10,000 on July 2, 1873 and what was once Vineland's railroad was consolidated with the New Jersey

Southern. Many of the Vineland rail line stockholders suffered heavy losses.

The Independent lost no time in attacking Landis, charging that he had never paid for stocks to which he subscribed in the Vineland railroad yet demanded payment for his position as president of the company after its demise. The newspaper also accused Landis of having "induced a large number of patrons to invest in it or to aid in its construction with labor or material" and now these "dupes," as the paper refers to them, had been "swindled out of everything they had invested."

The failure of the rail line and the attacks by *The Independent* couldn't have come at a worse time for Landis since he had also encountered troubles with the Wood family over debts he had accumulated from the indenture he had undertaken in 1863 and the credit extended by Richard Wood over eight years of land sales in Vineland.

February 12, 1869 was probably the last time Landis and Wood saw each other. The occasion was a visit Landis and Clara made to Philadelphia by train in the company of Wood and his wife. It didn't seem to bother Wood that Landis had yet to complete payment of the 1863 loan, despite the January 1869 deadline. Landis still owed $18,674.90. Over the next year, a little over half of it would be paid. But after the February train ride, Wood's health failed, and he spent the next month-and-a-half bedridden. When Wood died on April 1, 1869, Landis suddenly found himself doing business with Wood's son Edward, who was neither a friend nor a tolerant lender. Richard Wood seemed to have been more than willing to extend credit to Landis and overlook deadlines, but Edward was interested in resolving all standing debts as soon as possible. And it was at this time that Landis unwisely chose to challenge what he owed the Wood estate.

In 1870, Landis apparently dispatched his clerk, John Burk, to approach Edward about obtaining a larger bond and mortgage that tested the young Wood's patience and initiated an unexpected legal examination of deeds and records associated with Landis's sales and payments over the previous eight years. The proceedings began with a letter from Edward to Landis on March 29, 1870, addressing Burk's visit:

> The claim which he presented was for a much larger amount of land than your conversations with me had lead [sic] me to expect. I was too much occupied at the time to give Mr. Burk the attention which this matter deserves, and I referred him to my brother Walker who has given much attention to land titles in New Jersey, and from his report to me I do not think the executors can properly accept your claim without a thorough investigation by competent legal skill. I should not have felt justified in letting the [illegible] pass from my control if I had understood how large a matter there was behind it. I would like to have copies of the deed and of the mortgage and also any memorandum of facts bearing upon the titles in dispute in order to place the question before [Wood attorney] Mr. Voorhees and get an expression of his opinion what is right for us to do in the matter.

Edward may not have involved himself in the Landis matter initially, but he certainly immersed himself in Landis's claims for the next several months, committing himself to the task of assuring that the debt accrued was paid in full. After encountering Burk on May 27, 1870, Edward wrote Landis:

> I was lead [sic] to think that you might be willing to make some arrangement to settle all our interfering titles in a lump, so that we might both of us save the annoyance and expense, which attends the thorough investigation of a number of little land titles. If satisfactory to you I thought I would be willing to settle the whole list of questions as they stand by surrendering to you the mortgage upon your dwelling and retaining the United States Bonds to cover whatever balance there may be due to my father's estate upon the note given by you in redemption of your mortgage. If this seems satisfactory I shall be glad to hear from you by letter, as I have several engagements next week which I fear may interfere with my attending the next meeting of our council.

Wood's offer was a rather generous gesture. According to records maintained by Edward Wood and dated February 23, 1870, Landis had still not paid off his mortgage, but was apparently not ready to settle any debts with the Wood estate. This soon earned him the wrath of Edward, whose reaction was conveyed in a June 29, 1870 letter in which he reminds Landis that there are "several mortgages on which we have your guarantee" and "others which we have just cause to sue."

The letter's threatening tone did not seem to intimidate Landis, who, on July 1, 1870, had a legal representative respond to Wood's letter concerning the "unsettled account between [Landis] and the estate of the Richard D. Wood deceased." The letter states that "Mr. Landis is at present prepared to settle." As the correspondence makes clear, since 1863, Landis had paid Wood and his representatives, $125,788.14 for principal interest, leaving a balance of $8,562.70. Both Landis and Edward agreed that the balance was subject to deduction for exceptions made in the sale of land at $7 an acre. Landis claimed deductions for "necessary surveys" and other "exceptions," reducing the balance to $1,444.87. Landis proposed that if the Wood estate paid the balance, canceled the mortgage and returned the due bill and U.S. bonds and released all claims upon their part for timber on lands not yet sold, Landis would release any claims which may arise against the Woods in the future.

It appears that no agreement was reached during July since, by August 9, 1870, Edward, who was about to depart on a European vacation for ten months, sent a more acquiescent letter to Vineland's founder to address the "questions of title which I regret still remains." The letter informs Landis that

> you may think that in some degree this is my own fault and I do not deny that I have not hastened the investigation of the various points in question and vigorously as I might have done had I not almost been forced to feel that you intended to take some

advantage of me when you obtained from me the larger bond and mortgage, which I certainly would not have allowed to pass out of hands had I not been misinformed of the amount of your claims… In view of the assurance which you have given me, I cannot but believe that you were yourself misinformed upon this point, although you should have been better posted before asking for my consent to a transaction so vitally depending upon this question…you must not think that this question of the amount of your claim is immaterial nor must you think that I or either of my father's executors have ever had any idea of denying you any right that may be due to you under your contract with my father

Edward seems intent on resolving the issue, proposing that he wishes

to have these differences of titles settled by our yielding to you all those lands for which there is an unmistakable showing that the title was not in my father (sic) and by your settling with us for those which are still in doubt, taking our memorandums of agreement to hold you good in case of future loss…I have written you this long letter because I wish to deal frankly with you on a question which I feared might build some unpleasantness of feeling between us – an event which I should greatly regret both on account of our pleasant intercourse in the past and of the many interests we are likely to have together from the close neighborhood of our properties.

Landis apparently chose not to conclude the matter through compromise, resulting in the Wood estate placing the situation in the hands of a judge who did not rule in Landis's favor. The consequences led to paying off all debts to the Woods over several years, something Landis would accomplish by cashing in U.S. bonds twice a year as the Wood family accounts indicate. It seems, however, that Edward continued to examine his father's financial records and, on November 4, 1872, felt compelled to write Landis, confessing that when he compared Landis's papers to his father's books, "I find myself much perplexed as to the exact conditions [of] your affairs...the trouble is that some of these tracts seem to have been already allowed for or rather seem never to have been charged to you in the settlements made by my father...These matters are questions only of amount, but Father's books are not full and it will take some time to work it up. Have you not kept an account which would not show how much was originally charged in the deed to you and then what was allowed in separate items?" Wood concludes his letter by saying he would like to see Landis when the latter visits Millville.

Payments by Landis continued, but his records were not forthcoming. A lengthy correspondence, written on January 11, 1873 by Edward, notes that as far as "payments of commissions [to Wood], the Executor believes that receipts and other memoranda still remain" among Landis's papers.

By December 1873, according to a letter from one of Landis's attorneys, Bridgetonian William E. Potter, the next payment, after the removal of a property for which Landis was not accountable, was $4,042.50, most of which would be paid by U.S. bonds. The use of the bonds, Potter tells his client, "will nearly close the account." He also explains his attempt to have Wood pay for the court fees, a request that is met with a refusal.

The surviving written records of Landis's payments to the Wood estate end with a document dated November 23, 1874, presumably an indication the debt was resolved at this point. The next transaction Landis apparently had with the Wood family is recorded in a letter from Landis to Edward Wood on April 13, 1877, which reads, "Enclosed please find statement of the amount due me on the E. Thomps[on] Tract. This land was located by Ephram Dayton in 1732 and has been conveyed properly according to the papers I have examined down to Enoch Sharp. The land is within the bounds of the conveyance made by your father [and] made to me and I have paid for you the same. Trusting you will give this your early attention. I am very respectfully yours, Charles K. Landis"

Landis's stubbornness in resolving his debt with the Wood family cost him a considerable amount of money, certainly more than if he had accepted Edward's initial offer. But much more than money was at stake. Coming at a time when he was witnessing the decline of what had promised to be a successful railway line, defending himself weekly against the insults and mockery in the pages of *The Independent*, dealing with bouts of paranoia over his father-in-law exacting revenge and watching the free-thinking society he had founded slowly become a town in which the voice of his opponents and land speculators had grown louder and more powerful, Landis was poised to reach the nadir of his career. One or two of these problems would have been an inconvenience, but the combination of all five setbacks and their mounting tensions placed Landis in the most stressful situation he had yet faced. It would soon affect his marriage, his decisions and ultimately his actions

The first hint of change Clara noticed in her husband occurred in 1869. Clara's account of the marriage's early years for an article that appeared in the *Buffalo Courier* in1884 claims that her husband's demeanor had transformed, maintaining that "we lived happily during the year after our marriage, but from the time our baby was born [Landis] seemed to be changed. I do not know what caused it, but he became an entirely different man."

However, Clara's own behavior during the marriage was reported in an 1885 article published in the *Globe-Democrat* that claims it wasn't long into the relationship before Clara "became hysterical, and at times gave evidence of mental unsoundness." The condition described here was no doubt due the loss of the couple's first child. Both Landis and Clara were traumatized by the death of Henry, something that the births of Charles Jr. and Richard could only partially remedy.

By 1872, Clara observed that her husband's demeanor was becoming more critical, less tolerant and surprisingly abusive. During the custody trial she initiated in 1877, she recounted

> In that year, my husband betrayed at times most unreasonable jealousy in respect to me, and treated me with unkindness and abuse. He said to me substantially, at one time, "You are unfit to be any man's wife, and I have no respect for you. You and

all your family are a mercenary set and unscrupulous, and you have been injuring my interests and running after men." The interview in which these insults were given to me was protracted and much more was said by him insulting and abusive to me – all founded evidently on the insinuation of others, and not having the least ground of foundation in fact. It was the beginning of the serious trouble which has occurred between me and the respondent. I endeavored then and at all subsequent occasions to appease his unjust and acrimonious feeling toward me, and with partial success. But the respondent is a man of most unreasonable jealous temper; moody, morbid, self-willed and tyrannical, never thinking himself in the wrong, or at least, never willing to acknowledge it; and difficulties occurred, from time to time, until at last he became entirely estranged from me.

Clara's own demeanor would change over the next several years in what might be perceived as a defensive reaction to her husband's conduct.

The fact that Landis's paranoia had not only persisted but had grown worse was obvious not only to Clara but also to his friends and associates. In some cases, a degree of concern for his life was warranted, especially in circumstances involving individuals who felt they had not reaped what had been promised when buying land in the Vineland tract. But then there were others. In February 1872, Landis received a letter from a Millville individual who cautioned, "Sir, I hasten to inform you that you must not build no more [sic] C Churches in Vineland." The letter concludes with a threatening "You are warned in time. Now beware," and is signed by "Y. W. Chief." The "C" is certainly meant to stand for "Catholic," a term too abhorrent for the writer to commit to paper. But such threats were not imagined.

By August 1872, Landis began to display behavior that hinted he had become submissive to what he believed was his fate. According to John Burk, the town founder had convinced those who had gathered together before a Plum Street Hall speaking engagement with the editor of *The Independent* that there would be an attack on his life that night. When an attempt was made to convince him to remain home, he replied that the occasion was too important and that, should an attack commence, he would be the first victim. This incident would later be retold by Vineland physician John Ingram, who claimed that Landis stated *The Independent* editor would be the first victim, thereby turning the statement into a threat. The unlikeliness of such an utterance lies in the fact the Landis didn't use threats in this type of situation when his fears were so consuming.

As if to bolster the paranoia, *The Independent* newspaper had stepped up its attacks against Landis in 1872 under the editorship of its new owner Uri Carruth, who had been drawn to Vineland from Wisconsin, ironically enough, by one of Landis's Midwestern ads. A native of New York State, Carruth had studied law before turning to the newspaper trade. Moving to Berlin, Wisconsin, he established the *Green Lake Spectator* in March 1861, selling the publication to H.A. Phinney in October 1864.

Carruth and his family arrived in Vineland in 1868. They purchased the former home of G. T. Russell on the northeast corner of Walnut Road and the Boulevard, where they resided until 1875. Carruth became partners with William G. Smith in a printing business called Carruth and Smith, located on Landis Avenue near the railroad station and Landis's home and office. According to an invoice from the enterprise, the company was still in existence as of June 29, 1871, but the following month the partners would buy *The Independent*. By August 2, 1871, Carruth had become the sole owner and editor and seemed to meet with the approval of the town's "Independent Party," an aggregate of those who apparently opposed the town founder.

It has been hinted that Landis, on several occasions, sought to prevent a new onslaught of criticism by offering to pay for Carruth's silence but, if that is true, no deal was ever agreed upon. It was reported in the *New York Times* that Landis and Carruth had a falling out over an undisclosed matter; however, it appears that *The Independent's* editor needed little provocation to use his new acquisition as a means of persecuting the town founder's business ventures, speeches, articles, ideas, appearances, principles, lifestyle and opinions. Temperance was, of course, taken to task along with other components of Vineland's makeup. Landis was branded a dictator and it was the obligation of the paper to take him down.

On a curious note, Carruth was also affiliated with the local chapter of the National Grange of the Order of Patrons of Husbandry or, as it was simply known, The Grange, an agriculturally based group that was founded in 1867. While there is no direct evidence of any agrarian undertakings on the part of Carruth, he had served as an officer of the Green Lake Company Agricultural Society in Wisconsin and, in Vineland, edited a second weekly newspaper, *The New*

Jersey Granger, a publication affiliated with the organization of the same name.

The society had been created during a particularly low period in farming in the U.S. The Grange was a peaceful movement seeking to regulate transportation costs of farm products by rail and to promote within communities a positive relationship with agriculture, particularly from an economic standpoint. The group incorporated such ritualistic ingredients as secret passwords as part of its methods, reflecting its origins in the Masonic tradition.

The New Jersey State Grange was organized in 1873 at the height of the group's early national popularity which lasted until 1875. State and local Granges, for the most part, were politically non-partisan and included women and teenagers as members because of their place as workers on family farms. At a time when women were fighting for the right to vote, the Grange stipulated that four elected positions in the group's hierarchy had to be filled by women.

The beliefs of the Grange were in agreement with those espoused by Landis, particularly in championing farmers, women's rights and the community, which makes the vindictive streak leveled against Landis by Carruth a curiosity. Writing in the same timeframe as Carruth, Ezra Slocum Carr, in *The Patrons of Husbandry on the Pacific Coast*, recognized Landis's accomplishments and his connection to the purpose of the Grange. "All things considered," Carr acknowledged, "Vineland is perhaps the most single success in drawing off the over-crowded population of cities, and setting them at work upon the land; and it is unquestionably the most prosperous community in the United States...California cannot outvie in size and quality the fruit shows from Vineland... the luscious strawberries, peaches, melons—or the fresh vegetables... Speculation in uncultivated lands, which has been the bane of other settlements, never has occurred in Vineland, the advance in value invariably being upon the improvements of actual settlers, whether permanent or otherwise... [and] if anyone would know whether temperance and education are sufficient safeguards against crime, let him read the statistics of the police and poor expenses of this settlement for the last six years..."

Carr had witnessed the progress of Vineland in the early 1870s and his evaluation of the town took note of the evolution that had occurred in a short period: "In twelve years, there was a population of eleven thousand, mostly from New England. Fourteen thousand, and within the last year, twenty-three thousand acres have been added to the original tract...It has built one hundred and seventy-eight miles of excellent roads, twenty school-houses, ten churches, four post-offices, fifteen manufacturing establishments, besides shops and stores, such as would be required by a similar population elsewhere. In the importance of its agricultural productions Landis Township ranks the fourth in New Jersey. There are seventeen miles of railways on the tract, and six stations."

Regardless of these accomplishments, for the next several years *The Independent* was filled weekly with a number of articles, columns and editorials by Carruth condemning Landis. Some were without a byline, others used pseudonyms. Typical of his approach is an April 10, 1872 editorial in which he casts Landis as a prince dispensing benevolence when the mood strikes him:

You knew you could make no headway against the Prince. You talk of running for office! What insanity! No! No! You have missed your figure there and are reaping the reward of your impudence...Why not follow the noble example of your brother editors and fawn and truckle to your Lawful Prince? See how they have waxed fat and grown lusty on the rich morsels of fat that have fallen from the Prince's table...He may in his great goodness grant you his conditional pardon, and in pity for your unhappy state, even bestow upon you a few of those rich acres on the outskirts of the city of Landisville so you may once more sit in thankfulness beneath the shadow of your own vine and fig tree. But never, oh! Never again dare to oppose the Prince! If ye do, ye shall surely be cast out.

In the same issue, Carruth delivers another barrage at Landis for having written about the shade tree policy and maintaining what Carruth calls "brush land" that prevents the planting of trees in front of Landis's house.

In the April 24, 1872 issue, Carruth reports that Landis will devote his time to crushing *The Independent* by getting patrons to stop buying the newspaper. By now Landis had begun defending himself by writing articles for the *Vineland Weekly*, and each of his contributions were attacked by Carruth as well. A story, "The Way to Get Rid of an Unscrupulous Land-Shark," appears in *The Independent* as a not-too-carefully-disguised and unflattering tale of Landis as Patrick Killkenny, or Patrick K. At one point, after he is besieged by a mob and attack dogs, Killkenny takes refuge in a tree and announces his intentions to colonize an area, coax farmers and mechanics to work there and establish stipulations like temperance to attract the sober and the moral, until he is told, "dry up you old idiot," by one member of the mob.

On August 8, Landis launched a massive attack on *The Independent* in the form of a lengthy letter to the Vineland Historical and Antiquarian Society in which he discusses what he sees as the damage caused by the unending editorial attacks by Carruth in the *The Independent*. Acknowledging the onslaught aimed at him personally, he explains that the effects are far-reaching:

> The paper known as *The Vineland Independent*, from the time when it was started by its proprietor Hale, has been conducted in opposition to the interests of the Vineland settlement. When it passed from Hales's hands into that of Mr. Taylor, and the pen of Carruth was noticed in its columns, it became the vehicle of calumny and falsehood, until it finally threw off all disguise and all the restraints of propriety in the hands of Carruth as the sole proprietor. When the latter first became owner of it, I was given to understand that it was to be conducted in the interests of the place and, wishing all papers well that would contribute to such a cause, I advertised in it at the rate of $350 a year and continued to do so until I found that the paper was a public damage and that its sole aim appeared to be to injure the settlement. So long as its attacks were

directed against me, I was in hopes that they would do Vineland no harm. I felt strong in my cause, and my word, and thought that these spiteful attacks might perhaps gratify the envious, and thus relieve their hearts in some degree, and that I might, in this way, draw the fire which would otherwise be directed against the commonweal. In this, however, I was disappointed. There has been no occasion missed for detracting from the merits of Vineland.

Landis does not perceive *The Independent's* scathing articles as a personal vendetta on the part of the editor, certain that Vineland is the intended target of Carruth's wrath:

> I do not believe that, in all this, there is any personal feeling against myself on the part of the editor or co-editor of *The Independent*. I have never done Carruth, or Harrison his co-editor, the slightest injury; but, on the contrary, I endeavored to show my good will advertising, at considerable expense, in the paper, when I knew that the advertisement was valueless, but only to protect the interests of the place if possible; and owing to the peculiar reasons which induced Mr. Harrison's family to send him here, I extended toward him all the encouragement possible...I am convinced, after the most careful scrutiny, that there is only one object, either in the scandals against myself or against every enterprise or movement for the good of Vineland, and that object

is the injury of the place. What can be the inducement for this is a mystery... The result of it all is, however, that it has damaged the reputation of Vineland, until the common expression used in regard to it is that Vineland is a "fraud' and a 'humbug."

Landis disparages the paper's harsh criticism of the town's enterprises and how it has "maligned the character of the people by attempting to establish the idea abroad that our temperance law is a practical failure." He takes offence over *The Independent's* attempts to "stir up contention and misunderstanding of the part of its citizens as against myself, by the grossest falsehoods." Furthermore, he states that these personal attacks are affecting his business by preventing the sale of property since "strangers agree that if the Founder is a 'fraud,' a 'humbug,' and a 'swindler,'" terms Landis refers to as "choice epithets," they don't want to purchase land here. He then offers evidence of his accusations:

Neither I nor my agents have ever known a man to come to Vineland and purchase property here who was a subscriber for, or who had seen *The Independent*. I have known men to come here, to go around, and be satisfied with the place, and verbally agree to purchase property and order the [deed] made out when they would go into some store or the saloon where this paper would fall into their hands, and they would countermand the order. A late instance of the efforts produced by this paper occurred in the case of a man with a wife and five children, whose place was advertised by the sheriff under a mortgage. Although the place was offered at one half of its value, yet *The Vineland Independent* lost this man the sale of it; and he has not yet sold it. It will no doubt be swept from under him for a few hundred dollars when it is worth several thousand dollars.

By this point, the Board of Trustees for the VHAS must have been wondering why Landis had chosen to involve them in this issue. The explanation reveals that the town founder obviously required help in his ongoing battles with the paper. Vineland and some of its residents had become casualties and it was no longer Landis's war. He was beginning to understand it could not be won without reinforcements, even if the number of residents he could still count on were dwindling.

I have had none of our citizens to cooperate with me for a long time. Men who devoted themselves to the public welfare... have been so pursued and maligned, that they doubtless prefer to attend to their private business and let the interests of the public take care of themselves. Our best citizens seem to have become inert. It is a pardonable sensitiveness that hesitates about a course which will subject men to the risk of being scandalized, or having their families scandalized in a newspaper. That such things could exist in Vineland, and that such a paper could command advertising patronage and subscribers, has been a matter of the most intolerable astonishment to me, and of itself has formed with many an argument against the place. No such paper could live a week in any ordinary community…Perhaps these things are so because so many of the people are strangers to one another; because some of them do not take time to reflect, and because others are wholly employed upon their homesteads.

Landis's motive for the letter and for selecting the anniversary of Vineland to write it was "to clear me from all future responsibility in regard to the future of this heretofore prosperous colony. It is a time when all can, or should, lay aside their party feelings and personal prejudices and address themselves to the good of the community. May God grant that you may do this…It involves the question as to whether the future of our town shall be a grand success and an example to pattern after for all time, or whether our heretofore successful and beautiful Vineland shall only be another illustration of those numerous failures…"

The result of Landis's letter was a meeting a week later at Plum Street Hall to discuss the matter. When representatives of *The Independent* also showed up, there was, according to the newspaper's reports, "an attempt…to muzzle us in our attempt at a defense." The meeting was continued on August 21, with the newspaper proclaiming that "we are not to be heard on that occasion." In an article published on the day the meeting resumed, *The Independent* challenged Landis's letter and the residents' reaction in its pages, promising the publication would be represented at the event by Nelson Roberts, Capt. A.S. Hall, T.W. Braidwood, I.P. Fisher and others who were obviously sympathetic to the paper's belief that "nothing honorable or decent is to be expected" from "those who have so long misruled Vineland."

The article was emblazoned with a headline that carefully touched upon key words to convey the sense of impropriety and the conviction that only *The Independent* could protect the populace from the tyranny that Vineland faced: "FREEDOM OF THE PRESS. AN ATTEMPT TO CRUSH OUT THE VINELAND INDEPENDENT. AT PLUM STREET HALL TO-NIGHT! LET EVERYBODY COME! The Liberty of the Press is the Safeguard of a Free People. Shall Charles K. Landis Swallow up our Souls and Bodies we well as our Property?" The publication declared that all of Landis's charges against it were false and, once again employing highly charged words like "honesty", "fairness" and "Free Speech", trotted out an invitation to those who believe in such principles to join "the last great struggle of Tyranny. Let us see to it that the victory is with the right."

The newspaper also addressed the fact that Landis and Burk cancelled their subscriptions. "This sudden and crushing blow nearly took the breath away, but we happened to think that they would have to purchase of the news dealers, and then we felt better, and then again one of our friends came in and subscribed and paid for three new copies, so we are even again. If any of the eunuchs or others whose knees bend easily, wish to stop, we shall wait upon them with the greatest pleasure. We don't want anyone to take *The Independent* who lacks courage to say his soul is his own."

There is evidence that groups of subscribers at this time cancelled their subscription to *The Independent*, but the newspaper continued to publish. The assembly at Plum

Street Hall had given Carruth an opportunity that "proved to his own satisfaction" that Landis was the enemy of Vineland. It was followed by an affront claiming Landis was "palming off on editors worthless lots in Landisville, representing them as worth $150..." Carruth also wrote that he would end the feud if the VHAS would remove an unidentified newspaper, most likely the Landis-affiliated *Vineland Weekly*, from its archives and until then "we shall fight it..."

Over the next two years, as the dissolution of Landis's marriage continued, the attacks failed to subside, even during 1874 when Landis spent most of the year abroad to conduct business and remove himself from the anxiety caused by his wife and the press. Upon his return, Landis would discover his personal life a part of *The Independent's* columns.

Clara's subsequent account of her husband's demeanor during 1873 indicates that he apparently had begun to succumb to his own demons and those conjured by Carruth. Sadly, his temper was no longer confined to words or to his wife. Clara asserted that, in February 1873, her husband "became exceedingly violent and abusive to me, and that, in the presence of a visitor, calling me a damned mercenary b____ and using other violent and insulting language...he so far forgot himself as to seize me by the shoulders, push me to the door and tell me to get out of the house and have my child [Richard] in the street for what he cared, to communicate with my brother and that he should procure his attorney to make arrangements for a separation between us. This was within a month of my confinement with the youngest child...During the sickness, I took cold and was very ill with pneumonia, which rendered it necessary to procure a wet nurse for my child."

As the year progressed, Landis's jealousy became more pronounced. "In the summer of 1873," Clara recalled in 1877, "owing to my ill-health, I spent some time in the same boarding house and with the family of my sister, Mrs. Sands, and thus renewed an acquaintance which I had from childhood with a lad, then seventeen years old, the brother of my sister's husband. [Landis] chose to be jealous of this boy and without the least reason in my conduct charged me, in the most abusive and indecent way, of impropriety with him and with a design to make him my paramour. The violence of [Landis] was exhibited later, not only to me but also to others in our family and to our eldest little boy, whom on several occasions, he beat so severely that the child was injured by it for days. During the year 1873 this violence was displayed toward me the children and others and his jealousy toward the young lad, Sands, was expressed by him to me, not only in words, but in writing during my absence from home."

It would be enough to blame Landis's behavior on anxiety over personal financial pressures and *The Independent's* relentless attacks, but Vineland, along with the rest of the nation, was also facing the threat of the Panic of 1873, which had begun on September 18, 1873. On that day, Jay Cooke and Company, the prominent Philadelphia banking firm connected with the early stages of the Northern Pacific Railroad, suspended payments on notes it had issued, a prelude to its declaration of bankruptcy.

The failure of Cooke and Company sent Wall Street into an immediate panic, and over the next day, additional banks began to fail. By September 20, all trading was suspended on the New York Stock Exchange for the very first time. The government decided to pour money on the wound by announcing it would buy what turned out to be a total of $13 million in bonds. When, the following year, Congress passed a bill that the *New York Times* reported "would allow for more printing of currency to spur inflation and reduce the real value of debts," President Ulysses S. Grant vetoed it.

The rail industry played a significant role in the Panic of 1873. A total of 35,000 miles of track had been laid in the United States in the first eight years after the Civil War. The railroad was one of the biggest employers in the country, but it remained a risky business. Vineland's own investment in a rail line exemplified the difficulties in financing such a venture in the early 1870s. Unable to meet expenses, the Vineland Railway Company had been sold at a considerable loss several months before the Panic of 1873.

Just prior to September 18, the *New York Times* reported, "railroad and real estate speculation had been rampant, and values had multiplied to unheard of heights." The eventual consequence of the crisis on the country's rail industry was such that, according to the *New York Times*, "railroad construction dropped from 7,000 miles in 1873 to 1,700 in 1875."

Agriculture, another leading employer in the country and certainly a significant Vineland business, was another casualty of the Panic of 1873 when farm prices collapsed. Although B.F. Ladd's *History of Vineland* discusses the record grape crop sales in 1871, the chronicle makes no mention of farm sales throughout the next few years. And only several new businesses, each described as thriving, are noted during this time. Frank D. Andrews, editor of the *Vineland Historical Magazine*, acknowledged that in this period "the unprecedented growth of the preceding years had practically ceased, and doubts were expressed."

When it comes to the Panic of 1873, Vineland probably didn't have as bad an experience as other areas of the country, particularly major urban centers, which absorbed the brunt of the 14% unemployment rate by 1876. To help counteract the economic decline of his town, Landis prepared to undertake a trip to Europe to promote his town. Vineland's stability and growth would return within two years, well ahead of most of the nation, which required an additional several years to recover.

It was soon obvious that the economic recovery was easier to achieve than a reconciliation of Landis's marriage. By the start of 1874, the Landises had reached a crossroads in their relationship. The alleged abuses, jealousies and tirades on the part of Landis and the tantrums and fits attributed to Clara had become a steady part of their home life. Now it was about to invade their life outside of Vineland, as Clara recounted in 1877:

> In the early part of 1874, at Philadelphia, a difficulty happened between [Landis] and myself because of his beating the little boy Charles. Hearing the child cry, I rushed to his aid, and forgetting myself in my indignation when I found him severely whipping the boy, I slapped him in the face; [Landis] thereupon seized me violently, choked me and in great anger and with abusive language swore that he would kill me if I ever offered him another blow. I was then

enceinte [pregnant] since the preceding January, and the effect of this conduct was to produce severe illness for two weeks. Such instances as these, which though not always attended with violence, were numerous, tended to convince us that without adequate cause I had lost my influence over my husband and my position as the wife of his love, and that he had given the confidence and regard due me to others. I was, besides the whole of my married life either in a state of pregnancy or nursing children, having had, including one miscarriage, four births in six years, while I am now expecting to be confined again.

The miscarriage Clara refers to apparently occurred not long after the incident she describes above, probably March 1874, a month before Landis planned to sail to Europe for a four-month business trip to promote Vineland and establish Vineland Emigration and Land Agency offices to facilitate the relocation of those interested in settling in his town. For much of the 20th century, the European trip has been mistakenly represented merely as Landis's attempt to recruit Italian farmers to bolster Vineland's post-Civil War agriculture. Although he did attempt to promote his town while in Northern Italy, Landis enjoyed a brief stay there largely as a tourist. Recruitment in Italy was not as much of a necessity as it was in England, Scotland and France since he had already been promoting his town to Italian immigrants in Giovanni Francesco Secchi de Casali's publication *L'Ecod'Italia* or *Echoes of Italy*, an influential Italian-language newspaper for immigrants in the New York area. By 1873, at the height of the newspaper's popularity, information about Vineland could be found in its pages. In 1874, de Casali's publication reported that "250 of our hard-working and industrious compatriots bought land there which they allocated to fruit-growing and truck-gardening, in addition to raising grains. Most of them have built homes there with the intention of settling there."

Landis had also hired Carlo Quairoli to help the incoming Italian migrants with their adjustment in settling into South Jersey life. Schooled at the University of Milan in law, Quairoli had served as an assistant secretary to the Italian Prime Minister before migrating in 1870 to Hempstead, Long Island, where he supported himself as a laborer since he was denied legal practice because he couldn't speak English. In 1872, he grew disenchanted by the prospect of a life of manual labor and approached the Italian Council in New York about a passport to return to his homeland. Instead of granting him his request, the council instead informed him of a businessman from South Jersey who was looking for someone with Quairoli's legal skills and background to help him with the Italian immigrants relocating to his settlement.

He soon visited Vineland, met Landis, toured the town and decided to stay, engaging in work as a justice of the peace, a commissioner of deeds, a notary public in addition to his duties as liaison for the Italian families settling in Vineland. His association with these settlers over the next several decades would inspire him to put together a chronicle of the town's Italian community in 1911.

Despite the business purpose of Landis's upcoming voyage, Clara had hoped to join her husband on the trip and remained persistent about it until the miscarriage." I was convalescing from illness occasioned by miscarriage," she said in 1877, "and I acquiesced in his going alone – he saying he could not afford to take me – thinking I would have rest and peace..."

Clara was unaware she would soon earn Landis's wrath before he arrived in Europe. Now faced with a limited budget for clothing for herself and the children, she had gone shopping, with her husband's encouragement, most likely after the miscarriage. "I had not been expensive in my habits," she explained. "Both my own clothing and that of my children, owing to his complaints at the times, were of the most inexpensive nature...In March 1874, by directions of [Landis], I purchased some dresses for myself and my children, the bills for which were not presented till after his departure for Europe, and these formed a large part of the expenses to which he afterward took violent umbrage."

Landis had reason for concern when it came to Clara's spending. Three documents contained in the VHAS archives, two of which are incomplete, chart the Landis family expenses during the years Landis and Clara were married. In December 1868, two months after the couple's wedding, account records show that Clara spent $460. In 1869, however, the amount rises to $1, 624, a sum comparable to over $30,000 in 2015. The next three years show a significant decrease: $770 in 1870, $554 in 1871 and $323 in 1872. During the Panic of 1873, Clara's expenses rose again to $784, probably provoking Landis to curb her spending at the start of 1874. Records indicate that in the months of February and March 1874, she had limited her expenses to a mere $60, as her statements attest, but the most complete extant document of expenditures for that year reveals that after Landis's departure for Europe at the start of April, Clara undertook a spending spree that resulted in a total of $1,502 in expenses for the year.

When Landis set sail on April 7, 1874, Clara, expected him to return by August 1, but it would be December before Landis saw Vineland and his family again. Before departing, he had completed a series of articles on agriculture, horticulture and other topics and left them with T. C. Edwards, who would print these pieces in the *Vineland Weekly* during the founder's time in Europe. Landis would also send a series of correspondence to be published. Edwards later explained that, for the articles, he had been instructed "to attach [Landis's] signature and date each one to correspond with [Landis's] letter from Europe; I first saw the manuscripts just before he went to Europe...all were in his handwriting except one in relation to cranberries...sometimes I would modify some of the articles."

Within the first several months of the European trip, the Landises continued to bicker from both sides of the Atlantic Ocean via letters. Clara later made it clear that the arrangements with which she had been left when her husband departed were not to her liking:

> ...the arrangement was that I, with the children and his mother and sister should go to Cape May for the summer...While I acquiesced in this arrangement, it did not meet my wishes or my judgment. I had had trouble with Mrs. and Miss Landis...before. I feared a renewal of it. We were not

congenial to each other. Reflection, after [Landis] went away, satisfied me that the place had better [not] be abandoned, and so I wrote the sister... a kind letter, saying that I had changed my mind about going to Cape May and should stay in Vineland. She wrote her brother respecting this but in the month of May I received two letters, each referring to this matter, the contents of which were exceedingly unkind. They were especially painful, because the letters written to me from him before that – one by the [illegible], another on the voyage, a third from Queenstown, a fourth from Liverpool and a fifth from London – were full of fondness and affection. These I have preserved. The two in May, of which I have spoken, I destroyed immediately after their receipt. I could not bear to keep them."

Although none of the correspondence referred to by Clara survives, the content of one of the May letters was recalled by her in 1877:

On the 30th of May he wrote me another letter in which he acknowledged a short note from me of May 12 and reproached me for my silence. He says: "Do you not think it a long time, from the 23rd of April to the 12th of May, to write me or give me any information about the children? What is the use of calling me darling, or telling me that you miss, when I see it is irksome for you to write? Common civility bears more fruit than the ardent love you profess."

On May 10, while in London, Landis had written to Ellen Norton, Charles Jr. and Richard's nanny, advising and micromanaging her on the care of the children and the handling of Clara:

MISS ELLEN NORTON – I have been very glad to hear that so far the children have been well. This shows how much better Vineland agrees with them than the city, and is no doubt due to some of your own good care. I hope that while I am away you will do the very best for the children, and that God will reward you, and I will not forget it when I return…Help Mrs. Landis all you can, and if at any time you should have both children on your hands do not lose patience. Be sure that the children get their food at regular times, and that it is of the right quality: that they go to bed at regular hours; that little Charlie does not run out in the sun without protection to his head; that his underclothing is always kept clean and well mended and that the amount of flannel the children wear is not changed. If the children have not got what is necessary, speak to Mrs. Landis, and if she does not get the articles immediately, within a day after you report, go to Leavitt and get them yourself. There must be no delay about such matters. I do not wish the children to go to Washington under any circumstances as it will endanger their lives. This I will write to Mrs. Landis. Help Mrs. Landis all you can in taking care of the children and, when she is out, consider yourself their guardian angel. You have been [a] mother yourself and may thus know what a father's love may be for his children. It is from this feeling I write to you. Befriend me in this. And hereafter you will always had [sic] a friend in me, no matter what difficulties you may get into. Kiss the children for me.

Your employer and friend,

CHARLES K. LANDIS

Somehow, Clara discovered and retained the copy of Landis's letter to Norton. She explained in 1877: "I could not but consider the writing of this letter an insult to myself. I made up my mind that my secret enemy was the respondent's sister, Miss Landis. And I wrote her under date of May 25. 'Forget,' I said, 'that I have tried to be your friend, and that like Brutus, you have stabbed me. Let there be no semblance of friendship between us. I prefer an open enemy to a secret foe."

By the end of May, the accusations and criticisms seem to have ceased, but that may have been the result of Burk screening and withholding correspondence from Clara that may have potentially agitated Landis. In a letter from his employer's wife, probably received in early June, Burk is clearly being interrogated:

Sir,

Did you pass my 2 letters of 24th and 26th of May 1874 to Mr. Landis, also Ellen Norton's letter.

You will please state below here if so and if you do not reply – I shall take it as an acknowledgement that you have intercepted my correspondence.

Mrs. Chas K. Landis

Answer here

For the next two months, Landis seemed to focus on his trip and allow himself to revel in the sights and acquaintances he encountered. One of the more interesting experiences came during his initial stay in London where he encountered what he believed would be the next wave of technology. "I was riding on the top of an omnibus on Oxford Street, London," he wrote several years later in a surviving manuscript. "Looking down I saw a sign reading 'pneumatic tube transit for packages to Euston Station,' three miles away. I immediately alighted and made inquiries. I found that the tube was three feet in diameter, and that it would be perfectly safe to make a trip through it by one of the sliding receptacles in which packages were carried."

Pneumatic tubes, a system by which cylindrical containers were transported through a series of tubes by means of compressed air or vacuum, had been first employed in Victorian England to speedily convey telegrams from telegraph offices. In 1853, the London Stock exchange had already linked such a system to local telegraph stations. The sign that Landis happened upon was, no doubt, an advertisement by the London Pneumatic Despatch Company which, in 1861, had developed a pneumatic system for transporting heavy packages which was large enough to allow a person to fit into the tube. In 1865, the Duke of Buckingham and some of the company's officials were successfully transported by pneumatic tube to Euston Station.

Landis was struck by the idea of having himself transported in a similar manner to the same station and immediately inquired about the possibility. "I asked if it would be allowed," he recounted. "The clerk replied he thought it would, but that he would have first to get the consent of the superintendent, and that I should be on hand the next morning at 11 o'clock." That evening, Landis attended a dinner party and discussed his appointment the next day. While most were appalled at the idea of having themselves transported by such technology, two gentlemen, Captain Henry S. Clive of the Royal Engineers and Claud Moncton, a civil engineer, expressed interest and asked if the Vinelander wanted company. Landis said he did and the three showed up the following morning.

"We were laid flat in the tube, they at the bottom and I on top, being the lightest," Landis recalled. "The word was given, time was kept by their watches, and we arrived in a few seconds, I now forget how many. When released I saw seven or eight gentlemen on hand, the directors of the company. One stepped forward and said, 'Mr. Landis, how did you enjoy your ride?' 'Very much,' I replied. 'I suppose you have all taken it.' 'No,' he said, 'you are the first.'"

It is conceivable that the directors then in charge of the London Pneumatic Despatch Company had never been transported by tube since those who had accompanied the

Duke of Buckingham had done so nine years earlier and had probably since left the company or weren't present for this feat. But Landis's recollection of the trip having taken "a few seconds" is clearly misremembered. The 1865 transport had taken five minutes.

Landis remained quite impressed with the pneumatic tube system and, like science fiction writer Jules Verne, saw it as a means of future public transportation. "Of all modes of rapid transit whether by steam, electricity or anything else, I think that everything will be supplanted by the pneumatic tube," he wrote. "It was only a question of time. The past generation has seen the advent of the telegraph…The present has seen the telephone…but the present or next generation will see the advent of pneumatic tube transit carrying passengers with the greatest of ease from 500 to 1,000 miles per hour by pneumatic tube." Unfortunately for Landis, while the system continued to carry mail well into the 20th century, it never developed into a form of public transport.

Landis had resumed his journal upon setting sail for Europe in April, but the book containing entries for April, May and June, his early months in England, has been lost. His next book picks up in London on July 3. The entries reveal, in general, a relaxed lifestyle amidst the work he set out to accomplish, giving a clear impression that the change of scenery served as another motive for his trip. There are random moments of feeling "troubled in mind," but away from Vineland, Clara, public criticism and a breeding ground for his personal fears, Landis seems to convey a sense of rejuvenation, enjoying the company of the English or the solitude of a good book. Walking tours, visits with new acquaintances and sumptuous meals alternate with the creation of new pamphlets about Vineland, the promotion of emigration to the town and consultations with agents in his London office as well as in branches in Ireland and Scotland. And his usual bedtime, which consisted of anywhere from ten to eleven o'clock, was extended to the midnight hour on many occasions.

The Vineland Emigration and Land Agency established by Landis in London in 1874 was located at 12 Southampton Street, Covent Garden and run by J.S. Lowe. A pamphlet, entitled *Emigration to Vineland, New Jersey, U.S.*, circulated the following year and promoted Vineland through a reprint of a newspaper article that appeared in the *Philadelphia Baptist* on October 1, 1874, an explanation of the costs for lots, payment plans and a letter from Vineland resident W. Pollard to William Fithian sent during the time Landis was in London.

The *Philadelphia Baptist* article opens with the proclamation, "Vineland is the Italy of the United States," and proceeds to inform the reader of its large number of expanding farms, orchards and vineyards, its mild climate, its population of 11,000, its town's proximity to Philadelphia, Boston, Baltimore and New York and its fourteen places of worship and twenty schools. It announces that it provides over one thousand tons of grapes and many tons of additional fruit to various markets throughout the northeastern seaboard in the United States. The article also mentions that Vineland was only a ten-day journey from Liverpool, England.

The cost for British emigrants is announced at five pounds sterling per acre. For anyone paying the whole of the purchase in advance, there was a five percent discount offered. The alternative was to place a down-payment of one-sixth of the cost and the remaining amount in annual installments. Purchases of land could also be made in advance of an emigration planned for years later. Provisional receipts were given by the agency with official receipts from Landis replacing them in approximately six weeks.

The agency also provided "arrangements for the conveyance of passengers and baggage through to Vineland (which will save the passengers the risk of the impositions to which new arrivals are liable on landing) at the following through fares, per adult, from Liverpool," followed by a list of prices ranging from twelve pounds for a first-class cabin to six pounds for a second-class cabin and three pounds for a place in steerage. Passengers were encouraged to take as many household effects with them "as bedding and furniture are, at present, dear in America." Once in Vineland, a family could obtain "an excellent wood-built house, cut, dried and erected, in a short time, and especially adapted to the needs of the family, for about fifty pounds complete."

Pollard's letter fittingly presents an Englishman's view of his adopted home of Vineland, a sales pitch that provides the right appeal to fellow countrymen, even though it was certainly not the intention of the writer when it was composed. Pollard discusses his four hundred fruit trees which are part of his twenty-acre Vineland farm. "Intoxicating drinks are not sold there, and there are no drunkards, police, gaols or poor houses...We have no crime, no neglected little children, but peace, good order and prosperity." After discussing a speech of Landis's, Pollard suggests having Vineland's founder speak at some of the temperance meetings while in England. He then concludes with a hope that he will be able to send some fruit of "our own growing" next year as "this is the finest place in the world for growing peaches, pears and all other kinds of fruit."

The pamphlet offers a glimpse into Landis's marketing strategy for a European population. Until now, he had limited his ads to U.S. publications, but the enticement of prospective European settlers was probably seen as a solution not only to Vineland's recovery from the Panic of 1873 but from the damage land speculators had begun to inflict upon the town.

What may have begun as a business trip that also served as a part-time vacation, however, soon added yet another work-related item to its agenda. Three days after celebrating Independence Day at London's Criterion Restaurant, where "the only thing I saw in London to remind me of [the occasion] was a drunken American…dressed in full uniform and making an ass of himself in the worst of style," Landis notes in his journal the state of British street cleaning, tramways, park maintenance, sewerage and drainage systems, admitting that "in all these matters we in America are vastly behind the times. My national egotism received a beautiful setting down after I had been a while in Europe."

This unexpected diversion soon became an aesthetic tutorial. Landis's attention turned toward the architecture and designs that graced many of the cities he visited. He marveled at their beauty and economy and recorded his impressions in the pages of his journal. What he witnessed he intended to apply to Vineland, but these sights would also serve as ideas for his novel *A Trip to Mars* and as a design for the next town he would establish in South Jersey.

The journal entries of this period contain periodic references to his family back home. Landis mentions that he wrote a letter to Clara on July 4 and, on July 17, while in Glasgow, he purchases Highland suits for his sons and silk-lined dressing gowns for his mother and mother-in-law, an umbrella for his sister Matilda, a shawl for his sons' nanny and suits and socks for Burk's children. On July 25, he writes of buying "some very handsome Scotch pebble jewelry as presents to my wife and some friends."

Throughout his trip, Landis appeared especially enthusiastic about sites related to Shakespeare's plays. On July 22 in Scotland, he made it a point to visit "Cawder (sic) Castle, the scene of Macbeth's history and source of Shakespeare's play," which he discovered "was well kept up. They showed me the room in which Duncan was murdered. The ancestors' pictures hang in the hall. The grounds around it are very beautiful." He would later enjoy similar Shakespeare-related sites in Italy, always distinguishing between the historical facts and the legends created for tourists.

Upon his return to London, Landis attended a meeting of the Cogers Club, whose topics that evening included labor strikes and the agricultural laborer. Finding it necessary to impart his feelings on the matter, Landis spoke about the farmer having a right to a fair share of the profits. It would be one of the many occasions in which he defended and protected the rights of those in agriculture. But on this evening in London, such ideas were "not well received."

It was while in London that Landis encountered a twenty-three-year-old literary student by the name of William Adolph Baillie-Grohman. Near the end of his life,

Landis revealed in an introduction to Grohman's book *Life in the Mountains* how the two met: "In 1874...I began my acquaintance with him—meeting him accidentally at the house of a mutual acquaintance in a quiet country retreat on the sylvan banks of the Thames. It soon led to more intimate terms, as I was attracted by his entirely unconventional character, his fund of general knowledge, the result of wide reading and extensive travels. When I left England, he accompanied me on a pleasant ramble through France, South Germany and Tyrol."

On August 8, the anniversary of Vineland's founding, Landis, accompanied by Grohman, set out from Victoria Station for Paris wondering how the residents of his town were spending the day. In preparation for his trip to France, Landis had begun taking French lessons while in London, regretting the fact that he had not learned the language in his youth. Tutorials took up the middle portion of his days, with a review of his lessons afterwards. Speaking the language must have expedited the establishment of a French agency for the sale of his lands while in Paris because, by August 13, Landis and his companion traveled to Germany where they had a very short stay in Munich. As Landis would later recall, "I was then visiting [these locations] for the first time. [Grohman], however, knew...all the interesting old buildings, castles, museums, and art treasures and proved a delightful travelling companion."

By 10:30 a.m. on August 15, the two boarded a train for Matzen Castle, the home of Grohman's family. They arrived by 4 p.m. in a deluge of rain which did not prevent Landis from marveling at the snow-covered mountains surrounding the impressive castle that would serve as his home-away-from-home over the next month. His stay here would not be free from family issues, but the Grohman abode would become a sort of sanctuary and the company of his hosts would provide him with what was undoubtedly the highlight of his entire trip.

Located in the Tyrol, an area that would inspire both the Earth and Martian settings in Landis's novel *A Trip to Mars*, Matzen Castle dates back to the time of the Romans, who built it to serve as a fort against the Teutonic forces they were battling. The building contained a round tower and other structures built around a courtyard. The year before Landis's visit, its owner, Josef von Pfeiffersbergs, found that he could no longer afford the castle, which had been in his family's possession for 140 years. He sold the dwelling to Frances Grohman, daughter of the Irish Captain James Reade, the first Duke of Wellington's cousin. Grohman bought the structure by selling diamonds she owned. Landis's stay here preceded the renovations the new owner would undertake later in the decade but, on an early tour of the premises, he was informed of the plans for the restoration. The castle served as a summer home for Mrs. Grohman, her three daughters and a governess. Mrs. Grohman's husband, Adolph, remained at the family's other estate, while a son, Adolph, was away at college. William, who had relocated to London, was paying a visit.

Landis appears to have been immediately smitten by Frances Grohman's beauty and charm. They spent a considerable amount of time together during his stay, and he describes her as "a very young and beautiful looking lady," as well as "a most delightful conversationalist" and she would soon become a close friend and confidante of the

Vinelander. She and her sons and daughters would later be fictionalized as the narrator's hospitable Martian hosts in Landis's novel *A Trip to Mars*.

Two days after his arrival at Matzen Castle, Landis notes in his journal that his mail is not being forwarded from London to his current location. He expresses little concern over not hearing from home but admits how much he misses Charles Jr. "I appear to be cut off from communication," he writes. "I am so well situated, however, that I do not object to the cut-off. Last night I dreamed of my little boy Charley, that I was hugging and kissing him and listening to his pretty talk. I often dream of Charley."

Back in Vineland, Clara's expectations that her husband would return to the U.S. by the start of August seemed to consume her as the months wore on. A deposition-like report, found in the papers of Clara Landis and her trustee Charles E. Elmer, reveals that in 1874, during Landis's trip to Europe, Clara had "expected her husband home in July or August and a few days afterwards, she would ask [Elmer] about her husband's address." Clara said that "her brother [Richard] had already telegraphed Mr. Landis to the various steamships...[to] ascertain when Mr. Landis should sail back to this country as [Clara and her brother] were going to settle the matter with him on his arrival and that they would make it so hot for him that he would be forced to leave the county."

Unaware of the plans his wife and brother-in-law were concocting, Landis was enjoying his time with the Grohmans. Day trips to places like the village of Rattenberg and the town of Schwartz alternated with overnight stays in cities like Innsbruck where, according to records, Landis's purchases included two Blunderbusses, two pictures of saints, a picture of Venus on marble and one of the crucifixion on copper as well as two swords. He learned much of the history of the area and encountered both upper-class citizens as well as peasants, who he declared "show the refinement and taste of an old civilization."

On August 25, while in Haal, communications with his family were reestablished when Landis received correspondence forwarded from London. According to a journal entry, one letter addressed his decision to extend his stay in Europe.

> My brother-in-law is anxious for me to come home, on account of the conduct of _____ [presumably Clara] My going home now would be impolite, but yet I would go if it would do any good, which it would not. These things have racked my brain and torn my heart to pieces day and night and I will not write about them. Bad enough to think. It is a happy thing that I have confidence in God's help. It is my solace and rest.

Landis also heard from his clerk, who provided Vineland's founder with good news.

> [Burk] also writes me that the drouth (sic) is ended in Vineland. Thank God! Also that Carruth has ended his newspaper war upon me after a loss of $4,000. He remarks that my silence killed him. I think rather that the shallow falsehoods and scurrility he indulged in and the good taste of the people of Vineland killed

him. It is to be hoped that it may teach him the lesson that it is better to serve mankind than injure them.

The confidence that resulted from Carruth's decision to end his incessant tirades against Landis was unfortunately short-lived as the editor's printed jibes would resume and continue into the next year.

Two days later, Landis once again heard from home, but on this occasion the news was not like that of the previous letter. He reports in his journal:

> At the dinner time, received news from home that filled me with alarm about Charley, who is dangerously ill. Wrote telegram to my brother-in-law, R. W. Meade. On consultation with Mrs. Grohman, concluded to modify it, and finally not to send it…I decided to think overnight about my duty and the best course to pursue…Received news that my dog Lion has been poisoned. Alas! Poor Lion! An old friend and playfellow. The children will miss him, and he will play his tricks for us no more. When I left home, I feared my pets were in danger. This afternoon when I received the letters from home, I had arranged for a trip to the Achen Lake but postponed it in consequence. I prepared a dispatch to send to my brother-in-law, and Mrs. Grohman kindly consented to go to the telegraphic office with me and act as interpreter and attend the business. We walked there, but as previously stated, returned without sending the dispatch."

Landis spent the next day troubled and worried about his son and telegraphed Burk. That evening he received word from his clerk that Charles Jr. had "fully recovered" from the undisclosed illness. It's at this point in his journal that Landis admits he should "soon bring my visit [to Matzen Castle] to a close, but I am anxious to get letters, and besides it is difficult to part with the sunny spots of our existence, and my visit to Matzen has been one of them." Landis would enjoy the next two weeks free from news of unrest in Vineland. On September 6, he received letters from his sister Matilda and noted the significance of their content in his journal:

> "...read my letters. Two from my sister. She is still at Cape May and tells me very little about home...My sister sent me a slip from the paper to the effect that the High School at Vineland would be dedicated in a few days, and that President Grant would attend. I am glad of this for it will benefit the High School. One of my principal points of policy in establishing Vineland has always been to make it one of the first educational places in America."

On August 22, 1874, President Ulysses S. Grant arrived in Vineland for the dedication of the first official high school building constructed in the town. What Landis missed by not being in Vineland on that date commenced with Grant's arrival in Vineland at 11 a.m. by a special train that transported him from Long Branch, New Jersey, followed by lunch at the home of Board of Education President Henry Hartson on Seventh and Wood Streets. The founder was not able to witness the thirty-seven girls arrayed in white outfits with red and blue sashes who rode in the procession to Hartson's residence. His absence also prevented him from hearing Grant's brief speech at the ceremony in which the president proclaimed, "it gives me great pleasure to visit your thriving little town...It is pointed to as one of the greatest places for industry, prosperity and intelligence, and all of the improvements and progress I have seen and heard of have been accomplished under trying circumstances."

At the time he was reading about Grant's visit to Vineland, Landis had just returned from a trip through Austria with William Grohman. The tour included the village of Weissenbach which receives a journal note as a reminder to "visit this place again." On September 9, Landis writes in his journal that no letters had arrived and implies that he is waiting for one from Burk. He thinks that his clerk may have been experiencing "some domestic trouble" as an explanation as to why he had not yet heard from him. The next day, he reports,

> ...received a short note from my wife, and one from R. W. Meade, my brother-in-law. They confirm the desertion of my house, and I think my brother-in-law has helped to carry away the children. I await anxiously for news from my agent, Mr. Burk. There is one thing fixed. I will not abandon my children to this woman. Perhaps my instructions will suffice. If not, I will hasten to America after my October engagement in London.

Two days later, Landis writes that he cannot sleep owing to the troubling news from home. He awaits word from Burk, which arrives September 14. Landis notes in his journal that "this letter confirmed the information that my wife had left my home and taken my children away."

Landis soon abandons discussions of Clara and the children in his journal entries, but a letter presumably sent to Burk about the current situation indicates that the matter of the children has been resolved. Landis writes, "I like that you have been able to keep the children in Vineland," and provides instructions to contact Matilda and to be aware of the "movements of Mrs. Landis." The letter also orders that no one is to dispense "anymore deeds with Mrs. Landis' signature. It is unnecessary. Have others presented with my name alone." Furthermore, "give [Clara] no more money unless in very small [amounts]. Tell her you will pay the bills for the children. I will soon be back. I will know how to act when I get home, something I have not had for several years back."

Landis spent September 15 at Matzen Castle in the company of the Grohmans. The next morning, he "walked with Mrs. Grohman in the grounds for the last time. Perhaps not. Still in the hope of meeting this charming woman and her family again. I owe them much. A month of comparative happiness rescued from my otherwise sad life, and I will hereafter owe them my most pleasant memories."

Spending the remainder of the day, Landis had supper with the Grohmans and then left to catch the four o'clock train that would take him and William to Bazen. Once goodbyes were said, Mrs. Grohman accompanied her guest to the gate. Landis describes the parting like a poet, his meaning conveyed between the lines:

> Mrs. Grohman walked with me to the gate of the grounds, bid me farewell and turned back. I watched her retreating figure as tho it might be the last time. She looked back. I raised my hat. She disappeared, and I hurried out into the world…

While in Bazen, Landis purchased statues and paintings for Sacred Heart Church in Vineland. These and the other items he picked up throughout Europe were packaged and shipped well in advance of his departure for the U.S. But he was beginning to learn that his taste in selections needed work. He had begun to rely on Mrs. Grohman's opinion and when she arrived in Bazen on September 20, "her taste played havoc" with some of the things he had purchased since leaving Matzen Castle, particularly the paintings. This led to the decision "to have all my things taken to Matzen to be repaired and packaged and examined by Mrs. Grohman before they are sent off. All that may be considered bad will be left behind."

Before leaving Bazen, Landis inquired about how the town handled the insects that plagued the grape crops. At the time, Vineland was in the midst of its grape rot crisis during which attempts to remedy the affliction had not yet eliminated the blight. Landis discovered that black pepper and sulfur was used to eliminate the insects and writes that "this information may be worth untold sums in Vineland."

Once Landis secured an agent in Bazen, he departed for Venice. William accompanied him as far as Trent, then left in pursuit of antiques. Landis continued his travels, visiting not only Venice, but Verona and Desenzanoas as well. He found himself occasionally plagued by bad dreams about his son Richard, one in which the boy died and another in which he heard his voice.

Romantic poet Lord Byron had been a considerable influence on Landis in his youth and, while in Italy, Landis visited the Armenian monastery where the poet "spent six months of his life learning the Armenian language. In his letters…he states that he does it because he requires something which will give his mind some hard work in order to divert it from his troubles. This was after his separation from his wife. This philosophy is worthy of a heroic mind. It is rising above mental affliction instead of succumbing." It's sound advice that Landis seems to have attempted to follow throughout portions of his European trip.

A rendezvous with William was planned for October 4 in Trent, but the younger Grohman failed to show. Two days later, Landis returned to Matzen, taking a room in town until the Grohman's current guest departed the castle, but visiting each day and taking walks with Mrs. Grohman. His journal entries in Matzen are uplifting. "It was not long before we were steaming up the valley of the Inn [River] on the way to Matzen," he writes at the start of his return visit. "The art with which I have become acquainted at Matzen has given me new ideas concerning the human race and history," he reports on October 11, the day he moved back into the castle. "I now find myself observing everything as I go along – buildings, pictures, furniture and even small things, in order to fix in my mind the age and style."

On October 14, it was time to return to London. Before his departure, Landis received some advice from his host:

> I have noticed that you have sometimes been very sad, as though you had a great trouble, therefor (sic) I can sympathize with you. But you must never allow it to occupy too much of your mind. Think of it only when you have something to do in relation to it. For the rest, occupy your mind in study and action. This is a wide and beautiful world, and a mind like yours can accomplish and you will accomplish them – that I predict. Your nature is a grand and simple one, and your intellect is many sided. Never be discouraged or downhearted, nor allow small objects or people to worry you.

Landis arrived in London via Paris two days later. He enjoyed several nights of tranquil sleep before his anxiety dreams, no doubt brought on by his imminent return home, returned. On October 26, he writes that he "was suddenly wakened out of my sleep, dreaming of Charley. I was very sick the rest of the night. I dreamed that I saw him in a swing stretching his hands out to me and that a person was severely scolding him at a distance." At the time, Landis had no way of knowing that the scene in his dream would become a reality three years later.

News of his children arrived on November 2 in the form of a letter from Vinelander C.B. Campbell, who acknowledged that he saw Charles Jr. and Richard playing in the garden. The information confirmed that Clara and the boys had returned to their home on the Southeast corner of the Boulevard and the news improved Landis's sleepless nights, but his nocturnal unrest would reappear in the days before he set sail for America as he began wondering if his family would still be there when he arrived.

Immediately upon his return to London, Landis had devoted himself to several projects sure to provide temporary respite from his concerns and to satisfy his business and intellectual curiosity. Through the Temperance Alliance, he arranged for six speaking engagements that would take place in and around London during his last month in England. Vineland's reputation as a dry town was certainly known amongst the Alliance, and Landis enjoyed good attendance and a hearty response at his appearances.

Landis agreed to additional speeches in Manchester on November 24 and in Ashford on November 25, delaying his voyage home by several days. On November 26, he received an invitation to return the following spring for a two-to-three-month speaking tour of England and Ireland. The Alliance would pay for passage and all expenses. "This would be a good opportunity of doing some good," his journal entry for that day reads, but he had addressed his own place in the temperance movement in an entry a few weeks earlier when he wrote, "Have never been a total abstinence man, and always temperate, but find that I am much better, stronger, than when I drank anything. Have given it up for some time back."

With Vineland as his next destination and a dearth of communication from both his family and Burk, Landis decided to satiate the desire he had developed at Matzen Castle for more knowledge about the arts and European culture. Throughout this six-week London stay, he would read *History of Rationalism, History of Civilization,* and *Studies of Renaissance,* sometimes alternating between two at a time. He also visited the Geological Museum several times, on one occasion to receive a tutorial on the statues, pottery and china found there. "I am now finding great recreation in the intellectual reading I am now engaged in," he notes on October 28. "It is my medicine."

The October 28 journal entry also records a rather ill-fated moment. "Bought a saloon pistol for shooting at a mark," Landis writes. "This will be good amusement and practice." Less than five months later, it would serve yet another purpose.

Landis, in addition to securing office space for the Vineland Emigration Society at 12 Southampton Street in London, spent some of his time engaged in writing. Before leaving for the U.S., he completed an article, "The Social Science of Vineland" and made adjustments to his will, quite possibly the result of Clara's attempt to abandon him. The specifics about the changes remain a mystery, but the new will was executed at the U.S. Consul on November 10.

As December approached, Landis began arranging for his journey home. On December 1, he arrived in Liverpool and was stricken with a severe pain in his side, forcing the cancelation of a Southport speech he had agreed to give. The next day, he boarded his American Line ship back to America only to discover that its departure was delayed due to the discovery of smallpox on another ship in the harbor.

The following day, he picked up his mail, which included a notice from a legal firm from that summer requesting that Landis telegraph his brother-in-law once he arrived in Liverpool. After reviewing the rest of his letters, Landis requested a refund for his American Line ticket. He immediately booked passage on *The Republic*, a White Star Line ship, and later visited with the brother of Vineland's Captain Inman Sealby. He then retrieved his luggage from the hotel, boarded the ship and departed at 3 p.m. for what would be a pleasant voyage home.

Landis would arrive in New York on December 14 and set out for Vineland at 2 p.m. His family would be waiting for him, ready to welcome him back.

Chapter 5
Homecoming
(1875)

Within days of his return to Vineland, Landis had resumed his standard schedule. He made time for those who visited on December 15 and 16 but left with Clara and Burk for Philadelphia to see his mother and Matilda on the 17th. After another day of accepting visitors, he resumed his regular duties, which included examining a new school on the corner of Park Avenue and Third Street where he spoke with the students and teachers. He also visited the two locations he had set up to accommodate the Italian farmers settling in Vineland. One was New Italy, an area that became East Vineland in the 20th century, the other the unnamed northwest corner of Landis Township. He would later establish Landisville for similar purposes.

New Italy housed the first wave of Italians recruited by Vineland's founder. Not only did it provide the transplanted settlers enough land to establish their new farms, but it also created a reminder of their homeland. Landis was careful to title the streets of this area, relying on names that would be familiar to the new inhabitants: Venezia, Trento, Dante, Palermo, Pantera and the sovereign Italia.

Soon after establishing New Italy, Landis had turned his attention to the northwestern portion of Landis Township. To make way for additional farms, Landis extended Park Avenue beyond Delsea Drive, created Wheat and Garden Roads and then sold the land to the Italians. The settlers in this area were faced with the task of clearing the land, which was still largely forest in this area. Felled trees were brought to sawmills to provide lumber the farmers could use to build their homes as well as facilities to house livestock. When all was finished, they were left with acres of farmland they soon filled with fields, orchards and vineyards. "They have made great improvements," Landis writes in his December 28 journal entry, following it with his appraisal of the New Italy colony in which "the same speed and industry are evinced." On New Year's Eve, he hosted a dinner for many of the "Italian colonists," who provided the musical entertainment for the evening.

At Merchants Hall on December 30 Landis gave a two-hour talk about his European trip for what the *Vineland Weekly* estimated was an audience of 200 to 300 "highly pleased" residents. When William A. House and Rev. P.R. Russell had approached the town founder in mid-December about delivering an account of his experiences abroad, he agreed. The evening event was a benefit for the newly established Vineland High School Library.

Any tension between the Landises had dissipated by the holidays. Clara remained in Vineland throughout this period, taking walks with her husband and dining with him and various guests. As was his custom, Landis reported to his office on New Year's Day to catch up on business and hand out candy to any youth who came into the office to wish him a Happy New Year. Hoping that the two could ride their horses, Clara visited her husband, but Landis informed her he wouldn't be able to leave because of the work at hand.

Charles F. Kellogg was but one of a number of citizens who had stopped by Landis's office on New Year's Day to convey best wishes, but he was the only one invited to visit Landis's home later in the month because of their shared interest in architecture. When Kellogg showed up on the designated date, he was introduced to Clara. The evening consisted of Landis showing him architectural photographs. But according to Kellogg, "Just before I left he asked the question how certain articles that appeared in *The Independent* were received by the people of Vineland. I said that on the whole, [Carruth] printed them for fun." Having avoided the newspaper's attacks for much of the previous year, Landis was obviously still concerned about the effect Carruth could have on the town's residents.

Prior to Kellogg's visit, Clara had departed for Philadelphia for a week on January 2, 1875, staying with her cousin, Mrs. Ellis, but keeping in touch with her husband through letters. Meanwhile, the influence European culture had had on Landis began to manifest itself. Following Clara's departure, he took to reading Mrs. Charles Heaton's

1873 *A Concise History of Painting*, alternating it with Shakespeare's *Twelfth Night*, an appropriate choice for the season, He decided that Vineland needed an Art Association and established one by the following week with himself as president. And the Grohman family, particularly Mrs. Grohman who continued to correspond with Landis, clearly influenced his decision to hire a governess for his children, a matter he addressed in a letter to his wife and recorded in his journal.

> Wrote to my wife about a governess for my children. I do not like the idea of their being brought up by an ignorant Irish peasant girl. She does the best she can, however.

The Landis on view in this statement is someone all too aware of class.

The week was also spent working on another speech Landis would give at Plum Street Hall at the end of January. On the day he arrived back in Vineland, Landis had received a letter from a group of residents requesting he deliver a free lecture about his European tour. "Multitudes of our people would be delighted to hear you, who otherwise are deprived of that pleasure," the letter read, so a Plum Street Hall presentation was scheduled for January 27.

On January 15, Landis was approached by a committee of trustees from the high school, which had benefitted from his December 30 appearance. The group did not approve of the planned free lecture. By the following day, a petition signed by many of the residents requesting that the lecture not be canceled was presented to Landis, who was determined to proceed as planned.

On the night of January 27, an earlier claim that "multitudes of people would be delighted to hear you" had not been hyperbole. A newspaper account estimated 1,150 people filled the venue that evening with a number of other residents unable to gain admission to the eight o'clock event, which also included musical performances by local musicians. Clara was present at the event and afterward she and her husband attended a party.

Also during January, Landis prepared a speech he would give in Trenton before the State Board of the Agricultural Society, which was readying for elections that month. Landis's talk focused on the business advantages of New Jersey's proximity to Philadelphia and New York, a situation that Vineland had certainly utilized. After revising his speech on January 18, Landis awakened at 3 o'clock the following morning to catch the early train to Trenton where he delivered his lecture and ordered it to be published. That evening, he visited his mother and sister in Philadelphia, remaining in the city the next day before returning to Vineland on the 21st to discover a letter from England informing him that his article "The Social Science of Vineland," written during his European trip the year before, had been published in the journal *Frasier's Magazine* to good reviews. The magazine, established in 1830, boasted such contributors as Thomas Carlyle, William Makepeace Thackery and John Stuart Mill, so Landis undoubtedly took pride in having one of his pieces selected for print. He also received word from Mrs. Grohman that William had been climbing the highest mountain of the Tyrol, a very dangerous undertaking.

All this time, Landis was suffering from a cold, which did not deter him from business matters. With a good sleep serving as "my medicine when sick," he continued to work in his office and at home, investigating plans such as raising sheep in New Jersey, convinced that it would be well worth considering since there was plenty of wild land and sheep were a good "means of cleaning the land." He also tended to a new mill he had established at the corner of 6th and Quince Streets, purchasing a new steam engine for it and visiting the site on several occasions during the month while musing about adding a store on the property. He agreed to give a lecture on the Pinelands in early February and addressed students at Vineland High School on the afternoon of the 26th, after which he and Clara enjoyed a leisurely walk.

It appears that Clara's return from her week-long vacation in Philadelphia had prompted the couple to reconcile, as their public appearances certainly suggested. It is likely that it was in early January that the couple's youngest son James was conceived, but any romantic stirrings would be brief. By the middle of January, Clara began to show signs of disillusionment.

The version of Landis's journal from this period as published in the *Vineland Historical Magazine* during 1928 also presents an untroubled marital phase. But a comparison with Landis's actual handwritten journal reveals that the magazine's editors selectively excised any references to the couple's disputes and difficulties, particularly in entries from January 16 to March 8, 1875. The unpublished portions are revelatory in their candidness, disclosing such matters as

Clara's growing disinterest in Vineland and the couple's attempts to seek counseling.

According to the complete entries, we discover that the Methodist Landis had been accompanying his wife to Catholic Mass on Sunday at Sacred Heart Church during the latter half of January. The services were conducted by Father Peter Vivet, who also met with the couple for dinner and consultation at the Landis home on the 17th and 22nd and dropped by again on the 28th to counsel them at this critical juncture. As Landis reveals in his most personal and vulnerable diary entries, "My wife is very much discontented with Vineland." At dinner on the 22nd, he writes that the priest "had a long sensible and good talk with my wife."

Vivet would have another opportunity on the 31st to counsel Clara, but the matter had already been decided. At Clara's behest, the couple had signed separation papers on January 30. This was the fourth time such documents had been prepared, the previous three occasions having been prompted by Clara's brother Richard and dismissed by Landis with the statement "I did not believe it serious." But now, the matter had taken on an urgency that couldn't be ignored. "Since my arrival from Europe," Landis confesses in his January 30 entry, "my wife expresses so much dissatisfaction with life in Vineland that I think it inhumane to force her to stay here. Besides if I attempt it I fear for her mind or that she may do something desperate. May God give us both peace. This is a sad ending to my... hopes of happiness. I will be very sad hereafter." Landis then records that he "retired at 10 o'clock to my separate room," revealing that Landis and Clara were not sharing a bedroom at this point, something that would not have been suspected by those who witnessed their public personas at the time. He concludes the entry by proclaiming, "I would like to go away somewhere forever."

Clara's account of this day, however, differs significantly from that her husband's, particularly in the details involving which of them prompted the signing of the papers. According to Clara, it was Landis who proffered the suggestion of separation, but not before he recommended another solution to end their incessant squabbles." He insulted me," Clara revealed in a statement she made two years later, "by deliberately proposing that I should write him a letter asking him to place me in Kirkbride's lunatic asylum." If true, this recommendation would soon return to haunt Landis.

The failure of this proposal prompted Vineland's founder to offer a second recommendation to end their marital issues. According to Clara,

> About the middle of January, he proposed and stated his intention to make out articles of separation. I told him I would accede to his suggestion and sign the paper. He sent for his clerk and had a document drawn up, by which I was to have the youngest child; to be allowed $100 per month, and in consideration of this give up my right to what belonged to me by my marriage settlement. This last I did not understand at the time.

Discussion of a separation may have begun in mid-January, but the papers seem to have been drawn up around

January 30. John Burk later testified that Landis had remarked "that his wife desired separation papers; she was dissatisfied and did not wish to remain with him any longer; did not like the house and did not like the place. She was willing to take one child and leave the other. Mr. Landis would not consent to the separation of the children." Deborah Ryan, a cook hired in the late spring or early summer of 1874, was informed by Clara that Landis had the articles of separation prepared. Ryan later reported that, "Mr. and Mrs. Landis had some trouble and Mrs. Landis told me she was going to leave, that they had agreed to separate."

On Sunday, January 31, Clara was still in Vineland. That morning, Landis did not accompany his wife to Mass at Sacred Heart and instead took Charles Jr. for a walk. That evening, Father Vivet dined again with the Landises. When Clara hinted at going to Philadelphia, the priest attempted to discourage her but to no avail. "After he left, my wife packed her trunks," Landis records in his journal. "I tried to dissuade her from going but she insisted upon it." He concludes the entry with the self-diagnosis "anxious and in trouble."

At this point, Landis still held out hope that Clara would change her mind, but Monday would confirm his wife's decision to leave. She would also have her way in splitting up the children. Landis's complete journal entry for the day captures the details of her departure:

> February 1 Monday Got up early. Found my wife with her mind unchanged and determined to go. She spoke kindly however and seemed much affected. I urged her to postpone her journey, but she was sure we would both be happier. Little Dickie was very

sweet and affectionate. The train came, and they went away, my wife, Dickie and Mary the nurse. It made me feel quite downhearted to think that this was the end of my bright anticipations. Her brother Richard has been writing her letters bitterly abusive of me ever since I have come home, and I think he is the cause of the whole trouble. Walked down the [railroad] and got Mrs. Bagnell to take care of Charlie. I have sent for my mother and sister to take charge of my house. Charlie was very sweet and good all day. I went out with him in the afternoon for several hours. L. D. Black called and said he had heard of my affliction and offered to take care of Charlie... Retired a little after 9 o'clock. Had Charlie in a crib alongside my bed.

In 1877, Clara offered her account of that day and the next:

On Monday morning I left Vineland with grief which I cannot express but was impelled to hope that it was an escape from misery. I consulted with my counsel, Mr. H. B. Brewster, and showed him the articles of separation. He told me I had signed away my own and my children's right to my property.

Landis spent Tuesday, February 2 anxiously awaiting word from Clara. He passed the time by working in his office, visiting the mill with Burk and taking an afternoon walk with Charles Jr. but could not escape the fact that he was "terribly troubled in mind."

Ryan confirmed there were signs that Clara's departure took both a physical and mental toll on Landis. She claimed he would rub his head as if in great pain, lay on the lounge and sometimes retreat to bed during the day. He would tell Ryan to take Charles Jr. out for some air in the middle of winter, and she would take him to a neighbor's house to stay out of the cold. Ryan also witnessed another peculiarity during Clara's absence, noting in later testimony that, during meals while his wife was away, Landis "would talk to himself all the time and would talk as if he were in conversation with somebody although nobody was at the table with him."

Landis spent February 3 working and then dining with Dr. Bartlett and Cornelius B. Campbell. That evening, he was visited by Clara, who later claimed she had "returned to Vineland to ask my husband if [it]was true [she had signed away her rights to her property]. He said it was. I asked him how he could treat me so cruelly. He took a pen and wrote on the bottom of the page: 'This does not affect the jointure property, but only the income…'"

Once again, Landis's account differs from his wife's:

> In the evening, my wife came down on the 7 ½ o'clock train. She came in…with anger and said her allowance was not enough - $100 per month. It will require great effort to pay that, but I decided to make it $125 – I wanted her to destroy the papers of separation and come home but she would not. Said she might do so after a while. During the evening she was wild and profane in her language. All that

trouble comes from the letters that her brother Richard has written to her.

Clara did not return to Philadelphia that evening, remaining at the Landis residence that night and awakening the next morning at 5 o'clock to catch the 6 o'clock train. Her husband attempted to persuade her to stay, but she refused to listen. That day, February 4, Landis notified his mother-in-law about the separation.

Clara's departure once again left her uncertain as to what she should do. Viewing her actions as a mistake and taking stock of her financial situation, Clara seems to have reached the conclusion that she would have to remain in Vineland. On the evening of Friday, February 5, she, Richard and Mary returned home. Clara told her husband "she had had enough of the city." Two years later, she discussed other reasons for her change of mind: "Alone and without money, but for the remains of a small sum he had given me; enceinte and suffering for the loss of my eldest boy, I again returned to Vineland…" Landis, however, registered a mixed response that February evening, recording in his journal that he "was glad to see them," but adding the question, "How long will this last?"

According to Clara, Landis had been making certain statements in her absence that now circulated throughout the town:

> I again returned to Vineland to find, however, that his conduct and his words had spread throughout the village the report that I was insane and that my insanity was the theme of general village gossip.

Later trial testimony would demonstrate that Landis was prone to discussing his wife after her departure. On one occasion, he told a Vineland resident that Clara had gone away and left him and he "did not know what he was going to do, that she had threatened his life and that she would poison him, that he was afraid to sit down at this table or sleep nights."

Despite the unwelcome accusations, Clara chose to remain in Vineland and there is proof that she and Landis enjoyed a brief reconciliation during the next week-and-a-half. Except for a rather rude display toward her sister-in-law the day after she returned home, described by Landis as an occasion in which Matilda "was received most unpleasantly by my wife - no doubt with a view of driving her and my mother away," Clara put forth an effort to get along with her in-laws on their subsequent visits to Vineland, earning her husband's praise: "My wife afterwards changed and became more polite."

Clara also rejected her family's attempts to help remove her from Vineland. On February 6, the day after her return, Landis received "a dispatch of a most imperative kind from R. W. Meade to meet him at the Continental Hotel" in Philadelphia. Because the proposed meeting would occur after the departure of the last train back to Vineland, Landis rejected the idea, not wishing to incur the cost of spending the night in the city. He responded that he had no business to conduct and declined the invitation, writing in his journal that Meade "has been exciting my wife's mind to pursue a hostile course against me and without any sane reason."

Things settled down for several days. Despite zero-degree temperatures in the mornings and evenings, Landis continued his work at the office and the mill, delivered a talk on February 8 at the Baptist Church and read an essay by Montaigne each day. But on February 9, he reports in his journal that

> My wife's mother and sister sent her some more letters reviling and abusing me. What is worse, they sent them to Miss Morrell with the request that she should read them and consider the plea that I had tampered with their letters. They, of course, know better. Miss Morell brought them to my wife with a lot of tales of the idle gossip of people. Something must be done to prevent this.

On February 10, he writes that a new series of letters have arrived from his brother-in-law and that Clara has decided to take action: "In the afternoon R. W. Meade sent some more furious and insulting letters to my wife. She sent answers rebuking him for his interference and asking to be left alone."

Thinking the matter concluded, Landis left for Philadelphia on Friday, February 12, visiting his mother and sister and then traveling to Bird-in-Hand, Lancaster, Pennsylvania with the intention of luring to Vineland a group of Russian Mennonites wintering in the area. He had heard from their representative that they were dissatisfied with their stay in Kansas and offered literature on Vineland to be presented to the group's bishop. After spending a bad night in a hotel, Landis returned to Philadelphia, visiting his old friend Brewster and meeting with a publisher about an article penned by William Grohman.

Arriving in Vineland on February 14, Landis discovered a series of letters from Richard Meade "interfering with my domestic affairs." He also discovered that Clara's brother-in-law, James Hoban Lands, "had also written her advising her to leave me and offering her a home. This conduct is amazing – they must think that my wife will have loads of money to spend if she leaves me."

The following day, Clara received yet another letter from her brother, this time delivered by special messenger from Philadelphia, advising that she leave Landis and come to live with him, promising to give her, Charles Jr. and Richard a home. Landis writes that Clara "sent him a letter requesting that he will desist from interference. He is crazy."

It was probably during this period that Clara participated in a new parlor game played at the Landis home. The previous year, while in England, Landis had purchased a saloon pistol which would not have been considered a standard handgun at the time despite its use of a standard-size lead ball. He had expressed interest in using it for target practice as a form of entertainment. Now he set up two inch-and-a-half thick boards in a corner of the parlor and invited friends to join him and his wife on various evenings to shoot at the target. The later testimony of a guest of the Landises indicates that while Clara was not very adept at using a gun, sending one bullet flying into the parlor ceiling and through the floor of the room above, Landis was a fairly good shot.

On February 16, Landis dined with Father Vivet, having missed the priest's dinner visit over the weekend. The previous week-and-a-half had witnessed the return of his wife, her new cordiality toward his family and her rejection of her own family's bids to free her from this marriage. However, on February 17, Landis discovered that Clara had been giving away his European photographs. This turned out to be forgivable when compared to his other finding, "a letter in her papers from a young man in Philadelphia," which he immediately locked up in the safe, claiming its discovery was "very humiliating." He concludes that he will "reflect upon what can be done." That evening he gave a well-received lecture at Wilson's Hall in Millville, returning home at 11 o'clock and experiencing "a dreadful night, my wife disturbing me with her abusive language."

The next day, in an attempt to retrieve the letter, Clara had taken the keys to the safe from her husband's pocket during the night but had not used them by the time Landis discovered them missing. When she refused to return the keys, a locksmith was called. Upon opening the safe, Landis sent the letter to his Philadelphia office.

Clara recalled Landis's reaction to the letter in 1877:

> On occasions of altercations which arose he would ring the bell for the servants and bid them hold me as a dangerous lunatic. The first time he did this he had seized a letter which I had been reading. I tried to wrest it from him; he threw me upon the floor with violence, and rang the bell saying I had attacked him.

Landis soon decided to remove himself from Vineland for a bit, undertaking a trip to Washington, D.C. for post office business. His traveling companion was his good friend William A. House, who Landis describes in a later essay about the journey as "a lawyer, banker and local statesman of our town." The trip, which included brief stays in Baltimore and Philadelphia, occurred from February 18 to 22. During the journey, Landis and House toured a number of Baltimore churches before making their way to Washington. Once they arrived in the nation's capital, the travelers completed their post office business earlier than expected, and House suggested they pay a visit to the White House in the hopes of meeting with the president. Landis had been in Europe the previous year when Ulysses S. Grant had visited Vineland for the opening of the new high school building and now he decided to make amends for his missed opportunity.

Upon arriving at the White House, the two travelers were placed in a waiting room at the end of a dauntingly long line of visitors. Shortly thereafter, "an important looking individual" checked their credentials. Returning, after a brief time, he then inquired as to their business with President Grant. Landis informed him they had no business and had simply "come to see the President."

The man's surprise did not go unnoticed by Landis and House, but in a matter of moments, the two visitors were ushered in to see Grant, leaving all those who had spent most of the day in the waiting room looking "astonished and as though they thought we must be some princes or ambassadors." Landis and House found Grant in a moderately sized room "with a pile of clippings from newspapers before him." He cordially greeted his guests and immediately inquired about Vineland, calling it a beautiful place.

"I have a vivid recollection," Grant told the two men, "of its green hedges and long avenues of beautiful shade trees…you must have had a forester to select all those fine trees." When Landis told him that the residents themselves, under certain stipulations, provided the foliage, Grant complimented the Vineland residents and bemoaned the lack of such landscaping in the nation's capital. He said he hoped "this deficit in Washington will be cured" and expressed interest in visiting Vineland again.

"I do not think that this talk was merely complimentary or courtly," Landis writes, "as General Grant impressed me as being a very plain and sincere man…I have often thought of what he said and of his efforts, which have since made Washington one of the best and most beautifully shaded cities of the world, and what the example of Vineland may have had to do with it." Landis's visit with Grant would prove beneficial for him over the following year.

Arriving home around mid-day on February 22, Landis remained busy with his endeavors through the following day and then left for New York with Burk on February 24. For the next day-and-a-half, he and Burk conducted business. When it was time to depart, Landis writes in his journal, they "went to meet the 2 o'clock train in order to reach Vineland in the evening. As we were walking along the street… we met R. W. Meade, but I passed him without noticing him. I never intend to notice him again. He is a dangerous man."

On March 2, while in Philadelphia, Landis was confronted with a problem he believed he had already remedied. As he writes in his journal, "Called by request upon [Edward] R. Wood who told me that he was going to hold me responsible upon an old matter which I had guaranteed and where he had been guilty of [illegible] in not collecting the money when the property was worth it. I decline to pay it."

There is no further mention of Clara or her family in the remaining entries of the 1875 journal, only that Landis attended to business, met with various friends and acquaintances and read *Arabian Nights*, *The Odyssey* and *The Iliad*. While events seemed to have settled down in the journal entries, turmoil still existed, particularly in *The Independent's* printed barbs and in the Landis marriage, which was becoming more violent.

According to Deborah Ryan, the Landis cook, such conditions were clearly on display during the first few weeks of March:

> Somebody rang the bell so violently that it frightened me…When I got to the bottom of the stairs, Mr. Landis called, "Mrs. Ryan." I reached upstairs and Mr. Landis said, "Hold Mrs. Landis…" She said to Mr. Landis, "You ought to be ashamed to bring people up to see me." Mr. Landis said he wanted to put Mrs. Landis in a room so he could get away from her. Mrs. Landis was pushed in the room and Mr. Landis went into another room and shut himself in. He did not come down to dinner…about a couple of hours after he came down. I noticed he looked wild and pale. I frequently noticed after this a strange wild look in Mr. Landis's appearance at the table.

On March 14, according to witnesses, Landis was in a "frenzied state" about Clara, who threatened violence by stating, "I'll cut his throat from ear to ear" and warning, "I'll be the ruination of him yet." This was enough for Landis to summon his agent to find out how he could secure his will, fearing that he would be poisoned. Two days later, Ryan was called in and told by her employer to "Hold Mrs. Landis." Clara responded, "Don't put your hands on me, Mrs. Ryan." The cook was later told by Landis that if she did not hold her when he told her to, her services would no longer be required and revealed that Mrs. Landis had pinched him until he was black and blue, that he couldn't defend himself as if he had "lost the use of his arms," and that Ryan was afraid Clara "would do him harm."

That night, Ryan was awakened by a call. She went to the sitting room and found Landis on the sofa and Clara standing. Clara said she had been abused and that Landis had struck her. She then threw an object at him that hit him on the side of the head. Ryan brought her upstairs since Landis could not defend himself. Later, Landis asked if Ryan thought Mrs. Landis's "situation had anything to do with her conduct?" The "situation" to which Landis refers is most likely Clara's pregnancy.

On March 17, John Burk visited his employer, who mentioned that his wife had aimed a hammer at his head. Dr. Franklin Lane, the family's physician since October 27, 1872, was another witness to the goings-on at in the Landis household and reported what he saw in later testimony. On the evening of March 17, 1875, Lane was ill and retired early. He was interrupted by the arrival of Landis who, when told that the doctor was not feeling well and wouldn't be seeing anyone, insisted, proclaiming that this was a matter of "great importance." Lane finally agreed to see Landis, who said, "Doctor, I am in great trouble and I don't know what to do. I have been obliged to return from Europe without accomplishing the object of the journey, although it was promising important results, on the condition of my family. My trouble is too great to bear and I have come to ask you what to do, by God! I cannot bear this. My wife is insane."

Lane said he had heard from Clara that Landis had declared her insane "some time before." Lane also stated he had found her irritable at times, but that there was no evidence of insanity. Landis could not be quieted and wanted to know what to do. The physician told him if he felt she was insane, he should place her in an asylum and his visitor replied that, if he did, her family would be relentless in their pursuit of him. It seems that Landis's brother-in-law Richard had recently threatened to kill him. The conversation lasted two hours that evening. The only subject discussed was Clara and what Landis was to do, especially since he feared she would kill the children as well as himself and was afraid to return home. He requested that Lane visit the next morning and the doctor agreed.

On the morning of March 18, Landis asked Ryan to check his temple to see if there were any marks where the object thrown by Clara the previous night had struck him. The action had immediately prompted concern from Clara, who feared she had killed him. Landis hadn't slept all night because of the pain in his head, and Ryan confirmed that his temple was black and blue. Ryan then went upstairs to wake Clara, who, while Landis was having coffee, asked that breakfast be brought to her. When she finished her meal, Clara departed for Philadelphia, so that when Lane arrived, Landis had to explain his wife's absence and that she would probably be back that evening. Landis also confided that he had had a difficult night with Clara and showed the bruise he received on his temple, explaining that his wife had thrown a bracket [clock] at him. He declined to take medication.

Landis stayed in all day but that evening sent a note informing Lane that Clara had returned. The doctor arrived for the examination at 7 p.m. and found Landis walking up and down his hallway "under great mental excitement." Landis said he did not want his wife to know he had summoned Lane. She was already in bed and the doctor ascended the stairs to her room where he spent an hour examining her. She told him she couldn't live with Landis any longer and that she was afraid to remain in the house, that Landis's manners "had become unreasonable and at times furious." Lane cautioned her to do or say nothing, advice which Clara chose not to heed the following day. The physician concluded the examination by declaring she was not insane. Landis told him he was mistaken. After the doctor's departure, Clara prohibited her husband from entering her room and went to sleep. That night, Landis did not sleep.

On the morning of March 19, he was downstairs early and complained that his head pained him. He did not eat breakfast. Instead, Ryan found her employer pacing and rubbing his hands and his head. She recalled that "his eyes were like coals of fire." At 7:30 a.m., Landis went to his office across the street, complaining that he couldn't sleep, and then left the office. Distracted, he called a hired hand over three times to explain what work needed to be completed that day only to cancel the tasks when he later summoned the worker a fourth time. Revisiting the the office at 8:30, he did not attend to any business and left again. It appears that after returning to the house, Landis and Clara breakfasted together and this was when she decided to show her husband an article clearly written by Carruth and published in the March 18 edition of *The Independent*. It would prove to be Landis's breaking point.

The article read:

> A prominent Vinelander sat down by the side of his loving wife on the sofa and looked up at her eyes, and called her a duck, and a birdie, and rabbit and all the other endearing names. Then he told her he wanted she should learn the use of a revolver, so that in his absence, she could protect their home and silverware, and defend the honor of Vineland.
>
> Then he went off and bought an elegant seven-shooter and a nice target.
>
> Then he set up the target at one end of the parlor and gave her a first lesson in shooting. Then he told her he wanted she should practice every day. Then he went away for a week. When he returned he found the revolver on the other side of the looking-glass; the parlor door resembled a bad case of smallpox, and the furniture looked as if it had been indulging in wrestle with a Burlington County hail storm. Did he walk up to his wife and sicken her with all the endearing names of all the birds and four-footed beasts? Not much! He marched out into the street in

his shirt sleeves; with but one boot on and that patch over the big toe.

Then he went galloping up and down telling every man he met, confidentially, that his wife was *crazy*. Then he went on and tried to get her into a private Insane Asylum: yes he did, the *wretch*.

Later that day, Landis stated, "My wife handed that to me this morning, and reproached me with being the cause of it. But God knows, I was not. There is not a word of truth in that. I went to Europe to get away from this thing – but it has followed me there…" While Clara was apparently quick to accuse her husband of revealing private matters, Burk later testified that his employer had confided in him prior to the March 18 article that Clara was "apt to talk respecting his conduct, measures, etc. with outside parties" and that "Mr. Landis…believed it to be a fact that his wife made known their private affairs."

The most recent Carruth article elicited a response no one had thought possible. According to testimony from several witnesses, including Landis employee Benjamin Cook, Landis returned to his office somewhere around 9:30, complaining about the appearance of the article in the newspaper. He stayed several minutes and then jumped up and headed for home and then to his barn, which is probably when he countermanded the earlier work orders he had given the hired hand for the day.

Additional testimony recounts what happened next. Landis ran to the second level of his home, presumably to retrieve his firearm, and then left the house. He marched straight to *The Independent's* offices, a short walk away, with the English saloon pistol he had purchased the previous year concealed on his person, and encountered the foreman, Henry Wilbur. Landis asked if Carruth was in. Wilbur said no and then asked the town founder if he would like to see the editor. When Landis said he did, Wilbur sent the office boy to find his boss and told Landis to take a seat. The boy returned five to ten minutes later, saying he was unable to find Carruth. Wilbur sent him out again. According to testimony, no one noticed any weapon on Landis, only *The Independent* article Clara had shown him that morning.

After nearly twenty minutes, the editor, who had been on the floor below in the drug store operated by Dr. Edwin Bidwell, entered the office and discovered who his visitor was. Those outside the office claimed they heard no conversation between the two, but Landis stated afterward, "I asked Carruth if he wrote that article and he said he did, and would write another, and then I shot him."

Attempting to avoid Landis's attack, the editor ran into the newspaper's composing room, pulling the door shut behind him. He then reportedly "dodged his head back and forth for a moment, as though trying to discover the position of Landis through the two small panes of glass in the door..." Landis followed him, drew the pistol and fired, hitting the editor in the back of the head. The forty-nine-year-old Carruth slumped to the floor and lay unconscious while his assailant proclaimed to those around him, "I've killed him. God forgive me. I had to do it, I did it in the cause of God and humanity. There lies the man who has caused all the misery in my family." He was also reported to have said, "Oh, my poor crazy wife."

Dr. Bidwell was immediately summoned by Wilbur and entered the newsroom to find Landis in the doorway between the composing and editorial rooms, near Carruth, who was still alive, probably due to the type of pistol wielded by his assailant. The low-powder, multiple-shot handgun lacked the power to deliver the lead ball it had projected with the intensity of a standard pistol. Had Landis owned a regular gun of the era, the damage would have been much more gruesome and the outcome far more tragic.

Bidwell described the editor as laying on the right side of his face with no movement. He turned the editor over and discovered blood on his mouth, face and the floor from a wound caused when he bit his tongue during his fall. There was discoloration around his right eye. The bullet wound at the back of his head exuded brain matter "the size of a large pea." Bidwell probed the wound with his little finger to the inner edge of the skull to ascertain it had been broken.

In the meantime, Landis chose to surrender his firearm to Bidwell's son, who had just arrived on the scene and who, in turn, handed the weapon to his father. Asked if he wished to contact any lawyers in Philadelphia, Landis replied, "No, I don't want any lawyers. I don't want to live. This is the end. I wish I had shot myself." He also responded to a question about whether he had a pistol on him at that moment with the explanation "No, I gave it up."

Landis was soon removed from *The Independent* building. He would be held temporarily in the law office of his friend William House. As he was being escorted there, he encountered Clara, who described the moment two years later: "I rushed to the street and said to my husband, 'What, in God's name, have you done?' He put his arms around me.

I consoled him as best I could and went with him to jail."
Awaiting transportation to Bridgeton, Landis sat in House's
office, surrounded by a growing entourage: his wife, Deputy
Sheriff Thomas Cortis, Thomas Proud, Constable Lucius T.
Babcock and Freeman S. Hale, who had just returned from
relating the news to the Carruth family.

According to later testimony by James M. Dixon, Landis
was left alone in a room at one point. Dixon claimed to have
entered and attempted to help by mesmerizing or
hypnotizing Landis into a fifteen-minute sleep. Upon
awakening, Landis was not aware of what had transpired that
morning and reacted with grave concern once he was
reminded. He immediately pleaded with Dixon to telegraph
Dr. James McClintock, a Philadelphia physician Landis
hoped could examine and ultimately save Carruth.

Hale's subsequent testimony explains what happened
afterward. Upon the arrival of the carriage, all of the
aforementioned individuals waiting in House's office
boarded it and set out for the county jail. On the way, Landis
asked his wife if she felt cold. She replied that she didn't and
then inquired about the number of children Carruth had and
about the family's financial status. Landis cautioned her not
to say anything about it. "Don't talk," he ordered her.

The carriage arrived at Bridgeton and, as it passed the
telegraph office, Landis requested that Cortis contact
someone in Vineland to determine Curruth's condition. The
report the deputy sheriff was given said that the editor was
dead. Landis said nothing as he held up his hands to his face
to hide the tears.

When the carriage reached the jail and the entourage
entered, Landis asked Cortis to check if the news about

Carruth was accurate. The next report was that the editor was still alive but with no hope of recovery, to which Landis responded, "My God! Why have I been allowed to remain in this suspense?" Clara inquired about her husband's chances of eluding incarceration in a local facility or state prison if sentenced, but Landis proclaimed, "Do not flatter yourself – that is not the way they do it in New Jersey."

Landis was placed in the county jail by one o'clock that afternoon. He asked to borrow money from Hale, who did not have any. A similar request of Constable Babcock earned him a small amount that most likely was given to Clara so she could immediately telegraph Dr. McClintock. According to one account, Landis turned to his wife and said, "Tell him what it is or he won't come." After she was dispatched, Landis turned to Sheriff James L. Wilson and begged him to procure rope and to hang him while his wife completed her task.

Upon Clara's return, her husband advised her to go home to the children, but she refused to leave and allowed herself to be locked in the cell that night with Landis, whose speedy confinement probably saved him from violence when a crowd of residents gathered in front of *The Independent* building that evening, voicing threats of lynching.

From the time he entered jail, Landis was prescribed anodyne to sleep, but it was not always effective. He suffered many sleepless nights over the next several months, muttering and mumbling in the presence of the guards that his lack of rest was the result of the jail being overrun with snakes and rats.

Within hours of the shooting, Vineland resident Albert Moore had dashed off a letter to the Landises to offer his support. As a victim of Carruth's scathing articles, Moore empathized with Landis, writing, "…I can but say Carruth deserved it but I am very sorry he received his punishment from Mr. Landis. But for Mr. Landis I have a heartfelt sympathy. I know how year after year that vile man has wrapped up his slanders in a sheet around the hearts of our fellow citizens but I must say the opinions of such people are scarcely worth regard. On a level with Carruth, they are the parasites of society"

Moore's letter is an obvious attempt to bolster Landis by reporting that his real friends are filled with "sense, judgment and reason" and relates an example of how Carruth's articles have had a damaging effect on him as well. "I was paraded to the world as a barnburner under an assumed name," he reports, referring to Carruth's practice of thinly disguising his intended targets with pseudonyms. But he also feels compelled to warn Landis that his "enemies have the advantage… [and] will strive for a trial as soon as possible and finish you with a venomous hatred."

Offering to testify for Landis as he is sure others will, Moore cautions that the founder's friends "should not let their enemies know" their intentions. He is certain that a delay in the trial "will soften the public feeling on the one side and but help you on the other," adding that *The Independent's* files should be "procured" for Landis's defense. He ends his correspondence by stating he would like to visit Landis and offers "these thoughts in the spirit of a true friend."

Moore's letter reveals clearly the schism that had occurred in the town by the 1870s and highlights the concerns Landis supporters apparently faced at this time. But it is also somewhat prescient about how a delayed trial would soften the reaction of some citizens. When the case was tried the following year, Carruth's articles were not introduced as evidence, as Moore recommended, but would haunt the proceedings as well as the outcome of the trial.

Clara's response to the events that unfolded on March 19 seems to confirm that she did not think the article would propel her husband into a state of vengeance. Most likely she only wished to illustrate that his earlier attempt to have her committed had moved from chatter among residents to the pages of a newspaper. However, her guilt in the matter would become clear in a statement she made later that day. Expressing her hope that Carruth would survive, she then fretted over the possibility that her husband would be hanged for his crime before lamenting, "I am the cause of this. I ought not to have shown Mr. Landis that article. If anybody ought to be hung for this, I ought to be."

The pistol used by Landis would soon be identified as a British Bulldog and it was discovered that two of the five chambers of the gun were empty, but they were not consecutive chambers. The ball used was identified by *The Independent* as "a 7/16 conical bullet…believed to be half an ounce in weight."

By the time Landis had been placed in jail, Bidwell had managed to have staff members bring up a cot from his store and send for a physician. At some point it was decided that Carruth would remain at the newspaper offices for the next several days rather than move him to his home and risk complications with his health. *The Independent* reported that the patient "somewhat rallied and was rational, soon after a cot and mattress were improvised on the floor of the composing room, and he had been placed as comfortably as circumstances permitted thereon."

When Carruth was asked who his physician of choice was, he named Dr. Emory Rounds Tuller, a Vineland practitioner of homeopathic medicine, Samuel Hahnemann's 1796 alternative medical treatment that did not follow traditional, outdated and largely unreliable methods that science had just begun to question.

According to *The Independent*, Tuller arrived with his associate, Dr. Lewis W. Brown, and attended to Carruth around 11:50 on the morning of March 19. Bidwell claimed that three other physicians, including Dr. John Ingram, arrived but "did very little further than observe the examination of the wound." It was determined that the patient's pulse was 66 beats per minute during the examination, what *The Independent* called "small and oppressed." By 9 p.m., his pulse had dropped to 63, but Carruth remained conscious and rational, sleeping "at intervals through the night for about four hours and by 10 o'clock a.m. the pulse marked 60."

Despite the editor's preference for Tuller, another physician conducted an examination on the morning of March 20. Landis's interest in helping to save the editor's life and Clara's request that Dr. McClintock come to Vineland had produced results, even if they weren't the ones intended. Despite the fact that some six physicians treated Carruth over the next few months, McClintock was not one of them, having relegated the task to another doctor who, in turn, requested that his son attend to Carruth. Dr. S. W. Gross, referred to as the "son of the well-known expert in such cases" by *The Independent*, would be paid by Landis for his visits. With Bidwell, Brown and James Wiley present that Saturday morning of March 20, Gross arrived between 11 and 12 o'clock to examine his new patient. *The Independent* reported that "The object of his visit was explained to the patient, who consented to undergo any *necessary* operation, feeling no enmity toward Chas. K. Landis. Dr. Gross then proceeded to examine the orifice made by the bullet and extracted such loose pieces of bone as were found in that region. Using a flexible gum catheter, he probed the supposed course of the ball to the depth of two-and-a-half inches, and, failing to discover it, pronounced the option that it was *impossible to reach it.*" The probe of the wound was the first of several over the next two months.

Gross later testified that during this visit, he "enlarged the wound, by means of a conical incision with the view of seeing whether there were any splinters in the head and to detect the bullet; I removed nine fragments of splinters" and "thought it was not a hopeless case."

Before the examination by Gross, Carruth's pulse registered 66, but by the afternoon it ranged from 48 to 60 before stabilizing by 7 p.m. at 54. Despite Gross's appearance, Tuller and Brown remained Carruth's physicians of record and decided to allow the wound to remain open while the editor was placed in a continual reclining position to allow for drainage. That night, as Carruth slept well, Mary Robinson, his sister-in-law, arrived from New York. Because of the weak condition of Carruth's wife, she would serve as his main caregiver until April 21 and again from June 2 until October 24. Robinson later reported that upon her arrival in Vineland, a committee that included William House convened to arrange for the discharge of the local doctors on the following afternoon, two days after the shooting.

Upon awakening Sunday morning, Carruth discovered that he was only able to see out of the right side of each eye and managed to consume some beef tea and oatmeal gruel between sleep. His pulse would remain around 50 throughout the day, and he was undoubtedly uninformed of the attempt to dismiss his doctor of choice, a matter in which his family's decision would prevail. Tuller would remain Carruth's physician from March 19 until May 26.

At around 10:20 a.m. on Monday, March 22, Professor J.C. Morgan of the Hahnemann College of Philadelphia and Gross arrived in Vineland. Morgan would examine Carruth nine times in the next seven months along with a team of homeopathic physicians comprised of Morgan, A. R. Thomas, Brown and Tuller. Morgan had been summoned to determine if the ball had moved since Gross's examination two days earlier. According to *The Independent,* "the Professor proceeded to an examination of the bullet wound. At this time, Dr. Gross not being present, was waited on by Uri Carruth's family physician, and requested to attend, but declined on professional grounds, whereupon Dr. Morgan proceeded with his examination of the wound. It was found that the cerebral substance had closed up the track of the bullet, and that it would be injurious to make [a] further search."

On March 23, *The Independent* continued to monitor its editor's progress, reporting in that week's issue:

Tuesday, March 23, 9 a.m.

[Carruth's] pulse was registered at 46, fuller and stronger than the day before, but a little irregular. Slept well during the night. Appetite good this morning. Urine natural.

At 2:30 p.m., pulse [was] 54; rest quiet. He breakfasted on milk toast and baked apple.

At 3 p.m., [Carruth] partook of dinner of the same.

At 7 o'clock p.m., pulse [was] 52. Symptoms as favorable as could be expected.

March 24, 9 a.m.
Sleep [was] broken and more restless than the preceding night. Pulse 56, natural. No pain except a little throbbing in the wound. Appetite good, skin soft with a little perspiration at times.

At 9:20 p.m., after the wound had been dressed twenty minutes, the pulse showed no change.

At. 3:30 p.m., pulse [was] 56. Comfortable after motion from bowels at 10:30, following an enema of warm water.

The Independent also raised the question about surgery for Carruth: "It may seem to some that the attending physicians ought to have operated at an earlier period, but when it is considered how anxious Mr. Landis must be for the recovery of Uri Carruth, and that two experts had been telegraphed for by his order, from Philadelphia, it will be seen that mere humanity to the wounded man would lead to a postponement of the painful operation rather than risk its repetition." The newspaper praised the decisions of Tuller and offered as evidence the progress the editor had shown.

A view of the Carruth family following the shooting is provided in a March 29, 1875 letter by Portia Gage, which is in the possession of the Wilmette Historical Museum in Illinois. Writing to her son Henry, she reports:

> I went yesterday to see Mrs. Carruth, she is quite calm, but seems perfectly helpless, has no power to throw off the great load of grief that Landis has thrown upon her, but her sister, who is here from Clinton, Oneida Co., N.Y., is a full team capable of working through anything and everything. Mr. Carruth's sister is also here, the only relative he has that we know of, they are all at the Office yet board at Bailey's and have rooms there and at the "Ladies Store." Carruth has the best of nurses furnished by the Grange and Sovereigns [sic] but there is little prospect of his recovery."

Gage's letter is also a clear indication of how the aftermath of the shooting had divided the town. What remains striking is the personal view Gage offers about the sympathy for Landis conveyed by certain newspapers over the previous ten days:

> Isn't it perfectly outrageous to see the way the press talk of the affair. To judge by a great majority

of the articles we read one would suppose that Carruth was a perfect devil and Landis a God and the influential papers as far as I have seen find in Carruth's articles excuse sufficient for the shooting whilst if they were judged by their own rule there is not a political editor in the country that would not deserve to have a bullet put through his head. My opinion is that all of these excusatory and laudatory articles for Landis are written here and paid for as advertisements.

It is easy to discern from the letter that the enmity expressed by a part of the population toward Landis had continued to fester over the previous week. Gage's comments, which intimate a personal betrayal and include a condemnation of sympathizing residents, must have been representative of those who saw only Landis's actions as unconscionable and unfounded:

> I feel more anxious than ever to get away from here, feeling that it is not really safe to live in a place where a large proportion of the wealthy and educated class uphold the murderer and do not ever dare condemn the murder, probably feel in their hearts glad of it, at any rate that is the tone of talk, where those who worship Landis are fools enough to say anything, but the more shrewd worshippers, who get their bread and butter through Landis, say nothing pro or con.

The favorable report of Carruth's progress on March 23 would last less than a month. According to the *New York Times*, the patient's condition had become "precarious" again by April 18. The relapse was the result of a bullet splinter which had caused an injury in the victim's neck and had been treated by Brown with poultices that resulted in the exit of the sliver through the usual discharge of the wound. On May 7, Tuller conducted another probe of the wound to a depth of one-and-three-quarter inches to determine if the ball had moved. On May 12, Drs. Morgan and Tuller were summoned to examine Carruth to investigate if there was still an opening for discharges and if any foreign matter had fallen into the opening. During this examination, Morgan undertook yet another probe to a depth of one-and-three-quarter inches which, according to later testimony by Dr. A.R. Thomas, "must have passed through some uninjured portion of the brain" based on the direction of the probe.

On May 20, a third probe in a two-week period was undertaken by both Morgan and Tuller. Benjamin Williamson, in his summation at Landis's trial, reported that "when Dr. Morgan probed the wound...he probed to find the new direction...but Dr. Tuller took the probe and again passed it into the brain and through healthy brain matter. What tracks did it go through? Why the same one made by the probing on the 12th." Williamson also summed up the testimony concerning Carruth's doctors by saying, "No less than six physicians have had charge of the case, at times, none of whom consulted in regard to the experience of those who had previous charge of the case...."

From this point, Carruth's condition continued to progress favorably and, on May 22, the two doctors found him improved enough to be convalescent. On May 26, Dr. Gross also declared that the danger from the lodged bullet had passed, and Tuller and Morgan jointly gave a certificate saying Carruth was out of danger. The following day, Tuller was dismissed as the editor's doctor, at which time Brown became Carruth's attending physician.

According to James Nixon, who defended Landis during his trial the following year, it was around this time that Ingram and Bidwell were "called without Dr. Brown's knowledge. Ingram told Miss Robinson that "in order to save [Carruth's] life it would be necessary to open the protrusion [of an abscess]. Dr. Bidwell concurred in the opinion. Miss Robinson would not let it be done, or Carruth would not, and said that he 'did not want to be butchered anymore.'" In June, Brown continued the treatment of the past several months, removing a piece of bone one-eighth of an inch long and one-sixth of an inch wide that had appeared at the opening of the wound.

During Carruth's improvement, Landis remained confined in jail. He had given Burk power of attorney and his clerk had taken charge of all business matters in his absence. A journal, presumably maintained by Burk during 1875 and 1876, reveals that Landis's land sales continued to thrive during his period of incarceration. There were plenty of interested parties who toured the available lots, including individuals from overseas countries such as England. Exhibition of the sites continued through Landis's trial and beyond. In fact, by late 1876, Landis would approach at least one contact, James Skeerup, about steering more business his way, according to a letter dated September 2, 1876: "I hereby agree to pay you ten per cent commission upon all lands I may sell belonging to me, to parties you bring from Europe, or parties you may send from Europe, giving them a letter directed to me."

Within his first few weeks in jail, Landis received a curious letter from F. A. Bassett, an Albany resident acquainted with Vineland, who felt a need to inform Landis of the current situation of a former resident by the name of Sherry Garton. The letter mentions that Garton had earlier shared with Bassett a startling remark Landis allegedly made in reference to Carruth.

> I called upon Sherry Garton to learn the particulars and during our conversation he dropped this remark. I heard Mr. L. say that if he ever crossed his path, he would shoot him down like a dog. At the time I did not think much about it but the more I resolved it in my mind the more I thought this remark if dropped anywhere else might be used at your trial, to show premeditation on your part and to prevent anything of this kind I went to Sherry and called his attention to this fact, that such a remark might cause you considerable trouble. He promised me that he would not mention it to anyone again and said that he had not spoken of the affair to anyone except me. He meant no harm, he thinks as much of you as his own father and I am sure he would not intentionally say or [do] anything to your disadvantage. I do not think he will ever give utterance to the same again. I do not know as this information amounts to anything, but if you should think it did, I would advise you to write a letter to Sherry based upon old acquaintanceship

without giving him to understand that you knew what I have informed you of for he meant no harm…

The fact that Landis's alleged threat against Carruth echoes what his father-in-law reportedly proclaimed during his courtship of Clara is rather ironic and illustrates, if true, how far the founder had been driven by the editor's crusade. Bassett may be writing purely as a friend but it's difficult to overlook the overtones of blackmail carried in the letter. It appears the writer may be gently coercing Landis to help a friend in exchange for his silence about the incriminating information when Bassett informs Landis that Garton had fallen on hard times, left Vineland "under a cloud" and was employed at the Woods Hotel in Chicago for a meager salary. Bassett then suggests that Landis might use his influence to obtain a better job for Garton or "in some way place him under obligation to you."

After this recommendation, however, Bassett expresses his concern for Landis:

> I cannot express how sad I felt when I heard of your trouble and without dwelling upon this topic, which doubtless everyone is pouring into your ears, let me say that you have my sympathy and I hope and trust you will come out alright – I only wish I could do something for you.

Landis's purported incriminating remark was never mentioned at his trial. Whatever may have transpired as the result of the letter remains a mystery.

Landis's incarceration had afforded Clara the opportunity to finally abandon her husband and Vineland as she had been so inclined to do over the past year. A *St. Louis Globe-Democrat* article from 1885 reports that after the shooting, Clara "regained her mental equilibrium," but then "developed unmistakable signs of being a vixen in temperament, which disposition she assiduously cultivated in her language and conduct toward Mr. Landis…"

What had not been made public at time of the shooting, however, was Clara's pregnancy. So when she left Vineland on May 22, 1875, two months after Carruth was shot by her husband, it meant that Landis would not be with her when James was born in October.

Eight days after Clara's departure, Robinson met with Landis to begin discussions about a settlement with Carruth. By this point, the most recent diagnosis, which had declared the editor was out of danger, guaranteed the founder's release from jail, but he would be held a full week after the physicians' pronouncement. On June 2, Landis was released on $50,000 bail, yet he chose not to immediately return to Vineland, waiting instead until the end of the month when Carruth undertook a trip to New York.

News of the shooting had caught the attention of the country immediately. The *New York Times* reported the incident and even printed a follow-up article on the editor's condition a month later. Soon after, however, the national media coverage dissipated until an article by Carruth was published in *The Independent*. The editorial afforded the former editor an opportunity to comment on his condition and the events of the past several months:

Two months' constant wrestle with a hostile bullet in our brains has convinced us that we lack the capacity to develop a lead mine and publish an independent Vineland newspaper at the same time. Our impaired eyesight, shattered nerves and pulsating brain admonishes us that for the coming year we must not stray too far from the hospital. To our subscribers who, for the past four years, have read *The Independent* and paid for it, we hereby tender our acknowledgements. Those who have taken the paper just to help it along, never volunteering a dime or recognizing a dun, we shall feel it our duty, if we recover our health, to thank in person. We cannot omit to embrace this, perhaps last, free opportunity to thank our editorial brethren, who in their kindness of heart, have flattered our abilities, extolled our virtues and whitewashed our faults. The 'coyotes' of the craft who, taking advantage of our helplessness, have attempted to redeem past cowardice by yelping over our grave, we can afford to forgive and forget.

Newspapers like *The Daily Phoenix* of Columbia, South Carolina took advantage of Carruth's brief return to analyze the editorial and its writer. Calling the piece "his valedictory" the *Phoenix* comments that Carruth "steps from the editorial chair with considerable playfulness" and sums up the article by proclaiming,

As has often been demonstrated, an editor is endowed with that singular retentiveness of the mortal coil so frequently remarked in the domestic cat. Carruth affords a fine instance of the terrific grip the members of the journalistic guild have upon the continuity of their sojourn upon this terrestrial ball. Whether it is a fear of the hereafter that makes them cling so desperately to life or a consciousness that without them mankind would be miserable, is a matter for the profession alone to determine. Carruth's humor, however, has a graveyard suggestiveness about it that reminds one of a sportive skeleton.

On June 17, *The Nashville Union and American* of Tennessee reported that Carruth "cannot see the left side of anything as ordinarily presented...At the same time the right eye has acquired what is termed "telescopic vision." He can perceive distant objects hardly discernible to other men, with wonderful clearness, but cannot judge of their distance, often imagining that buildings a long way off are quite near. This affection is doubtless temporary, and after some experience he will be able to determine distances as well as any one-eyed person."

Shortly before the newspaper's report, Gross had visited Carruth on either June 14 or 16, having been summoned by a telegram from House and a letter from Robinson and, according to later testimony, the physician found the editor in excellent condition and "could see no reason why Carruth could not have recovered." He was also asked to visit the patient "should any brain troubles originate," but never received any such requests. Additionally, newspaper accounts of Landis's trial report, "Mr. Carruth told [Gross] he wanted to go away from Vineland because he was nervous. Here was a disposition to go, a desire to get away. Dr. Gross visited him and asked his symptoms, and getting answers to his enquiries he told him he was well enough to travel and could go to New York. Dr. Morgan had told him to remain. He went in spite of these precautions, as if courting death."

Gross's later testimony revealed that he was already aware of why he had been asked to perform another examination. He said that following his visit with the patient, he "went to Landis's office; an opinion was wanted whether Carruth could travel to New York and I made an examination to see if he could travel safely." Carruth's desire to "get away" had been prompted by Landis's offer of a settlement which, the founder stipulated, had to be conducted outside of New Jersey. The location would be Clinton, New York where Robinson lived. Landis's proposals could serve only as a civil settlement in the matter of the shooting. Despite its outcome, he would still have to face criminal charges.

Gross had sanctioned the journey, but specifically warned the patient to avoid excessive drink, anger and the sun. Robinson later complained that Gross had not questioned her brother-in-law efficiently enough about his condition. Brown acknowledged the gradual improvement of the patient in June, but, like Morgan, he and the rest of the homeopathic physicians who had periodically treated the editor over the past three months cautioned against the trip. Robinson claimed that Carruth was aware he shouldn't go.

Carruth left Vineland for New York on June 24 in order to consider proposals from Landis for a settlement. "Mr. Landis told me that he would do all in his power to make reparation for what he had done, and that no one regretted it more than he," Robinson later reported in her trial testimony. She added that she was informed by Landis that any settlement could not take place in New Jersey.

Battling incessant pain and impaired vision, Carruth traveled across rough roads and arrived in Clinton, New York, on June 26, settling into the home of his sister-in-law. With the various doctors acknowledging his improving condition, Carruth spent his time playing croquet and visiting friends. Meanwhile, Landis engaged himself in the prospective settlement, but wouldn't arrive in New York until July 30. With him was William House, who participated in the negotiations.

Cornelius B. Campbell explained in later testimony that he had accompanied Carruth, his wife, four children and Miss Robinson to Clinton. Both the trip and Campbell's involvement had been suggested by House. According to Campbell, who would depart the day after arriving, "Carruth was well, or seemed to be, at the start; had good appetite on the way; bore the fatigues of the journey well..." Campbell "looked out for the comfort of Carruth and attended to the matter of procuring passage for him and family and facilitating the journey in other ways."

Upon his arrival in New York, Landis made an offer of $5,000, which was rejected by Robinson. A second offer of cash and 370 acres of land, which raised the amount to $12,000, was also rejected, largely because the editor would have had to pay taxes on the land. Landis and House suggested that Robinson inform her brother-in-law that this was the best offer to be made and that he risked getting nothing if the matter entered the legal system, but no agreement was reached at the time. In fact, during negotiations, Landis never met with the editor of *The Independent*, Carruth refusing to confer with him until a satisfactory settlement had been worked out. In her testimony, Robinson stated that her brother-in-law was not convinced of Landis's remorse over the shooting.

Without a settlement, Carruth undertook the journey home on August 5, arriving in South Jersey two days later. Upon reaching the Camden depot, the editor, in a purely serendipitous moment, encountered Landis in the waiting room but refused to shake his outstretched hand. Sometime after their return to New Jersey, however, Landis and Carruth did reach a settlement. According to Robinson, a larger undisclosed offer was made and accepted but, while the papers were being drawn up, Carruth's condition worsened so that a trip outside the state became impossible.

Two weeks after returning to Vineland, Carruth summoned a physician, possibly Dr. Ingram who would later state that he ceased serving as the editor's doctor after September 25. Afterward, Campbell saw the editor, who was complaining of pains in his head and sleeplessness. Campbell reported that he went riding with Carruth and also saw him riding with others and that the attending physicians at the time offered no objections to the activity.

As hope for a legal settlement with Carruth dwindled, Clara gave birth to the Landises' fourth son, James Montevert Landis, who came into the world in Huntington, Long Island, New York on October 20, 1875. He would be called "Monte" by his family.

Three nights later, on October 23, Carruth was seized with convulsions and vomiting after eating dinner. Despite having been discharged the previous month, Ingram was summoned and made a late-night visit that lasted into the early morning of October 24. According to subsequent testimony, Brown was apparently also in attendance. Ingram later reported that his patient's symptoms at that point "were pain in the head on sudden movement, dizziness, sleeplessness, difficulty of articulation; [the patient] complained that he could not use his limbs with his accustomed facility. He was not willing to talk, it made him nervous." Carruth fell into a coma and died between two and three o'clock the morning of October 24, seven months after the shooting had occurred.

With Carruth's demise, Landis's re-arrest was imminent, but a letter written by John Gage to his son Henry on October 24, reveals that a faction of the editor's sympathizers was not going to waste any time or take any chances in bringing Landis to justice. Gage informs his son that "the papers were all made out for Landis's arrest beforehand and they did not want his death known outside as long as they could keep it...and if Landis is not arrested he will be soon as the news gets out."

Gage's wife Portia also wrote Henry concerning Carruth's death and corroborates her husband's account that the matter remained hushed until it was certain that Landis was in custody. She also appears more sympathetic toward Landis than in her March 29 letter. "Carruth's death was kept a perfect secret," she writes, "until the... officer [presumably Constable Babcock, the arresting officer] saw Landis go into his barn; when the barn was surrounded and Landis arrested and taken to Dr. [Hosea] Allen's office where they came pretty near having a fight over the poor man, the Landis party claiming that 'this court has no jurisdiction over the case'...The friends of Carruth i.e. the officers in charge claimed him as their prisoner arrested on charge of murder...poor Landis was again sent to Bridgton."

Both Gages did not limit their accounts to the events that unfolded that morning. John appraised the situation of Vineland's founder, offering his opinions about a just outcome: "Let Justice take its course though if law should condemn him to be hung I should hope law might not have its course though he should be confined in a prison so strong that he could not get out and so good that even his friends could not complain but would unite with his enemies in keeping him there until he became worthy of the confidence of all [the] community and could be discharged a good citizen." Portia seems to have viewed Landis's situation as more tragic than Carruth's, writing, "Surely 'the way of the transgressor is hard.' I should prefer that any of my friends should be in the place of Carruth, rather that of Landis."

The warrant for Landis's arrest was issued by Hosea Allen, Cumberland County Justice of the Peace. The basis for the warrant was a complaint by Vineland newspaper editor B. Frank Ladd, who accused Landis of causing Carruth's death by shooting him. According to Allen's ledger, subpoenas were issued for Ladd, James Wiley, Edward Wright, Millie G. Case, Dr. L.W. Brown and Bradford P. Foster, all of whom were rounded up and sworn in, subsequently testifying before Allen about what they had witnessed concerning the crime and Carruth's condition over the previous months.

Leverett Newcomb, representing Wiley, Wright, Case and Ladd, presented a similar account of what had transpired on the day of the shooting. Brown identified himself as Carruth's attending physician and explained that he had seen the deceased "often during this summer" and on the evening before he died and that he thought his death "was occasioned by the pistol shot." Foster, who testified that he had spent much of the time over the previous week with Carruth, found him "very uneasy and restless" and was with him when he died that Sunday morning.

Landis had produced no witnesses at the time to defend himself against these testimonies and was placed in the hands of the sheriff and into the county jail in Bridgeton. Costs for his arrest were tallied at $22.95, but only the court costs of $4.40 were paid at the time. The constable cost of $18.55 was still pending when the proceedings were placed in the ledger.

A.R. Thomas and a fellow colleague of homeopathic medicine caught the early train to Vineland on October 25 to participate in the autopsy. Their account of the post-mortem examination, which appeared in the November 1, 1875 edition of the *American Journal of Homeopathic Materia Medica and Record of Medical Science*, revealed information that had otherwise escaped previous examinations. The bone fragment removed when the wound was initially dressed accounted for the damage to the brain tissue while the impairment to Carruth's vision had been the result of "increased pressure" rather than an actual injury. It was also discovered that the trajectory of the bullet had not been straightforward once entering Carruth. Instead, it had turned slightly to the left before lodging one-and-a-half inches below the surface, which was why none of the probes conducted encountered the bullet.

In addition to these findings, the report also identifies that the path of the bullet had been "closed over by a thin membrane" and that there were three abscesses near the area of the bullet, the first of which had filled "the greater part of the posterior lobe with about two ounces of thick, greenish-yellow pus." The homeopathic journal confirms that an early proposal to surgically open a section of the skull where an abscess might have formed had been rejected by Carruth and his family.

A Cincinnati physician, Francis Dowling, who evaluated the medical and autopsy reports prior to the Landis trial, blamed the existence of the abscesses on the probing conducted by Gross and Morgan. Dowling maintains that the silver probes, plunged into the wound two-and-a-half inches by Gross and one-and-three-quarter inches by Morgan, who struck two parts of the brain in the process, correspond to the locations of the abscesses described in the autopsy report. Dowling posits the question of whether Carruth's death was the result of the bullet or the abscesses. "The facts of the case go to show that it must be attributed to the latter," he writes, "...A bullet...which thus becomes encysted in the cerebrum, may remain years, even a lifetime, without interfering materially with the functions of the part. Abscesses, on the other hand, in almost every instance prove fatal, sooner or later, if they are not evacuated by surgical procedure, death being produced by the interruption to the performance of the functions of the brain...the abscesses were three in number, situated in the posterior lobe of the right hemisphere, not far from the surface. Would not the use of the trephine, and puncture of the abscesses, have been feasible and justifiable under the circumstances?"

Dowling was most likely unaware that any surgical procedure had been ruled out by Carruth and his family. There is no way to determine what might have occurred if surgery or treatment of the abscesses had been pursued or what Landis might have been spared over the next several months. The impending trial would turn out to be one of the most anticipated events of Cumberland County, but it also captured the interest of the nation as Bridgeton transformed into the site of a media circus with reporters from Philadelphia, New York and beyond conveying the details concerning the legal fate of the founder of Vineland, New Jersey.

Michael Landis   Mary Landis

Matilda Landis   Charles K. Landis

Clara & Henry Landis   Charles K. Landis Jr.

Richard Landis   James "Monte" Landis

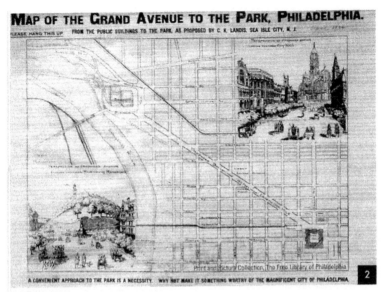

Landis's Philadelphia Parkway Design

Charles K. Landis

Uri Carruth

The Landis home, southeast corner of Landis Avenue and the Boulevard

Landis's office, northeast corner of Landis Avenue and the Boulevard

(All photos courtesy of the VHAS)

Chapter 6
Trial
(January 1876-February 1876)

By the time of Landis's trial, Uri Carruth lay buried in Sunset Hill Cemetery in Oneida County, New York for several months, but his Vineland legacy had yet to be determined and would require the patience of the key players in the legal battle as well as that of the public. The shooting the previous year had garnered headlines throughout the country, but that would pale in comparison to the trial coverage, which would turn into a media event that invariably satisfied the curiosity of readers nationwide. In the end, the verdict would continue to divide citizens, local and national, for over a century.

Ever the astute attorney, Landis assembled an impressive team of lawyers from both New Jersey and Philadelphia. He selected Philadelphia attorney and friend Benjamin Harris Brewster as well as Vineland counsels William House and James H. Nixon and E. M. Turner, Bridgeton attorneys Col. William E. Potter and Charles E. Sheppard and Elizabeth resident and ex-Chancellor Benjamin Williamson. They faced prosecutors James R. Hoagland, District Attorney, and Jacob Vanatta, Attorney General. The presiding judge was Alfred Reed.

The trial was set to begin at the County Courthouse in Bridgeton at 10 a.m. on Tuesday, January 11, 1876. Hours before the start time, a huge crowd of Cumberland County residents had lined up, each hoping to gain entrance to the proceedings. Anticipating the surge of attendance, the courthouse had devised a system whereby each waiting individual would be handed an admission card that would allow access to the upper level of the courtroom until capacity was reached. That Tuesday morning, at ten o'clock, admission cards were handed out and the line directed upstairs where the cards were turned in for a seat. It took only a few minutes to fill the room, leaving the vast majority of the crowd no opportunity to witness the trial that day. The overabundance of attendees would continue for the duration of the hearing.

While the constables were tending to the crowd, several of the key players in this legal drama were en route to Bridgeton, including Judge Reed and Williamson. A reporter from the *Times of Philadelphia* who, having missed the train to Bridgeton the day before, wound up on the same railway car from Camden carrying Reed and Williamson, took advantage of the opportunity to observe and report on the pair. "He is a young man, not more than thirty-five years old," the journalist writes of the trial judge. "He dresses well, even approaching the top of the fashion and if met on [Philadelphia's] Chestnut Street would be taken for anything else but the presiding Judge of a New Jersey district such as he holds the scales of Justice for Cape May, Salem, Cumberland and Atlantic Courthouses." Williamson is described as "a large English-looking man of about forty-five or fifty, coming from Trenton, where he is well known as a leading equity lawyer."

Also on the train were some witnesses for both the defense and prosecution. Landis's team had chosen to focus on two areas, the first demonstrating that Carruth's death had been caused by malpractice on the part of several of the physicians attending to the deceased editor, so Drs. Gross and Thomas felt they should arrive early if they were to take the stand over the next several days. Isaac Kay, superintendent of the Providence Hospital for the Insane, and Dr. Horace A. Buttolph, superintendent of the New Jersey Asylum in Trenton, both of whom were required to observe the proceedings from the start before they testified, formed the backbone of the Landis team's second line of defense which was to prove that the defendant had been insane at the time of the shooting. They had also rounded up nearly one hundred witnesses from the Vineland area and Pennsylvania to appear over the course of the hearing.

The first day of the trial wasn't able to begin until an hour after its scheduled start and it was a bumpy start. As proceedings commenced, it was obvious that two key players were missing from the courtroom - Brewster, who was reportedly sick, and Landis, whose absence was not explained. Once minor business was completed, it was discovered that three witnesses for the prosecution, E. C. Wells, Dr. Bidwell and J. D. Holden, had not arrived and Hoagland refused to continue without them present. Reed demanded they be procured and penalized immediately and declared a recess until 3 p.m. Once adjourned, the court was informed the reason for the missing witnesses' absence had been a delayed train and that they would arrive shortly.

When the trial resumed in the afternoon, Landis appeared in the courtroom, accompanied by Matilda, who had been serving in her new capacity as caretaker for the Landis children since the departure of Clara the previous May. The *New Jersey Patriot* reported that Landis's "demeanor was such as indicated that he had full confidence in his attorneys and was strong in the hope that no serious punishment would be visited upon him for his crime."

The afternoon session focused exclusively on assembling a jury, a task that would require two-and-a-half hours, with the defense challenging twenty prospective jurors and the prosecution ten. In the end, four were set aside or excused. Those selected for the trial were George W. Dummitt, Thomas Ludlam and Francis Reeves from Millville, David O. Frazeur and Joseph M. Ware from Bridgeton, Benjamin F. McKeag and Jonathan Cox from Maurice River Township, Dallas L. Compton from Commercial Township, Joseph A. Minch from Hopewell Township, Elmer Biddle from Deerfield Township and Jacob Richman and jury foreman Thomas Proud from Vineland.

The inclusion of Proud and Ludlam are curiosities that did not escape the attention of some in attendance, including the *Times of Philadelphia* reporter, who commented that "two circumstances connected with the drawing were noticeable to close observers, and give every reason to believe that Landis has at least two men on the jury who favor him." Reed had already explained that the defense and prosecution would be allowed to challenge a prospective juror only until he had been sworn in. Proud, as expected, received no challenge from the defense, but the prosecution chose to wait until his hand had already been placed on the Bible to contest. Potter immediately argued that it was too late for the prosecution to declare its opposition, and a heated debate among attorneys began. Vanatta insisted that only after a juror had kissed the book was the right to a challenge halted and Reed concurred. It was then decided to consult the law books for clarification. During the wait, two other jurors were selected. When the review was completed, it was discovered that Potter was, in fact, correct and the court had no choice but to swear in Proud.

Ludlam's situation was not a matter of confusion over procedure, however. As the Bible was about to be placed in the prospective juror's hand, Ludlam addressed the court, candidly explaining that he should not serve on this jury since he had made known his support for Landis prior to the trial and that his bias was well known. Reed informed him that he could not be dismissed until a challenge was made but, for whatever reason, neither Hoagland nor Vanatta chose to dismiss him and the Millville resident was sworn in. No doubt Landis and his legal team scored this moment a victory.

Once the selection process was completed, Reed decided that the jury should be sequestered for the duration of the trial. The members would stay at the City Hotel in Bridgeton for what was initially thought to be approximately a week. No one anticipated that the trial would continue for four weeks. At 5:30 p.m., court was adjourned.

When the trial resumed Wednesday morning, the battle was ready to begin. Preliminary arguments would be heard for several days before a seemingly endless array of defense witnesses testified. On Wednesday, Hoagland presented the prosecution's opening arguments and medical witnesses testified as to the treatment Carruth had received. By Thursday morning, Potter presented the defense's arguments in a three-hour speech. He said it would be shown that the editor's condition improved until September 1 and that the continued probing of the wound and the neglect on the part of the attending physicians to remove a protruding abscess at the opening of the wound, thereby eliminating the inflammation, led to the patient's demise. He also stated that the defense would show that Landis had undergone a descent into insanity since 1872 and that since his return from Europe, he had displayed conditions that concerned his family and friends.

The defense attorneys may have realized early on that their medical argument wasn't as sound as they had hoped. The number of physicians who treated Carruth during his last seven months made it difficult to point a finger at only one doctor since examinations, probes and treatment overlapped among them. It was clear that the homeopathic physicians Tuller and Morgan were targeted for the malpractice, but Gross, a witness for the defense, had conducted the deepest of the probes on the editor's wound. In addition, the claim by the defense that the refusal to remove what was thought to be a protruding abscess would be laid to rest when Dr. Brown took his turn on the stand two weeks later to explain that the protrusion was actually a bone. In all, there were fewer days devoted by the defense to the medical argument of the case.

On the other hand, the question of Landis's sanity received considerable examination, taking substantial time during the proceedings on all six days of the trial's second week and four out of five days in the third week. It's likely the defense team realized this was Landis's only chance at acquittal and acquired Drs. Ray and Buttolph to examine the defendant and to provide testimony in order to support its claim of insanity.

Potter's account of the chronology of Landis's actions on March 19 takes some liberties with the order of events, placing the time that Landis first read Carruth's March 18 article near 10 a.m., immediately after which he reportedly retrieved his gun from the second level of his home and departed for *The Independent* offices. It's conceivable that painting Landis's crime as the result of a rash and impetuous decision lent credibility to the insanity plea, but more importantly it conveyed no sense of premeditation.

Over the course of three weeks, the defense managed to parade close to one hundred witnesses onto the stand to testify that they had each encountered a situation in which Landis's demeanor bore suspicion and concern. The range of peculiar actions included wild-eyed looks, disheveled appearances, quirky actions or various combinations of the three as proof of a diminishing sanity. While witnesses for the prosecution claimed they observed no unusual behavior, some even pointing to rational moments that contradicted certain testimony elicited by the defense, Landis's team managed to paint a somewhat convincing picture of a haunted man. The fact that much of this testimony bears a striking resemblance may be insight into the defense team's coaching tactics.

The strategy of Landis's lawyers was not confined to Vineland and area residents, however. An attempt was made to demonstrate the defendant's insanity was hereditary by calling George M. Kline, a lawyer from Lancaster, Pennsylvania, to testify that he had known Landis's grandfather, John Landis, whose mental faculties, he asserted, had diminished after becoming an alderman. He "soon became incapable of attending to his business; from that time to his death was under continuous restraint [and] surveillance [was] necessary for his safety. His mind wandered, and his conversation was incoherent. Late in life he was violent; on one occasion he assaulted his son Jesse with a chair; tried to knock him down and escape from restraint; he was for years under continual guard; for his own good confined most of the time to his room."

Occasionally, a defense witness would discuss Landis's paranoia, some of which predated the 1872-1875 period on which the insanity argument centered. This testimony is clearly the most convincing and may have contributed considerably to the outcome of the trial. The fears of retaliation from Landis's father-in-law, the desperation in assembling an armed team of bodyguards to be ready for the arrival of a vengeance-seeking group by train and the uncertainty of when an assassin's bullet would find him were public revelations that must have been most painful for not only Landis but the townsfolk as well. The paranoia and recent domestic struggles revealed demons that could now be seen by everyone.

The amount of witnesses brought in by the defense slowed the trial, but Landis's team was not willing to risk defeat for the sake of expediency. The case would drag on to a fourth week, when the two sides finally delivered closing arguments. It wasn't until Thursday February 3 that Reed was ready to charge the jury. He told the members, "I need not say to an intelligent jury that no friendship, feeling, ties, prejudice or bias, nor sorrow for the dead or pity for the living should warp or influence your absolute sense of justice. Here we know no man or men; we only know the State of New Jersey and the defendant, and to render a true verdict between them."

Reed spoke to the jury for a considerable amount of time that day, explaining the choices facing the members and the details of the law pertaining to the case. According to a manuscript of Reed's statements, the judge began by charging the jury to return with a degree of murder if they decide that Landis is guilty. "There can also be returned a verdict of manslaughter," he added. "Under our present statute, a verdict of not-guilty of murder, but guilty of an attempt to murder may also be returned." And, he said, a verdict of not-guilty can also be rendered. "If, however, that result should be reached in this case on the ground that the defendant was insane, then you should be prepared to certify that fact upon your coming in."

Reed told the jury that the prosecution "insists that the defendant has been proven guilty of murder in the first-degree," that the murder was deliberate and premeditated and that the intention to kill existed at the time the wound had been inflicted. "If it is proved also that Carruth died from the effect of that shot, it presents a case of willful killing – it is a case of murder in the first degree."

As for Carruth's death having been caused by the use of silver probes by the doctors, Reed explained to the twelve men that in circumstances such as Carruth's, "probing is a usual method" and that "I think it does not appear that the use of the silver probe is an unusual thing…" Reed also told the jury that it must determine whether or not Drs. Tuller and Morgan are "guilty of a violation of the ordinary [method] of treatment" and if the probing was the cause of the abscesses. "When, however, a dangerous wound…is inflicted and death ensues, the person who inflicted it cannot shelter himself behind the plea of erroneous treatment. Neither will the refusal of the wounded man to submit to a surgical operation nor his neglect to take proper care of himself change the rule."

Concerning the plea of insanity, Reed warned the jury of the conflict of not punishing a person who has suffered from a "mental disease," but also acquitting someone whose insanity is not real. He stated, "these conflicting interests demand the most careful and conscientious considerations of all the facts that surround each case that justice may be done to the state and to the accused."

Reed also defined the term "insanity" as meaning "that degree and type of mental derangement which by the rules of law makes the defendant irresponsible for the [committed] act," and reminded the jury that the insanity of Landis's grandfather needed to be weighed with the other testimony. The jury, he said, must see if there is proof of insanity and if "the testimony all together proves the existence of that degree of insanity which renders the defendant incapable of committing crime."

The judge added that "if you believe that at the time he fired this shot he was unconscious by reason of disease of the mind that he ought not to do it, he is to be acquitted but if he was conscious that he was doing what he ought not to do he should not be acquitted whether he was partially insane or not. Anger has been said to be a brief madness, but it is not a madness which is recognized by the law as an excuse for acts done through its influence."

Once transcribed, Reed's speech to the jury amounted to nine pages that discussed the "guilty by murder" verdict and twelve pages that explained the "not guilty by insanity" verdict in addition to two pages of summary on each point. When he was finished, the deliberation began.

The jury's confinement to the City Hotel had, by now, extended to more than three weeks, but the members were not yet finished. The deliberation lasted three days. By Saturday morning, the jury had acquitted Landis on the charges of first-degree and second-degree murder but found itself stymied on the charges of manslaughter and intent to kill. *The Independent* later reported:

> On Saturday morning the jury came into the courtroom and asked to be discharged. It was impossible, they said, to reach an agreement, and if the Judge should keep them confined until the autumn leaves fell to the ground, so desirable an object would be no nearer accomplishment. But the Judge was deaf to their entreaties and refused to let them go…All through the long day they discussed

the matter, balloting at intervals, but without coming any nearer an agreement…

The jury then decided to take a different approach on the remaining charges. Thomas Proud later told *The Independent*, "Do you know how we found a verdict? Why, down on our knees, praying to God to direct us in the performance of our duties." Mr. Dummett added, "For hours we have been striving with each other, until on our knees the verdict we have rendered came to us."

The Independent's coverage provided details that included a first-hand account by a member of the jury: "Every juror agreed to submit the matter to the decision of the great Father and to remain in honest and silent prayer for direction, and then arise and cast a ballot as directed. 'Long and earnestly we prayed for direction; the struggle was hard and strong; and then we arose and voted, and every vote was for acquittal. I cannot tell you how we felt or what we did when the result was known, for it beggars description. After we had agreed we sang with full hearts, praise God from whom all blessings flow, and told the constables to ring the bell.'"

Around 9:50 on Saturday night, Bridgeton residents, some already asleep, were informed that a verdict had been decided by the ringing of the courthouse bell. It wasn't long before the courtroom was filled to capacity. Landis entered with Matilda, escorted by Sheriff Hampton. James Nixon and Potter were there, as well. *The Independent* reported that "a breathless silence came upon the audience, and there was an awful moment of expectancy." Proud read the verdict: "We find the defendant, Charles K. Landis, not guilty on the ground of insanity." Landis's reaction was "electrical" according to the *Bridgeton Daily. The Independent* reported, "The face so full of painful anxiety and fear lit up with a smile and brightness, and instantly he grasped the hands of his counsel, Hon. James H. Nixon and Col. Wm. E. Potter, while a look of honest gratitude displaced the smile."

The decision was instantly met with criticism and derision. Newspapers were soon filled with acidic responses to Landis's acquittal. Others came up with questions like the *West Jersey Press* which wanted to know what had happened to the type of "Jersey justice" that had accounted for "more executions in Cumberland County for capital crimes in the last thirty years than in all the other counties in South Jersey combined."

Yet some of the publications, like the *Brooklyn Daily Eagle*, attempted to weigh in on the circumstances that led to Landis's actions the previous year:

> Carruth was a mixture of a thug and an imp, who used a few pounds of type to attack a man and his family, because the man had committed the offense of succeeding and being thought of better than Carruth. He plied his attacks at the outset for blackmail and then with redoubled deviltry because blackmail was refused. He succeeded in driving Landis' wife into temporary insanity and that effect of the attacks, added to other attacks, wrought up Landis to the pitch of frenzy and disorder that led him to shoot some honest lead into the dirty head of his assailant...There is no reason in saying that Landis was justified. He was not, either legally or morally,

but that question is disposed of by the provided eclipse of his reason. That Carruth was served right, which is conceded, does not show that Landis did right, at all. Had he known what he did, he would not have been without great extenuation, but it would have fallen far short of justification. His situation today must reveal to his returned reason the unwisdom [sic] of his course. The recoil of his deed has lost him his family. It has lost him his health and his usefulness. It has made him a vagrant mourner among men, over desolations that time can neither blunt nor repair.

Like other pieces written at the time, a *New York Tribune* editorial didn't seem to believe in Landis's insanity but, like many, concluded it was "as good an excuse as any for an acquittal which was to have been expected from the outset."

The most surprising response to the trial's conclusion, however, came from *The Independent*, the vehicle used by Carruth to cast his barbs against Landis. In its February 12, 1876 edition, under Editorial Notes, a piece titled simply "The Verdict," reveals a startling stance for the publication. By this time the paper was under the editorship of E. G. Blaisdell, and its content had dismissed the type of scathing criticism and satirical folly favored by Carruth. The unsigned editorial, most likely written by Blaisdell, reads:

> With the issue of the trial, which has resulted in the acquittal of Mr. Landis, no true friend of Vineland has any reason to be dissatisfied. It has followed as the natural sequence of causes, which were remote

from and anterior to the unfortunate act which placed his own life in jeopardy and made him amenable to the just laws of his country. Back of all that, the pain he had endured at the hands of his victim and his outraged domestic life were remembered to his good and reacted in the sympathy of men in his behalf. In the eyes of those who sat in judgment of his life, what he had done and what he had suffered outweighed in importance what he did in one sad moment of unconscious forgetfulness of right and, in consideration of the wrong that had been inflicted upon him, they sunk the minor point of the wrong that he had done another.

The editorial then acknowledges its agreement with the trial verdict before pointing an accusing finger at the irresponsible journalism previously practiced by the paper:

The ends of justice are met, and justice tempered with due mercy restores to him his rightful liberty. No one can deny that it belongs to him…the result of the trial is an impressive moral argument in favor of a necessary change in the laws relating to the freedom of the press. We as a community, in our own bitter experience, can attest to the real requirement of some speedy modification of this character. Until the laws protect men, not only in their rights to property, but most of all in their rights to character, and insure the sanctity of domestic and social life, we cannot expect that wise counsels will prevail, or that men assaulted with pens dipped in gall will keep within the bounds of reason, Our experience here in

Vineland of the effects of a journalism that aims to destroy, and not build up or promote the true interests of the people, has been a sorrowful and exceedingly bitter one, but if it teaches…men and women all over this land that there are private and domestic rights and privileges, pertaining to individuals and society, which are not to be violated by pen or tongue with impunity, it will not have been amiss.

However, it was the Philadelphia *Public Ledger's* appraisal of the Landis verdict that probably recognized the decision for what it truly was, stating that it "may be regarded as a reliable evidence of public opinion in the matter." The article acknowledges the two points argued by the defense but offers that "supplementary to these two legal points was another element, not pressed as a legal point, but still entering into the surroundings, and making an atmosphere favorable to the defense. This was the great provocation suffered by Landis from the gross personal attacks upon his family published by Carruth's paper. These were not criticisms upon or censures of a candidate for office, or of a public officer in his public capacity for official misconduct but were invasions of the sacred privacy of family and home."

The article ultimately states that after the jury acquitted Landis of the two serious charges, "they could agree no further, and no other logical explanation of their failure to agree can be given than that they gave great force and influence to the gross provocation suffered by the prisoner through the vile publications attacking his family and home."

The conclusion of the trial meant that everyone could finally go home, except for Landis. Based on the decision, he was detained in order to determine if he was safe to return to society. After another week of psychiatric examinations, Landis was deemed fit for release on February 14. He returned home where, on February 15, he wrote his friend Cornelius B. Campbell "My Dear Campbell: When you called upon me I was in bed, resting. I will be very glad to see you and any other friends."

Chapter 7
A New Normal
(March 1876-December 1879)

The trial may have been the legal conclusion to the Carruth affair, but it's doubtful Landis achieved full closure on the issue, as reports of his private life would reveal after his death. Many friends commented that he seemed sadder after undergoing the experience.

As for Carruth, while his body had been buried in New York, his debts had remained in Vineland. A series of invoices sent to the editor's accountant in 1876 reveal that Carruth owed a considerable amount of money, some of it dating back as far as 1872. An invoice from R.H. Forestal and Co., sent after Carruth's death, shows unpaid bills dating back to 1873 and amounting to $252.43 including $8.53 in interest. There is a June 12, 1876 bill for $43.25 in purchases and rentals from 1872 to 1875 and another bill dated June 22, 1876 for $369.39 from Lewis Brown for what appear to be the late editor's funeral services the previous October. Another notice identifies an unpaid balance of $119.22 from May 1875 that is to be paid by the Carruth estate to Robert Sylles. The evidence is an indication that Carruth had already been in debt for several years before his slow demise incurred additional costs.

In the fall of 1876, Landis received a threatening letter from a recently jailed resident who seemed intent on reviving *The Independent's* crusade against the founder, particularly the newspaper's earlier accusations of Landis offering editors of publications "worthless" land in exchange for ads promoting Vineland. The letter, dated November 7, 1876, was from a man named Moore who discusses how Landis was one of the individuals who brought undisclosed charges against him. The purpose of the letter is to let Landis know that "I am now compelled to show the public the truth and allow them to decide." He continues by writing that he

> has a good memory of a large portion of the editors who have published your advertisement, as well of many who have refused. I shall give them a truthful statement of the most gigantic swindle ever known…you have the advertisement in 386 papers at a considered valuation of $100. Many refused not thinking it sufficient. Now I will show you some figures, 386 at $100 equivalent to $38,600.00. We now take the 386 lots 50 x 50 feet that makes about 70 acres of land at a cost to you of not over $70,000. Now take the cost of labor, paper, envelopes and

stamps you will be amply paid $2,000 which will be far more than actual cost, which gives you $38,000 profit. I completed this statement on Sunday, and left it with a friend who, when I direct, will see it is circulated…After the election is over you will have the pleasure of having many to call to view their property. I shall remain in Vineland and as my name is known to many as well as my writing I think we can call it square.

It had been customary for Landis to offer editors around the country land in Vineland or Landis Township as payment for ads placed in their papers. Many accepted the offer, like the editor of a newspaper in Cedartown, Georgia who wrote Landis on July 4, 1876:

Dear Sir – your letter of a recent date proposing to give me a deed to a town lot in the town of Landisville or Vineland in pay for advertising has been received. In reply I will say that I will accept the proposition and will insert the advertisement before receipt of the deed. Write me and let me know what the tax is on property there – when it is given in and when paid. Yours truly, Thomas Gibson. I will leave the selection of the lot to you.

Moore's threats remained idle since the following year, Landis continued his practice undisturbed, as the following letter from a West Virginia editor reveals:

Having fulfilled our mutual agreement in publishing the attached advertisement, I now desire you would send me a [illegible] deed for lot set apart as mentioned in contract for me. You will please have it put on record...

Other papers in which Landis advertised in exchange for Vineland or Landisville property in 1876 were *The Malden Mirror*, Massachusetts, *The Panhandle News*, West Virginia; *The Norfolk Reformer*, Virginia; *The Sunday Morning News*, Buffalo, New York; *The Marksdale Expositor*, Marksdale, Ontario, Canada; *The Plymouth Index*, Pennsylvania; *The Burlington Daily Sentenal*, Burlington, Vermont; *The Turners Falls Reporter*, Turners Falls, Massachusetts; *The San Benito Advance*, San Benito, California and *The Union Register*, Mt. Gilead, Ohio. The locations demonstrate the geographical range covered by Landis's promotions.

Evidence of the popularity of this type of bartering among editors can been seen in a letter Landis received in February 1879 from L.B. Hatch of the *Middlesex Newspaper Company* in South Farmingham, Massachusetts concerning the deed to Vineland property that the newspaper had received in exchange for ads. Because of a change in management, the newspaper found the land "of no value to us," but if Landis would cancel it and issue one for the new management "you will confer a great favor."

Landis chose to remain in Vineland throughout 1876. His life returned to a somewhat normal state, and with his sister Matilda now part of the Vineland household to help care for the children, a duty she continued to perform for the next decade, he was free to undertake new endeavors. While in Europe, he had proposed the idea of writing a book on Italian antiquities and was encouraged by Mrs. Grohman to pursue the project. It seems likely that he began working on the project within this frame of time. He envisioned a book about "the form and decoration of china and porcelain in the style of art" as it originated in Italy and illustrated with graphics to accompany the prose he would write. A manuscript of the work, entitled "China," indicates that Landis completed the text, but it appears the graphics for the project were never completed, and the book itself never appeared in published form. Writing had always been a necessary endeavor for Landis and, in the aftermath of the Carruth ordeal, it was undoubtedly therapeutic.

Landis would eventually receive an answer to the question as to why Carruth made a career out of persecuting him. It arrived in the form of an undated four-page letter by Isaac N. Wilson, who had been an employee of *The Independent* for two months. Wilson explains, "For some years I have felt that I ought to make known to you, facts in my possession regarding the late Uri Carruth and his object in conducting *The Vineland Independent* in the manner he did. I was employed by him for several months and quitted [sic] his employ but a short time before he met his fate. I had many conversations with him; he frequently read to me the articles he had written, casting ridicule upon you and your Vineland venture, while you were in Europe."

Wilson's letter reveals that the circulation numbers announced for *The Independent* had been favorably skewed ("he claimed for *The Independent* a circulation of 5,000. While I was with him, it did not reach over 800") and the dubious methods Carruth employed in gaining advertising revenue for his paper ("he wrote little novels about the employees in the Ladies Store of Vineland to compel the [owners] to advertise in his paper. While their advertisement was in his columns, he was silent; when they removed it by reason of depression in their business, he recommenced his stories, choosing such of the girls as had no defenders...")

The term Wilson uses for Carruth's method is "blackmail," and such extortion extended to Landis as well. "I asked Mr. Carruth upon one occasion," Wilson writes, "why he pursued the course he did, seeing it cut off his circulation and lost him friends? He replied, 'It is the only way to conduct a country paper. Never let the people know who you mean to strike next.' Upon another occasion I asked him the secret of his animosity to you. He laughed as he said, 'I will make him give me half he is worth to get rid of me.' There was no avoiding the conclusion that his attacks were intended to drive you to purchase his paper in order to silence it. Blackmail."

Confronting Carruth about his 1874 series of articles, "Letters from Europe," which mocked Landis's European trip," Wilson pointed out the risk of publishing such pieces: "I said to him, 'Mr. Carruth, these articles are injuring the circulation of the paper; the people laugh at your ridicule while at the same time they curse you as an enemy of Vineland. Mr. Landis will return some day, and if he is the man I think he is, he will horsewhip you within an inch of your life, and the people will applaud his act. If he is not, you will get shot. You are pushing this too far, Mr. Carruth, and there will come an end to forbearance.' He laughed and said,

'Landis hasn't courage enough to shoot a dog.' 'He may find courage enough to shoot you, I replied."

Wilson explains that, after the March 19 shooting, "I held [Carruth's] hand while he said, 'Isaac I pushed it too far, too far; I don't blame him for avenging himself, but I do blame him for shooting me down like a dog in my own office.' He thus quoted my own language and seemed to recognize the fact that he reaped as he had sown."

Wilson's humble postscript is evidence of the sincerity of his letter and his purpose: "Please forgive me if this communication stirs painful recollections. My sympathies have always been with you. I do not know that what I have written will be of any use to you; in the hope that it may, I have written it. As I stood by Carruth and heard him speak, I could not help believing that he justified you rather than himself."

It is not known how many people learned of Wilson's revelation or if it made any difference to those whose opinion had been obstinately maintained over time. Even Clara's facts had become protectively selective in the years following the shooting. In an extensive account of her life, published in the *Buffalo Courier* in 1884, Clara presented Landis as the sole victim of Carruth's published attacks with no mention of her own alleged mental ailments as reported by *The Independent*. She relays matter-of-factly that her husband "… was arrested for shooting a newspaper editor who published slanderous articles concerning him, but he was acquitted." Curiously, Clara dates the shooting five years earlier than when it occurred.

The most startling statement about Landis delivered in Clara's account contends that "twelve months later he killed a neighbor who had won a lawsuit from him but was acquitted... after a trial which lasted two years." She continues by asserting that "at this trial I first learned of my husband's enormous wealth...Shortly afterward, I left him and went to live with my parents."

The statements are strewn with inaccuracies and falsehoods, but whether they stem from misremembering or from an attempt to tarnish her former husband's reputation or from something else entirely will never be known. There is no evidence of a second Landis trial, which would certainly have drawn considerable media attention for its alleged duration and for occurring so soon after the Carruth scandal. Clara never attended Landis's trial in 1876 and it seems surprising that she wouldn't have had an inkling of her husband's worth during their marriage. The pre-nuptial agreement she signed, his business ventures, which included land sales with which she was involved, and his reputation in their years together would have been enough to indicate his wealth. Finally, her father's death on April 16, 1870 would have made it impossible for her to return home "to live with my parents."

Clara also reported that after separating from Landis she had been "so overcome by sorrow that I tried to find forgetfulness in a foreign land. In July 1876, I took my youngest child [James] and servants and sailed for Europe. I traveled there for three years." However, it is clear that she had returned to the U.S. by the start of 1877 to follow up on a legal matter she had initiated.

In early 1877, one year after his acquittal, Landis found himself back in a courtroom as a result of Clara. In early 1875, prior to Carruth's death, Clara sought a separation that would grant her custody of Charles Jr. and Richard. Several months after she had departed the Landis home for good, she petitioned for a writ that was granted August 9, 1875 and that could allow her custody of all three children once the couple's youngest son James was born. She claimed that she had separated from Landis on grounds of cruelty. Her custody claim was based on a law passed in 1860 giving the mother the right of custody of her children under the age of seven in situations of separation. Prior to this, the father had been guaranteed custody.

Landis's legal team, Benjamin Williamson, James Nixon and Benjamin Brewster, all of whom represented him during the murder trial the previous year, responded to the writ by branding Clara an improper guardian who deserted her husband in 1875 when he needed her most and declaring that the separation of the Landises did not meet the requirements of the 1860 law. They also argued that an 1871 law dealing with custody matters was a repeal of the 1860 law on which Clara based her claim. In the meantime, Landis retained custody of the two older boys, but was warned that he must be ready to relinquish guardianship to his estranged wife at any point.

Testimony was presented in early 1877. Individuals out to discredit Clara as a fit mother offered a variety of tales that painted her as uncaring, selfish and distracted. Ellen Norton, who served as nanny to Charles Jr. and Richard, testified that on one occasion, while Clara was away, Richard became sick and Norton had to summon his mother three times before she returned to Vineland. Apparently, the doctor arrived ahead of Clara. Norton also claimed that the children received no attention from their mother

According to other testimony, there was a time when Clara was in Jenkintown, Pennsylvania and Charles Jr. became ill. His mother was telegraphed and, upon returning to Vineland, did not tend to her son but went horse riding to visit a friend instead. But for every witness who had an example or two of how Clara was unfit as a mother, there was another who attested to her appropriate conduct as a parent. According to them, her kindness and care were on display constantly. Dr. Lane, the Landis family physician at the time, countered the testimony given about her return from Jenkintown, saying that Clara was in the room during his examination and that he had always witnessed her kindness to both children when visiting.

Two former Landis family physicians concurred and helped weaken the Landis legal team's argument with their testimony. It was reported that "Dr. Lansing, who attended the family from 1867 to 1872...was socially intimate with the family. He says hers was the ordinary care of a careful, painstaking mother towards her children...Dr. Brewer speaks in the same manner."

The decision was scheduled for February 16 at noon at the courthouse in Trenton, New Jersey. Unlike the murder trial the previous year, the spectators numbered only a few, but included an unnamed reporter whose article would appear in the *Independent Hour* newspaper of Woodbridge, New Jersey and who provided a detailed record of the events that unfolded during the several hours in the courtroom that day.

S. H. Grey and Cortlandt Parke, Clara's lawyers, and Williamson and Nixon, having arrived early, consulted for an hour before the start of proceedings. Landis, Charles Jr.,

Richard, Matilda and a nurse arrived at the designated time. "He placed the eldest boy, Charley, who will be six years old in March next alongside of him on the chair," the Independent Hour reported, "and he took the youngest, Dickie, who has just turned four years, in his lap, where the little fellow reclined during the proceedings…Mr. Landis looked fully ten years older than he really is. His hair is of a silvery hue, and his moustache and whiskers are nearly as white. His face was pale, his eyes were sunken and his features altogether portrayed a downcast sullen disposition. He was attired in a light gray suit."

Clara, "under the protection of her brother, Captain Richard W. Meade, was early on hand." She and her brother sat behind Landis and the boys. "Mrs. Landis looked in robust health and buoyant spirits. She was attired in a neat navy-blue suit and a plain black hat without a veil."

Judge Alfred Reed, who had presided over the Landis murder trial, read the decision at one o'clock, during which time "little Charley now and again looked back at his mother, but she did not seem to recognize him at any time." Reed explained that the 1871 custody law was a supplement that dealt specifically with divorce situations and did not take into consideration matters crucial to the 1860 law. He declared that it was not a repeal of the earlier law. He also concluded separation of the Landises did, indeed, meet the requirements of the 1860 custody law. In examining the evidence offered on Clara, his conclusion was that

> without reference to the testimony of the parties themselves, and their immediate relatives, I do not think, upon any or all the points upon which

testimony has been taken, it has been proved that the mother is of such character and habits as to render her an improper guardian for such children. By force of the statute, an order should be made that the children be discharged from any restraint by the father, and that they shall be delivered, and remain in the custody of Clara M. Landis, the mother, until they severally attain the age of seven years.

The decision deeply affected Landis and his sister, who rose and, with the nurse, gathered the children to leave the courthouse by the main entrance. Clara stood immediately and headed for the antechamber near the entrance. She was stopped by Parke, who attempted to persuade her not to confront Landis, but her decision had already been made. She encountered Landis in the chamber and, as the *Independent Hour* reported, "a scene ensued which will not soon be forgotten." The moment, captured in the newspaper article, shares an eerie resemblance with Landis's dream three years earlier in which Charles Jr. reached out for his father while being scolded by an unseen figure:

The children, on being taken from the custody of their father, commenced crying and screaming. Charley sobbed out, "Oh! Papa, papa, where is my papa? I want papa! I will not leave him! Kill me – kill me or let me go to my papa" Little Dickie sobbed piteously. The wailing was kept up for nearly an hour, and it could be heard all through the building. Mr. Williamson tried pacifying Mr. Landis, who was greatly affected. Mrs. Landis talked to her husband, but he refused to be consoled. The door of the chamber was closed, and even then the heart-rending sobs of the children could be plainly heard.

Matilda, it was reported, was also deeply moved, having cared for the boys over the previous two years. Yet she made no attempt to interfere. "After an hour's agony," the newspaper reported, "the children were taken by their mother and uncle, Captain Meade, who conveyed them to a carriage which was in waiting outside, and then drove to a railroad depot where they took a train to Mrs. Landis's home in Jersey City. Mr. Landis, dispirited, nearly heartbroken, walked up the street to a hotel and in the evening took his departure for Vineland."

Clara's victory in the custody battle closed the door on a brief but important chapter in Landis's life, one that saw him establish a family only to have it removed with the very legal tools he had used for his own protection. But his wife hadn't been the only person looking to deprive him recently of things he loved.

During the murder trial the previous year, Landis's position as postmaster was vehemently challenged. According to an 1885 article in the *St. Louis Globe-Democrat*, a sort of insurrection was mounted by a Vineland resident not identified by the newspaper. This individual eyed the postmaster position, which paid $1,200 a year, and took advantage of Landis's incarceration to work up a petition that he circulated among the town. After receiving numerous signatures, he, along with a group of friends, departed for Washington to win the appointment of postmaster.

The Vineland contingent met with President Ulysses S. Grant, who had recently visited his visitors' hometown upon the opening of the new Vineland High School facility. Upon learning of the purpose of the group's visit, Grant invited them to join him in the auditor's room of the postal department. Once there, the president requested that the auditor review the accounts of postmaster Landis. Grant was soon informed that the Landis accounts "were square and correct in every particular."

The Vineland committee did not accept this as sufficient reason for Landis to continue to serve as postmaster and argued that because the founder was in jail on charges of murder he should be replaced. Grant acknowledged that he understood the circumstances but ended the meeting by telling the Vinelanders that "the only charge against him is that of shooting an editor, and I do not consider the charge sufficient to justify me in making any change. Good day, gentlemen."

With that, the committee left Washington and returned to Vineland, unsuccessful in their efforts to oust Landis as postmaster and challenge his authority. What these individuals failed to realize was that while Landis met with criticism and opposition from certain residents of Vineland, his reputation in Washington, particularly with a president who had witnessed first-hand what the founder had accomplished, was untarnished. Landis would serve as postmaster for two more years before resigning.

Landis wouldn't resume his journal until summer 1878. The previous three years had been filled with difficulties and disappointments and the opening portion of his July 31 entry, which was excised when the journals were published in the

Vineland Historical Magazine, contains a brief assessment of those intervening years. Having recently regained custody of Charles Jr., Landis explains that he has his son, mother, father and sister living with him before declaring "after three years of the most horrific experience such as rarely falls to the lot of man, I have decided to resume this journal or rather notes of a journal, which it had better be called."

It isn't long before the 1878 entries display traces of a restless Landis, frantically searching for a new project to fulfill his business needs. "Doing nothing in Vineland," he writes, "and having plenty of assets which are unavailable, I must do something – what shall I do?" He confesses that he is "not able to stand work now," and spends his days visiting the Italian community on Garden Road, reading Thomas Carlyle and traveling to Philadelphia in the hopes of obtaining a loan he believes will not materialize.

His first notion is to provide Vineland with a lake. "Not having the means to do it myself, I have put it in the [Lake Company's hands]," he writes. "Attended a meeting in the evening of the Lake Co. about passing the deed. They declined to take the deed at the time and appointed a committee to report the next night." Landis's journals mention Blackwater Pond as a site and it's possible this was, at one point, considered. The town also had previously entertained the idea of building a race track but abandoned the notion as they soon would reject plans for the lake.

It wouldn't be long before Landis would pursue the lake project on his own and, over the next several years, he would set it in motion. According to research conducted by Patricia Martinelli and Mark Demitroff of the Vineland Historical and Antiquarian Society, the Beaver Lake and Dam

Association was begun at a meeting held at Union Hall for the consideration of a Vineland lake on January 24, 1879. A dam was constructed in the vicinity of Mill Road over the next two months and, in April, the Beaver Lake Association, which included Landis, was organized. However, by August the lake was condemned for unsanitary conditions and the project was abandoned, yet Landis continued to pursue it into 1880. As for the race track, Vineland would eventually establish one in the form of the Trotting Club, most likely during the 1880s, but it, too, seems to have been short-lived.

During 1878, Landis first considered adding a sugar plant to Vineland although his efforts seemed to have stalled in the early 1880s. He helped organize the Italian Silk Growers Society of Vineland and worked on establishing a farmers market on Wednesdays and Saturdays. His work for the town may not have been full-time as it had been, but he still devoted considerable energy to his creation.

In his journal, Vineland's founder bemoans the fact that travel has been the great motivator of maintaining his journal and muses that his "life appears to be filled with untoward events at all times. I have always longed for peace and quiet, but it does not appear to be my fate to possess much of it. I can recognize that it may be all for the best, especially if this is a world of probation, which I believe it is…Oh for strength that I may show myself superior to my trouble and still be of some good in the world."

On August 4, 1878, Landis visited Coney Island while in New York. The trip seems crucial in determining the direction he would follow over the next several years. Praising the hotels he toured in the Coney Island area ("they are upon a grand and convenient scale") and other locations

("I saw a bronze fountain…I think would do credit to Italy"),
the seeds of a new project were planted, a resort inspired by
the European sites he had witnessed four years earlier during
his stay in the Tyrol, a period he now referred to as a "happy
time."

During a visit to Boston that August, Landis began
contemplating the establishment of what he called a
"sanitary and art city" that would consist of "different styles
of architecture on different streets. Room for fountains,
monuments and breathtaking places. Each house to have a
garden in front and trees for shade. To be cut off from all
sewers and sewage utilized. Drainage only for clear water.
A building to be erected for a library, reading room,
gymnasium, baths and public hall. Floral, art and literary and
musical societies to be organized." He planned on pricing
homes at $1,000 to $2,000, an offer he placed at half "the
ordinary price."

His 1874 visit to Europe had given him the perfect model
for such a project, England's Shaftsbury Park Estate, and he
would return to this idea early in the next decade. For the
moment, elements of his design for this utopian project
would first find their way into the novel on which he was
currently working and the seaside resort project that would
take shape the following year. In fact, one of the most
striking feature of his upcoming resort would be the
realization of a separate sewage and drainage system he had
already discussed in his plans for a "sanitary and art city."
For his new settlement, Landis would abandon the idea of
cesspools, requiring each building to have above-ground
receptacles composed of iron or brick and concrete for the
containment of human waste. Residents would be required

to remove the waste from the island. These precautions prevented diseases like cholera that had been a problem in urban areas that allowed waste to contaminate drainage.

The business trips Landis undertook at the time were not enough to diminish the financial difficulties he faced. Recent New Jersey legislature threatened the repeal of the charter of the Philadelphia and Cape May Short Line Railroad, a system he had "considerable money locked up in." To add to the difficulties, the Landis Township Committee had raised his taxes $800 without any notice and was looking to collect on August 6. "I have nothing to pay them with," Landis confesses in his journal the day before. He admits that he has "$350,000 worth of property on hand and about $75,000 coming to me from contracts of sale of land…upon which I can collect very little" and fears that he will lose it all. "There is no confidence among the people," he reflects in his journal. "The policy of contraction and paying off the National debt like a great boa constrictor has squeezed the life out of many people and it is tightening around me every day."

Landis resorted to approaching the Wood family for a loan of $600 for three months and was turned down. His financial situation had reached a point where he agreed to become a salesman for the Woods for a tract of land in Cumberland County that would earn him a 3% commission if he was successful in selling it. Ultimately, however, Landis relied upon sales of his land to stir a financial resurrection, selling property at a reduced rate of $15 per acre which increased the number of buyers as well as the amount of acreage sold. Still, he grew despondent, writing, "I work hard but my mind is much disturbed about financial matters. I shall do my duty, after that I shall trust to God, who has never yet deserted me."

An attempt to borrow money by giving contracts as collateral failed. Landis reasoned that, with his taxes and debts, "$45,000 would pay everything off and free me," but admits that he never "was a skillful borrower, never possessed the art, never tried to do it before." He was able to convince the tax collector to accept $100 and delayed the township's advertised sale of property until later in the week in order to legally investigate the matter and file a claim against the township for previously overpaid taxes. He hired William House to represent him. But by August 15, Landis was feeling a bit desperate and offered half of his unsold Vineland land to a prospective buyer for "about $53,000."

It was during this year that Landis accepted an offer to have the Venetian artist, Vincent Stepevech, paint his portrait for $400, a fee that would be paid in 16 acres of land. The offer was made by Secchi de Casoli, the editor of the Italian-language newspaper *L'Ecod'Italia* in which Landis advertised Vineland. Landis met with the artist at de Casoli's home in Elizabeth, New Jersey on August 12 and on August 26, but it was a visit to Stepevech's New York studio that convinced Landis this was the person to paint his portrait. On September 4, the artist visited Vineland and was shown five lots he would receive in payment for his work. The following month, Landis began sitting for his portrait, which was completed the next year and now hangs in the Vineland Historical and Antiquarian Society building.

At home, Landis spent considerable time with Charles Jr., "very thankful to God that I have got him." There were visits to the park, to Philadelphia and to other sites as well as attending the celebration of Vineland's seventeenth birthday, during which "Charley...enjoyed himself immensely." Landis also enrolled his son at a private school that met in the basement of the Congregational Church on the corner of 7th and Elmer Streets. The class had seven other students. The proud father seemed to savor his time with his son, doting on him in a way that wasn't repeated with his younger children.

One of the things that captured his attention during 1878 was the local efforts of the Greenback Party and its convention, and Landis made room in his schedule not only to attend meetings but to lecture and apply his legal skills to this group's cause. This national political organization took its name from the term for the paper money issued by the North during the Civil War that was not backed by the gold standard. Greenbacks lasted for some time after the war, even surviving the passage of the Resumption Act in 1875 that returned things to a gold-backed currency. The Greenback Party saw a problem with the gold standard because it was controlled by banks and not the federal government, thereby giving an advantage to the wealthy industrialists over common laborers. The movement was established in 1873 by mostly farmers in their pursuit of reform and initially lacked laborers in other fields of work because the Panic of 1873 had considerably weakened unions. In 1877, the onset of national strikes and the intervention of federal troops opened the door for other workers to join this political organization.

The party would dissolve in the late 1880s, its efforts unproductive during its final decade, but during the late 1870s, it succeeded in placing twenty-one members in

Congress, including one from New Jersey. According to Elizabeth Sanders's *Roots of Reform: Farmers, Workers, and the American State, 1877-1917*, "the year 1878 proved to be the electoral high point for the Greenback Movement..."

Landis's interests were reflected in his involvement during 1878. Always a proponent of the farmer, he saw the movement as a means of providing agricultural laborers with an opportunity to remain above debt by championing a currency not backed by the gold that gave bankers a share of the wealth. The platforms of the newly christened Greenback-Labor Party were associated with the Grange, the agrarian organization whose local newspaper had been published by Uri Carruth. The two movements overlapped in advancing the interests of the farmer as well as welcoming the women's vote. It did not approve of speculators who bought "unbacked" currency at a deflated cost with gold-backed notes and then solicited Congress to allow them to redeem it for a profit. It also endorsed the eight-hour work day and opposed the use of state and federal suppression of any union strikes.

On August 25, 1878, Landis wrote resolutions for the Greenback Convention seeking the repeal of the Resumption Act, a campaign that would be pursued vigorously over the following year to no avail. On the afternoon of September 12, he attended the Greenback Convention, observing the proceedings and noting that "railroad corporations had the influence to have voted down every resolution against them. They will always own the conventions I fear."

The corporate control, however, did not deter him. Two days later, he was reading *The Advocate*, a Greenback-Labor

Party publication which he proclaimed was "full of information." He continued his research into the party's stance with a book about money written for the organization by Marcus Pomeroy and followed it with a steady diet of pamphlets and books "on the Greenback question." At an October 3 meeting, he addressed an audience of substantial size on the Greenback-Labor issues. But over the next year, his fervor diminished as a new major project began to consume most of his time.

It was in 1878 that Landis began to reconnect with individuals and locales of his past. During a stop in Hammonton, Landis paid a visit to his former partner, Richard Byrnes, but discovered that he was away. He also stopped in to see Andrew Hay, a farming acquaintance from the time Vineland was founded, at his home in Winslow, only to discover that, instead of the healthy businessman he had heard Hay had become, his friend was now an invalid. Landis also undertook a trip on August 14 to Lancaster, Pennsylvania where, as a youth, he had visited family and created memories that were now stirred upon his return. In his journal he describes the Catholic Church and revisits the Lutheran Church, which he calls "the finest steeple in the state with four apostles, life size, upon it," and recalls that he "used to look upon them when a boy and wonder if they would ever change" now concluding that "there is no change yet."

Landis spent much of 1878 working on a short novel entitled *A Trip to Mars*, a story of imagination that centered on a character journeying into space. Landis may have begun work on it over the previous year or so, but 1878 is when he clearly made a concerted effort to complete the book. A journal entry, dated August 2, 1878, reveals that he is in the midst of writing his "article, book or whatever it may turn out to be, called *A Trip to Mars*," admitting that "it takes a deal of hard thinking and I am a slow writer. Oh, for the pen of [Sir Walter] Scott or [Charles] Dickens," struggling at times with "lethargy or laziness," yet persevering with the project into the following year when it was presumably completed.

This fictional tale concerns the adventures of a nameless narrator who is rescued by a Rosicrucian community in the Tyrol region of Austria and decides to join them. He is mentored and befriended by the learned Count and, with the advanced technology of the Rosicrucian society, they are able to plan and execute a two-man expedition to the Red Planet where they encounter and explore Martian society. The book is a mix of adventure and philosophy that allows Landis to both entertain and examine relevant social issues of the time.

A Trip to Mars manages to distill the features of the best of 19th century science fiction into a blend of philosophical and scientific discourse and action-packed sequences. The science of the novel is careful not to borrow too freely from Jules Verne or other authors' methods of space travel and relies on the narrator's own learning process to make the flight plausible for the reader if not for the world of aeronautics.

Landis frames the novel with explanations about a traveler's discovery of a tin in Africa containing the Mars manuscript, which contends to be an eye-witness account of the events described. In concluding the book, he provides a comment from "the editor" on the sudden ending of the story and speculation on whether there is more to the tale, promising that "a diligent search shall be kept up for the remainder nearby where this was found." While the technique serves to dispel any disbelief that might accompany an early science fiction story, the execution here is only passable and not as effective as it would be in a later fictional works by Landis.

Landis's 1874 trip to Europe, particularly his extended stay at Matzen Castle in the Tyrol, figures prominently in the novel's settings. From the beginning of the book, the narrator describes the paradise of earth as being between Salzberg and the Alps, between Holl and Innsbruck, locations Landis discovered when visiting the Tyrol. While out for a stroll during a violent storm, he is rendered unconscious by thunder and awakens in a Medieval-style room where he meets his rescuer, the appropriately named Count Matzen, proprietor of the castle where he has been taken.

The Rosicrucian community is housed in the mountains of the Tyrol, and the narrator's descriptions of the scenery are reminiscent of Landis's accounts of the area in his journal entries. On August 15, 1874, the day of his arrival at Matzen Castle, Landis writes that it was "raining hard" and that "mountains around [were] covered with snow; hundreds of streams pouring down the mountainside." On August 24, he writes that Matzen Castle "command[s] a view of the mountains, the valley and the winding and swift rushing Inn [River]..." When the narrator of *A Trip to Mars* is placed before a window during his recuperation, he describes the view in a similar fashion:

I saw before me a green valley through which stretched a river. At the borders of the valley were high and broken mountains. It had rained the night before, and thousands of cascades were falling down their rocky sides. Some of these mountains were crowned by old castles and at different places were to be seen old convents and monasteries.

Landis had the opportunity to visit some of the monasteries mentioned by the narrator of his novel. On August 19, he and the Grohmans trekked to the town of Schwartz where "we visited the monastery which, with its long Gothic arcades and old glass, was wonderfully impressive. We then went to the old church, a vast building...We also went through the churchyard, all filled with gilded crosses and crucifixes and kept in the best order." Schwartz is somewhat similar to a village the narrator of *A Trip to Mars* visits late in the book and describes for the reader: "In the center was a beautiful old palace, brown with age. The spire of a church rose behind it, but the main portion of which was hidden by the palace, and the spire was surmounted by a gilded cross."

Landis's visit to the Tyrol is not the only autobiographical strand in the novel. The author's involvement with the secret society of Freemasons would have given him insight into the Rosicrucian society from which the Masons were descended. And Clara's desertion is also present in the novel. When the narrator is offered a place in the Rosicrucian community and an apprenticeship in the ways of the secretive group, he chooses to return to the girl he loves back in America. But she has run off to marry someone else, and the narrator, filled with despair, retreats to the Tyrol to accept the offer he was given.

Aboard the ship that carried him back to Europe, he attends a lecture about Mars given by an astronomer. He eventually convinces the Count that the Rosicrucian advancements in technology might make a trip to Mars possible in order to meet the inhabitants they already know are there. The two of them are eventually launched into space, escaping Earth's gravity and placing their crude space vehicle into the line of Mars's gravitational pull.

At first, the narrator is fascinated with the new culture. One of the things that impresses him early on is the way a Martian city is laid out, and its resemblance to Vineland is not coincidental. The 66-foot wide main street is described as immaculately clean, with trees lining the avenue to provide shade. Sidewalks are paved with bricks and flower gardens fill the yards of houses for purposes of health and ornamentation. There are also other streets that are narrow with taller houses.

Landis's tendency to promote the features of his town can be found in other sections of the novel. The importance of trees is discussed by members of the Martian family who host the narrator and provide him with most of his knowledge of the planet. The family consists of thinly disguised members of the Grohman clan who served a similar function when Landis visited the Tyrol, and their graciousness, intellect and love of nature and art are transferred lovingly to the fictional Martians. When they venture into a discussion of trees, they echo Landis's own philosophy that their purpose is not only aesthetic in providing shade and practical by serving as homes for birds and bearing nuts and fruit, but historical as well, linking later generations with the one that planted it. Isole, the name the narrator gives to the mother of the Martian family, explains: "We found in long ages past that man could not live without the trees. They attract rains, prevent droughts, prevent sudden changes in the atmosphere, afford homes to birds who not only fill the air with song, but they eat the insect destroyers of our fruits, vegetables and grains. Besides shade, the planting of trees is morally elevating. The man or woman or child that plants a shade tree, does something for someone else than themselves. Something for future ages, and the mind and feelings are broadened, deepened and liberalized by the thought that follows the act. In our schools all this is taught. Children are taught to know that in order to be happy themselves, they must seek the welfare of others…"

Temperance is also explored in the novel and its treatment reveals what Landis may have ultimately hoped to achieve with his Vineland settlement. When the narrator inquires about drunkenness, he is told by the Martians that it was a problem solved thousands of years ago. The system of training and marriage relations had the effect of making people happy, so there was no need to "narcotize or etherize their senses." Isole explains:

> This in a high degree is a mental vice. A temporary suicide. It is akin to insanity. When people were taught music and were secured the sweets of conjugal and paternal love, and the wolf of want was driven from the door by our adoption of our human form of

government, the joy of life was found in existing, not in flying from it..."

In the novel, Mars is a re-imagined version of Earth. The ornamentation of many Martian homes seems to derive from Ancient Greece and, because of the inability to translate names from the Martian language, the narrator gives each of his new acquaintances names from Greek antiquity. Martian villages also bear an uncanny resemblance to the towns Landis toured during his time at Matzen Castle. In a similar fashion, Martians resemble humans but govern with a different set of laws and limitations. The foundation of their principles, we eventually discover, consists of a palpable human system of ideologies reminiscent of our own late 19th century schools of thought. In this way, Landis's book is more akin to Jonathan Swift's *Gulliver's Travels* in which the various lands visited contain recognizable traits of English society. Landis may not be interested in Swiftian satire, but he does intend to debate the various issues pervading the novel by slowly unraveling the ideological threads for both the narrator and the reader.

The novel may also be read as the dream of the narrator who, at the start of the book is rendered unconscious by the storm. The remainder of the book contains hints that the events are merely the fabrications of a dream state. "Though I have met with great surprises, yet could imagine that we had not left the earth," the narrator tells the Count. A village visited later in the novel reminds the narrator of places he's seen in Europe and he admits he would have thought he had awakened from a dream if it weren't for seeing his companions.

Ultimately, Landis manages to use his fictional work to express opinions on various matters with impunity. When the Martians explain that their government cares for citizens in need by evenly distributing funds among them, the narrator takes umbrage over the existence of such a welfare system. The more he discovers about social systems of the planet, the more he finds himself in opposition. Having discovered he is in a society without taxes, class systems and big government, he argues that it is better to be taxed, to have rich and poor and to have communications and travel controlled by private ownership. He learns that women on Mars must marry by the age of twenty and men by the age of twenty-four. Those who refuse are made warriors, with the women preparing traps and snares, working in hospitals and providing other prescribed services. Some marry while warriors and return home. The narrator calls all this madness.

The young on Mars are trained mentally, physically and industrially and are given an inheritance from the state when they start out on their own. They then set to work, using the "skill in the arts" they have learned. The inheritance from the government comes from
the property of those who die. Citizens are allowed to own property if they use it as a residence or a business, but anything unoccupied cannot be privately owned. Individuals can make up to $100,000, but anything beyond that is given to the public treasury, which uses all inherited money to provide for the people in terms of care for the elderly, maintenance, programs, etc. Those who contribute a lot are seen as benefactors and may have statues erected to them, and there is an abundance of statues on Mars. The author

treats such socialistic tendencies with disdain but allows the Martian leader to defend his stance:

> That order only should be followed which is for the good of the parents, the children and the state. In ages past, when our laws of inheritance were different, and when all went for hundreds of years to the eldest son, and afterwards to all the children, share and share alike, it was found that the pure natural affection of the child was sometimes corrupted by sordid influences, and frequently there was most disgraceful litigation over the property at the death of a parent. They appeared sometimes to be as bad as a lot of vultures ready not only to devour all that was left, but even destroy the good name of a father to accomplish their purposes. It was also found that the prospect of wealth without labor made idle children and sometimes those worthless, who otherwise might have been valuable and happy citizens. Consideration, therefore, for the welfare of all parties and that of the Commonwealth induced the change and it has been found to work most happily.

It's conceivable that the novel's stance against socialistic or communistic tendencies arose from a contemporary movement known as the Republic of Industry, which was derived from the philosophies of Jean-Baptiste Andre Godin, a French industrialist who developed a self-contained community in the late 1850s in Guise, France. The community provided housing for nine hundred of his industrial workers within a development known as the Familistere or Social Palace. In addition to a factory, there were three four-story buildings that provided housing for the workers as well as stores, recreation rooms and courtyards.

Godin, whose ideas were based on Francoise Marie Charles Fourier's concepts of a co-operative society, had aided in the funding of Le Reunion, an intentional community in the area of what became Dallas, Texas. Its failure provided Godin with the understanding of how a successful version of such a utopian venture could be undertaken in Guise.

The Republic of Industry was an American offshoot of Godin's project. It nicknamed itself the First Guise Association of America and published a pamphlet entitled "A Concise Plan for the Reconstruction of Society." The booklet is dated October 20, 1876, and it was printed in Vineland since the location it had secured for a U.S. version of the Familistere was 319 acres of land "three miles from the beautiful village of Vineland, on Landis Avenue, running directly to Bridgeton." The organization felt that communism was "a standard of human excellence to be attained," but saw it as a future accomplishment that would be achieved through practical implementation of work and equality and the elimination of selfishness and the conditions by which society enslaves women. It rejected the institution of marriage in the same way the free-love movement of the 19th century saw matrimony as threatening to women who marry into an abusive relationship.

Landis would certainly have been apprised of the Republic of Industry's local plans and would no doubt have been aware that he had received mention in the organization's pamphlet. "Mr. C.K. Landis of this place has done more to develop its capabilities than all others combined…" John Wilcox writes in one of the essays before he levels a criticism against Vineland's founder as harsh as the first statement was complementary: "One mistake has been made that has resulted in disappointment to many who came here with bright hopes. That mistake cannot be remedied in isolation. A thousand families cannot run a thousand little homes on five or ten acres each, support a team and secure the necessary outfits for so many homes and meet the necessary expense for living from year to year."

Maintaining his group's agenda, Wilcox then explains how the mistake could be corrected if "the same number of families, with the amount of capital to make a scanty provision for so many homes, with all the land combined as the basis for an association, could erect a magnificent palace capable of accommodating all with all of the comforts and luxuries that the wealthy classes enjoy." Such a notion would have been taken as an affront by Landis, and the anti-socialistic themes in the novel may well derive from this Guise-like local experiment, for which there is no evidence of it ever coming to fruition.

In the end, what destroys the Martian society's sheen of perfection for the narrator is the discovery that, in order to maintain a society without jails, drastic measures must be taken. It is explained that prisons were eliminated thousands of years earlier because it was determined that disease made someone a criminal and either an individual had the disease or not. Around the time of reforms for individuals who were deformed or diseased or simply classified as "idiotic children," the state concluded that a diseased brain or nervous system produced criminal acts and should be treated as such. In the event of two convictions for a crime, a person was counseled on each occasion about right and wrong. In the case of a third conviction, he or she was put to death since it was no longer deemed a disease. The rationale behind such actions was that it rid society of a permanent criminal class.

The narrator questions whether this isn't inhumane but is told that it protects the citizens from the inhumane acts of the criminal. The Count says that if Earth could adapt this, it would provide more happiness for people. The narrator then asks how drunkenness is handled and is told that it is treated as a criminal act and subject to the same consequences, especially since drunkenness leads people to selfishness and passion that, in turn, lead to other crimes. The narrator doesn't agree with treating drunkenness as a crime and is informed that the Martians had the same outlook for several thousand years yet determined that drink is the cause of not only crimes but deformity and idiocy as well.

When asked by the narrator how the great doctors had reformed the laws for those deformed, diseased or classified as "idiotic children," he is told they are all put to death with an anesthetic. The narrator is shocked. He is informed that the Martians felt the same as he does thousands of years ago, but then discovered that the criminals and drunks were "largely recruited from the children of the deformed, diseased and idiotic" and that "allowing them to live simply was giving life to suffering, disease and crime." The Count agrees, saying that this is the same "advanced idea as the most learned physicians upon the Earth," and as soon as people achieve sufficient intelligence, this will be the way of Earth as well.

Landis's warnings about the practice of eugenics in the U.S. was prescient. Several years after *A Trip to Mars* was completed, the U.S. government became intent on preventing "impurities" from infiltrating America and established safeguards against immigrants. Congress passed a law to prohibit those considered "mentally defective" from entering the country through Ellis Island, even though such a task was impossible to achieve with 5,000 immigrants awaiting inspection on a daily basis. But by the start of the 20th century, monitoring was possible thanks to a screening system devised by Henry Herbert Goddard, the future Director of Research at the Vineland Training School. It was only after World War II and Nazi atrocities that any favorable outlook on eugenics faded.

Mars may be a glimpse of Earth's possible dystopian future, but its evolution is not yet complete in the book. The arrival of the Count, whose introduction of steam power and guns to this world, may guarantee its inevitable destruction. The novel contains a series of action sequences, all of which center on the testing of firearms against outlying creatures that raid the Martian society for food and prey. The last and best of the action sequences, which takes up a good portion of the second half of the book following the protagonists' foray into dangerous territories, is a riveting sequence that makes the reader wonder how long it will be before the Martians become the species hunting food and prey in these other territories.

Although there is no record of its progress in 1879, the novel was probably completed during this year since Landis shared the manuscript with an acquaintance early in 1880 in the hopes that it would be published. Filled with the reminiscences of his European trip as much as it addressed the futuristic mode of space travel and debated the social systems of the 19th century, the novel would be shelved and wouldn't see publication until 2015, when it was made available by the Vineland Historical and Antiquarian Society and Stockton University. Until then, there had only been vague rumors of its existence and it was usually dismissed as simply legend. Yet it stands as a significant achievement, both literary and entrepreneurial, for in a way, *A Trip to Mars* allowed Landis, if only in print, to found yet another colony, albeit one that did not entirely meet with his approval.

On Christmas Day 1879, Landis wrote a children's story entitled "The Lion and the Prince of the Fairies," which was presumably the work he submitted to *St. Nicholas Magazine* the following month. It was rejected, prompting Landis to write, "My attempts to be an author are very discouraging. How do people get their writing in print? That is the question." The failure to publish *A Trip to Mars* and "The Lion and the Prince of the Fairies" would sidetrack Landis's literary aspirations for over a decade.

By 1879, aware that any attempt at maneuvering himself into the town's politics would be fruitless, he had begun to consider establishing a shore resort shortly after the June newspapers were announcing that he had been granted a divorce from Clara on the grounds of desertion. He closed the door on that chapter in his life and began another, writing in his journal as the 1870s drew to a close that he "must do something." And that he did. According to Michael Landis's journal at the time, his son visited New York and Philadelphia regularly throughout the first six months of 1879 in pursuit of real estate deals.

By the middle of the year, the acquisition of property at the South Jersey coastal location known as Ludlam's Island would become the focus of his attention. His schedule would consume so much time that he put his journal on hold until the final days of the year when he reported that he had already accumulated over one-hundred-and-fifty signatures of Ludlam's Island property owners willing to sell their lots in order for his new town to be born. He was now divorced from Clara and Richard had returned to the Landis household in Vineland. All that awaited was a new decade for new opportunities.

Chapter 8
Temperance

From the start, Landis felt that Vineland should remain dry, free from the temptations of alcohol and, despite several attempts to change that rule, the founder's wishes were preserved into the 20th century. The *American Heritage Dictionary* defines temperance as "moderation and self - restraint" and "abstinence from alcoholic liquors." In his *Autobiography*, Benjamin Franklin placed it at the top of his list of necessary virtues in achieving moral perfection. The Tarot card for temperance depicts an angelic figure balancing liquid between two containers. It was the subject of a full-scale, largely female-led movement in the late 19th century to eradicate the use of alcoholic beverages. And, for Vineland, it served as one of the stipulations demanded by the town's founder for those settling here. But the choice to eliminate alcohol from his community had more to do with Landis's vision than his own religious or political convictions.

In the year 1851, temperance advocates were handed a victory when Maine passed a law mandating that the entire state would be dry. The door to prohibition was now open and temperance groups from other states, according to *The Library Company of Philadelphia*, shifted "goals from keeping people away from liquor to keeping liquor away from people."

Landis, while practicing law in Philadelphia in the 1850s, would have been familiar with temperance propaganda in the form of woodcuttings of the time and might have read Philadelphian T.S. Arthur's novel *Ten Nights in a Bar-Room*, part of what became known as temperance fiction, which revealed the sordid and depressing effects drink had on individuals and families. In addition, Landis would have seen how temperance activists, who were usually also involved in the antislavery and women's suffrage movements, associated drinking with the devil.

Yet Landis, like Franklin, pursued a personal goal disconnected from any movement. Franklin could have been describing the outlook of Vineland's founder when he wrote, "Temperance first, as it tends to procure that coolness and clearness of head, which is so necessary where constant vigilance was to be kept up, and guard maintained against the unremitting attraction of ancient habits, and the force of perpetual temptations." But, whereas Franklin's intentions were to achieve his own moral perfection, Landis's vision was more concerned with the effect temperance would have on the planned community of Vineland.

Charles Nordhoff, in his 1875 book *The Communistic Societies of the United States*, quotes from Landis's 1874 address before the New Jersey State Legislature in which Vineland's founder declares that he had not selected temperance as a founding principle because of any philanthropic motives. "I am not a temperance man in the total-abstinence sense," Landis told the legislators. "I conceived it to be of vital importance to the success of my colony. If in this thought I had seen that liquor made men more industrious, more skillful, more economical, and more aesthetic in their tastes, I certainly should then have made liquor-selling one of the main principles of my project."

Landis was aware of how the sale of liquor could jeopardize the mental acuity and physical labor necessary to develop his settlement yet realized the success of his town risked being compromised by the exclusion of saloons. In "The Social Science of Vineland," he acknowledged that "many persons had the idea that no place could prosper without taverns - that to attract business and strangers, taverns were necessary." As new settlers arrived, he understood that those who subscribed to total abstinence were a minority and accepted "that to benefit an entire community the law or regulation would have to extend to the entire community. In examining the evil I found, also, that the moderate use of liquor was not the difficulty to contend against, but it was the immoderate use of it."

He concluded that, of those who regularly imbibed, "few or none ever became intoxicated in their own families, in the presence of their wives and children, but that the drunkards were made in taverns and saloons. After this conclusion was reached, the way appeared clear. It was not necessary to make temperance men of each individual."

It is generally believed that Landis attempted to shun liquor altogether in Vineland and the surrounding township during the earliest decades, but that is not true. As he explained, "it was not necessary to abridge the right or privilege that people might desire of keeping liquor in their own houses, but to get their consent to prevent the public sale of it; so that people, in bartering, might not be subject to the custom of drinking, and might not have the opportunity of drinking in barrooms, away from all home restraint or influence. In short, I believed that if the public sale of liquor was stopped, both in taverns and beer-saloons, the knife would reach the root of the evil."

The founder personally met with residents to discuss the matter. He refused to treat the issue from a moral perspective, instead explaining that

> I was not a total abstinence man myself, but saw clearly the liability to abuse, when liquor was placed in seductive forms at every street corner; that it incited crime, and made men unfortunate who would otherwise succeed; that most of the settlers had a little money to begin with, sums varying from two hundred to a thousand dollars, which, if added to a man's labor, would be enough, in many cases, to obtain him a home, but which, taken to the tavern, would melt away like snow before a spring sun; that new places were liable to have this abuse to a more terrible extent than old places, as men were removed from the restraints of old associations, and brought

into the excitement of forming new acquaintances; and that it was a notorious fact that liquor-drinking did not add to the inclination for physical labor. I then asked them, for the sake of their sons, brothers, friends, to help establish the new system, as I believed it to be the foundation stone of future prosperity.

Landis had no problem convincing the earliest residents, particularly those who had already witnessed the effects of liquor sales in the western states. As he points out in his writings, the prohibition of the sale of alcohol in Landis Township was not the result of a unanimous decision by temperance advocates but was based "upon broad social and public principles." Vineland began life as a dry town, but some residents were not in agreement with the founder's outlook. By 1863, it became necessary to legally defend its temperance-based status.

The first town temperance meeting occurred on June 10, 1863, during which a committee was established to record the population's reactions to a dry town. A report the following day showed an overwhelming majority in favor of temperance, with Benjamin B. Bowen and William Hilton the only two residents against it. Four citizens chose not to express an opinion.

But Landis's vision was already challenged by a man identified by chronicler A. G. Warner only as Rollins, the owner of a grocery store on a corner of Landis Avenue and the Boulevard. Rollins's name does not appear in the survey taken by the temperance committee, but it was obvious where he stood on the topic of selling beer to boys and wood choppers in the township. Another meeting was called, and the perpetrator of the offense was confronted. Rollins defended himself by saying that he was licensed by the U.S. Government to sell liquor and had no intentions of halting his sale of alcohol. Despite an impassioned argument from Landis, the gathering accomplished nothing. However, the organization's members had already pledged to "withdraw our custom or patronage from any store that may sell alcohol" and after adjourning, a group of them met unofficially on the street and Rollins was confronted again about discontinuing his sale of liquor. Having been advised by friends, in the interim, about a projected loss of business, the store owner agreed to the crowd's demands and soon left the region.

The incident led the settlement to collect 228 signatures for a petition that prompted a law declaring the sale of alcoholic beverages in Vineland punishable by a fine of fifty dollars or imprisonment or both. The sale of liquor became unlawful in Landis Township as well.

Eleven years later, Landis told New Jersey State Legislators that "the results in Vineland have convinced me that temperance does conserve the industry of people…is conducive to a refined and aesthetical taste… [and] can be sufficiently secured in a community."

In his 1882 account of the founding of Vineland, Landis was even more specific about his reasons for establishing a dry town:

> I knew that, for years, rich people would not come to such a banquet as this, where they would not be permitted to buy [land] on speculation. It was

337

therefore important that people should have the full use of their health, strength and faculties, that they might be able to labor with all their might and, efficiently, and also be happy in their homes, with all of which liquor sadly interferes. In fact, I had never known a sober man to be a pauper. I also knew that the temptation to drink would be much stronger in a new country than in an old one, and that wives and families would be terrified if the evil of drink were to be added to the trials they would be called upon to endure.

During its early years, Vineland took temperance seriously. The town was founded on the principle that the sale of liquor was not to be a component, thereby ensuring that its citizens maintained a clear and focused vision. In an untitled and undated manuscript, Landis discusses Vineland's continued growth, taking the opportunity to mention that "its temperance principle, founded upon the ballots, is like a dove folding its wings of peace over many a little household." The movement met with little opposition early on, but those in favor of liquor sales grew as the years progressed and the rallying cry of prohibition would eventually be silenced in an unexpected fashion.

Warner explains that "every year it is submitted to a vote of the people whether any tavern shall be licensed to sell liquor." The publication of Warner's account of the town was 1869, eight years after Vineland's founding, and he reports that in recent elections "there was not one vote cast in favor of liquor selling." The reaction was seemingly the result of Landis's founding principle, but as time passed it seems that a considerable amount of campaigning and preaching on the part of several temperance organizations sustained the movement's march into the 20th century, but not without challenges along the way.

Landis remained interested in societies that had managed to control drunkenness, particularly those he encountered during his European trips, and was impressed by the effect it had. He even read up on reports on the effects of alcohol. In 1880, he examined a study that showed that, of the students graduating from Cambridge College that year, those with the highest averages contained one smoker for every ten and those with the lowest averages contained nine smokers for every ten. He concluded that this demonstrated "tobacco, as well as alcohol, is a paralyzer to the intellect instead of a stimulant."

Around 1887, Landis drew media attention for a letter addressing the issue of temperance in Vineland. An extant clipping from an unidentified publication explains that, in his letter, Landis addressed an uprising of anti-temperance sentiment and, quoting from a *Philadelphia Daily News* article, reveals that the letter appeals to residents to support temperance in the upcoming election. He chooses to conclude his letter with a well-delivered, clear-cut directive to the citizens of Vineland: "Here is what you have done, citizens of Vineland. After twenty-five years…the work of your hands is to be taken away from you. We have with God's help…made Vineland into a temperance town and no man shall take it from us…Will you allow the slander to stand, that we are worse than Sea Isle City? Or will you come out boldly at the ballot box on Tuesday – the 28th of August – and crush this thing into insignificance and nothingness with the prerogative of the free-born American citizen?" He reminds them of their civil rights, telling them to "exercise them and down the sentiment which does not respect our rights as citizens who have made the place what it is. You came to a temperance town. You have a right to a temperance town. Show your right at the ballot box and cast a vote 'against' the sale of intoxicants."

Residents did just that, and Vineland remained a dry town, but it wasn't long before a new threat arose. In the fall of 1891, Vineland prepared for the biggest challenge to its temperance law. A letter from Landis would not have much effect this time, but although the odds seemed to be against them, Vinelanders were ready to rally behind Mayor C.P. Lord to fend off this new threat of liquor sales.

The menace itself had taken shape the previous winter when New Jersey Governor Leon Abbett proposed and successfully campaigned for a bill whereby County Excise Boards could be appointed in each of the state's counties to override any restrictions local governments might establish concerning the licensing of saloons. A petition of one hundred signatures was all that was required to secure a board whose powers could fill towns with any number of establishments that served liquor.

The law directly threatened Vineland's temperance code and Millville's seventeen-year dry state. By September, Bridgeton succumbed as saloons sprang up throughout the city. Applications for licenses in Millville indicated the Holly City would be the next to fall. But as of October 16, when the *New York Times* ran a story on the controversy stirring in Cumberland County, Vineland had not yet received any requests for licenses, and the town was determined to keep it that way. The town railed against Abbett, calling his law "an outrage" and christening the governor the "Czar of Jersey." The *New York Times* reported that residents saw fit to boycott anyone in the community who favored an influx of saloons. Street corners were filled with embittered citizens whose chatter was comprised of the details of the excise law.

Soon enough, Abbett was being accused of buying the support of the liquor dealers in the state, with the *New York Times* pointing out that the governor was once the solicitor for the State Liquor Dealers' Association. Vineland planned to battle the new law from all fronts. Its legal approach, however, had to contend with an oversight in its own charter. When, as a village, the municipality was first granted a charter in 1864, it provided that the residents would have the right each year to vote on the issue of allowing alcohol to be sold within the town. Annually, the vote had overwhelmingly, although not always unanimously, rejected the sale of liquor. The most recent election had upheld the temperance lifestyle by a vote of 614 to 31.

When Vineland was incorporated as a borough, however, it had failed to include in its charter the same provision for an annual vote on the sale of alcohol. While elections still included the topic on its ballots, the misstep gave prospective saloon owners ammunition in their battle to establish their businesses in Vineland.

But Vinelanders weren't merely brandishing legal weapons. When Borough Councilman Charles W. Wiley was asked by the *New York Times* what he thought would be the result of anyone opening a saloon in the municipality, he responded, "I think he would be given a coat of tar and feathers...I believe the women of this town would throw eggs at the man who started a saloon. He would not be received in anybody's family, and he would need a regiment to protect his place of business. Another regiment would watch for his patrons, and they would be severely let alone by the better element of the place."

City Solicitor Henry S. Alvord, who questioned the constitutionality of the excise law, also provided a clear picture of how the residents would deal with saloon owners. "I would not be surprised," he stated, "to see a vigilance committee formed to ride the saloon keeper out of town on a rail...I would not be surprised to see a mob burn his buildings."

Vineland would successfully fend off the arrival of saloons until 1933, so the verbal threats never became reality. But Landis, while not condoning the proposed actions, provided an explanation that reveals something about the early settlers. "Many people who are living here had been drinking people," he told the press. "They came here because they knew there was no liquor to be had, and they could not resist it if it were to be had at local saloons...they hoped to be away from the temptation, and now that there is a possibility that saloons may be opened – perhaps in the buildings next to their own houses – they are violent in their denunciation of the proceedings that made this possible."

The temperance movement here was not without a headquarters. According to an informative lecture given by W. F.Tower before the Vineland Historical and Antiquarian Society in 1911 and printed in a 1930 edition of the *Vineland Historical Magazine*, Temperance Hall served as the center of the local movement, housing various meetings, lectures, activities and rallies. Tower, a resident of Glendale, California at the time of the lecture, stated that his involvement with Vineland's temperance groups was during the 1880s and 1890s and cited that the first organization he joined was the Independent Order of Good Templars, a society comprised largely of "young people of both sexes."

Tower informed his audience that the group followed the principles of "total abstinence for the individual and prohibition for the state and nation, and without doubt, the educational influence exerted was good and wholesome." He estimated the membership of the local society at around 250.

The Vineland Temperance Union, Tower said, was another organization that consisted largely of young members who were intent on spreading the word of prohibition. The group would meet each Monday night at Temperance Hall. The gatherings were comprised of not only talks and discussions, but musical performances as well. The youthful members, Tower explained, were "urged to develop the talent of recitation and vocal and instrumental music and thus builded [sic] for future usefulness and awakened and cultivated a deep interest in the traditions upon which Vineland was builded [sic], an infinitely better training than the moving picture and cheap theatres of today."

In addition to the hall hosting the Union, it also served as a meeting spot for the Loyal Temperance Legion, a headquarters for Sunday afternoon gospel temperance gatherings and the site of regular and public meetings of the Woman's Christian Temperance Union as well as an outlet for the organization's public library. Tower said that on one occasion, the hall was utilized for a special meeting of the Borough Commission for a hearing on a curfew law.

During his lecture, Tower brought up a curious incident concerning the use of the facility. He remarked that a group called the Law and Order Society "met [there] to consider ways and means to preserve the temperance principles of Vineland by punishing offenders" and went on to explain that this group succeeded in preventing a man identified only as Stetser "from enjoying a license for the Borough of Vineland, granted by the odious County Excise Board in the year 1892."

According to the *Vineland Times Journal* this organization, the Law and Order League, had been "composed of noble-spirited citizens...so powerful that [Vineland Borough] administrations had done little to stamp out the under-the-counter sales of liquor." The article attributes the effectiveness of the league, which was finally abolished in 1915, to the group's generous offer of $50 for each conviction. Over time, it seems, the meetings and discussions for the cause required some additional help.

For decades before the national declaration of prohibition, the borough and township had annually voted down the issuing of liquor licenses in the area. But in 1933, the year temperance finally met its match here, the *Vineland Evening Times* delivered an interesting bit of information in a December article. "It was learned," the story reported, "that the people of LandisTownship voted in favor of issuing licenses one year, but no one applied..."

That year, according to the *Times Journal*, was 1907. The use of voting machines in place of the traditional ballot box apparently had been introduced two years earlier, and area

344

residents were not pleased with the devices. In 1906, the *Evening Times* published notices about when and where instructions on the use of the machines were provided in the town. There is also a report that the new devices would be used for at least another year due to the state's failure to pass a bill that would have allowed municipalities to choose their voting method.

So, in 1907 residents throughout Landis Township set out on the first Tuesday in November to cast their votes on candidates and the issue of the public sale of alcohol. But, as the *Times Journal* article reveals, "in that year the traditional [poll designation of] 'No License'...was somehow left off [the machine], and when people, as usual, voted 'no,' they were in reality voting against the 'no license' clause...and in favor of issuing licenses." The newspaper stated that Benjamin Stevens, who began a reign as mayor of Vineland in 1912, "recalls that every minister in town during that election unwittingly voted against the clause."

The townsfolk at the time apparently did not find this amusing. There are no reports in the *Evening Times* of the confusion in the voting, and the election results reported to the public reflect the usual victory of the temperance movement. According to the newspaper, borough voters not in favor of granting a license won 63-26, while the township standings had 667 voters against licensing over 80 who favored it. Unsurprisingly, the voting machines were soon abandoned. Regardless of how the results are read, it is clear that temperance concerns were not unanimous. Voices of opposition were beginning to make some noise, but the din wouldn't be loud enough for a while yet.

In 1919, the United States approved the 18th Amendment to the Constitution which declared the prohibition of liquor throughout the country. The Amendment took effect January 17, 1920. Six days earlier, Dr. Thomas S. Brock, pastor of the First Methodist Episcopal Church in Vineland, gave a Sunday night talk on "The Passage of Booze" in anticipation of the law which would take effect the following Saturday morning at 12:01 a.m. Brock told the listeners that "America is a paradox in that it permits some things to grow up on its soil without molestation and then when it becomes an evil rises in its might and smites it to the earth forever. The best illustrations of this principle is [sic] the growth of slavery and the liquor habit."

The day before the new law took effect, the citizens of LandisTownship were invited to a ten-minute address by former Judge Royal P. Tuller at the high school at 3:15 p.m. The talk was coordinated by the Woman's Christian Temperance Union which, according to an *Vineland Evening Journal* article, "was instrumental in having text books on scientific temperance instruction placed in the public schools, whereby the youth of the land were taught the truth about alcohol as it effects [sic] the human system."

The next morning at nine o'clock, bells and whistles sounded in Vineland to signal the start of Prohibition. But for the borough and surrounding township, it was business as usual since the law simply demanded of the rest of the country what had been commonplace in Vineland. And while it was certainly a vindication for local temperance organizations, the new Amendment would actually prove to be, in a mere thirteen years, the undoing of the township's seventy-two-year-old dry state.

346

U.S. Prohibition lasted from 1920 until 1933 and was riddled with contradiction. While the temperance movements rejoiced in their victory, locations like Atlantic City used the period to reach the pinnacle of their popularity by providing free-flowing liquor with impunity, the result of well-connected politics. The 18th Amendment had opened as many doors as it had closed, and it remains the only amendment in American history to be repealed.

Thomas M. Coffey, in his book *The Long Thirst*, writes that, on February 16, 1933, the U.S. Senate voted 63-23 to send the 21st Amendment, which would repeal the Prohibition Law, for ratification by state conventions. On February 20, the House of Representatives did likewise with a vote of 289-121. Prior to that, President-elect Franklin D. Roosevelt had appealed to all citizens to buy liquor only from licensed dealers. It was the government's plan to wrest control of liquor sales from the bootleggers and speakeasy owners who had been providing alcohol for the past thirteen years.

Coffey reports that after Roosevelt took office on March 4, he asked for modifications in the Volstead Act, which provided a basis for the 18th Amendment, so that light wines and 3.2 percent beer could be sold. On April 7, the *Evening Times* reported that "real beer, 3.2 percent alcoholic, flowed freely in Vineland and Landis Township, as well as surrounding vicinities in South Jersey and elsewhere in 19 States, starting at 12:01 this morning." The newspaper added that residents purchased bottles of beer for 8 to 15 cents each or glasses of the brew for 5 to 10 cents each in restaurants, stores and clubs, and that sales began immediately after midnight. There were apparently no bells or whistles to summon in the sale of alcohol in Vineland, only the sound of empty glasses and bottles being placed on tables and bars. The *Evening Times* article also stated that there were no arrests for drunkenness throughout Vineland and Landis Township.

By the following day, the paper reported that price wars were anticipated, with over 100 individuals selling beer in Landis Township. Nearby areas like Newfield and Buena Vista Township were setting the cost of a license at $20. By April 11, the Landis Township Committee passed a resolution that also required a $20 fee for 3.2 beer and wine licenses.

In June, New Jersey became the fifth state to ratify the amendment. Vineland and the rest of the country enjoyed the limited sale of alcohol until December, when the 21st Amendment repealed Prohibition. But unlike neighboring Millville, which voted to grant liquor licenses only days after Utah's ratification of the amendment on December 5 made it official, Vineland and Landis Township chose to wait a bit longer to clarify the terms of the State Liquor Control Act.

By December 20, the *Evening Times* reported that the borough would grant yearly liquor licenses. There would be a limit of only four retail establishments and six distributors, with respective fees of $1,500 and $1,000. Club permits were a mere $350. Criticism was leveled against the limitations and fees, which residents felt favored clubs. By December 26, all permit fees had been reduced to $350 and limits on the number of retailers and distributors was lifted. On December 29, Landis Township unanimously approved its Liquor Act which charged $350 for a retail license and

$200 for a distribution fee. With it, one of Landis's earliest and most guarded tenets came to an end.

Chapter 9
Exile
(1880-1889)

"The New Year opens hopefully," Landis writes in his journal on January 1, 1880. "Prospects are brighter for business than the past." The 1880s would prove fruitful but not immediately. The decade began with Landis still in debt and restless from a lack of projects. The work he had begun in turning Ludlam's Island into Sea Isle City was still several years from completion and the changes Vineland was currently undergoing were beyond his control. It would take patience and perseverance before Landis would be able to restore himself to the level he had reached two decades earlier.

Landis had already abandoned his tradition of greeting residents in his office on the first day of the year. He had continued to fall out of favor with the leading residents of Vineland and shied away from political town meetings while restricting any comments about decisions that shaped the town for his journal only. He chose instead to concentrate on improvements he could introduce on his own or in collaboration with his closest allies. By this point, many residents had determined the direction the future of Vineland should take, and that included a new plan to separate from the township.

In 1878, the State of New Jersey had passed the Borough Act, which allowed a township with four square miles or less and a population under 5,000, to become an independent borough through a petition and referendum process. The act stipulated that the borough government must consist of an elected mayor and council whose six members would have staggered terms over three years. Vineland was about to become one of many municipalities in the state to take advantage of the new law in what has been referred to as "Boroughitis."

B.F. Ladd's *History of Vineland* reports that a town meeting was held on the evening of March 23, 1880 to decide whether or not Vineland should incorporate under the Borough Act. The issue, Ladd writes, had already been discussed by the Board of Trade and at previous public meetings. The March gathering concluded with the near-unanimous adoption of resolutions that would soon change the status of the municipality.

On May 26, an election resulted in 181 votes in favor of incorporation and 122 against. An election was set for October 5 to determine which members of the Republican and Citizens Parties would constitute the town's first mayor-council system. The entire Republican ticket was narrowly elected and Quartius Wright became the first mayor of Vineland. In compliance with the Borough Act's requirement of staggered terms for council members, Albro S. Brown and Henry Hartson were elected to the council for three years, Solon S. Gould and John P. Ashworth for two years and E. Morley and H.B. Reese for one year. The powers of the borough officials had been clearly designated so that the mayor would preside over meetings but vote only in the event of a tie. The mayor also would nominate appointed officials who must then be confirmed by the council, which also had the power to override a mayoral veto by a two-thirds vote.

Landis chose to address the borough issue in his journal and was still uncertain by March 23 if he supported the proposed change. He had decided to remove himself from the proceedings so did not attend the meeting that night, "knowing that it was held only by those who favor it." His journal entry declares that "Vineland has been the best governed place in the state and at the lowest rate of taxation. We have paid our war debt and have a surplus on hand." He confesses that he has always opposed a city charter "in defiance to the marked corruption of the time," stating that the town has had a good government "because we have had so little of it," and citing that "a city charter would have ruined the enterprise." The only advantage he sees in a borough charter is that "it may stave off indefinitely a city charter," which was one change he did not deem necessary for the town.

Landis refrained from casting a vote on May 26, explaining in his journal that "we have had the best governed place in the state, principally because the great majority of voters are taxpayers. In a year or two a majority of voters in the borough will be non-taxpayers. Tho' I established the excellent laws of this township, which has been so great a success, only two persons have asked my opinion about the borough. This is a commentary upon life and human conceit."

His decision not to vote may have been an extension of the tirade he delivered in his journal the previous month when, on April 17, he declared, "in the future I shall mind my own interest and that of my family a good deal more than that of an ignorant, thankless and unappreciative public. What the public most admires is selfish power. The symbols they love are the Eagle, the Lion. The heroes they love are those that do men most harm – soldiers of the most rapacious kind. These ideas are forced upon me against all my feelings, my predilections and what I should like to see. They seem to leave a choice of but two things to a man, to step out by suicide, which must be a great sin, or to meet the world sword in hand, accept the issue and pursue a crafty, selfish policy, to lead and save oneself from being beaten…"

October 5, Election Day for borough officials, seemed to afford Landis the opportunity to reflect on the previous decade: "I cautiously keep out of these local politics…when I did vote at them, they used to call me King and they got up a party which they called Independent, outside of the regular parties, for the sole purpose of opposing me and my projects for the improvement of Vineland." He cites the Independent Party's financial contributions to the newspaper of the same name, which he claims, "defeated a great number of my measures for the industrial development in Vineland." He itemizes their efforts to stand against him, noting that "they had a committee to intercept visitors at the [railroad] platform to prevent them from buying from me" and published "disparaging articles" and sent "anonymous letters when I was negotiating for any great improvement." The most revealing moment of the October 5 entry claims the Independent Party members "sent letters to the Italian minister against Vineland" during Landis's 1874 European trip to promote and encourage settlement here.

Landis accuses Nelson Roberts, a mayoral candidate for the new borough who would lose the election by seven votes, of being "one of the worst of the party." What has hurt him the most, however, was how the population of Vineland "cry out that I have designs upon their privileges… If the people of Vineland had possessed any sensibility or gratitude, they would have given me this election, but the truth is their envy is so excessive against [my] being unquestionably the Founder that they studiously ignore me unless they have some favor to ask. Men who have worked against me for years, if they get into trouble, unhesitatingly come to me for advice or assistance and I never can refuse it when I find them in trouble. Is this not one cause of it all? Bad people think they have nothing to fear. I notice that it is the hard natures that succeed in the world and are respected."

There was other evidence at this time of interference with Landis's vision of Vineland. Trees planted early in the town's existence, particularly those in what is today Landis Park, had been cut down. "It is painful for me to see my wishes so little regarded," a journal entry reads. Landis also laments that "The Pennsylvania [Railroad] controls all the papers in Vineland and that [rail]road is no friend of mine…"

He accuses the train system of "bringing their own man into the [*Vineland*] *Weekly*, a certain Horace K. Flint, for the purpose of controlling its columns. He is, of course, opposed to me."

Still, Landis devoted a portion of his time to improving his settlement. He sought ways for more Irish immigrants to settle in the town and examined the possibilities of establishing a sugar refinery in Vineland. For the latter, he contacted Girard Sugar Refinery in Philadelphia and sent a sugar culture from a Vineland farm. The news was encouraging, but apparently the capital wasn't forthcoming. Landis also undertook the task of implementing a foundry, which became his only successful Vineland endeavor in this period. He also kept tabs on the lake projects the town had pursued, reporting on April 1, that "Beaver Lake, which as I prophesied is going to pieces, a failure unless they can get more water." Eight days later, he discussed with William House "some plan to put up a dam on the Blackwater."

Landis's divorce from Clara the previous year had presumably closed the door on that relationship and that period of his life, and his business ventures since then indicate that he had turned his attention away from his failed marriage. However, on April 22, he received word that Clara had recently returned from Europe and an old wound began to fester once again. By April 27, he confided in his journal that a despondent mood had overtaken him since hearing news of her. The passage, a portion of it excised when published in the *Vineland Historical Magazine*, conveys the sense of despair he was experiencing: "My domestic misfortunes have produced a degree of despondency that I find it impossible to shake off. To be disappointed so sadly where one expected consolation and sympathy and, in a manner to make it irremediable, is dreadful. Everything in life has since appeared so empty. May God give me strength to get over it, but it is a long time now since it occurred, and the Abyss only appears the more awful and dark."

However much the past intruded upon Landis at this time, his salvation seemed to be his sons. Both Charles Jr. and Richard were now in Landis's custody, having returned to Vineland when they had reached the age of seven, and considerable time was spent with them during the year, attending events, taking walks and sharing stories. But even here the past intruded. Charles Jr., who on a cold and snowy day the previous January 5 had been confirmed at the Episcopal Church in Vineland by Bishop Learborough, was attending a private school and had run into a problem of being bullied there. Landis brought the matter to the school master and, although it apparently was remedied, the incident had left him with the fear that "I shall not be able to send my children to school in this place," a statement that seems to imply the abuse may have been the work of children whose parents did not hold Landis in high regard.

Despite his optimism over brighter business prospects for 1880, Landis had entered the year with more financial difficulties than before. With debts haunting him, he continued to rely on land sales to cancel them, only to encounter a significant lull in buyers for a good part of the year. "I find it difficult to sell property and collect money," he writes in a March 1880 journal entry, lamenting that he could have accrued a million dollars had he not prioritized the success and improvement of Vineland, the "realization of the designs of the colony," over the profit margin. "There are very few people who could be made to believe this fact," he writes.

His desperation was apparent in his journal entries. In January he was offered a deal by lawyer Leverett Newcomb to sell a farm for $3,000, a price Landis claimed was not even a third of what it was worth. Lamenting in his journal that "you can never get the value of property if people think you are pinched," he offers his appraisal of Newcomb as "a legal pirate" who "will take all the advantage of that estate and of myself that he can." The lawyer's most unforgivable flaw, as Landis sees it, is that "he forecloses upon poor people and extorts money from them." The next day, still consumed by an urgency to sell lots, homes and buildings in order to pay his debts, Landis signed the papers for the sale of the farm.

By April, with debt letters arriving regularly from individuals like his trial attorney Benjamin Brewster, he complains that "the times are very dull. I find it impossible to sell anything by advertising or by any amount of effort." The dearth of sales lasted until a family purchased $2,000 worth of property in late June but did not signal an end to the lull. Using the money from sales to slowly settle what he owed meant that Landis needed to raise funds for Sea Isle City expenses by making investment deals with people he knew. This accounts for some of his visits across the Delaware River at this time.

The trips to Philadelphia were usually for the purpose of business, but occasionally they included socializing. He encountered Richard Byrnes in Philadelphia on May 6, commenting that his former partner was "happy and cheerful as ever." However, Landis's travels were not confined to the City of Brotherly Love. Trips to New York had become more prevalent over the previous year and, like the jaunts to Philadelphia, business sometimes gave way to opportunities that reacquainted him with individuals like Wallace Holbrooke, an early clerk of Landis's who was now in the publishing trade. One of the more interesting chance encounters Landis experienced early in 1880 occurred during a business trip to New York when he met Clara's uncle Charles A. Meigs, whose home was the setting for the wedding of Landis and Clara in 1868. With all that had transpired over the next ten years, it might be suspected that this moment of serendipity ended badly, but Landis records that Meigs, now employed as a bank examiner, "was very glad to see me…" and agreed to provide "a good letter of introduction" to a businessman with which Landis intended to meet.

Landis made his way to Staten Island on February 7 to visit Meigs and his family, who were delighted to see him. "We talked over old times, the old romantic days and when they used to visit me in Vineland," he writes in his journal. Revisiting the site where he had been married, Landis reflects, "Here I used to come when I was rich, prosperous and in love – now it is all gone! …Here was the place of our courtship – among these trees I often wandered full of joy and home. From this door I started in the carriage with my wife after our marriage, bright and buoyant. I was pleased at the confidence and elasticity with which my wife sprang into the carriage." It must have been obvious that the trip would serve as a painful reminder, but it also seems to have provided enough solace for Landis to muster a new resolve: "But with a stout heart, there is fortune yet to be won. There is one thing certain, I have my dear children and the rest of my family and here is love and a good deal to live for." After returning to Vineland on February 9, he concludes that "I feel happier for the visit."

Always a voracious reader, Landis chose this timeframe to immerse himself in copies of John Bunyan's *Pilgrims Progress*, which he shared with his sons, and Mark Twain's *Roughing It,* which he proclaims the best book by the author. He also read several works by the English novelist Maria Louise Ramé, who published under the pseudonym Ouida. But it was Cervantes's *Don Quixote* for which he seems to have had a particular affinity. One of the comments in his journal refers to the title character as a "poor enthusiast" and muses that "it set me thinking. I think there has been a good deal of the Quixote about some of my own experience. All enthusiasm, instead of recognizing the cold selfish logic of the world." But Don Quixote wasn't the only individual with which Landis identified at this point in his life. William Penn received his attention as well, especially since the Quaker had had his own problems as a founder. "It is about the same with all [founders]," he writes. "The experience of William Penn was terribly bitter. Whilst living in the colony, colonists placed themselves in constant opposition to him from jealousy and envy." The situation was all too familiar.

For Landis, the arts were never restricted to simply one form. During one of his visits to New York City, he took in a production of Gilbert and Sullivan's *The Pirates of Penzance* at the Fifth Avenue Theater. The comic opera had debuted twelve days earlier and while proclaiming the work "very good," he qualified his evaluation by claiming that it was "not so good as *[H.M.S.] Pinafore*." Landis even made time for the sculptor Tureni to create a bust of him. The idea had been Matilda's and the finished piece was delivered July 5 and placed in the parlor. He also attended performances by the Vineland Theatrical Company and regularly entertained guests.

It was also during this period that Landis wrote about his church attendance in his journals. Now a member of the Episcopalian faith, he did not usually disclose information about his churchgoing in these private entries. The significant exception had been during the final months of his marriage in early 1875 when he attended Catholic services with his wife and met with Father Vivet in an attempt to save his eroding relationship with Clara. By 1880, however, he would be seen attending Sunday services with Matilda, but to say it was with regularity would not be accurate. A spiritual individual who never hesitated in financially helping a number of denominations in Vineland establish their places of worship, Landis apparently was not someone committed to the observance of weekly worship and his journals and correspondence were rarely used as a forum for his private views on God, religion and faith. A notable exception occurred during 1882, when a sermon about "how we should not ask God for temporal blessings but for spiritual strength to bear up with our afflictions, trials and calamities" and how "these things were often blessings in disguise to fit us for the eternal world which worldly prosperity could not do" received an approving "well taken" in his journal entry. The relevance of the sermon to events in his life had certainly not been overlooked.

Mostly what his entries do reveal is that he was, on more than one occasion, moved by a service or music that he considered to be good, but he could also be critical of a sermon he felt was lacking. Yet there were also Sundays in which he remained at home either reading or sitting in front of his house talking to passersby. At other times, his work took precedence and he visited his office instead. Over the next two decades, he would continue to attend church irregularly, enjoying the sermons offered in 1882 by the new rector, Mr. Egbert, and even returning to Catholic services while traveling outside of the U.S.

On March 7, 1880, Landis records in his journal that he had been "taken with a severe pain in the lungs," a foreshadowing of a condition that would worsen over the next ten years and require periodic retreats to warmer climates during the 1890s.

When it came to business ventures, Landis did not restrict his focus only to Vineland. He sought other projects, including the possibility of forming a telegraph company in conjunction with William House that was initiated in June. While Landis continued to act as agent, seeking out interested parties, his personal investment diminished when, at the contract signing, he deemed the venture "not altogether satisfactory" and decided he would "not use much time or money upon it."

Also in June 1880, Landis undertook the most ambitious of his projects, something he referred to as an experiment in New York. He drew up a map of his plans and two months later visited the Equitable Life Insurance Company in New York to see if it had a large tract of land available near New York City for the development of an enterprise reminiscent of Shaftesbury Park Estate in the Battersea area of South London. Landis had visited the British location in 1874 during his travels through Europe and was inspired by it. The

London site, a residential estate consisting of 1,200 two-story homes at the time, was in its second year of construction during Landis's visit. What no doubt appealed to him the most were the wide streets lined with trees and the concept of providing residences for every social class.

The idea of taking his expertise to the New York area was appealing, especially since Vineland, he felt, no longer afforded opportunity for his real estate plans or, as he wrote in a journal entry for August 22, 1880, "I have no sea room to do business in Vineland. I also want a wider field." He found 180 acres of land on the Hudson River opposite Central Park and, as he had with his past enterprises, ensured that railroad access was available. Acting impulsively, he also consulted with an assessor in Fairview, New York, convincing him "to agree to send me descriptions and prices of farms for sale in this and the adjoining townships." He also looked into acquiring tracts of land in Newark and Jersey City, New Jersey as well as in Virginia. These new enterprises continued to be explored over the next several years without fruition.

Already suspicious of how his endeavors might be perceived, Landis turned down a request from the current editor of *The Independent* asking him to provide a biographical sketch to be included in the newspaper's recognition of the lives of twenty successful men. "Upon reflection," Landis reports, "I decided not to send it. Bad use of it might be made of it and the lesson of my life teaches me the persecuting to which I have been subjected as if pursued by the very fiends of hell, that the constant effort to do good is not only unappreciated but subjects one to incessant and ruinous persecution. Self-protection in this world requires a good deal of the tiger and shark in a man."

The restlessness that pervaded the first half of 1880 would disappear as the Sea Isle project became Landis's primary focus. Work continued on obtaining property on Ludlam's Island, also referred to as Ludlam's Beach, the site of the planned resort. The gestation of this project is a highly productive phase for Landis, a return to the entrepreneurship he exhibited in the formation of Vineland. Over the previous year, Landis had been drawn to the Jersey shore, not by the opportunity to create a resort town but by another concern. According to Jeffrey M. Dorwart in his book *Cape May County, New Jersey: The Making of an American Resort Community*, Landis had originally turned his attention to Cape May County in an attempt to thwart the monopoly the West Jersey Railroad had secured in the area when it established a new rail system in the county. What stood in his way, however, was raising the funds for such an endeavor, and the project collapsed before it really got started. Landis then decided to follow the old adage, "If you can't beat 'em, join 'em," and approached West Jersey Railroad heads William Sewell and John C. Stevens about helping to develop Sewell's Point and Poverty Beach, but as Dorwart reports, he was rebuffed by the bosses.

Although nothing came of these plans, they had managed to draw Landis's attention to this shore area where a good amount of property was waiting to be developed into resort communities. In particular, the barrier islands of the county were promising investments and Landis was ready for a new challenge. He set his sights on Ludlam's Island and began doing what he did best – designing a city. Joseph Ludlam had originally purchased the island in 1692. The location was initially used for cattle grazing and cattle was still found on the island as late as the 1870s prior to Landis's involvement. While Ludlam named the location after himself, the inlets at the northern and southern ends were christened with the names of two early intrepid individuals of the area, Corson and Townshend, respectively.

Landis hadn't had the opportunity to revitalize an already established settlement since Hammonton, but the criteria in this shore location differed from that of his earlier agricultural communities Landis wanted a seaside resort modeled on the sights he had witnessed during his 1874 trip to Europe. This was to be a U.S. version of Venice, complete with a canal, an opulent hotel and a respite from the bustle of the urban environment. He would base his new town on his ideas for a "sanitary and art city" from two years earlier and utilize some of Vineland's design, such as a wide main avenue and the appeal of a healthy climate, to forge his new project.

According to Dorwart, Landis "prepared sketches for the proposed city, complete with a design for a protected harbor and a thousand-foot wooden pier and pavilion. Landis envisaged a seaside city with an elaborate canal and drainage system and public baths and fountains somewhat like Venice, Italy. He wanted to build Italian-style piazzas and public buildings decorated with Renaissance artwork, sculpture, and statuary."

The designs also included a grand hotel modeled in part on a Rockaway Beach facility. Landis's hotel would incorporate "a tropical garden, an aquarium, a theatre, hot and cold salt water baths in rooms, [and] circulating libraries" as well as "wide verandas." Landis also considered the area a prime location for a marine science lab and would eventually approach the University of Pennsylvania about establishing such a research facility there. Not every facet of the original design for Sea Isle City would be realized, but the working plan provided a solid blueprint of a town that could set itself apart in attracting settlers and tourists.

In his pursuit of titles of ownership to property on Ludlam's Island, Landis had turned up information that the Ludlams, a landowning family who had significantly increased their property holdings in the 18th century through sheriff sales, had heirs who had moved to the Midwest. However, not all the families of the island's prominent landholders had relocated. Thomas E. Ludlam, described by Dorwart as a "prominent Dennis Township businessman," met with Landis, who soon surrounded himself with a series of investors, like Philip P. Baker, a Cumberland County legislator and merchant from Vineland, Jonathan Cone, whose steamboat traveled the route from Cape May to Philadelphia, and John Wright, a Camden County resident and heir to the fortune held by the Cooper family.

The pieces would come together slowly in the creation of Sea Isle City, much slower than what Landis had been used to in the establishment of Vineland, Hammonton and Colville. A substantial amount of business needed to be transacted and technical details needed addressing before this island could be transformed into the envisioned resort.

One of the items that needed attention was what Landis had always considered an important ingredient in the success of a newly founded town, transportation. The fact that there was no rail system on or in vicinity of Ludlam's Island did not deter him. He was aware that the location was ideal for tourism, as was his chief engineer H. Farrand who, in an undated letter, told Vineland's founder that "with proper railroad facilities, and lots offered at a reasonable price, I do not see why this place should not become as great a resort as Atlantic City..." Landis had already written of the importance of a railway in a journal entry and, consequently, was quick to secure an alliance with West Jersey Railroad director William Sewell. Dorwart writes that Landis and Sewell worked out a deal that "led to the establishment of a railroad branch line from just north of the South Seaville station (known as Sea Isle Junction) across the marshes to Ludlam's Beach in 1882."

Construction seems to have gone smoothly during the year it took for the railway to be built, but that doesn't mean there weren't problems. From the start, Landis faced a series of challenges from the rail company. According to the South Jersey Rails online site, as of September 15, 1979 "West Jersey Railroad inform[ed] Charles K. Landis that his development at Ludlam's Beach is not a paying proposition and that he should invest more money in improvements, and if successful, West Jersey Railroad will build a branch there."

By December 10, 1880, according to Christopher T. Baer's online chronology of the Pennsylvania Railroad, the West Jersey Railroad apparently felt that the project was worthwhile enough to "make a proposition" to Landis to "provide rail and rolling stock for a branch to Sea Isle." However, it would be the founder who would have to oversee the construction of the train line.

Regardless of the situation, Landis, like Cervantes's protagonist, continued his pursuits undaunted. By early 1880, people had already expressed interested in purchasing lots on Ludlam's Island. Landis, in a February 2 journal entry, addressed his enthusiasm and funding concerns for his new endeavor. "I live in the hope of getting this enterprise started," he writes. "It is dreadful to be able to see what can be done, and then be cramped for the want of a little means. Perhaps this is a part of the discipline we are destined to undergo in this world of probation."

By February 14, he had "arranged for more money for Ludlam's Island" in order to pay for the rest of the title and to prepare a road to the island. That project would require the passage of a bill in the New Jersey State Senate, which would be completed the following month, allowing for the creation of what Landis termed "a wagon road to the Island [that] opens up all the Island on the coast to the main land." All of these accomplishments he found "encouraging."

By April 1880, the process of procuring titles to Ludlam's Island properties was slowly nearing completion. Burk had spent the previous months tracking down landowners and on April 3, Vineland's founder wrote that he had "decided to send Mr. Burk out West to get signatures for the Island to close it up if possible..." The clerk was dispatched later in the month to Ohio and Illinois to visit with the Ludlams, the Edwards, another New Jersey family and others about selling their share of land. He returned May 3 with what Landis called "a good many signatures for the Island."

Burk shared with his employer accounts of the locations he had just visited. The information triggered in Landis a need to re-evaluate his local achievements. "Mr. Burk gives glowing accounts of the West," he writes in his May 4 diary entry. "He says that I stand well there. Wonder if my efforts would not have been more fortunate for myself out West than in N.J. In this state I have never received any kind of recognition for what I have done and never had any assistance. Have never been placed upon a single State Committee or recognized in any way, whilst many honors have been heaped upon men who have never done anything for the State, the public, or any but themselves."

Landis spent much of May and early June planning the resort. Traveling by train and boat, he joined his associates in the Sea Isle City venture for a tour of the island on May 28, declaring afterwards that "the party appeared to be pleased."

On June 19, the Brief of the Title of Ludlam's Island was completed and sent to Judge Clements in Haddonfield for review. Landis seems to have grown impatient with the gradual progress of the enterprise but maintained a busy schedule that always included the development of new ideas for his current venture. He would have to be tolerant of the pace of his project for nearly another year before sufficient funds and an interested public could ensure a successful promotion.

After taking several mortgages in the early stages of establishing his resort, Landis finally undertook a move that clearly provided him with an advantage in this new enterprise and in his frustrating quest to pay off his mounting debts. He recorded this decision in the September 24 entry of his journal: "Established mortgage of $10,000 Ludlam's Island and cancelled the other mortgages. Paid $2,050 for this money. It give[s] me however, the control of the Island.

I negotiated the matter through Henry Whelan. The commission and what has been expended comes to $7,500. I got $1,000 and expect to get the balance in a few days. This will pay my taxes and stave off some of my duns...I shall now establish the Island enterprise soon as possible."

As early as February 1880, Landis had been contacted by individuals interested in purchasing property in Sea Isle, but buyers needed to wait another year before they had their chance to become official residents. According to Dorwart, Landis incorporated, along with Burk and Baker, the Sea Isle City Improvement Company "to sell land and build houses, hotels, docks, seawalls and piers." Landis would serve as president of the group, with Burk as secretary and William House as treasurer. Dorwart also reports that Landis "offered one million dollars in capital stock, provided tours for interested investors and directed installation of gas, waterworks and electric lighting."

According to 1881 promotional material reproduced in *South Jersey Magazine*, the Sea Isle City Improvement Company, with a Board of Directors consisting of Landis, Burk, Baker, House, Seaman R. Fowler, Henry Hartson and Benjamin Swain, Jr., owned "960 acres of landing, fronting three miles upon the Beach and embracing 5,405 town lots" north of the railroad. The property south of the railway was "a private enterprise."

By spring 1881, advertisements for Sea Isle began appearing and the selling of property commenced. Proclaiming the availability of lots "50 feet front by 110 feet deep," the ads offered beachfront locations and corner lots for $250 and others for $150. Landis also provided a map of the town displaying the sixty blocks on one side of Railroad

Avenue and seventy-six blocks on the other side containing property for sale. Each block was divided into twenty-four lots. Tours were available seven days a week, with a "surveyor always present to show lots."

Landis's map not only identifies the lots advertised by the Sea Isle City Improvement Company but also highlights the sales that occurred in the first two months of promotion. By June, much of the beachfront property had been purchased as well as a considerable amount of lots on the next two blocks closest to Railroad Avenue.

The advantages afforded those purchasing Sea Isle City property was carefully outlined in the engineer's report, which was used to entice interested buyers: "The island is 6 ¼ miles in length…and is surrounded by the Atlantic Ocean, Ludlam Bay and a navigable channel called the Thoroughfare, furnishing excellent advantages for fishing, sailing and still water bathing. A beach, 150 feet wide, extends the entire length of the Island [with] unusual facilities for walking and bathing which are not excelled by any watering place on the coast…the advantages the beach affords for bathing are excellent, there being no undertow perceptible, and in this respect peculiar."

There is one other thing the map of the town illuminates when examined carefully. While there are a series of streets named after aquatic items such as "Dolphin," "Pearl," "Coral" and "Shell," other roadways bear names that were not particularly indigenous to the area until the establishment of Sea Isle City: "Whelan," "House," "Hartson," "Swain," "Fowler" and "Landis." But it's also curious to note that certain street names in their early form, before numbering became the commonplace method of identifying them, form an autobiographical trail of the resort's founder. The names reflect various components of Landis's life such as his earliest literary influences, the poet Byron and his contemporary, Percy Shelley (today's 63rd and 64th Streets), his previous accomplishments (Vineland and Hammonton, the current 53rd and 54th Streets) and his travels (Italia and Paris, the modern-day 42nd and 43rd Streets).

Plans for the West Jersey Railroad to provide transportation for prospective buyers were also underway. Construction of the line had begun on May 25, 1881 and Don Wentzel's research identifies that work began in Woodbine and extended "five miles across a meadow to Sea Isle City." He identifies that "151 tons of 40 lb. iron rail and 6,160 [railroad] ties were brought into Sea Isle to Townshend's Inlet a distance of 2.42 miles." By January 7, 1882, Landis notified West Jersey Railroad that he had graded a right-of-way from Seaville to the meadows and requested assistance from the company in completing the project through the meadows to his new settlement.

It wouldn't be until six months later, on June 2, 1882, that the passenger line from Seaville to Sea Isle City officially opened. The new tracks provided what Landis needed to guarantee a continuous flow of visitors to his new town, but his work with the railroad wasn't yet finished. Baer writes that, on March 22, 1883, Landis contacted the West Jersey Railroad, saying he had built "an excursion house at Townsends Inlet south of Sea Isle City and built a light railroad to it," and that he offered the company "a right of way the length of the beach and to build another excursion house at Corsons Inlet at the north end of Sea Isle City to be done by June 1," to which the railroad "agree[d] to negotiate for a railroad running the length of the island from Corsons Inlet to Townsends Inlet." The following month, the company approved the extension, but required Landis to build it at his expense if it failed to do so.

The sale of lots in Sea Isle City began in 1881, two years after the project had originated. The success of the venture can be measured by the immediate purchase of a number of properties available, and one of those sales offers a rare look inside the process of buying a piece of a new Landis enterprise. According to a published account by Richard M. Atwater concerning his experience in obtaining his lot in the Sea Isle City sale, Landis's astute planning had paid off. The arrangements to extend the railway system to the town and to promote the convenience of its location to South Jersey residents as well as Philadelphians had captured people's attention.

For Atwater, the popular seasonal retreat of Cape May proved to be an expensive and inconvenient location for a summer home and he decided to consider the newly established Sea Isle City. Its accessibility from Millville's rail lines and its "broad and smooth and hard" beaches caught Atwater's attention, but so did the island's pronounced flaws such as the "broken range of sand dunes at the high-water line to "a low marshy stretch, flooded by storm tides and in several places swept through by surf." The beaches, however, "made one forget all that was behind it," and the "extension of the railroad would bring it within easy reach." Sea Isle City became "the line to follow."

With the railroad extension completed in the spring of 1881, circulars advertising the new resort had been distributed. Atwater reports that he received his copy on

April 21 and less than two weeks later found himself the owner of a beachfront property. By his account, "I attended the Auction of Lots in Philadelphia on May 2 and bought the first lot fairly sold. It was the central front lot in the block containing the largest clump of cedar trees on the island. I acted on the advice of Edward Cooper to buy a front lot or none."

Atwater went to work immediately, hiring an architect and a contractor and buying materials in Camden for the construction of his house in the new Landis resort. During preparations, he made a series of visits to the island. On one such occasion, he "took a survey of its good and bad elements and noted the desirable lots." Atwater's description of Sea Isle City in May 1881 reveals something similar to the origin of Vineland twenty years earlier. "A number of street posts had been set up – a path had been blazed through the jungle – a wilder spot could hardly have been found on which to plant a colony…," he writes.

Construction of the house began June 9 and by July 6, "we moved into it such as it was," Atwater writes. He had chosen to reside on the island despite the flaws he witnessed, but those faults would remain. It wasn't long before Landis was confronting challenges from weather conditions instead of railroad companies and money lenders with which he had been dealing.

According to Dorwart, a brush fence was used as a seawall meant to guard what was considered prime beachfront properties from the damaging surf. Unfortunately, the fence offered little protection and beach erosion became a serious problem.

In addition, the railway tracks into Sea Isle City were consistently washed away. Dorwart reports that Landis found fault with the way the railroad had dealt with securing the track but counted on the recent addition of a mud bank to help control the situation. It didn't. In September 1882, a violent storm raged through the island, scattering sections of the track as if they were pieces of a model railroad. Dorwart reports that the tempest also "swept away entire sections of the tack as well as the railroad bridge across Ludlam's Thoroughfare, a deep channel that connected Ludlam's Bay to Townshend's Inlet. Landis hired a crew of twenty Italian-American railroad workers to repair this vital lifeline to the mainline."

Landis was capable of mending what the forces of nature had destroyed in his resort town, but the next damaging blow would prove irreparable. When he first conceived of creating a seaside resort modeled after the European cities that caught his attention during his overseas trip, Landis relied upon Burk to carry out much of the legwork required to establish the town. But in May 1881, Landis fired Burk after sixteen years of service. According to Dorwart "apparently Burk had some deeds signed over to him rather than to Landis and allegedly swindled Matilda Landis, Charles Landis's sister, out of shares of Sea Isle City." However, records of a court case resulting from a lawsuit initiated by Matilda tend to exonerate Burk of the accusations leveled against him. They also shed light on how Landis conducted some of his business at the time.

The lawsuit behind the case is one of the more bizarre occurrences associated with Vineland's founding father. Matilda brought suit against both her brother and Burk in order to annul an agreement between Landis and his clerk that took place two months before Burk's firing.

According to the 1886 *Central Reporter: Cases, Courts of Last Resort, New York, New Jersey*, the issue of the case can be traced back to when Burk began procuring titles for the Ludlam's Island properties. According to the clerk's testimony, he had an arrangement with Landis whereby he "was to ferret out the title and buy the different interests in the beach; that Landis was to advance the money and Burk was to have a half interest in the property; that his work in the matter was to be independent of and additional to his employment as bookkeeper, etc., for Landis; and that the half interest was to be given him in consideration of his extra work in ascertaining and obtaining the title."

Records show that by the time of his dismissal, Burk, who was paid $1,100 a year by Landis for his clerical services, had spent two years obtaining titles from 400 different individuals and incurring expenses in the amount of $800, which he paid out of his pocket. The agreement with Landis over the half interest in the titles stood until March 19, 1881, when Burk was offered and apparently unwillingly accepted $58,000 in lieu of the title interest. The full amount would be conveyed in the form of $40,000 of stock and forty town lots that would be selected by Landis. The deed to this agreement was recorded April 7. Burk was fired May 18.

The Sea Isle stocks were priced at $50 a share, but Burk contended they were "at a high estimate, about $35 and that the stocks had no immediate value inasmuch as there was a mortgage of $10,000 upon the property conveyed by the company." He also testified that the lots selected for him by

Landis consisted of "963 acres of unimproved beach, strand and marsh."

The intent of Matilda's lawsuit, curiously enough, was to annul this renegotiated agreement between Landis and Burk. Her claim was that, in October 1880, Landis had agreed "to purchase Ludlam's Island for her" and completed all necessary financial and legal arrangements in order to give her ownership. Under those circumstances, the suit argued, she was neither apprised of nor consented to the agreement that gave Burk $40,000 in stocks and forty lots in the town. The argument was as bold as it was outlandish, and judging from the case records, the court thought so too.

The attempt to convince the judge the Sea Isle City project belonged to Matilda failed, the transparency of the scheme provoking an annoyance clearly evident in the case record published in *Central Reporter: Cases, Courts of Last Resort, New York, New Jersey*: "Although the suit is ostensibly against Landis as well as Burk, it is not only thoroughly amicable so far as the former is concerned, but it manifestly is in fact his suit. It is impossible not to conclude, from the reading of the testimony, that the enterprise of buying Ludlam's Island and establishing there a seaside city was Landis's and not the complainant's."

Burk provided testimony that proved devastating to Matilda's case. Landis had argued that Matilda's ownership of the Sea Isle City project was proof of a recent plan to give his father, mother and sister "the benefit of his property to the exclusion of his wife," whom he had divorced immediately prior to launching the Sea Isle City venture in 1879 while still facing a series of unpaid debts. Burk, however, claimed Landis's distribution of his assets was, in fact, "done to put the property out of the reach of Landis's creditors."

Those creditors may have included the widow of Uri Carruth. According to a letter by Hosea Allen dated July 16, 1881, Mrs. Carruth, who apparently had remained in Vineland with her children after her husband's death, had brought a lawsuit against Landis, and property under Landis's ownership, as the letter makes clear, could figure into any settlement that might have been reached.

The court found credibility in Burk's accusations, citing the fact that, in February 1879, "Landis conveyed parts of his property by voluntary conveyances to his father and mother...and to the complainant a very large amount of his real estate, for the expressed consideration of over $100,000," concluding that "it would seem that this arrangement had reference to something else than any claim his wife might make, seeing that there was, as he testifies, an antenuptial [sic] agreement between them..."

The most convincing evidence that the Sea Isle City enterprise belonged to Landis and not Matilda came in the form of a lawsuit brought against Landis, Burk, Matilda and the Sea Isle City Improvement Company in 1886 by Henry Whelan, an associate of Vineland's founder, over money he claimed he was owed as a partner in the Sea Isle City endeavor. According to the case, Landis, without notifying his sister of his plans, promised Whelan a conveyance of $100,000 in stocks and entitlement to half of the island.

According to a document filed by Landis on May 29, 1886, Whelan claimed the Sea Isle City founder owed him $11,477.86 in light of agreements signed in 1881. Landis countered that it was Whelan who initially owed $7,364.30

in reference to the same agreements and $8,861.86 as of April 30, 1885. Calvin B. McLean, a veteran bookkeeper for the Pennsylvania Railroad which, according to Landis, also had not received payment from Whelan, reviewed the signed agreements and other material at Landis's request. His study reveals that the land pertaining to the suit was the southwest portion of the island. In his affidavit, dated April 1, 1886, McLean says that he worked with Landis's Sea Isle City bookkeeper, J. Harvey Cochran, and reports a debit of $14,728.61, "which, according to the agreements, should be divided between the said Henry Whelan and Charles K. Landis, attorney in fact for Matilda T. Landis," accounting for the amount Landis had initially sought from Whelan. Scrutinizing the April 30, 1885 records, McLean discovered that the amount had increased to $17,723.72.

Landis had also received a total of $8,000 in loans from Whelan during the time he was organizing Sea Isle City and claimed that he had paid back the full amount along with a $2,000 bonus. He also reported that he thought his dealings with Whelan had been through the business Townshend, Whelan and Co., discovering later that his transactions had been only with one man.

Landis's arguments against Whelan's suit included his claim of a document of trust that was, on October 30, 1879, signed by Burk and witnessed by J. Hunter Ewing, Whelan's son-in-law "showing the true ownership of the island to be in Matilda T. Landis," with no mention of Whelan as part owner. Landis tried to be careful in stating he was merely acting for Matilda in the matter of these legalities, but there is evidence that he was not always successful. At one point, he contends that "for all the valuable land conveyed by me to the said Whelan, he never paid one dollar of consideration."

Landis brought suit against Whelan in the Court of Chancery, asking for a review of contracts with Whelan from May 2 and 3 and on November 11, 1881. The first of these contracts was signed by Landis, but not as attorney representing the interests of Matilda. The others were signed on behalf of Matilda, including an August 13 agreement among Matilda, Whelan and the Sea Isle City Improvement Company which did not seem to play a part in this legal battle. Additionally, Matilda filed a suit against Whelan, requesting that all deeds with Whelan be cancelled "on the ground of fraud and want of consideration." However, this would not turn out to be one of Landis's victories. The case against him awarded Whelan half the island, clearly acknowledging that Landis "exercised the most absolute and complete control over [the deal]."

As for Matilda's suit against Burk, its purpose does not seem to have been solely an attempt to retain stocks and property promised to Burk. As Dorwart notes, "The disenchantment with Burk arose less from the alleged theft of properties than from Burk's development of a competing barrier island community on Five Mile Beach to the south," which would become Holly Beach.

The author reports that several weeks before he was fired by Landis, the clerk had established the Holly Beach Improvement Company. His partners included Dr. Aaron Andrew of Vineland. Hiring William H. Bright to run his real estate office, Burk soon turned the Holly Beach location into a successful resort that even boasted some former Vinelanders as permanent residents.

By the time Matilda's lawsuit was dismissed in 1886, developers like Burk and Landis's former associate Philip Baker had transformed all the barrier islands except Avalon into vital seashore communities that provided competition to Sea Isle City. Baker, who was instrumental in establishing Wildwood, even earned considerable attention when he hosted President Benjamin Harrison at his seaside resort.

On May 16, 1882, the first elected officials of the new Sea Isle City were chosen. The resort's first mayor was Martin Wells and the first city council consisted of James P. Way, Roger Dever, William L. Peterson and Hudson E. Ludlam. The town was promoted as a year-round resort and even in the 1890s, interested visitors/settlers were told to contact Landis at his Philadelphia office.

During the final stages of establishing and preparing Sea Isle City as a resort site, Landis's father took ill, suffering from heart disease and dropsy for much of 1882. He died at 6:20 p.m. on Thursday, September 7, just short of his 77th birthday. Landis had been at his side, holding his hand. The burial in the family plot at Siloam Cemetery, where Henry was interred years earlier, took place at 3 p.m. on Saturday. "I always tried to do my duty by him," Landis remarked in his journal after his father's passing.

A December 30, 1882 document by Marcus Fry, now Landis's chief clerk, reveals that Landis, designated as his father's heir, transferred his inheritance to his mother Mary on that date. The transaction may have been another way to prevent creditors from coming after it for monies owed.

Around the time of Michael's death, Richard began maintaining a journal for a brief period at the age of nine, obviously inspired by his father's diary. His account covers the timeframe from September to December 1882, when Landis was completing work on Sea Isle City. Unlike his father's entries, which do not provide much insight into family dynamics, Richard's record offers a glimpse into the Landis household and a better understanding of the relationships and daily routines of the family.

It's likely that Richard had the opportunity to maintain a journal at this time because he, unlike Charles Jr., wouldn't begin his school year until the winter, although his classes at Braidwood Art School began around November 12. He is keenly aware of his brother's schedule, noting almost daily that the eleven-year-old Charles Jr. departs for school at 9 a.m. and returns at 4 p.m. The journal reveals the relationship between Richard and Charles Jr. as a bit aloof. They play ball, enjoy sleigh rides and spend time ice skating together, but there is no sense of camaraderie conveyed in the entries. Competition, instead, seems to be a defining factor.

During autumn 1882, each sibling is working on carving a model sailboat, but it's obvious they are working separately on these projects, and only Charles Jr. shows the initiative of taking his boat to three area businesses, including a blacksmith, to have it hollowed out. In a similar fashion, Richard reports that he is writing a story, "A Tiger Hunt in India," but notes that Charles Jr. has also written his own tiger story, completing it on October 22 and sending it off to a periodical in the hopes of publishing it.

Richard's commentary about his father primarily focuses on his absence due to work on Sea Isle City, which, he reports, "is getting to be a nice place." But his daily observances of Landis's business trips offer an alternate view from the one presented in his father's journals.

Richard's entries convey a sense of loneliness and concern that his parent may have been too busy to notice. Landis was rarely at home during this period, spending his time mostly at his office on Locust Street in Philadelphia and at Sea Isle City, but ample time was also devoted to his growing interest in New York real estate.

Even Michael Landis's diary had taken note that his son had been visiting New York, sometimes for extended stays, as early as 1879. Each new venture would require Landis to be away from Vineland longer, and his absence was having some effect on the family. According to Richard's diary, Landis would usually return home most evenings, but there are several instances noted in which he would be away overnight. While Matilda was apparently in charge of caring for Charles Jr. and Richard, there are more than a few times in which she undertook shopping trips in Philadelphia or elsewhere. On these occasions, the boys were looked after by Landis's mother, who had a room at her son's house.

It's clear from the journal that Richard was precocious for a nine-year-old. He was reading Washington Irving's multi-volume biography of George Washington, *Don Quixote* and several other books during this four-month period. His day usually consisted of waking between 6 and 7:30 a.m., having breakfast and then reading, writing in his journal, working on the boat model or running errands for his Aunt Matilda. He occasionally played with Charles Jr. when the latter was home. He also reports that, on September 28, 1882, "we are cleaning house this week and painting, although it is doubtful the family actually engaged in the work.

Other entries inform us that there was a family dog named Spottie and that Charles Jr. played accordion. Richard reports that "Grapes are plentiful this year," in a September entry that reflects the attention Vineland's grape crops were receiving because of black rot, but later writes in the October 1 entry that his father is disappointed in the grapes in his vineyard this season.

What is most revealing in Richard's journal is that there is no mention of Clara or the youngest of the Landis siblings, James Montevert, in any of the entries. Since James would have turned seven in October, requiring that he be placed in his father's custody, it might be expected that his name would be referenced in the journal, but there is no mention of him, indicating that he was not delivered into his father's care immediately upon his seventh birthday. Landis's absence from home during much of autumn 1882 may have delayed his youngest son's entry into the Vineland household. It is likely that he joined his brothers at the start of 1883.

Richard does write that William Adolph Baillie-Grohman, his father's good friend from his 1874 European trip, visited in early December and stayed with the family. It was expected that he would remain for three or four days, but his stay in Vineland lasted until December 11, when he departed for Philadelphia at 5:50 p.m.

In November 1883, Landis, in need of a change of location, arranged a trip to Florida with G.W. Bently, an old acquaintance. In New York, Bently, who was suddenly required to appear in court, informed Landis that he wouldn't be able to join him, but the Vinelander decided to proceed on his own. Because he chose this time to resume his journal, Landis provides details of a whirlwind tour of Florida that began with his departure from New York on the steamboat

Nachachee on November 10 and concluded with his return by train to Vineland on November 20. The trip included stops in Jacksonville, Sanford, Kissimmee and St. Augustine, all of which afforded Landis the opportunity to examine the orange groves and rail systems of the area. He learned a considerable amount of information from passengers on the *Nachachee* and continued his education by visiting with a Mr. Phelps, the owner of a successful orange grove in Sanford.

Landis also witnessed the gradual disappearance of the grand estates that had filled the South, "houses built with thick walls of concrete and overhanging piazzas. They are disappearing, however, bought up by wealthy Northerners who are building shingle palaces in their places." Homes weren't the only remnants of the Old South. There was a veteran of the Confederacy who spoke with Landis about the battles he witnessed.

His traveling companions for much of this short trip were the Browns, a Georgia couple. When Landis decided that he wanted to return home, they accompanied him on the train as far as Savannah. In the final portion of his return journey, Landis estimated that "there is a great future for Florida" in its cultivation of tropical fruit. As he approached the Northern states, the warm weather he had experienced in the South gave way to cooler temperatures and, arriving in Vineland at 4:50 p.m. on November 20, he discovered his family suffering with colds.

The following year, Landis requisitioned a lighthouse for Sea Isle City, an addition he had first considered as early as 1880. The urgency of such a structure stemmed from the recent shipwrecks that had occurred off the resort town's coast. The barrier island's location had always been the site of such occurrences, including one that had transpired around the time Vineland was being founded and which changed the fate of two cousins traveling from Europe, steering them to a life as Vinelanders in the process. But Landis felt that the existence of a Lifesaving Station in the town was not enough.

According to a 1999 *South Jersey Magazine* article, "Ludlam's Beach Light" by Philip W. Bur III, Landis requested government help for the establishment of a lighthouse. Aid arrived in the form of $5,000 authorized by Congress on July 7, 1884. By December, the United States Light House Board, established in 1852, designed the plans for a frame lighthouse and living quarters. A site on the beach at 31st Street near Lifesaving Station Number 33 was selected and purchased in 1885. The structure, which consisted of a white frame building adorned with green shutters, was built the same year. At a salary of $500 per year, Joshua H. Reeves was hired as the first Sea Isle City keeper, having already served as assistant keeper at the Barnegat Lighthouse. The new town's new addition commenced operation on November 3, 1885. The site was reinforced to protect it from high tides and the grounds also included a storage shed for the lamp oil and a privy in the back of the building. The beam from the lighthouse could, in clear weather, be seen 11 ½ miles from shore.

In the final days of 1884, Landis undertook another trip to Florida, this time for the express purpose of examining a railroad project out of Jacksonville which he was considering managing. The trip ran longer than his last and would enlist train transportation both to and from the South.

Departing on December 27 from Philadelphia, he arrived the next day in Jacksonville where he met G.W. Bently. Except for Jacksonville, this trip would focus on towns the Vinelander had not seen on his previous visit. He arrived in Leesburg the following day, impressed by a town that had begun twelve years earlier with lots that had sold for one to two dollars. Now worth $300 to $700 each, the lots indicated the growth the town had experienced. The population was 1,000 and it had become a railroad center.

Leesburg began to whet Landis's appetite and, by the time he arrived in Clermont the following day, his journal entries began to exhibit evidence of his entrepreneurship. In Clermont, he encountered a town that consisted of former Vinelanders, all in a panic over the halting of work at the local mill and at the construction site of a new hotel. Work had ceased because of the non-payment of wages, something Landis called "a fatal mistake in such an enterprise." And he remarks that "I could take this enterprise and make it a grand success if I had it myself."

He reacquainted himself with the former Vineland residents and stayed long enough to enjoy the sights of the area, including the lakes, but continued to contemplate the temptation of investing in the settlement. "I think if I had this location," he confides in his journal, "I might make a beautiful place." Even after returning to Jacksonville to conduct his business with the proposed railroad, which was to run through Clermont, he continued to contemplate the idea, writing, "If I had a good tract of land in the right place in Florida, I could get up a model settlement." But both the railroad project and Florida settlement failed to secure Landis's involvement.

The following day, January 4, 1885, he departed for New Orleans where he met former Vinelander John Zucca and his family, who now owned a fruit store. He enjoyed their company over the next ten days as he took in the sights of the city and surrounding area and experienced the culture which reflected what he had witnessed in Europe. Other than a mishap of falling and skinning his leg in the Zucca yard, he had a pleasant time that gave him an opportunity to meet up with J.F. Cooke of Cape May, who was working as a government agent.

But New Orleans was not one of Landis's favorite places. He complained of high prices, dirty streets and the lack of art. The only sad feeling elicited upon his departure was over the friends he had left behind. He had gained weight throughout the trip, increasing from 145 pounds at the start of the trip to 157 by the time he left on January 13. He was anxious to return to his family but concluded that "my trip has been a great benefit to me. [It] has strengthened me in every way."

Upon his return, Landis began to use Sea Isle City as a place of self-exile, spending much more time there and even listing his shore home at the northwest corner of Marine and Central Avenues as his address. The Vineland estate remained but, for the moment, served as a second home. Through the rest of the1880s, Landis didn't so much cut ties with the newly christened Vineland Borough as take a vacation from the settlement that needed him less and less.

Still unwilling to commit to any new major ventures in Vineland in 1884, Landis had turned his attention to designing a thoroughfare for Philadelphia, the location where he began his professional career and still maintained an office. Envisioning a roadway that would connect the city's business and political center with Fairmount Park, Landis planned a Grand Boulevard or Parkway that would reflect the sumptuous look of Europe in the City of Brotherly Love.

The idea for such an avenue did not originate with Landis. As early as 1858, the Philadelphia City Council had proposed the construction of two boulevards that would run between the suburbs and center city, but the plan, which included the improvement of streets, never advanced any further. According to *Historic Landmarks of Philadelphia* by Roger W. Moss, "a proposal dating from 1871 argued that if the park was truly to benefit the people of Philadelphia, it 'must be brought within reach of all. It must be connected with Broad Street and with the centre of the city by as short a route as possible; and the avenues which lead to it must be made elegant and attractive.'" Once again, this was as far as the plan would get.

Using the 1871 proposal as inspiration, Landis developed a design for just such a boulevard that would resist the city's grid structure and cut diagonally from the site of the current City Hall to the southern edge of Fairmount Park. The European look he envisioned reflected the designs from which he created Sea Isle City. Interestingly, Landis's approach predated the 1893 Chicago World's Fair and its French neoclassical White City, a Beaux Arts setting that would give birth to the City Beautiful movement that would follow and provide the initiative to complete Benjamin Franklin Parkway. Landis was at least ten years ahead of the movement when he devised his parkway plan.

It appears, however, that Landis's efforts to sell the idea to the city did not receive his full attention until late 1888. A map illustrating the design of his intended road began arriving in the mail of businessmen and city leaders at the start of 1889. For three years, Landis courted these Philadelphia connections in an attempt to earn the city's approval for his plan.

Extant correspondence about the proposed project reveals that the parkway, which was to be one mile in length and one-hundred-and-fifty-feet wide, met largely with approval and endorsement from those who viewed the map. Landis initially sent copies to certain Philadelphia businessmen to stir interest in his proposal and it worked. Throughout the first six months of the year, there was a continuous flow of requests for copies of the map along with responses of encouragement. "The suggestion has everything in its favor," one reply read, while Thomas S. Morton proclaimed "the plan has long been an ideal which I hoped most of all municipal improvements might ultimately go through and must take a very vivid interest in all that tends in that direction...the Avenue as proposed would undoubtedly be the greatest and most strikingly beautiful thing of the whole city, be of benefit and advantage in a myriad of ways, and the town would gain more benefit from the expenditure of a million dollars in this than in any other way." Charles B. Lynch, whose Market Street business sold watches, jewelry and silverware, wrote to say that he was framing his copy of the map and displaying in his window to inform the public.

By March, the reaction to the parkway had begun to spur questions. Morton reported to Landis that he had been asked "if the Avenue will cut any portion of Will's Hospital building and I have answered that it will not. Am I right?" Morton also offered the first indication of the political side of the project, mentioning that an undisclosed acquaintance interested in the project had asked "if you would be willing to meet the mayor by appointment and, with your engineer, carefully explain the plans to him?" He assures that "such appointment can be arranged." It was most likely what Landis had been waiting for, although there is no record of him meeting with Edwin Henry Fitler, who was then mayor of Philadelphia.

C. H. Showaker, who apparently experienced an unsuccessful run for City Council after he contacted Landis, wrote that, when elected, he would support the plan and "push it for all it's worth," and Morton reported that "an important member of the select council resides on West Logan square just south of where the Avenue will run, hence it is likely – especially as I understand that he owns other properties in the same neighborhood which would be vastly benefitted – that he would favor and take an interest in the project."

The business contacts Landis made during his first two years of promoting his design for a parkway failed to generate enough interest in Philadelphians, but one particular factor most likely served as a deterrent to the plan. For the project to be implemented, it was necessary for the city to acquire and destroy buildings in the path of the projected avenue. When the parkway project was eventually approved in the 20th Century, approximately 1,300 buildings that stood in the path of the boulevard were demolished. While businessmen and investors always saw an advantage to the parkway, concerned citizens from the start decried the destruction of such a large number of homes.

By December 1890, Landis received a letter that presumably prompted renewed vigor for the project and resulted in a new and more illustrious set of supporters. The letter, from William H. Capp, suggests that Landis take advantage of the circumstances that had recently developed in Philadelphia.

> Just now when we are having so much promise from the Committee of Fifty and the newspapers about the New Philadelphia, for which we have all been waiting so long, I hope your Boulevard Entrance to the Park from Broad and Market Streets will be taken up and receive the attention which its merits deserve. In today's *Ledger* I notice a long account of what various physicians have to say concerning the need of playgrounds, breathing spaces etc. Certainly the park would be much more frequented if some such wide, open and attractive avenue from the heart of the city led to it. Should you still feel like publicly manifesting an interest in a matter which relates to the best interests of the park and the city at large, I am sure that a general exhibition and advertisement of your excellent map with explanations, just now, in the proper quarters, would do much to enlist the popular favor in behalf of the plan. I have heard of no plans of improvement for the city which to my mind, seem to promise so much for the pleasant convenience of the citizens and at the same time will attract strangers of leisure to spend their money here.

The Committee of Fifty for a New Philadelphia, which Capp references in the opening of his letter, was the newest of reform groups determined to shut down the Republican political machine that had been ruling the city. *Cities in American Political History*, edited by Richard Dilworth, reports that "as with other major cities, what truly ran Philadelphia during this period was a corrupt political machine. In Philadelphia's case it was a Republican machine. Political corruption was in fact rife throughout Pennsylvania, and perhaps the worst excess in the city [was] the thirty-year-long construction of Philadelphia's City Hall from 1871 to 1901 at the cost of $24 million."

According to Peter McCaffery**'s** *When Bosses Ruled Philadelphia: The Emergence of the Republican Machine 1867-1933*, the political machine "was challenged by successive public watchdog committees, such as the Citizens' Municipal Association (CMA, 1886-1906) and the Committee of Seventy (1904 to the present), while in the electoral arena its supremacy was contested by a series of committees and third parties sponsored by nonpartisan reformers. These included the Citizens' Committee of Fifty for a New Philadelphia (1890-92) ...these reform groups differed from their predecessors, such as the Citizens' Municipal Reform Association (CMRA) and the Committee of One Hundred, in organizational breadth, depth, coherence and duration."

Most importantly, the Committee of Fifty for a New Philadelphia was comprised of prominent Philadelphia businessmen, some of whom were about to become supporters of Landis's parkway plan.

A month after Capp's letter, Landis received further encouragement and advice from Thomas S. Harrison of Harrison Brothers:

> I have looked with a great deal of pleasure at your plan of the proposed new avenue to the Park. The design is very excellent and undoubtedly just what is wanted, but I think that, while the improvement is being made it should be thorough, and to this end it seems to me that the boulevard, if possible, should be made three hundred feet [wide] instead of the one hundred and fifty, so as it compares with the Champs Elysees of Paris. I would suggest that it might be well for you to see Mr. Edward T. Steele, Mr. W. W. Justice and other similarly prominent gentlemen south of Market St. with a view to getting them to call a public meeting in furtherance of your project.

Landis responded to Harrison with a suggestion of a public meeting to promote the parkway, but Harrison's response favored a different approach:

> My thought was not for a public meeting at once. It was that a circular should go out, signed by a few reputable citizens, to a certain number of public-opinion-making men, that those men should be invited to a private conference, and that that conference suggest the best method to pursue to gain the end. All this cost[s] money and it seemed to me that the "conference" would make a small assessment, which would give the funds for printing

etc....I "talk" the new avenue now to all I meet, who will give me attention.

By April, Landis had impressively secured the support of Justus C. Strawbridge, one of the more prominent businessmen in Philadelphia. His advice echoed that of Harrison:

> Your circulation of the map of the proposed Boulevard to the Park has awakened much interest. I think the same map with new reading matter suggesting that if the people unite and pull together they could soon have the new drive to the Park. I would circulate at my own expense a large number with such an appeal to the people – if you would permit the use of your plans.

Within days, Landis granted permission and Strawbridge responded immediately:

> I thank you for the ready permission to use your plan of the Grand Av[enue] to the Park. I want to interest such men in the project as Mr. Drexel, Geo. B. Roberts, John C. Bullitt. Will you tell me who prints them for you and if I can get the plate? I want a copy sent to every member of all our driving clubs.

Landis may have been blinded by the prominence of these estimable gentlemen, failing to recognize that his second wave of powerful business contacts would inevitably doom his parkway project. Justus C. Strawbridge, Anthony J.

Drexel and William W. Justice were all members of the reformist Committee of One Hundred. Strawbridge was also an Officer of the CMA and a member of the Committee of Fifty, Justice was a member of the Committee of Seventy, Committee of Ninety-Five and CMA. Drexel was also a member of the Finance Committee of the CMRA. Even John C. Bullit's Bill, which became the Philadelphia City Charter, would have been perceived as an enemy of the Republican political machine controlling the government. With such allies, Landis guaranteed that political endorsement of his plan would be denied.

As of September 1891, Landis was still fulfilling requests for maps, but by 1892, during Edwin Sydney Stuart's term as Philadelphia mayor, he abandoned the project, having never successfully navigated the political waters of the city to win the necessary support he needed. It's curious, then, that in 1892, after Landis had finally conceded defeat, the project was resurrected under the auspices of another individual. According to Roger W. Moss, "proponents of such a boulevard succeeded temporarily in gaining political support for an 1892 refinement of the Landis scheme created by James H, Windrim, the City director of public works...Windrim's plan called for a 160-foot-wide boulevard boldly sundering the rigid grid of Philadelphia streets from City Hall, across Logan Square, and on to Fairmount Park. Then the scheme fell afoul of Philadelphia's notorious Republican political machine..."

In 1893 the Chicago World's Fair had introduced the City Beautiful movement with its White City exhibit, inspiring the beautification process of America's urban centers. From

1907, when Philadelphia, amid continued debate, granted approval to Fairmount Parkway, as it was originally dubbed, until 1917, when the avenue was redesigned by French planner Jacques Greber, Landis's name had receded and soon disappeared from the project altogether. Yet, despite all the architects credited for the completed parkway, Landis's original vision can be seen in the finished form, demonstrating that his plans were the first serious attempt at building such a grand avenue.

In 1926, Philadelphia hosted the Sesquicentennial International Exhibition or World's Fair to celebrate the birth of America. The Borough of Vineland secured a booth at the event as a means of promoting the town in the more competitive 20th Century. At the event's conclusion in November, Vineland bestowed upon a representative of Philadelphia's mayor a map of Landis's parkway design. It was treated as a revelation, but unbeknownst to both the givers and the recipients, numerous copies of that map had already circulated among the businessmen within the City of Brotherly Love nearly forty years earlier.

As Landis was readying his Philadelphia parkway project in the mid-1880s, Charles Jr. had, in 1886, entered the Pennsylvania Military Academy in Chester, Pennsylvania. He had completed his early education at private and public schools in Vineland and studied land surveying with his father's clerk Marcus Fry before attending the Military Academy. One letter Charles Jr. wrote to his father indicates that he was rather content at this new facility. In this correspondence, dated January 13, 1887, he writes,

Dear Father,

   I arrived here last Friday evening and found my room-mate in good health…There are new cadets and some of the old ones have left. Aside from this I do not think that… Colonel [Hart]'s death will interfere with the hither-to-good course of affairs. A large picture of him has been placed in the Assembly-room. It is draped in mourning and presents a fine appearance.

The letter then conveys the studies Charles Jr. was undertaking in the new semester and his enthusiasm for one of the classes.

   I am now studying trigonometry, chemistry, German, drafting, epistolary composition and Bible. I think that chemistry will be a most delightful study. The method by which it is here taught demands a great deal of experimenting by the pupil aside from the study of theory. This has many advantages over others.

After describing the new mathematics room as large, well-lighted and more conducive for study, he addresses several family matters: "You may tell my aunt [Matilda] that the watch has been keeping time well and that as yet I have had no difficulty with it. My Jaeger flannels are very comfortable." He calls the weather "disagreeable," describing recent snowfall, fog and rain and concludes with "I suppose that all things at home are the same as when I left there. Give my love to grandma and my aunt. Hoping to hear from you soon, I remain your affectionate son, Charles K. Landis Jr."

It was during the late 1880s that the life of Charles Jr.'s mother had reached the type of contentment her son describes in his letter. When Clara Landis began her European travels in July 1876, she was still legally married to Charles K. Landis and had custody of their youngest son, James Montevert. This was not the first time she had traveled abroad, according to an account given in the 1960s by her grandson, J. Meade Landis, in which he reported that she had been educated abroad and became fluent in French and German. She had been denied the opportunity to join her husband during his 1874 voyage to Europe, resenting her exclusion from what became nearly a nine-month excursion. Now, free to traverse the Atlantic Ocean of her own accord, her trips over the next several years seemingly began as a retreat from her marriage but eventually became a reinvention of herself.

An 1885 article from the *St. Louis Globe-Democrat* reports that Clara "was furnished money from Landis with which to travel abroad." It may account for how she was able to afford servants at the time. But, unlike her husband, whose European activities are precisely recorded in a journal, Clara left very little trace of her life abroad. It is known that she returned to the U.S. at the start of 1877, appearing in Trenton for her custody battle with Landis. She may have returned to Europe with all three children during 1877 but, by March 1878, the seven-year-old Charles Jr. would have returned to Vineland. Her whereabouts in early 1879, however, are verified as Nice, France, where she met and fell in love with Baron Von Mutzenbach, whom she credits with building "the celebrated bridge over the Rhine at Coblentz [sic]," despite modern sources crediting Robert Gerwig with designing and managing the construction of the Koblenz Bridge.

Back in the U.S., Landis seems to have been following the exploits of his wife and her new love interest. According to the *Globe-Democrat*, "Landis learned some facts concerning the conduct of his troublesome spouse which enabled him to get a divorce." News of her romance with a ranking European figure may have been enough for Landis to do what he hadn't done three-and-a-half years earlier. A June 1879 announcement in an unidentified newspaper confirms how fast Vineland's founder reacted to the news: "Charles K. Landis, of Vineland, has been granted a divorce on the ground of desertion." It's probably no coincidence that the finalization of the divorce occurred in the same timeframe as the marriage of the former Mrs. Landis and Von Mutzenbach. It seems that Clara was simply awaiting the legal end of her first union. With her second wedding, she became a countess.

Clara later told reporters that she and her second husband "lived happily," but it turned out to be only for a short period. By the spring of 1880, Von Mutzenbah died. And Clara returned to America for a brief visit. A journal entry in Landis's diary that April confirms that "Mrs. Landis" has returned to the U.S."

Returning to Europe sometime that summer, Clara lived with the baron's family in Wiesbaden, Germany. The *Globe-Democrat* reports that Baron Von Mutzenbach "actually possessed some property," and his widow was reported to have a legacy of $10,000 per year left to her, to be paid as long as she did not remarry. It seems as if Clara was financially settled for the rest of her life, able to live comfortably on the annuity provided by her husband's will and free to travel between Europe and America whenever she pleased. But a letter from her sister changed all that.

According to Clara's account, published in the *Buffalo Courier* in 1884, "I accepted my sister's invitation to visit her at Washington." Clara booked passage on a steamer headed for America and, on November 3, 1880, unknowingly embarked on a path that abandoned both her Washington visit and her annuity. Aboard the steamer, she met and immediately fell in love with Gerald Moore, who had set sail for the U.S. in hopes of remaking himself in a land known for new opportunity. During the voyage, Moore courted Clara and, upon their arrival in New York City, they married. The newlyweds settled in New York and Moore took a job as a secretary at the Co-operative and Accident Life Insurance Company. Unbeknownst to the former countess, her husband had begun reinventing himself before they met.

Moore's past soon began to surface through an encounter with Thomas Lodge, who had happened upon the newlyweds in New York City. It turned out that Moore's real name was T.J. McAfee. Born in 1852, he had become the breadwinner for his family at the age of fifteen following the death of his father. He accepted a position at a music store and over the next ten years was promoted to manager. Near the end of his tenure, the store became embroiled in an embezzlement scandal in which one business partner had defrauded another. By this time, McAfee, never a participant in the illicit activities, had taken to spending most of his non-working hours in the local pubs. The focus of his ruminations there was his recent marriage to Mary Lodge, a local shop-girl who, according to McAfee in a later interview, was "a person of unrefined manners and entirely without education" and whose mother worked as a housekeeper for a boardinghouse. He had failed to heed the warnings of his own mother who had vehemently disapproved of the union.

McAfee contemplated a way out of his marital dilemma, choosing to inform his wife that he had embezzled the money at his workplace and now needed to flee the country. He set off alone from Dublin, his marriage not even a year old. Upon his arrival in Paris, he made the first of several fateful decisions by assuming the name of Gerald Moore. He then traveled to Marseilles where he booked passage on a steamer bound for America. When he met Countess Von Mutzenbach, he fell in love. "I saw in her the woman who could reclaim me from the depths of degradation into which I had fallen," he later declared. However, he refrained from revealing the lie about his involvement in the embezzlement scheme and the fact that he was married to Mary Lodge, consoling himself with the idea that there was no need to obtain a divorce if he remarried in the U.S. since he had previously wedded in another country.

By her own admission, Clara first learned of her husband's true background and legal complications from Thomas Lodge, Mary's brother. The couple hired a lawyer they mistakenly felt could be trusted and, failing to remedy the matter, decided to separate, Clara demanding that Moore remove himself from her life. Leaving New York, Moore traveled to Connecticut, pursued by detectives Lodge had hired. Meanwhile, Clara reconsidered her decision and realized her "love for him was too intense." They reunited in New Jersey, taking a train from Patterson to Chicago and then St. Paul where they intended to proceed to the West Coast. St. Paul, however, proved attractive enough for the couple and they settled there with McAfee working in the stationery trade, free from threatening legalities, East Coast detectives and Lodge. But escaping the past turned out to be more difficult than they imagined.

By 1884, Lodge had determined the whereabouts of the couple and arrived in Minnesota with Mary. Her presence added weight to the legal plight in which McAfee had become hopelessly entangled and it was obvious the couple's attempts to outrun these matters by journeying across the U.S. had reached a dead end. When, on August 14, 1884, McAfee, was arrested on charges of bigamy, their lives would take a most unexpected turn. By the time McAfee appeared before Minnesota Judge Brill in St. Paul that October and was sentenced to three years in Stillwater Prison, national attention had focused on the couple. But if Clara had been shy of the press during her years in Vineland, she had become media savvy by late 1884.

She wasted no time planting her story in the press. She gave an extensive interview for an article that was syndicated in many newspapers, including the *New York Herald* and the *Buffalo Courier*. In that piece and others, Clara recounted her story from her early days in Brooklyn as the daughter of Commodore Richard Warsam Meade to her time married to Landis and her subsequent divorce and second marriage to Von Mutzenbach. The purpose of the interview can be viewed as a means of eliciting the sympathy of readers and survival may have been the motivating force behind it.

After McAfee's arrest and incarceration, Clara faced difficult times and not always from reporters. Having terminated a $10,000 annuity provided by her second husband's will when she married McAfee, she now faced a series of troubles that began with eviction from the Pleasant Avenue rooms the couple rented from the Hetheringtons. "Mrs. Hetherington has been very kind to me," Clara explains in her interview, "and told me to stay at her house until any trouble was over. She went to Detroit the very day my husband was arrested, and her husband turned me out into the streets. I had pawned everything I had to raise funds to engage lawyers for my husband, and for the first time in my life I was homeless, friendless and without a penny. To add to my misfortune, I had a baby but a month old." The infant was the couple's first daughter.

In the interview, she describes her difficulty in trying to raise money for lawyers by selling items for a fraction of their worth. "One lawyer here charged me $30," she says, "and to procure it I was obliged to part with a sealskin sacque worth $125. After receiving money from the East I tried to get it back but was unable to until yesterday, when it was obtained through the kindness of Judge Eagan." Curiously, she doesn't identify whether her benefactor "from the east" was a family member or her first husband, who certainly would have followed the media's coverage of McAfee's scandal.

"But why worry you with these petty details?" Clara asks the reader. "My God, you cannot comprehend…what I have suffered. Ever since my husband's arrest, Lodge has tried every means to turn me against [McAfee], and failed, [and] has even attacked the purity of my life. I am a heartbroken and weak woman but let him beware. I shall remain here during the three years of my husband's confinement, and then I trust God that we may be once more united."

After her eviction, Clara found temporary lodging for three days thanks to a woman she met before a Reverend Gilbert "interested himself in my behalf and procured for me my present resting place." According to a December 1885 article in the *New York Tribune*, Clara had been taken in by the Women of the Home for the Friendless in St. Paul. The situation was a far cry from the conditions she was used to during her marriages to Landis and Von Mutzenbach, but her determination to remain with McAfee and to win his release were her guiding forces over the next year.

McAfee was also interviewed at the time. Giving a brief overview of his life, he focused his attention near the end of the article on his present situation and Clara. He begins by stating that he is willing to serve his three-year sentence "in order to free myself from what was once my [first] wife. In regard to my present wife I will say nothing that will associate her with my former life. She has reclaimed me from my fallen condition and had I but met her in the first place I should have never been disgraced."

Shortly after her husband's incarceration in November 1884, Clara decided to relocate to Stillwater, Minnesota. McAfee was in the territorial prison just north of the town. There is little known about the time he spent at the correctional facility except for a curious bit of information that emerged in the *New York Tribune* on December 31,

1885. "Since his incarceration, McAfee has saved aside from the small allowance for good time, some $25 a month, earned as a bookkeeper," the report reads. Meanwhile, Clara set to work trying to facilitate the release of her husband. She petitioned the right people, taking her cause all the way to the state government and Governor Lucius Frederick Hubbard. The petitioning was successful and, in December 1885, thirteen months after he was imprisoned, McAfee was released from Stillwater and immediately became the center of media attention once again.

Two months after her husband's release, Clara left Stillwater with the couple's child and relocated to Hudson, Wisconsin and spent the next three months waiting for McAfee to join them. There is no recorded explanation as to what motivated the move, but there are accounts of what McAfee was up to from March until May 1886.

Clara's husband lost no time in filing for divorce from Mary Lodge. Mary had arrived in Minnesota in 1884 in order to prove the bigamy charges leveled against McAfee. According to the *New York Tribune*, Mary remained in the U.S., living with her brother in Minneapolis. "She is still McAfee's wife," the report states, "but will seek a divorce." It was obvious, then, that McAfee would encounter no resistance in his attempts to dissolve the marriage. The only problem he met with was the wait until the processing of the divorce was complete. Ironically, he spent his time at Stillwater Prison, not as an inmate but as the correctional facility's accountant, earning "a lucrative salary," according to a *New York Times* article from 1886.

At the end of May 1886, the divorce was official, and McAfee traveled immediately to Hudson, Wisconsin. The family reunion was followed by what the *New York Times* called a "remarriage" of the couple. "The second marriage ceremony," the article reports, "was performed by the Rev. L.L. Kneeland, of the Baptist Church. Mr. and Mrs. McAfee are both communicants of the Episcopal church, but the Rev. Mr. Slidell refused to marry them on account of conscientious scruples on divorce." The article is revealing in that Clara, a Catholic through much of her life, had converted to the Episcopal faith.

After scandals had plunged her into an unwanted spotlight twice in a ten-year period, Clara seemed to have finally achieved what she probably desired all along – the opportunity to melt into the oblivion of an average life. And she succeeded, for the most part. Other than the birth of the couple's second daughter, there are very few traces of this family after the bigamy scandal had subsided. It would be a non-eventful existence until Landis's death provided a very brief, yet intriguing, glimpse of Clara's life at the time.

Chapter 10
The Final Decade
(1890-1899)

Landis would begin the 1890s in much the same way as he had spent the start of the previous three decades – engaged in a series of projects that kept him busy and content. Over the first several years of the 1890s, he would undertake improvements in Sea Isle City, even entertaining the notion of establishing a race track in the resort town, an idea that did not survive beyond the discussion stage. He still maintained an office in Vineland from which he largely conducted his business and also reported on occasion to his Philadelphia office. He would spend more time writing fiction in favor of his journal and even publishing a work of historical fiction. His propensity for creating new towns led him further west into Cumberland County with plans for a new settlement and north from Sea Isle City for another resort. His yearning for new experience and knowledge would spur his wanderlust throughout the decade and into the year of his death. It would be his final ten years and he filled them with the richest of accomplishments.

In late 1889, Landis undertook a second journey to Europe. Like his first in 1874, this trip mixed business and pleasure. But it was a wiser and more seasoned Landis who traveled to Holland, France, Italy and Egypt. Whereas his leanings fifteen years early had been to learn about cultures and accumulate antiquities, this expedition was filled with more musings about family, class and personal reflection. Instead of being plagued by the anxiety that hounded his previous overseas travel, Landis undertook the trip at a time when he feels "I have much to be thankful for in the past year," and his journals reflect a more meditative state, perhaps nurtured by his advanced age and awareness of mortality. The entries at times display examples of his personal resolve and on occasion serve to debate unresolved subjects, while the writing style offers evidence that Landis had by now achieved a mastery of style and form. Instead of simply describing the scenes he witnesses, he explores the narratives of the people and the cultures he encounters, intermingling them with his thoughts and evaluations to create a written tapestry that would surface again in the fiction he would produce several years later.

Landis did not begin his journal at the start of the trip when he departed New York on November 23. Instead, he commences his account on December 8 in Holland, where he would begin his study of sea defense methods used to reinforce coastal towns. In 1888, severe storms and unusually high tides had pounded Sea Isle City, requiring temporary repairs to the sea wall protecting the lighthouse. The following year, a September storm wreaked havoc on the town, threatening the lighthouse and forcing its keeper to vacate the structure after finding it necessary to remove the lamp to prevent its destruction. The recent addition of a new sea wall survived the storm but the old wall, parts of which were still being used, didn't. Such threats convinced Landis that he should research sea defenses in European countries facing the same conditions as his resort. He would also talk to experts about the marine lab he envisioned for the town. This trip and its findings would be one of his last significant investments in the resort before returning full-time to Cumberland County and his home in Vineland.

Landis traveled on the French Transatlantic Steamer *Gascoigne*, enjoying what he says was a "pleasant voyage" for the first few days before he encountered a wounded sparrow he believed may have been harmed by the sailors because of their superstition that it was an omen. He revives the bird but does not see it again during his journey across the ocean. "How like some of us poor mortals, who also in thought and soul get far beyond our depth," he records in his first entry. "I sympathized with the little sparrow as I had seen the time when I had as tho' 'on some sea of trouble.'" The entry is indicative of the ruminations Landis would entertain throughout the trip.

Arriving first in Paris, Landis enjoyed a visit to the Louvre and the Eiffel Tower before setting out for Holland to meet with engineers concerning designs of dyke protection that might be useful in Sea Isle City. In his first meeting, he discovered that "the main reliance was upon jetties and afterward embankments. All was upon a slope, both jetties and embankments, front and behind…top water was allowed in case of a spring tide to go under the wall. Soon saw that I could adapt this principle to Sea Isle."

Landis was taken with the Dutch scenery and on several occasions expressed hope that his artistically-inclined son Richard would one day see these sights. While sight-seeing, his mind never strayed far from New Jersey, formulating ideas that would be beneficial to the state. In Ijmuiden he even devised a plan for a canal that would cut across the state from the Delaware River "near Bordentown, over to the Raritan Bay, connecting the Atlantic Ocean with the river Delaware. It would be 27 miles and worth millions to the country and the commerce of Philadelphia," but concluded that his idea would most likely be opposed by the Pennsylvania Railroad.

After a week in Holland, Landis noticed that he has not seen any signs of drunkenness and, inquiring about it, learned that new laws had mandated that anyone arrested a third time for drunkenness spends one year working in a drunkard's asylum. "It would be a good idea to have these asylums in the [U.S.]," Landis states in his journal. "They can always work upon the land for nine months out of the year and the rest of the time they could do something." He obtained a copy of the law but could not find anyone to translate it for him and resolved to undertake that task when he returned home, concluding, "if the law is a good one and practicable in America, I may have it passed in my own state."

During his visits to Amsterdam and Strasburg, Landis neglected his journal for a few days, chiding himself that he must "do better in the future." He once again mentions Richard, hoping that he might "someday take sketches or make paintings of such villages as these" and purchasing German beer glasses and other items from which his son can work on still life paintings.

While in Germany, Landis began his observations of the poor and what he calls the "cruelty of class." Leaving for Italy on January 1, 1890, he would continue his examination of the class system amid the familiar sites he first witnessed just over fifteen years earlier when such a topic was not a concern. At Pompeii, he confesses he is mystified because he is assigned a guide while others simply follow the crowds for tours and confesses that it has happened in Holland and Germany as well. He praises the Italian government, proclaiming, "like some other nations it now takes care of its poor." The people he encounters in Naples "all appear to me to be workers but cheerful over their work," yet the concern and horror he expresses in witnessing young girls carrying baskets of dirt or stones upon their heads, he realizes, is his alone.

While in Italy, Landis was vocal about what Italian emigrants, many of whom had come from poverty in their home country, had accomplished in Vineland. "These are the kind of men who improve a country and make it better," he states. "Who ever saw rich men laboring? At best they are parasites. What mistakes conventional people make on these subjects. Who settled America but poor people? Who do the best work now in America but poor people? And how soon they or their sons become worthless when they get rich?"

Art, both natural and man-made, is a significant topic Landis returns to in his journal. He writes that the citizens of Naples can marvel at a public garden filled with trees, statues and fountains. The museums and galleries, educational systems in their own right, are open on Sundays. He becomes aware that "the human form in the nude state is familiar to them on all sides. The statues in the streets and public gardens on all sides." Landis was given a private performance of the tarantella by four women who, as was the custom, were nude during the dance. When he protested that it wasn't necessary for them to disrobe, his host explained that the women would misunderstand and take it as an affront.

Landis attended operas while in Italy and visited museums, but it was the art of nature that seems to have captivated him the most during his trip. He returns to certain sites to marvel at the natural beauty on display and concludes at one point, "when we look upon these works of Nature antedating history, we feel like mere ephemera."

In the mountainside village of Mola, he is taken with the beauty of the landscape, the simplicity of the peasants and the isolation of the location. He praises the village and "the sublimity of Nature softened by its beauty" and notes that he is "here among the simple children of Nature, in the absence of the artificial and conventional. I feel that it would all harmonize with my soul."

For Landis, nature provides a more enduring art form than those produced by man and his reflections on such matters suggest a concern about his own achievements in Vineland and Sea Isle City, a perception that developed over the passage of time. Surveying the ruins of the

412

Mediterranean towns and villages through which he journeys, he is struck by the sense of impermanence. "What a lesson of the mutability of human things," he writes, "where there were so many vast buildings so little should be left." Such concern over the demise of things may have been fueled by his own health issues. He mentions on more than a few occasions of having difficulty breathing and complains of many "bad nights" due to his condition.

Landis did not confine his dining to hotels and restaurants. Meals were also taken in small villages with families who seemed to dote on the American and his companions. Commenting on the health of some peasant girls, he concludes that "their poor food does them more good than our luxurious eating does us. They are well, they sleep well and eat well and may be happier than the rich." He is overwhelmed by the bond evident in the families he meets throughout Italy, remarking that "conjugal and paternal love are the two sweetest things on earth, and those who in life have missed them, have missed what millions cannot supply the place of, and yet many a poor peasant is blessed with both." Later, Landis poses the question, "Can a man be happy without a family?" and answers, "I do not believe it."

"My study is humanity," Landis proclaims in one journal entry, and his examination of various cultures during the trip attests to that. While in Palermo, Sicily, he dines at a restaurant named for the American president Lincoln. There is also a street bearing his name. Landis is told that the reason for the popularity of the U.S. leader "was due to him as a friend of human freedom." Landis calls this true fame, adding "the assassin's bullet cannot kill such a man – his example lives with its unceasing influence."

By the middle of January, Landis had made the acquaintance of John Hale Sheafe, "one of those sybarite Americans who wander continually over Europe." The two would visit a number of towns and sites together, spending evenings at their hotel drinking wine, reciting from the poetry of Burns and Byron and discussing a variety of subjects. By the end of the month, Landis seems to have tired of his traveling companion, citing differences in taste as a good reason to depart from the company of his new friend. But that same day, he experienced a change of heart, realizing he "felt an attachment to Sheafe for some things" but admitting he felt no sympathy for things like his companion's suspicious nature.

The decision not to abandon Sheafe would soon become significant. On February 1 Landis awoke from a dream in which he was home again. Until then he had been able to stave off the urge to return home by consistently writing letters to his sister, his sons and friends, but now he was unable to shake the homesickness that had taken hold of him and was convinced that it was time to travel back to the U.S. He shared his decision with Sheafe, who proceeded to explain that, although he himself missed his wife, he would not consider returning to America before April in order to witness the splendor of the European spring. "Whilst I have a fierce countenance and apparently act with temper, but really act with reflection," Sheafe counseled his friend, "you with a placid face and sensible talk act from impulse. Where, oh where, has that heart of yours lead you in its day?"

Landis may not have been used to someone talking to him that way, especially an individual he had known for less than a month. But he confesses in his journal that "though I hate the idea of the character he gave me, from my secret knowledge of the past, I know he diagnosed very well, and yet I denied the charges." Sheafe's talk convinced Landis to remain in Europe and ponder his fellow traveler's assessment a bit further.

Throughout the journal entries of his second European trip, Landis discusses his love of animals. In his lifetime, the Vinelander counted the dogs that were his pets as part of the family. These included such faithful canines as Jake, Snap, Spottie, Tanner and Pete. Even Matilda owned pets including a dog named Jack. The rights he championed for women and African Americans extended to animals as well. During his time in Sea Isle City, a seal appeared at Townsend's Inlet one day and was shot by the first person who saw it, its carcass left on the beach. Landis called the incident "a brutal act," pointing out that more seals might inhabit Sea Isle City if it weren't for hunters. "The idea that man," he reasons, "because he is a man, has a right over all other animal life is an erroneous, unconscionable and a brutal doctrine, and must be a sin for which he must be held responsible." Landis didn't simply make idle threats. Within two days, he had drafted a law "to protect seals that visit our waters from being killed." These views also applied to animals used to haul and transport heavy goods. When, in Italy, he witnessed the mistreatment of a mule by its owner, he swore in his journal, "Oh God! How I wished to cowhide that driver. I should like to have him for an hour to give him a lesson of kindness to animals."

By the time Landis reached the island of Capri in early February, he was keeping company with the American artist Charles Caryl Coleman and the American writer Francis Marion Crawford. Coleman, who was born in 1840 in Buffalo, New York, had settled in Italy years earlier, first in Rome and then Capri where, in 1870, he transformed a convent into the Villa Narcissus, a palace of art housing vintage works and his own paintings. His style is photographic in nature and Landis no doubt introduced his son Richard to Coleman's works. Crawford, fourteen years younger than Coleman, used the Italian setting in which he had been living for his novels. In 1890, his book *A Cigarette Maker's Romance* was published and it's likely that his follow-up, *Khaled: A Tale of Arabia*, was being written at the time of Landis's visit to Villa Crawford, the former Villa Renzi.

Receiving an invitation to have coffee at Coleman's villa, Landis visited the artist as he was working in Capri instead of his Rome studio, completing paintings he planned to take to America when he traveled to see his mother in March. Landis refers to his host as a gentleman and "an eminent artist." He continued to meet with Coleman over the following week, taking walks through the countryside and rendezvousing at the artist's villa, sometimes with Sheafe, for discussions and musical performances. It was through Coleman that he learned of Crawford's nearby residence. Landis had read all of the novelist's books and admired his unconventional ways, including his preference of spending time with the peasants and even joining a fishing expedition that ended with the writer sleeping on the beach with his companions rather than at a first-class hotel.

Landis makes clear his contempt for those who judged Crawford as crazy for his refusal to assume the mantle of the upper class. "God, can people be such idiots," he exclaims. "Such ignoble natures, if they cannot understand Crawford, might they not suspect there is nothing in themselves? No, their minds are too small for anything beyond a groove of the narrowest conventionality."

Throughout his time in Capri, Landis continued to suffer from ill health and it was Coleman who offered the visiting American a solution, advising him to travel to Cairo, Egypt. The artist explained that the warmer climate would help and offered to write Landis a letter of introduction to a friend who had recently opened a studio there. Landis made arrangements to take a steamer leaving February 12 for Egypt and then settled into his hotel to read Robert Louis Stevenson's *The Master of Ballantrae*. The next day he discovered the boat that would take him to the steamer would not leave on time for the rendezvous, and he settled back into Capri. The delay led to the purchase of one of Coleman's paintings that is now in the possession of the Vineland Historical and Antiquarian Society.

The purpose behind the purchase was not to enhance the Historical Society's archives, however. Landis reveals in a later diary entry that he called on Coleman to pay for the painting in advance, thinking that the artist might be able to apply the earnings to his upcoming trip to America. Landis records that he bid farewell to Coleman and his house staff and explains that "this picture is perfectly lovely and will be a help to my son Dick. He will copy it."

Having to wait several more days to catch a steamer to Egypt, Landis spent his nights suffering from incessant coughing. But he was resolved that the Egyptian climate would assist in his recovery, writing that "I wish to return home well that I may be able to put some strong work into my business. "

What may be most surprising about Landis's outlook as he neared the age of sixty was the comfort he expressed in reflecting on what may be considered his bleakest moments. His writings reflect an acceptance of what had happened with the Carruth incident and a better understanding of himself in this later period of life. While touring one site with Sheafe, Landis listened to his companion describe the place as a prison. The Vinelander comments in his journal that it was clear Sheafe had never spent time in a prison. More telling is the counseling he provided for his traveling companion in which he recalled Plato's metaphor of the soul as a charioteer and human passions the horses. In recounting the talk, Landis alludes to the shooting of Carruth when he admits "I succeeded in mounting the chariot and my greatest effort is often necessary in holding these steeds and preventing their throwing me again." He also expresses no bitterness or regret over his marriage in passages that discuss love, family and motherhood.

On February 16, Landis set sail on the maiden voyage of the *Tara* for Egypt, the setting he chose for his first attempt at writing a novel five decades earlier. Sheafe saw him off and the two made plans to meet in Florence before the Vinelander's return to the U.S. The *Tara* carried 400 English emigrants, 175 of whom were traveling to Australia. Among the passengers heading there was a clergyman and his three daughters who became the Vinelander's companions until reaching Egypt. The clergyman carried a revolver to protect himself and his daughters and later offered it to Landis when he volunteered to take the vicar's daughters on a horse ride once they arrived in Egypt. The American was uncomfortable carrying the weapon and cajoled the clergyman into joining them and pocketing the gun. While there were no moments that provoked gunplay, they discovered that other passengers had been beaten and stabbed in a café. Landis attributed the incident to liquor, and his stay in Egypt prompted him to reveal the reason he found drunkenness so distasteful. "Some of the sweetest girls I have ever known," he confesses, "have only lived to be the victims of drunken and unworthy husbands."

Spending his last hours with the vicar's family in Port Said, Landis takes them horseback riding and, as the owner of a horse himself, demonstrates kindness by offering his horse an apple and stroking its nose and neck. Shortly afterward, the *Tara* resumed its journey, taking the clergyman and his daughters with it and Landis was alone in Egypt. He would wonder later about his English companions, admitting that he thinks of them often.

At the time of Landis's arrival, Egypt had been under British rule for eight years, a situation that gave evidence of some resentment from individuals the American met. Landis became interested in the situation of the farmer there and felt that those involved in agriculture had benefitted from a moderate and stabilized tax under the British. But he rails against certain conditions, including the educational process. Visiting a university in Cairo, he witnesses various lessons being taught, all which involved the Koran. "I discovered no other study," he writes, "no geometry, no natural history, no sciences…thus Egypt becomes the victim of the sciences of the Western world and any nation with this science can become the master of her wealth...."

Landis sees failings such as these as indicative of human nature. "What animal is more foolish and stupid than man?" he asks. "It is man alone that, turning his back on the laws of nature, accepts some man insane upon religion or something else and goes on for centuries making a fool of himself until he accepts some other dream , whilst all the while he violates the laws of nature and common justice – and his inner conscience and understanding."

While Landis found his hosts a highly "talented and noble people," his concerns about the emphasis on religious teachings may have stemmed from witnessing the exclusion of women from ceremonies of worship. "Think of the baseness and selfishness of any religion that would discriminate against woman," he writes. "Any religion that makes such a mistake about sacred womanhood...I do not feel much interest in."

Landis's illness had caused him to neglect his research concerning the Sea Isle City marine lab while in Europe, but his stay in Egypt remedied both matters. Within the first week of his arrival, he reports that his health is greatly improved and that "the temperature is that of summer weather... and I am getting entirely well. What a relief to be rid of the coughing in the morning and to have rest from it at night!" His improved condition allowed him to contact Dr. Charles S. Dolley of the University of Pennsylvania about the lab. He had also been in contact with his Camden lawyer Edward B. Leaming about getting the necessary legislation required for the lab, but was informed that nothing could be done until his return to the U.S.

Landis wished to immerse himself in the Egyptian culture and partook of their food, coffee and even a Turkish pipe. He favored places like Ismolia, founded by an individual who planted trees in the desert, brought water and dirt from the Nile River and established "a beautiful little city well shaded." Such settlements, no doubt, reminded him of his own accomplishments and their success spoke a universal language to someone like Landis.

For a short period, Landis spent time in the company of an English coal merchant by the name of John B. Kneen, who had lived in Egypt for twenty years. Dining with the British businessman on a few occasions, Landis felt comfortable having found a new companion. But within a short time, Kneen returned to Alexandria. Landis was later to lament, "I no sooner make an acquaintance than they are gone."

At the suggestion of a fellow traveler, Landis ventured on a journey down the Nile River. The experience would take him to the sights of Luxor, Karnac and Philae, exposing him to the sights of Egyptian antiquity and working-class lives. His concentration was just as much on the farmers as it was on the ruins and tombs that filled the major cities. For Landis, the irrigation system employed by those engaged in agriculture was fascinating and he marveled at the bountiful crops that resulted. He noticed that entire families were engaged in the processes of the working day and noted that there were no bad farmers in Egypt. Yet he was appalled by the curfews set by the British in urban areas in which residents could not leave their homes at nightfall or even leave the town without prior permission. The consequence of any such violation led to arrest and the Vinelander equated the circumstances to serfdom.

Each visit to temples and ruins produced increased amazement in Landis's journal entries. He explains his philosophy of sight- seeing as an exercise in pleasure and instruction, "that the natural operation of the mind for any profit was first to receive a strong, vivid impression – this generates an idea – this idea may produce something in conversation, writing or thought or memory. It is this process only that fills the mind with beautiful pictures and with wisdom." Still, witnessing an American flag or an American mission couldn't help but summon a sense of pride. And when he encountered several women who were more than familiar with Vineland because of friends who had been there, it was the pleasantest of surprises.

Landis's explorations included visiting ruins on his own before daylight one morning despite the danger of which he had been warned. But his determination prevailed, and he describes the beauty of the experience: "A profound silence reigned over all things, and in the soft rays of the moon and the shadows cast, the vast pillars, colossi and broken buildings looked more sublime than ever."

On March 15, his fellow travelers arranged for a group portrait while in Luxor, the former Thebes. Landis misunderstood when the photo was to be taken and missed the session. The other passengers suggested that he take a separate photo, and he agreed. The next day, his birthday, he visited the photographer to make arrangements and together they "went to the temple of Luxor built 1,600 years before Christ, where it was taken." The photograph, which Landis picked up during a return visit to Luxor five days later, reveals how age and ill-health had taken their toll on the fifty-seven-year-old Vinelander.

Although he traveled with a largely unchanging group of people, Landis did not strike up the kind of friendship he had recently developed with Sheafe or with the Grohman family during his 1874 trip. He remained in the company of a dozen travelers for a period of fifteen days and developed good relationships with them, mentioning them in his journal entries, particularly Luise Schluessner, a writer who earned everyone's affection and the nickname "the German lady" because of her ladylike demeanor. He accompanied them to various sites, dined with them, regaled them with anecdotes and even offered them his views on animals ("I stated my belief that animals have souls...What a dreary place heaven would be with only men and women."), but he had not found a traveling companion with whom he felt comfortable enough to share his thoughts and concerns as he had done with Sheafe. When he advises a Russian man on his way to the U.S. about American law and the judicial system favors women, he carefully avoids any details of his 1877 custody battle.

Still, he records in his journal the names and addresses of his traveling companions on what was dubbed the Toski Expedition, noting that "one of the most painful things about travel is the parting with people for whom we contract sentiments of friendship – so often to part forever." On March 31, eleven passengers embarked on their own journeys elsewhere. Landis would do the same the next day.

With his health vastly improved, Landis had taken in the breathtaking sights without any further medical issues. At times he had become meditative and speculative, as he did when his discovery of the red granite of one region provoked questions about the future. Noting that the granite had existed for 4,000 years, he wonders "who will be here at the end of the next 4,000 years? What nations? What civilization?" Before departing Alexandria for Greece, he concludes that "when the body is master of the soul, man is lower than the brute, but when the soul is superior to the body, he is akin to the God that made him."

Upon reaching Athens, Landis was consumed by the classical architecture and the history of the Greek civilization. He summons the poet Byron, quoting his "Maid of Athens Ere We Part" and recalling the writer's visit to these lands earlier in the century. He spent several hours touring the city on his own, losing himself in the culture. During his stay, he visited the sights, enjoying the fact that he was there for the anniversary of Greek independence. And his time was spent with new fellow pilgrims, primarily the Beckwith family, who accompanied him to Italy for a return visit. This time he toured Salerno and Amalfi before returning to Capri to see Coleman about the painting he purchased. The artist had already left for America and had taken the artwork with him, obviously with plans of connecting with the buyer during his time in the U.S. A letter from Coleman, written from Clinton Place, New York and dated May 6, 1890, confirms this. He writes that he isn't sure if Landis had returned yet from Europe but was sending an invitation to his exhibition "in the chance of you being here." Explaining that he would be going back to Europe sometime in August, he added that "if I don't see you before, I will send you the picture." Another letter from the artist on May

424

28 finds Coleman happy that Landis and his family were very pleased with the painting.

Also absent from Italy on this occasion was Sheafe, who was to meet the Vinelander in Florence. Landis makes no further mention of him in his journal, so it's probable that he had decided to return home to his wife now that he had been able to experience a portion of spring in Europe.

Naples, Rome, Florence and Genoa completed Landis's visit, giving him another opportunity to reexamine some of the sites he had seen in 1874 and to experience some other locations he had missed. He visited the homes of Dante and Michaelangelo in Florence as well as the Pallovini Gardens in Genoa where, he notes, in 1874 he "drove to this place with Captain Clive but could not get in, owing to the hour being too late." Upon seeing the tombs of the Medici family, he observes the amount of money it had cost to create such a crypt and, in a critical moment worthy of Shelley's "Ozymandias," concludes that it "serves only to illustrate the insatiable self-importance and vanity of Medici. Where will it all be in time? Like those of the Egyptians, empty of the so valued dust of the proprietors and but monuments of the futility of the attempts to preserve that dust from the operation of those laws of nature which are always working to restore it to its original elements."

With each site, however, Landis drew closer to the end of his trip. While in Egypt, he had already dreamed once again of being home in Vineland. When he visited the U.S. Consul in Genoa, a Mr. Fletcher, he was informed that the dignitary was sending his daughter back to the U.S. and had booked passage for her on the steamer *Gascoigne*, the same ship on which Landis would be sailing. Landis agreed to look after her on the voyage home.

Landis and Miss Fletcher departed for Paris, where Landis had the opportunity to visit the Julian Academy of Painters, an illustrious school that had taught some of the greatest contemporary artists. It was a place he was considering for Richard's studies and he was impressed by the work of the students as they painted portraits of live nude and clothed models, noting that "the rate of tuition is only 300 francs a year and the professors are among the most eminent artists in Paris." A subsequent visit to the Arc de Triomphe was the final site he witnessed on this journey. The next day, May 3, he writes that "the shores of France faded away from my sight and this was the end of my European trip."

Upon his return from Europe, Landis's illness, which had been under control while in Egypt, returned for at least the month of May, according to a reference Coleman made in his May 28 letter, but it would recur, and his health continued to be an issue. A receipt for medical services rendered by Doctor C. R. Wiley reveals that Landis made eight visits in November 1893 and seven the following month before his condition seems to have improved somewhat for an extended period. In April 1895, however, he once again made seven visits to Wiley throughout April.

Landis still wasn't ready to resume life in Vineland full-time in 1890. He settled into Sea Isle City once again, remaining throughout the summer, intent on implementing his plans for establishing a marine biology lab in the town. His proposals to the University of Pennsylvania had not generated a favorable response. The implementation of the sea defenses he had researched during his European excursion seemed easy when compared to persuading the Philadelphia university to undertake a lab project that had not yet received widespread interest in the U.S.

Marine biology institutes had not been in existence very long when Landis presented his plan. The oldest of such laboratories in the world was the Station Biologique de Roscoff, which had been established in France in 1872. Around the same time, Swiss-born Jean Louis Rodolphe Agassiz was spending his final years establishing a school devoted to the study of marine zoology on the island of Penikese in Buzzards Bay, Massachusetts. The location, along with $50,000, had been provided by philanthropist John Anderson. The school would not last very long after Agassiz's death in 1873, but it paved the way for the first official zoological institute in the area when, in 1888, the Marine Biological Laboratory was established in nearby Woods Hole, Massachusetts. The lab became an educational and research center in the areas of biology, biomedicine and environmental science.

Prior to his departure to Europe, Landis had spoken to the University of Pennsylvania about references that could provide access to various European scientists with whom he could discuss his proposed project. On December 8, 1889, he reports receiving "letters from the University of Pennsylvania at Phila. To Prof. P.P.C. Hack at Leiden; Prof. Alfred Girard, Paris, to Prof. H. deLacoze, Dutchneis, Bas Pyrnees, France; Prof. Ed. Graeffe, Triest, Austria; Prof. Brone, Plymouth, England; Prof. Marion, Marselles, France; Prof. Mobius, Berlin; Prof. Dopn, Naples."

The letters, he claimed, would "assist in gaining information as I desire to establish a first-class Aquarian and Biological Institute at Sea Isle City." Landis also writes that he "received by letter a telegram from Washington sent to my office in Philadelphia, that letters from the State Department would be sent for me to the American minister at Paris. I wrote for them at once. These letters are to the U.S. ministers in Holland, France and Italy, instructing them to obtain all the facilities for me that are possible to get."

Two days later, Landis sent his letter of introduction to Professor Hack in Leiden and received "some valuable information from him." By January 11, 1890, while in Naples, Landis wrote to Edward B. Leaming of Camden, asking him to organize the company of The Aquarian and Biological Institute, suggesting names of those he felt should be considered as directors.

"This will be upon the plan of that at Naples," he writes in his journal, "and is one of the most needed institutions in America on account of the great value of our fish and oyster interest. This will require action before Congress, the legislatures of New York, Connecticut, Rhode Island, New Jersey and other places to raise the money." Landis determined that the cost for the marine lab would be at least $500,000 with an additional $50,000 endowment fund per year. "Money is constantly raised for things much less necessary," he adds, "and perhaps its merit will carry it along even if I, from want of health, fail of my accustomed energy. We must try."

Upon his return home, Landis continued to put his plans for a marine lab into play, but it wasn't until the start of the following year that he aggressively pursued the project. In

January 1891, he offered to provide the University of Pennsylvania a site in Sea Isle City for the proposed lab. The offer now caught the attention of the college. On February 22, he invited Charles S. Dolley from the university's biology department to visit the resort. Dolley's credentials made him an ideal candidate for the new facility. He had taught biology at Swarthmore College and the University of Pennsylvania and had served as a lecturer in the Central High School of Philadelphia, in the School of Pedagogy for men of Philadelphia and in the Wagner Free Institute of Science. His research had already taken him to Bermuda, the Bahamas, the Chief Marine Laboratories and Fish Commission Headquarters in Europe. He had spent time in London, Paris and Berlin, and Landis was impressed that he had spent several years at the biological department in Naples and had also visited Capri. His achievements seemed to promise a successful future for the resort institute if the university agreed to it

After surveying the island, Dolley noted that Sea Isle City was favorable for a lab because it was a mud beach. He arranged for Landis to meet with the university president, Dr. William Pepper. On February 25, Landis met with Pepper at 8 a.m. to discuss the lab. "Arrangements were discussed and concluded," he reports in his journal, "and Dr. Pepper drew up the writings. They are to be ratified by the trustees next Tuesday. Dr. Pepper said that it might be considered done."

On March 1, Landis met with a contingent of professors from the university to tour Sea Isle City and examine a proposed site for the lab. The following day, the bill for establishing a marine biology station in New Jersey was introduced in the State Senate. On March 4, Landis was in Philadelphia, where he learned that the college had not accepted his offer, instead referring the matter to a committee for review. Dolley assured the Vinelander that this was standard, but Landis decided to call on Pepper the next day. The president admitted that some of the trustees were concerned with how the lab would be financed. Speaking with Dolley afterward, Landis was told that the trustees would be assured that there would be financial support for the lab and that there would be no difficulty in receiving approval. Eight days passed without word of a decision. Landis returned to Philadelphia March 13 to meet with C.C. Harrison, head of the university's finances, who bluntly told him that he did not see any way to fund the lab. Landis interpreted the declaration as meaning the university expected him to pay for it. "This is out of the question," he proclaims in his journal.

The following day, a meeting with Harrison and Dolley proved more favorable, probably because Landis had made it clear the funding would not be provided by him. Harrison promised to reconvene the committee and "take some action." At this time, Landis recommended that Dolley be made director of the new biological institute if it received university approval. On March 23, Landis, who had been ill for a week, dragged himself to a meeting of the university committee. Whether or not his presence influenced the proceedings, the plan for the Sea Isle City lab was approved and the offer of a site accepted. "This is the greatest work I have yet done for Sea Isle, in some respects," Landis writes in his journal. The next day he visited Governor Leon Abbett in Trenton to discuss the bill dealing with the lab, learning that it had already passed both houses and was ready to be signed by the governor. On March 25, the official site for the lab was finalized, having been selected by Dolley, Joseph Leidy and John Adam Ryder.

The next day, twenty students from the university's biology department visited Sea Isle City, touring the island and examining the proposed site for the new institute. Landis treated them to dinner and then returned home to continue reading the novels of Tobias Smollett. On April 18, the bill for the marine lab became law. Construction of the building commenced, and it was projected that the college's summer-school studies in biology, which would supplement the year-round investigation of fish and crustaceans, would begin June 1 under the direction of Dolley.

According to research by Dr. Harry Gershenowitz published in 1982 in the *Vineland Historical Magazine*, the expenses for the lab's inaugural summer session the following year totaled $3,732.71. The highest costs were $360 to cover the wages and $250 for pound net, with supplies, equipment and repairs constituting the remaining expenses. Landis had committed an advance of $2,500 of the $3,100 promised, but the university remained anxious over funding for the project, with Harrison informing Dolley by letter that the Board of Trustees was questioning how the lab was to be maintained. "I would like you to consider from what source the attendant expenses will be derived," he instructs the new director. Pepper also weighed in with a similar request and was informed on June 6, the day the lab budget was submitted, that Dolley would be visiting Vineland the next day to talk to Landis, who had informed the director two days earlier that "he would advance an

431

additional $500 if we needed it for equipment and summer expenses." Landis's earlier fears over having to fund the lab were becoming a reality and, on June 23, Pepper launched yet another appeal for money in order to purchase glassware.

Because of a report from *Forest and Stream: A Weekly Journal of the Rod and Gun* published August 20, 1891, we have a physical description of the Sea Isle City marine lab, dubbed the University of Pennsylvania's School of Biology. The site on which it sat was roughly three blocks from the beach and close to the railway line. The lab itself consisted of a wooden two-story building which, according to the article, was efficiently equipped with a pumping plant that provided a supply of salt water for the aquaria and also contained a wide variety of boats, tow-nets and pound-nets among its materials.

Many years later, J. M. MacFarlane, one of the first professors who had the opportunity to work at the lab, recalled the building as "a severely plain frame structure...which showed only unfinished walls within." He explained that the routine at the lab consisted of "companies of two, three or four teachers and disciples" who would "daily trod the long mile of boardwalk or shoreland [sic] from their Sea Isle rooms as an after-breakfast appetizer, and we held Socratic discourse; survey[ed], discussed and analyzed the plants and animals [that] daily reached the biological dragnet whether from land or sea...Half-hour sallies were often made to nature's territory around and the captured spoils were discussed round the long table that became familiar to all as our center of action."

The lab was authorized by the State of New Jersey and met with an exemption from taxes. The state also extended to the station the right to fish freely in the waters within New Jersey as long as it was for the purposes of research. Plans for the publication of monographs on some of the investigations undertaken by the lab were also announced.

The institute's opening earned it mention that October in the *New York Times*, which erroneously credited it as being the first such marine biology lab in the U.S. According to *Benjamin Franklin and the University of Pennsylvania: Bureau of Education Circular of Information No. 2, 1892*, "the laboratory accommodates sixteen investigators and twenty students. Besides the laboratory building the station is furnished with suitable engines for pumping purposes; storage tanks for fresh and salt water; collecting apparatus, such as seines, weirs, dredges, and trawls. Three sail-boats, one large barge, and six row-boats are owned by the laboratory and used for collecting in the bays and thoroughfares. A private dock has been built for the use of laboratory boats. The laboratory building was erected in May 1891, and the entire summer season was spent in getting apparatus into place and perfecting the various appointments of the station. The scientific work was therefore necessarily limited. That which was done consisted of some experiments in practical oyster culture conducted by Prof. John A. Ryder, of the University of Pennsylvania; a collection of the fishes of the locality was made by Prof. E. D. Cope, of the University of Pennsylvania, and a large collection of invertebrates was made by Prof. Hall, of Haverford College. In July 1892, the second season in the existence of the Marine Laboratory, the summer school was opened..."

An eight-page catalogue highlighted the courses in General Biology and Microscopical Technique, Botany and Zoology being offered at the marine lab during the summer of 1892. The accomplishments of its researchers that year were given an account in the *University of Pennsylvania Bulletin* in February 1893. The report acknowledged that "the course of instruction at the Marine Laboratory of the University at Sea Isle last year was conducted by Prof. J. M. MacFarlane, who gave twenty-five lectures on Botany, with practical demonstrations, and conducted five extended field excursions. Mr. J. Percy Moore delivered twenty-five lectures in Zoology and conducted a number of zoological and dredging excursions..." The report also recognized the aquaria as "a very attractive feature of the marine laboratory. The tastefully designed grotto in imitation of rock work, the result of the ingenuity and zeal of Dr. M. J. Greenman, added not a little to the instructive character of the surroundings of the establishment and enabled visitors to form some idea of the beauty and delicacy of coloring of many of the animal and plant forms indigenous to the adjacent waters."

The account identified that sixteen students worked during the summer on their own research as well as that of the university's. Advanced students working on experiments with oysters had abstracts of their experiments published in *The Proceedings of the Academy of Natural Sciences of Philadelphia, Nature* and *The Annals and Magazine of Natural History* in London. Two studies associated with the Pinelands were also undertaken: "Mrs. Kathleen Carter Moore was occupied with a study of the anatomy and development of the common lizard of the pine forests of New Jersey" while "Mr. P. P. Calvert reports as follows upon...twenty-five species of Odonata – dragonflies were recorded from Sea Isle and the adjoining mainland..."

One of the more revelatory occurrences during the lab's second year took place in July and August when "sixty-one species of fish were taken in the waters of Ludlam['s] Bay and the adjacent thoroughfares and inlets. The locality evidently constitutes an important breeding ground, as young of the year, representing thirty-four species, were found, without special effort in this direction. Several of these young forms have hitherto been undescribed." Additionally, the fauna of Sea Isle and surrounding areas "was found to be much richer than at first supposed. Sea-anemones, sea-cucumbers, sea-urchins, starfishes, sponges, polyps, worms, crustaceans, insects, mollusks, fishes, sea-turtles, and other indigenous land reptilian of the neighborhood were found to be more than adequate to maintain the supply of material for study and research, and which was obtained at no great cost of time and labor."

The report also made clear what was still lacking in the lab after a year of operation, stating, "A great desideratum to the laboratory, however, would be a light draught launch with which to explore the inlets and thoroughfares for zoological and botanical purposes. A dormitory building near the laboratory would render its advantages to students much greater, as such proximity would greatly economize their time and tend to reduce living expenses."

The account also mentioned that the recently established aquaria, "this valuable adjunct of the establishment, it is to be hoped, may be still further enlarged in the near future." It's possible the *Bulletin* had hoped that Landis would be reading this particular volume and provide the provisions listed, especially since it noted that "Mr. Landis, the donor of the Laboratory buildings and grounds, also interested himself in its welfare."

The Sea Isle City marine lab managed to lure such renowned names as Thomas Montgomery, who had worked with Agassiz but, according to Gershenowitz, the lab had to be closed after several years due to lack of funding and, in May 1894, "Landis sued the University for the $3,000 that was used for the construction of the Laboratory of Marine Biology. The University purported that Mr. Landis made the first introductory proposal for a scientific laboratory and that the entire matter was an honest misunderstanding. Dr. Pepper indicated that the University had intended to return the no-longer used building and land and equipment as financial compensation to Mr. Landis for his donations. Mr. Landis counterblasted [sic] that he had sent three unanswered letters referring to his initial claim. In July 1894, the Board of Trustees of the University settled with Mr. Landis by reimbursing the requested money, interest and full litigation costs." The reacquisition of the investment, however, probably served only as partial compensation for the failure of the project.

In early 1891, in the midst of creating the marine lab, Landis began working on plans to establish the town of Gardenville along the Maurice River past the western reaches of Vineland. Similar to the colonies already formed in nearby Alliance, Rosenhayn and Carmel, the site would house Jewish emigrants involved in manufacturing. By late February, work had already begun on the main thoroughfare, Grand Avenue, a one-hundred-foot-wide road, one of many "broad and beautiful avenues" envisioned by Landis for this location which would consist of one-acre plots and a park.

During this period, Landis had contacted the Jewish philanthropist Baron Maurice de Hirsch, a successful industrialist and banker whose organization was committed to resettling Jewish immigrants in rural locations, including South Jersey. Many Jews had been driven out of Eastern Europe in the latter part of the 19th century, the result of threatening economic conditions and anti-Semitic pogroms. Many had settled in urban centers like New York and Philadelphia, living in tenement dwellings and eking out a living. Relocating them to rural areas improved their living conditions and economic opportunities.

Landis suggested that de Hirsch establish a horticultural school in the Jewish community of Alliance so that diseases and remedies of fruit could be studied locally. The suggestion was undoubtedly prompted by the discovery four years earlier of a cure for the black rot that had plagued Vineland's grape crops for nearly twenty years. The recommendation seems intended to stave off any future blight that might arise.

Landis was also hoping to entice the de Hirsch Foundation into providing funding for Gardenville but, according to an entry in Landis's journal, a February 25 meeting with the secretary of the group in New York City made it apparent that the philanthropist was "as yet unprepared to act in the purchase of land." Still, Landis reserved hope for his new community and purchased a zinc statue of Hebe, the Greek goddess of youth, for his new colony before leaving New York. Over the next month, the statue was placed at Grand Avenue.

In early March, Landis came across an 18,000-acre tract of land belonging to the Coxe family that he felt de Hirsch might be able to use. A journal entry discusses the land but does not identify its location, yet it seems that it was somewhere between Vineland and Sea Isle City. When Landis took the time to visit Mrs. Coxe, she mentioned she had not yet been to Sea Isle City and extended an invitation to Landis to stay for the weekend, an indication that he was not nearby either of his settlements.

Landis's March 5 journal entry reveals that he attempted to aid the de Hirsch organization by presenting a plan for the development of the 18,000 acres to one of the foundation's trustees, Mayer Sulzberger and, in a letter sent to Sulzberger on March 6, made a generous offer to "lay it out" for them. There is no further mention of the project in Landis's journal.

Gradually, it became apparent that there was no interest on the part of de Hirsch or his foundation in funding the Gardenville settlement and, by the middle of March, it seems to have been confirmed that funds would not be forthcoming. Landis's journal entries become sporadic after March 6, but there is one final mention of his Grand Avenue and the statue of Hebe on March 26 when he reports that Matilda and his youngest son James visited the completed road. Landis makes no mention of Gardenville; instead he refers to his unrealized project as only a "new Avenue I have opened from Landis Avenue to Almond Road."

The failure of the de Hirsch Foundation to fund Gardenville left Landis with an unused design for a settlement that he felt would fit de Hirsch's new Jewish community of Woodbine, which was being organized in

Cape May County. The plans Landis envisioned for his own colony were passed on to the Woodbine colony, as Jeffrey M. Dorwart reports: "The original Woodbine town plan had been prepared by Jeremiah van Rensselaer and William S. Townshend for the Cape May and Millville Railroad, but the final design adopted by the Jewish-American leaders of the colony followed the plan that Landis gave in March 1891 to Mayer Sulzberger, a leading trustee of the Baron de Hirsch Fund and the Jewish Colonization Association, which financed the Woodbine settlement."

In July 1891, the Baron de Hirsch Foundation bought the Woodbine tract with the exception of property belonging to Nathaniel Holmes located near the railroad station. Dorwart sums up Woodbine's success with another nod to Landis. "Woodbine became the most ambitious – and in the short run most successful – Jewish-American agricultural and industrial colony in the United States," he writes. "It presented the same quasi-utopian vision that drove the Lakes in Ocean City and Charles K. Landis in Sea Isle City as they sought to provide an escape from industrial machines and urban decay by establishing planned, healthful communities in rural Cape May County."

For the next several years, Landis seems to have conducted his business from Vineland. He did not maintain a journal during this time and there is no surviving correspondence. Early in 1894, he resumed his journal when he undertook a journey to Mexico. The trip may have been arranged because Landis had been suffering from what had now been diagnosed as grippe. His fifteen visits to Dr. C.R. Wiley in November and December of the previous year seems to indicate that a trip to a warmer climate was warranted, especially since it had proven beneficial four years earlier in Egypt.

Landis does comment on how his health in Tampico "is improving wonderfully," but he also seems to have had a business agenda for the trip, having proposed a European emigration plan that he calculated would bring an annual flow of 20,000 emigrants to Mexico to "take up lands, start new industries and stimulate those now existing." It was similar to a plan utilized by Buenos Aires, but Landis foresaw himself managing the Mexican project. The proposal seems to never have been attempted but, unfortunately, Landis's pencil-written journals of the trip have survived only in fragments and his business dealings are not part of the entries that survive.

The extant selections begin in mid-March in Tampico where Landis witnesses an odd occurrence. He learns that prior to the railroad system there, "all goods were consigned to merchants in Tampico from whence they were sent in the packs on donkeys to their different destinations," but unlike the circumstances of the towns Landis founded, the railway proved to be detrimental in Tampico. "After the railroads were built, [the goods] were consigned to the railroad and by them sent to the back cities," Landis explains in his journal. "This at once deprived the merchants of Tampico of all of this business and the thousands of men and donkeys it deprived of work who were engaged in the transportation. Many of the inland country places benefitted by it at the expense of Tampico."

As he had done on previous foreign journeys, Landis takes in the sights of the towns he visits, paying attention to the people, the buildings, the landscape and the historical connections. While visiting a Catholic church in Tampico on March 18, Palm Sunday, he reminisces briefly on his visit to a Catholic house of worship four years earlier in Egypt. But his recollections are not confined to pleasant memories of past experiences. At one point, witnessing a grisly attack on a carcass by buzzards, he is reminded of "the directors of corporations of 'Burrough Officers' [one of his terms for the politicians in charge of Vineland] at home. The work of the buzzards, however, is a good one, whilst the other is robbery."

As was his wont, Landis saw opportunities for development that could benefit the country. While in Victoria, he considers that "this would be a great country for grape and olive growing." In Montemorelos, he muses that "it might be a good thing to build a coast railroad, connecting the most direct way with the railroad system of the U.S. through Texas. This would gather up all the products and travel of the hot region of Mexico and take them to other parts of the nation."

Anxious to receive news from home, Landis traveled the three-day journey to Monterey to collect his mail and prepare for his emigration proposal. The surviving journal entries end on the eve of the presentation of his plan.

The year 1894 also saw in Landis a renewed interest in his literary endeavors. His recent journals had already demonstrated a maturity of style and the several works of fiction he produced during this period contain the same graceful approach as that of his non-fiction. Just as he was inspired by science fiction in writing *A Trip to Mars*, Landis delved into other genres to produce these new efforts.

The first is a work of historical fiction best categorized as a lengthy short story, which provides an interesting glimpse of Landis as author. The story, published under the title *Carabajal: The Jew, A Legend of Monterey, Mexico*, is a retelling of the life of a 16th Century Portuguese expeditionary of Jewish descent, Luis de Carabajal, who was appointed governor of the area once known as New Spain, the territory that now incorporates much of Central America, Mexico and Texas. According to Landis, he was inspired to tell the tragic tale of this figure after his trip to Mexico, where he claims to have come across the history of Carabajal. He was able to weave a twenty-seven-page account that was printed by Cloyd and Smith, a Vineland publisher, later that year.

Landis begins his story with Spain's King Philip II obtaining a loan from Carabajal and bestowing upon him the governorship of New Spain, where he could establish new colonies and recoup his investments from the revenue within those settlements. The king's self-interest, Landis intimates, is matched only by his contempt for the man from whom he is borrowing money. Soon, Carabajal is setting sail across the Atlantic with his family, soldiers, several Catholic priests and others interested in starting a new life.

Upon arriving in New Spain, the governor establishes a number of settlements within the newly created Kingdom of Nuevo Leon. In his colony, located on the site of Santa Lucia, Carabajal addresses the physical and aesthetic concerns necessary to build a thriving community, but for the first few months, he establishes martial law, expecting an attack by the Yako Indians. After sending couriers from another tribe to a northern location to act as spies, he awaits their reports about the Yakos.

When word arrives that an attack is imminent, he takes his small army and travels to engage the opposing forces away from his town. Once he finds an area of rock to fortify and hide his army, a decoy unit is dispatched to lure the Yakos to this location. The plan works, and the Indians are cut down in the ambush. Rather than celebrate, Carabajal begins planning for the revenge that will be unleashed by the tribe.

It isn't long before couriers bring word that the Yakos have enlisted the aid of the Apaches in a new attack on the colony. This time, Carbajal relocates the colonists to a mountaintop should their efforts to thwart the attack fail. He then sets out as before. Because the two tribes are traveling separately before rendezvousing near Nuevo Leon, he attacks the Apaches in the same fashion as the earlier ambush against the Yakos and is victorious. The Spanish then attack the larger Yako forces during the night, winning yet another battle.

Landis tells us that, with the threat eliminated, Carabajal sets up the conditions he felt were necessary to nurture a successful colony, such as building roads, schools, churches and businesses. Indians are not used as slaves, he reports, and because the governor believed in equity, the Indians who work in the nearby mines are given a share of the profits.

Nuevo Leon grows in wealth. But with the threat of attack now curbed and the colony prospering, Carabajal becomes expendable in the eyes of the clergy. Resenting the governor's religious background, the priests establish their own Inquisition and secretly imprison the governor and his family so the public will not know. Carabajal is aware of their intentions and accepts his fate, but when he learns of his family's incarceration, he immediately dies of a heart attack. After the members of the governor's family are burned at the stake, Jews and Indians of Nuevo Leon gather the various tribes in the surrounding areas and use them to avenge what the local Inquisition has wrought.

The choice of Carabajal as subject is an inspired selection, affording Landis the opportunity to address his own concerns and still tell a tale that is rather captivating. The historical figure, a Jewish-born Portuguese expeditionary, who converted to Christianity before returning to Judaism because of his wife, is a successful businessman who does not relent, even in the face of the Inquisition's abhorrence of the Jewish and Muslim faith. If we limit his legend to just these facts, he can be viewed as a hero. It's not surprising that Landis was attracted to Carabajal's accomplishments as a founder of the Nuevo Leon settlement and he wonders, in the story's opening, "who could have been the consummate and daring genius who established it?" However, there are more than a few liberties taken with history.

Landis writes that "the facts of the...legend of [Carabajal] were picked up during a two months (sic) sojourn in Monterey in the winter and spring of 1894." It is true that his visit to Mexico included a stopover in Monterey. The fragment of the journal Landis maintained during this trip confirms that he arrived in Monterey at 5 p.m. on March 22. Since many of the entries were written in pencil and have faded over time, all we know is that he remained there until at least March 24, the last date of the surviving entries. There is no mention of encountering any manuscripts or accounts related to the legacy of Carabajal.

Landis must have learned of Carabajal's legend at some point during his stay, but not all of the details he provides in his story can be considered fact. In the Appendix to his tale, Landis writes, "The written accounts of the period of time relating to Carabajal are meager and contradictory..." Whether or not that was the author's way of excusing the liberties he had taken with his retelling isn't known, but the 1894 account is certainly filled with alterations and omissions.

Landis employs the basic details of Carabajal's life: he was appointed governor of New Spain in 1579, traveled with his family to the New World, established new colonies, including Nuevo Leon, could be brutal in dealing with outside tribes of Indians, and faced charges before the Inquisition. There seems to be no historical precedent of a loan to King Philip II, but Carabajal was allowed to use the profits of the colonies to recoup his personal expense in the expedition.

Some other historical points and geographical information are brushed over by Landis, most likely in favor of expediting the narrative, but these missing details reveal the true extent of Carabajal's achievements in New Spain. According to *Spanish Exploration in the Southwest, 1542-1706*, "...in 1579 Luis de Carabajal was authorized to found the new Kingdom of Nuevo Leon. This province was to extend two hundred leagues north from Panuco, thus embracing much territory now within the state of Texas. In (or by) 1583 Carabajal took a colony inland, opened the mines of San Gregorio, and founded the capital city of Leon, now Cerralvo, a few miles south of the Rio Grande. Within the next few years several points were settled between Cerralvo and Monterey, and in 1590 Carabajal founded the Villa de Almaden, where Monclova

now stands. While there he was arrested by order of the Inquisition and taken to Mexico, leaving Castaiio de Sosa in charge."

What Landis has deliberately chosen to overlook is Carabajal's career-long involvement with slave trade that began early on when he lived in Africa for thirteen years. He was engaged in Indian slavery during his first visit to New Spain and apparently continued these dealings when he returned as governor. These actions did not meet with the approval of the Spanish government and, while Carabajal was arrested by the Inquisition for promoting Judaism, it is rumored that his work in the slave trade may have been the real cause of his arrest. At the time, Spain was seeking to secure a peace settlement in a war with the Indians in New Spain, and slavery was strongly discouraged. Then again, this may simply be an attempt to obscure the religious implications of the arrest.

Historically, the Inquisition arrested Carabajal's daughter who, after torture, implicated her entire family, most of whom were eventually burned at the stake. Carabajal was charged with heresy and, unlike the title character in Landis's story who receives a death sentence, earned only a six-year exile from the colonies he had established. He died in prison while waiting for his sentence to be carried out.

In many cases, these alterations of historical fact do help propel the story while creating an alternate legend, one that Landis uses to his advantage. The reader is provided with hints that the tale should not be taken as pure fact when, after the massacre at Santa Lucia, Landis writes that no one was left alive to tell the tale of Carabajal. If no one remained to tell the tale, then how did Landis discover it? Even the author's curious transformation of the Indians who threaten Carabajal's colony from the historical Yaqui to the fictional Yako can be seen as an admission of the liberties taken with fact since Landis would have become familiar with the Yaqui tribe during his travels through Mexico. It seems then that the manuscripts purportedly consulted by Landis are merely a literary device to lend credibility to the tale in the same way Nathanial Hawthorne uses a similar technique to engage readers in the opening of *The Scarlet Letter*, providing a realistic-sounding situation in which to set his fiction.

Of all the changes Landis made to the historical tale of Carabajal, however, perhaps his decision to banish slavery in Nuevo Leon and to include an equal share of the profits for the colony's indigenous mine workers are the most relevant. With those alterations, the settlement becomes much more familiar to Vineland readers and establishes an uncanny kinship between author and subject.

Landis credits the success of Carabajal's Nuevo Leon to the principles applied in building the colony. If we examine these guidelines found in the alleged source manuscripts discussed in the Appendix, we discover they include "agricultural and manufacturing development," "the educational and the aesthetic," the establishment of "free libraries," and "wide and spacious" roads planted with "rows of beautiful trees of different varieties" so that they can attract "birds which are essential in the cultivation of fruits by destroying insect enemies." Houses, we're told, should be "set back a certain distance from the roadside, and thus afford room for flowers and shrubbery. And it is stipulated that the founder should provide access to markets for the sale of agricultural and manufactured products and "see that the inexperienced colonists should not fall into the hands of dishonest consigners or commission men, and in this way be robbed of their toil."

Interestingly, in Landis's written account of his founding of Vineland, he tells us that the development of "the best of schools and different industries" was part of the design and that, for agricultural concerns, "I wanted land more suitable to fruit than to grain." In addition to eventually establishing a free library, Vineland would create roads like "Landis, Chestnut and Park Avenues to be 100 feet wide...all lined with a double row of shade trees." Homes were to be "set back...at least twenty-five feet in order to afford room for flowers and shrubbery" and "shade trees should be planted along the entire front...to afford a harbor for birds, which I regard as all important as against insect enemies in the fruit country." Train access to Philadelphia was available for farmers and manufacturers from the start, but a short-lived local enterprise was also established to connect Vineland with New York City.

As for "consigners and commission men," a Landis journal entry, written on February 23, 1891, reads: "Sent my law to the Governor for the protection of the farmers and fruit growers from being defrauded." On October 18, 1895, a year after the publication of *Carabajal*, he writes, "I have endeavored to protect the farmers against the robberies of the commission men and many of our local politicians are commission men. This largely accounts for it. I have also endeavored to establish a public market [that t]he shop-keepers, green grocers are opposed to and many are local politicians so that upon the whole they have decreed that I am a dangerous character."

The parallels cannot be coincidental and, even with additional details and regulations added to accommodate the Mexican culture, the tale becomes an allegory of Vineland. Louis Harap, in his book *The Image of the Jew in American Literature: From Early Republic to Mass Immigration*, comments on the direct connection between the New Spain colony and the town Landis established in 1861: "Landis quotes from what he says is Carabajal's manuscript, in which the aims of the colony were set forth, much as Landis himself had done for Vineland. The venture, says the manuscript, should not be in a 'mere mercantile spirit,' but rather 'more in a parental spirit.' Development of the colony should be both agricultural and industrial, educational and aesthetic. There should be free libraries, lectures, 'intellectual entertainments,' dancing, calisthenics, and music. Indeed, the likeness between the principles attributed to Carabajal and those that governed Landis's conception of Vineland… is unmistakable."

If we choose to read the story as allegory or parable, the connections might paint Landis as a misunderstood visionary and a threat to local politicians. Landis was forced to watch as his power was stripped and his role diminished so that, by the 1890s, his unflagging work for the betterment of Vineland was void of town support.

Landis also works into the story of Carabajal an unmistakable parallel with his own family's history, something he had never endeavored to address in his earlier writings, including his journals. It can be no coincidence that six years prior to constructing *Carabajal*, Landis became aware of an achievement by one of his Pennsylvania relatives.

In a letter, dated February 15, 1888, Levi S. Reist of Lancaster County, Pennsylvania informed Landis of some details from his family's history, including ancestral martyr Hans, and reported that David B. Landis's book on the Landis ancestry was nearing publication. "It will be a very interesting work," Reist tells the Vineland founder. "He has gone back to Switzerland and France." There is also mention of a province in France called Landis, "so it seems of a French name as well as German."

The letter and eventual book seem to have provided Landis with what might have been his first account of his family's 17th century history, in particular Hans Landis, the last Swiss Mennonite martyr and the deeds perpetuated by the Council of Zurich and the Reformers whose persecution of Mennonites led to the Landis family's exodus from Europe.

The Mexican Inquisition had been an extension of its European counterpart, initiated to reinforce Catholicism from the perceived threats of other faiths. When the Inquisition arrived in New Spain, it surprisingly didn't dwell on what was considered the paganism of the indigenous Indian tribes. Because there were many parallels between the Indian's belief system and Christianity and because missionaries became protective of the tribes after seeing the harsh treatment they received from the Spanish and other explorers, the Indians were not the primary targets of religious zealots. However, many Portuguese Jews, whose families had suffered exile in the late 15th century if they chose not to convert, journeyed to New Spain during the 16th century in search of opportunities and were perceived as a threat in the eyes of the Mexican Inquisition.

In *Carabajal*, the title character's encounter with the Inquisition is remarkably similar to that of Hans Landis's own experiences with the Council of Zurich in 1614, only twenty-four years after the historical Portuguese expeditionary had been arrested. Unlike Hans, who was beheaded, Carabajal dies upon hearing of the incarceration of his family, thus escaping execution at the hands of his tormentors. But he is perceived as being as much of a threat as Hans is to the Reformers, and the suffering inflicted on the rest of his family can be compared, in some instances, to the treatment experienced by Hans's family.

The account of the persecution of Hans and his family in *Martyr's Mirror* provides an interesting perspective when compared with the conclusion of Landis's telling of the Carabajal legend:

> ...they sentenced him from life to death, and hence, in the month of September of the aforesaid year, 1614, for the sake of the truth he was beheaded as a true follower of Christ. Which they nevertheless would not acknowledge but pretended and persuaded the common people to deceive them, that he was not punished and put to death for his religion, but for his obstinacy and disobedience to the authorities.

Carabajal may be the most personal of Landis's fiction and remained his only literary work to have been published during his lifetime. He seems to have discovered, in the final decade of his life, a way to tell his own tale and that of his ancestors allegorically.

Probably written around the same time as *Carabajal*, *Autobiographical Sketch of a Tree* is an eight-page story by Landis eventually published posthumously in Vineland in 1910. "We all love the companionship of a tree," Landis wrote in his journal on September 21, 1878, and he put his belief into practice by allowing trees to be a prominent part of Vineland. So it's not surprising that a tree would become a protagonist in one of his literary works.

The story uses a form that dates back to the earliest literature in which inanimate objects are personified in order to convey a unique perspective of human life. Such tales ask of their readers a suspension of disbelief for their narrative to work. So, in the opening of Landis's story, the narrator confesses "Mr. Editor, whilst sitting one day upon a bench underneath an old tree, a manuscript fell upon my head and turning over the leaves I read as follows." What ensues is the tree's autobiography. The original manuscript of the story, written on notebook paper, reveals the original title as *Autobiographical Sketch by a Tree*, which upholds the idea of the tree as author.

There is little doubt that Landis had encountered the genre earlier in his life since his reading habits always included a versatile range of subjects. The 19th century had produced its own versions of such tales like Annie Carey's story *The Autobiography of a Lump of Coal; A Grain of Salt; A Drop of Water; A Bit of Old Iron; and A Piece of Old Flint,* published in England in 1870 and certainly available for Landis's perusal during his 1874 trip abroad. Carey's narrative, according to Paul Collins in his 2004 article "You and Your Dumb Friends" in *The Believer* magazine, improvises "on an old theme. The conceit of an inanimate object's memoir is ancient; the seventh-century poem *Dream of the Rood* features a tree holding forth on just what it's like to be cut down, carried out of the forest, and then pounded through with nails to crucify Jesus Christ...More often inanimate narrators are used for no more nefarious a purpose than promoting clever fiction...But *The Autobiography of a Lump of Coal* is something different. It is neither satirical nor reverent; it is not a promotional gimmick." And the same can be said of Landis's work. After all, as Collins notes, "A talking lump of coal...is a fine way to get better acquainted with the science of geology."

If Vineland's founder did not encounter Carey's work while in England, he would certainly have been aware of James Fenimore Cooper's *Autobiography of a Pocket-Hankerchief*, a work that manages, at one point, to explore various ideologies through the perspective of a woman's handkerchief. So, why not a tree that isn't hewn? Beyond their practical function of providing shade and housing birds, trees, according to Landis, are links to future generations. Once planted, they can connect residents of a community for hundreds of years as overseers of that town's development and guardians of its history.

In Landis's story, the tree, which has been around for over 500 years, describes its existence, having provided shade for people, a place to sit and read, etc. It recalls various time periods, including the era of "steel-clad" men and offers dialogue between birds, an explanation of how it was kept alive by plentiful rains until a time when the tree needed to extend its roots to find an underground spring to sustain itself. By now the spring has gone dry. It notes its favorites among the people who have spent time under its shade, including a silver-haired man who has read, written and admired the landscape while sitting under the tree. It calls him a "poet of nature." It's possible to perceive this gentleman as the sixty-one-year-old Landis, aware of the integrity of nature and its gift to humankind and recognizing in it the solace of old age.

Landis also produced "How the Mayors Do in Japan: A Story," an undated, unpublished and rather interesting short work that may also date from the 1890s. The tale involves a group of Japanese citizens who "had heard of European and particularly American Civilization and they became ambitious to have a mayor." They appoint Hi-Glee, whose name "signifies good fellow," but whose actions betray a morally questionable individual. The people pass ordinances for the mayor, who finally decides to hire Petti Fog, a smart lawyer who teaches the mayor everything about the law. Hi-Glee realizes he can use the ordinances against the people, declaring each of the following as breaches of the law: the singing of the birds, the crying of babies, the drinking of wine at certain times, the writing of love letters, the eating of too large a dinner, too small a dinner or having no dinner at all.

These new laws now demand the hiring of an informer, Hi-See, who is described as an "opium eater, an alcohol drinker, a gambler, a thief, a bicycle rider, a burglar, a counterfeiter…and everything that was horrible." He spies on the citizens, reporting them to the mayor, who fines each one. The penalties leveled at the "innocent Japanese," as Landis refers to them, make the mayor a rich man. When the people have had enough and demand that the mayor issue a warrant for Hi-See's arrest, Hi-Glee explains that his informer is actually a religious man who prays loudly in church. He also tells them that he is a man of temperance and "only drinks to keep the liquor away from other people." He couldn't possibly have him arrested on the charge of stealing because money is the root of all evil and therefore taking it from the people is preventing the citizens from becoming evil. The people attempt to mutiny and hold a meeting during which a grey-bearded man explains how Hi-See is an informer who brings Hi-Glee business. The gathering immediately breaks up without accomplishing anything, and "the people left the hall looking sad, but very, very wise."

Landis concludes the manuscript with the name Anacharsis in parentheses, a reference to the 6th century B.C. Scythian philosopher considered to be a forerunner of the Cynics. None of the works of Anacharsis have survived, but he is credited with a belief in moderation, particularly with drinking, something with which Landis would have identified. But Landis also seems to be endorsing the modern interpretation of the Cynic's disbelief in human goodness, as evidenced by Hi-Glee, Hi-See and American politics. But it's also easy to discern a parallel with Vineland Borough's governing body and Landis's perceptions of how the town was being run. While there is no direct indictment of the townspeople in the story, their lack of action in the face of their new-found enlightenment calls attention to the tolerance Landis probably saw as enabling those in power.

Since Landis's literary phases can be traced to the 1840s/early 1850s, late 1870s and early 1890s and Vineland's legal status as a borough began in 1880, it seems likely that this short story dates from the early 1890s, a time when his own patience was running low for the town's leaders. The style of the story is simple and direct, rendered without embellishment, much like a folk tale or a fable. Whereas in *Carabajal* there is vengeance undertaken for the actions of the Inquisition, the fact that there is no come-uppance for Hi-Glee by the end of "How the Mayors Do in Japan," no triumph of good over evil, speaks to Landis's continuing development as a writer and his ability to supplant the overt elements of the story with a subliminal message, that of the townspeople creating and then perpetuating their own nightmare.

Another work by Landis that appears to have been written in this same period and was uncovered by the Vineland Historical and Antiquarian Society in 2018 is an unfinished tale that uses Vineland as one of its settings. The surviving manuscript consists of twenty-two pages of a projected novel entitled *The Information Bureau*. While there is no authorship or date contained on any of the pages, the handwriting, narrative style, subject matter and autobiographical implications bear too strong a resemblance to Landis's other writings.

It's obvious the manuscript is a first-draft that was abandoned too soon in its development. Unlike many of Landis's surviving handwritten originals, *The Information Bureau* appears to have been committed to the page in a hurried fashion, presumably penned as the inspiration flowed. The cross-outs, inserted words and numerous illegible passages make it one of the more challenging of Landis's texts to read, and sections of the story are compromised by the indecipherability of sections. But what can be discerned offers an intriguing glimpse into an amalgam of plots, settings and timelines that make it arguably the most complex fictional work undertaken by Landis.

The manuscript opens on a scene at the Vineland rail station on the Boulevard where the Ellerys, a couple visiting the town, arrive on the 9:58 train. They are met by the narrator of the work, who reports, if the manuscript's legibility can be trusted, that he has been a resident here since 1889. Mr. Ellery learns about the industriousness of the residents, many of whom, he is told, had relocated from New England.

There is mention of the Vineland Historical and Antiquarian Society (VHAS) and hints, derived from the dating of the Declaration of Independence, that the Vineland setting of the novel is early 20th century, probably late 1920s. And there are comments about the Information Bureau, an establishment at Seventh and Elmer Streets instituted by the playfully named I.M. Bright, who may be the narrator, and U.R. Brighter. The Bureau pledges that it can provide answers to "important questions [that] have to be solved" for a "very moderate fee."

During a walk on "the Avenue," the Ellerys, consider visiting the Information Bureau, but Landis interrupts their plans to address a bit more background of this mysterious institute, identifying its connection with the narrator and its formation through an unfortunate series of events involving public library employees losing their jobs and becoming involved with the Information Bureau. Still, he withholds information of its true nature.

In the third chapter, the reader experiences both a geographical and temporal shift to a British setting during the time of U.S. colonialism in what we later learn is 1693. This subplot involves a character identified as Sir John, who is looking to cross the Atlantic after Mary, the woman he loves, chooses to marry another man, but not before pledging his loyalty to her and her husband and accepting their financial gift, which he says he will consider a loan. He tells the couple that labor is in "great demand" in the colonies, "and you know I can work."

Forlorn yet eager for adventure, John sails from Liverpool. Inspired by the setting sun on the ocean and the emergence of the evening star, he philosophizes about the phases of life and these musings accompany him across the Atlantic. John and he fellow passengers, half-starved, lacking sufficient drinking water and suffering from seasickness, finally arrive in Annapolis, Maryland. John is not impressed with Annapolis and, having heard about a Quaker settlement he later references as William Penn's a short distance away, he decides to travel there.

Meeting a group of adventurers headed for the same location, he joins them, "all his earthly possessions in a pack." Arriving at Penn's tract, John discovers that workers are in high demand and he takes a job with a merchant who has just opened a store. Using the loan from Mary and her husband, he soon invests in land that he can subdivide and sell to "newcomers" and purchases two-hundred acres for himself. The merchant for whom John works has an attractive daughter who reminds him of Mary, and he falls in love and marries her. This portion of novel ends with John being offered a share in his employer's business.

This chapter of the novel seems to serve as a modified and fictional account of how Landis's grandfather John arrived in Pennsylvania, ignoring the Austrian/Italian origins of the Landis family and its religious persecution in favor of a lovelorn protagonist making his way to the colonies while on the rebound. Any element of religious freedom is merely implied by the mention of "Penn's tracts."

John's diligence in establishing himself in the New World intimates that his success in the novel will eventually extend to a wide sector of Pennsylvania and the birth of an American heritage that will reach to Vineland. John's sale of lands to "newcomers" even mirror Landis's own real estate ventures

The final pages of the manuscript return to 1920s Vineland and the Information Bureau, where a dialogue ensues between the narrator and Mrs. Brighter concerning the success of the business. Much of the writing is illegible, making it difficult to discern all the information imparted before the narrative abruptly ends.

It's possible to date the creation of *The Information Bureau* to the early 1890s through several factors. The interest Landis displayed for his family history in that period is not evident in any other decade, but there is also his choice of locating the Information Bureau on Seventh and Elmer Streets in proximity to the VHAS facility during the 1890s. The Historical Society's building, donated in 1890 by Daniel Morrill, originally sat on the organization's Peach Street lot but was transported to Seventh Street between Grape and Elmer Streets in 1893 and would have been adjacent to the

Information Bureau in the novel, certainly no coincidence in Landis's fictional manipulation. The irony that the current Historical Society facility sits on the site of his Information Bureau would not be lost on him.

The Information Bureau's references to the town's public library and sudden unemployment of librarians is another way of dating the writing of the novel to the early 1890s. It was in 1892, that Vineland's Library Association closed its doors, donating its book collection to the VHAS. Landis would have seen the lack of a library as a vacuum in the town, and the fact that his novel's Information Bureau is begun with the help of former librarians might be interpreted as a fictional remedy.

In February 1895, Landis decided to have a three-ton safe transferred from his main workplace to a rear office in order to rent the front office space. The work was completed two days after Landis undertook a second trip to Mexico, departing Vineland by train on February 13, accompanied by Charles Jr. as far as Camden. He traveled to New York to commence his journey to Vera Cruz. The only journal entry, from March 11 in Guadalajara, reports that Landis was anxious to return home, which he was about to do. It may have been health reasons that convinced him to take a second trip below the border, but records show that during April of that year he made seven visits to Dr. Wiley before his symptoms seemed to subside.

As summer 1895 arrived, Sea Isle City had self-propelled itself into a moderately successful seaside resort and was poised to enhance its growth. Newspaper reports at the time indicate that train service on the Pennsylvania and Reading Railroad lines from Philadelphia to Sea Isle had been reduced to ninety-seven minutes from the previous two-hour run. The tourist trade was flourishing, drawing vacationers as well as fishermen to the town. A $200,000 improvement plan, including an artesian well, a waterworks plant and the addition of fifty cottages, was implemented in July and promised to usher in future prosperity.

The workings of the city had been left to the municipal government over the past decade as Landis became preoccupied with his Florida visits, the Philadelphia Parkway plan, the European trip, Mexican tours and literary work. But by mid-1895, Landis was busy promoting another settlement he had recently founded, and he was probably hopeful that this would meet with more success than his recent Gardenville project.

Whale Beach is one of the more curious ventures undertaken by Landis. This strip of land, located at the northern point of the barrier island that contains Sea Isle City, houses a beach stretching approximately one-and-a-half miles and spanning the northern portion of Sea Isle into a section of Corson's Inlet, today's Strathmere. Its history rarely, if ever, credits Landis with its founding, and the name of the location, which does not usually appear on maps and has never been incorporated, has no known derivation, although legend has it that it was a place where whales would beach themselves. The Sea Isle area was known in the 1700s for its whaling industry, but there is nothing to directly connect it with the naming of Whale Beach. By the 1940s, it was well-inhabited with many houses filling the beach and, despite two devastating hurricanes over the next twenty years, approximately one hundred houses still filled the community in 2001.

Recent reports indicate that the location sits atop a former marsh, making it a vulnerable area for storms. Whether or not Landis was aware of this when he undertook the settlement isn't known, but in his promotion of the resort he called it "one of the finest beaches in America." In a handwritten notice composed to advertise his newest creation, Landis draws attention to Whale Beach's proximity to the Sea Isle City rail station (two miles), Philadelphia (sixty miles) and Atlantic City (eight miles), its bathing, sailing and fishing opportunities, and its "desirable social surroundings and protection from intrusion." He states that lots would be sold "only to people of good character and to be built upon within a year." The beach, he attests, is "smooth enough for bicycle riding." Anyone wishing more information is told to contact William D. Squires 238 South 4th Street, Philadelphia or "Charles K. Landis, Founder."

Landis had been spending time in Whale Beach in June 1895, overseeing improvements, such as the addition of a landing. With his health slowly failing, it's doubtful he mustered enough strength to provide the devotion necessary to nurture a project like this, and it's likely that the selection of Squires to assist had been the result of his condition.

Fall 1895 was a particularly busy time for Landis, but not all activities were pleasant. On October 17, he was forced to offer the remaining Vineland lots he had been selling for $200 each to "a syndicate for $50 each" as a "consequence of heavy taxation." Landis was convinced that "the people have determined "to tax me out of the place if they can, the result of a feeling that they are now independent of my efforts." The high taxes were the result of political economist Henry George's single-tax theory, a popular outlook at the time which proposed the idea that any economic value assigned to land in a community should belong equally to the residents rather than titleholders. Favoring land value tax, a system whereby the wealthiest individuals are taxed the heaviest, George believed that such "rent" would allow the land to be common property," a semi-socialistic philosophy in conflict with the anti-socialist views espoused by Landis in *A Trip to Mars*.

Landis's economic views had always been grounded in capitalism. He championed workers' rights, both personally and legally, and remained outspoken about his concern for their well-being, but there are more than a few occasions in which his journal entries clearly view a distinction between social classes and remind us that he is in a superior position. On one occasion, while riled by a servant who had abandoned her employment at his residence, Landis professes, "we may find fault with servants, but we cannot do without them." It is difficult for him to understand the resentment of the Egyptians against the British because these English invaders provide a fair taxation system for the farmer. For the most part, the social position of the lower class is treated as pre-determined and self-contained. These views would soon manifest themselves in matters of his own family.

Curiously, Landis and George would have agreed on a mistrust of land speculation and the necessity to provide good wages for the working class, but the latter's single-tax theory targeted individuals like Vineland's founder, and Landis didn't like it. He resolved to sell the land he had earmarked as "the main-stay of my old age." He surmised that his defense of the farmer, which included authorship of a law passed in 1891, and his endeavors to establish a public market had earned him the wrath of "the commission men" and "the shopkeepers [and] green grocers" who also served as Vineland politicians. He also decided to "defend himself against "exorbitant assessments, which mean confiscation" by attacking it from a legal standpoint, an exercise that could only prove futile in light of the progressive movement spearheaded by George. Sending Charles Jr. to Trenton to "apply for quo warrants writs on both Vineland and Sea Isle," Landis learned, upon his son's return, that he had been refused.

But Landis continued to sell lots over the course of the last several months of 1895, so he had not depleted all the property he owned. He also had Marcus Fry purchase two-hundred acres in New Italy in order to facilitate the draining of the lowland in the area. He learned, after digging began for a drain, that white clay had been discovered and decided to pursue it in the possibility it could turn out to be "a profitable and valuable industry." At the same time, he was also pursuing legal action against a blackmail attempt that had apparently arisen recently and involved someone in Philadelphia. Landis was reluctant to provide details of the matter in his journal, writing only that it is "an atrocious case" that has him distracted and employing as his attorney Charles Jr., who had immediately hired a detective and began looking into the matter. Afterward, entries do not refer to the progress of the matter.

Landis spent time re-reading the works of Plutarch he had first read in his youth, enjoying both the history and the storytelling. Still a member of the Masons, he attended meetings. He was asked to consult about sea defenses for

Ocean Grove and Long Branch. At one point, he and Matilda visited the Pennsylvania Art Industrial Building in Philadelphia, unexpectedly encountering their sibling Beulah. In what seems to be a moment of nostalgia, he stayed overnight at the Girard Hotel in Camden, a place where "I used to stop in the fifties." Recalling that it was considered "one of the grandest hotels in the country," Landis now saw it as old-fashioned. He spent the evening thinking, no doubt about his youth, his life and mortality.

Thoughts of death seemed to consume him at this time, and the Girard Hotel was a reminder that "all the people who used to be there are dead." Earlier that autumn, while contemplating the recent death of a Vineland resident, Landis mused that he had "seen an entire generation of Vinelanders join [death's] march. When will my hour come?" Hearing about the passing of a Hammontonian, he had known, he lamented that all the individuals who had spent time at a particular house in Hammonton were now gone. "How old I feel when I see the swath that death has mown among all I knew in youth," he writes. On a day in which he felt physically poor, he concluded that "I may say that I live in the hopes of death. I am very weary."

However, death was still a few years away for Landis, despite the retirement of his Vineland journals on November 23, 1895. During his remaining years, he would maintain only a foreign journal when he once again sought a warmer climate to improve his health in the final months of his life. Traveling to Jamaica, he discovered that the therapeutic conditions he had experienced in Egypt and Mexico were not to be found in this island country.

During the late 19th century, electric power plants had begun springing up throughout the United States and were either shareholder-owned companies or municipally-owned/federally-owned electric utilities. Vineland decided to establish a municipally-owned plant because of a lack of interest from private utility firms who viewed small towns as offering no promise of high revenues in exchange for the substantial setup costs to connect it to electrical power.

The discussion of electric street lights in Vineland can be traced back to 1893 when Mayor Charles P. Lord first addressed the issue. During Mayor Joseph Mason's second term, which began seven years later, electric lights slowly began to replace the gas lights that were common in the 19th century.

In 1899, Landis, unyielding in his service to his creation, served as president of the Maurice River Water and Electric Power Company of Vineland, N.J., which was working on a proposed water power development for the town, a precursory plan to the eventual establishment of Vineland's own electrical plant.

In a surviving record of the company, Landis explains that "in the Borough of Vineland there is constant application for electric power from outside manufacturers, who wish to come there on account of its nearness to the great markets, railroad facilities and other advantages...I thought it advisable to have these water powers examined by a competent engineer and reported upon and by advice, I selected Mr. C.C. Vermeule...of our State Board of Geology who...refers to the Maurice River as a water power..."

Using Verneule's calculations, Landis provides an estimated net profit of $68,415 from the proposed plant. At the time, Vineland boasted fifty-two manufacturing sites that would be served by a Vineland-based electric company and Landis observes that "Alliance, Brotmanville, Rosenhayn and Carmel, between Vineland and Bridgeton, are manufacturing places that all want power." He concludes by stating, "Since the advent of electricity and the transmission of power, there has been a complete revolution in the value of water powers. It has made possible what heretofore was not possible and valuable that which in some cases heretofore has had no value. A power which is central to three industrial cities and so near Philadelphia and New York as to be practically in the greatest market of the United States, must naturally be of the value that has been estimated for it."

In the same document, Vermeule explains the prospective plans by stating that he has "examined three sites for the development of power. One of these sites is at the crossing of Almond Road and Maurice River, the next is half a mile above the crossing of Sherman Avenue over Maurice River and the third is on Muddy Run where it is crossed by the New Jersey Southern Railroad. I have made estimates in detail of the cost of developing power at these sites…in order to be able to deliver a stipulated amount of power at all times, and at the same time use the water power to its full capacity, it becomes expedient to equip our power stations with steam for occasional use in dry weather. The economy of water power under these conditions arises from the saving of fuel and labor whenever there is sufficient water to operate the plant or any part of it."

Any further involvement Landis may have had with the Maurice River Water and Electric Power Company is not known as there is little surviving correspondence from this final year of his life. He would not live long enough to witness the existence a power plant in Vineland. A year after the Maurice River Water and Electric Power Company report, an ordinance was passed in the borough to allow for construction of the electric plant. By 1903, the electric utility had 200 customers. By 1912, street lighting had expanded beyond the center of town and into side streets and, by 1916, through West Landis Avenue.

Landis would never witness the existence a power plant in Vineland, but his involvement with the Maurice River Water and Electric Power Company was evidence that his workload he had maintained for four decades had not dissipated much. In addition to serving on the Power Company board, he also followed his traditional daily regime of land sales and business trips. The details of Landis's routine near the end of his life are preserved in several accounts provided by George G. Walker, who was interviewed by the *Atlantic City Press* and the *Vineland Times Journal* in 1957 and 1962 respectively.

Walker, who was employed by Landis at the age of fifteen and who swept floors, ran errands, made pin maps of lumber-wood lots and received payment installments from those who had purchased land from the town founder, reflected that "the office was busiest on Saturday afternoons because most sales were on contract, and they would come in once a month on a Saturday to make payments on them." Any business that he couldn't handle, Walker explained, would be referred to Arthur Russell, another realtor in town.

Walker's reminiscences reveal that Landis questioned land purchasers as to whether they had any knowledge of farming and "if they didn't, Landis would try to discourage them from buying, unless they could obtain some agricultural help from someone in their own family." Landis had always sought experienced workers to farm the property he sold and, in 1880, had offered somewhat of an explanation for his aversion to selling land to novices when he witnessed what he called "poor farming," referring to it as something a child would accomplish. "Such people can never make a living at farming," he concluded. "Why do they attempt it?" Walker's account reveals that by 1899, Vineland was witnessing an influx of settlers without the agricultural experience necessary for success. Landis's strict demands probably did them a favor.

Walker's other duties included exercising his employer's horse, Major, who was quartered in the livery stable behind the Landis home. Domestic chores, according to Walker, were handled by two servants, Ameilia Robinson and Mrs. [Henrietta] Thomas.

It seems that Landis had also developed a new approach for enticing Italians to settle in Vineland at the end of the century. According to Walker, he had established a friendship with a Philadelphia restaurant owner named Gotti and provided him with "illustrated views of Vineland" to display in his Christian Street establishment to catch the interest of Italian families. Landis made regular visits to Gotti's restaurant and spent time in Sea Isle City as well. He did not spend a lot of time in his office.

Landis's mother and Matilda had continued to live with Landis in Vineland, with Matilda no doubt caring for her sibling and parent. But at 11 a.m. on February 14, 1896, Landis's mother died suddenly from heart failure after being treated by Dr. Wiley for other undisclosed complications. She joined her husband at Siloam cemetery in the Landis burial plot.

At this point in his life, Landis was spending less time with his two youngest sons, whose life choices gradually provoked estrangement from their father as the decade had progressed. Only Charles Jr. would maintain a healthy relationship with his father during the elder Landis's final years.

Landis's sons had spent the 1890s establishing careers and lifestyles largely away from the Vineland residence in which they had grown up. Marriage and other commitments would form a large part of Charles Jr. and Richard's lives during the decade, leaving only James Montevert in the company of his father by the time he turned twenty in 1895. They had all entered adulthood, but Landis would remain ever watchful and protective of them.

Although Charles Jr., a member of the Philadelphia Military Academy's class of 1890, had appeared agreeable to his new educational circumstances at the start of his second semester there, records show that he did not graduate from that facility, turning his attention to the study of law in the offices of Henry S. Alvord. He was admitted to the New Jersey bar as Attorney in 1892.

In 1893, the wedding of Charles Jr. and Minnie Rosenbaum occurred in the early morning hours of Thursday, June 15 at St. Paul's P.E. Church in Georgetown, Delaware, hometown of the bride. The ceremony, which included the administering of Holy Communion to the newlyweds, began at 6:30 a.m. and concluded a half-hour later. Rev. J. Cooper Kerr, a chaplain stationed at Fort

Wingate in New Mexico, was the officiating clergyman and the ceremony included a blessing of the rings as part of the event.

While one newspaper account identified the groom's father and Richard, in attendance, there is no mention in any of the reports that James Montevert attended. In fact, Charles Jr. selected as his ushers William Holmes of Philadelphia, Simeon Pennewell of Greenwood and Charles W. Cullen and Col. Everett Hickman of Georgetown. His best man was Richard W. Rosenbaum, the bride's brother.

The bridal party, which included the bride's sister Phoebe as flower girl dressed in a "frock of white China silk" and carrying "a bunch of La France roses", entered the church as Mrs. H.E. Paynter, organist, played the "Lohengrin Bridal March." The floral decorations described by the *Evening Journal* hid the altar "in a mound of blooming woodbine daisies, evergreens, roses and handsome potted plants…" The bride, carrying roses and smilax, was clad in "a gown of two-toned bengaline of the bluish-gray shades with brown velvet trimming" and a hat that "matched the gown." In addition, "chains of daisies tied with handsome ribbons the color of the bride's gown roped off the aisles of the church."

The bride was escorted by her father to what was described as a parasol "made of choice flowers" under which the couple was joined in matrimony. During the ceremony, Paynter played variations of "You'll Remember Me" and concluded the event with Mendelssohn's "Wedding March." Following English tradition, the church bells were rung after the service.

A reception at the home of the bride's parents, Mr. and Mrs. R.A. Rosenbaum, immediately followed. The couple had also hosted a reception for the bridal party and invited guests the previous night. Those in attendance included Landis, Mrs. Westcott of Trenton, Judge Carrow and his wife of Merchantville and Mr. and Mrs. Craft of Camden

A gift described in newspaper accounts as "a set of cameo jewelry, consisting of lace pin and sleeve buttons that are over 300 years old, having been discovered at Pompeii" was presented by Landis to his daughter-in-law. It was also reported that the bride received other valuable presents from guests.

Following the breakfast at the Rosenbaum's home that morning, the newlyweds caught the 8 o'clock train for Sea Isle City where they spent the remainder of the morning and afternoon. They needed to remain close since a wedding reception given by the bride's aunt, a Mrs. Leach, was held that night in Vineland. It was announced that the newlyweds would settle in Charles Jr's hometown where he would continue his law practice. That was true for a while, but the couple would soon settle in the location where they spent their first day as husband and wife together - Sea Isle City.

The most notable person missing from this occasion was Clara Landis. Charles Jr.'s estrangement from his mother, which certainly had been fueled by her victory in the 1877 custody battle, had grown considerably over the past two decades. The decisions she made since leaving Vineland had altered her lifestyle several times, but they had also contributed to distancing her both geographically and emotionally from her second-born son.

Charles Jr. did not settle into a job after the wedding as might have been expected. In a letter to his father most likely composed after leaving Vineland, he writes that he is thinking "about my future and duty. I am ready to do anything for my future when the chance comes…I think that most failures are due to ambitions beyond means or opportunities…I am doing nothing at present but housework. It has been almost impossible to find the time to prepare this short statement." He informs his father that his wife is making lace, possibly as a means of income.

Charles Jr. was eventually admitted to the bar as Councilor in November 1895, and moved his practice to Sea Isle City, where he specialized in real estate law. Two of his clients were his father and his Aunt Matilda, for whom he won disputes with the Vineland municipality over what Vineland Mayor Benjamin Stevens called "assessments of their extensive Landis holdings in the Borough and Township."

Over the course of the 1890s, a daughter and three sons would be born to Charles Jr. and Mary. In a surviving booklet from the couple's wedding, entitled "Our Marriage Vows," there is an entry written by the proud father that records the birth of each child: Mary Rosenbaum Landis, born November 15, 1894, Charles Klein Landis 3rd, born October 30, 1896, Robert Rosenbaum Landis, born November 24, 1897, and Gordon Meade Landis, born March 7, 1899.

Unlike Charles Jr., Richard had selected a career as an artist early on. Landis had encouraged his sons to be well-read and engaged in artistic endeavors from a young age. He sent Richard to Vineland's prestigious Braidwood Art School beginning November 12, 1882. The school was founded by Philadelphia artist Thomas Braidwood and seemed to have captured young Richard's imagination, so it must have been surprising to discover that his father disapproved of the artistic field as a career choice when Richard reached the age of college. It seems that Landis found the artist's life a poor choice for income. To his credit, Richard continually implored his father to change his mind.

While vacationing on the island of Capri in February 1890, Landis received a letter from Richard who pleaded that he be allowed to pursue his artistic inclinations. "To receive the letter in this beautiful place seemed very much in keeping with the request. Is it not better to be happy than rich," Landis muses in his journal, "With his love of art, to him it will be a perpetual source of pleasure, and perhaps pleasure to others. Is it not a great thing to make one mortal happy in this world, greater than the conquest of a city?" Landis's decision was accompanied by the purchase of a Charles Caryl Coleman painting in Capri for Richard to copy and a visit to the Julian Academy of Painters in Paris to determine if it was where his son should study.

Instead, it was soon decided that Richard would enroll at the University of Pennsylvania. The choice of the Philadelphia institution, which had just opened its Architectural School, coincided with Landis's overtures to the university in establishing the Sea Isle City marine biology lab. It afforded an opportunity for the father to keep tabs on his son. By the following February, Richard's extra-curricular activities as a ladies' man instigated his father's intervention. In a journal entry for February 17, 1891, Landis writes, "Richard had a folly in regard to a young lady older than himself (he is only 17). The young lady got engaged to a Southerner and Richard wrote her a letter complaining of her perfidy, which she sent to her betrothed. He came on and sent Richard a challenge in a vulgar way with many insulting phrases. Richard, boy-like and tho' this person was a man of 25, went down to the Continental Hotel where he stopped and gave him a terrible beating."

Landis reacted immediately, threatening to have the man arrested for issuing a challenge. The Southerner promised to leave town as long as Landis didn't follow-through on his threat. Agreeing to the proposal, Landis soon discovered that his son's opponent had not upheld his part of the deal. Taking no further action, Landis dined with Richard that evening, recording in his journal, "I shall do what I can to protect my inexperienced son. The lady is certainly foolish and cannot care much for the man she is engaged to, to get him into such trouble." The incident made Landis wary of his son's exploits and keen to keep track of those closest to Richard. Apparently, he also continued to cast a disapproving glance at the women who captured his attention.

Richard probably completed his studies at the University of Pennsylvania by 1894. A newspaper report around this time explains that he had sailed for Madrid, Spain for one to two years to continue his art studies. There is no doubt that while in Madrid he encountered the works of Diego Valazquez and Alonzo Cano, two 17th century Spanish painters who would be an influence on his own work. It is also likely that this European visit included some time in Germany as well.

Before leaving for Madrid, Richard was commissioned, apparently through the efforts of Dr. Mary Dunlap of the Women's State School in Vineland, to paint a portrait of former New Jersey Senator Alexander G. Cattell, who had also served in the State General Assembly and was chosen by President Ulysses S. Grant as a member of the first United States Civil Service Commission. The Republican senator had passed away in April 1894 prior to Richard's departure and the young art student, it was reported, would complete the portrait abroad, undoubtedly working from a photograph of the politician. By the following year, this and another commissioned portrait by Richard hung on the walls of the Women's State School.

While in Europe, Richard probably completed a portrait of his Aunt Matilda, a painting that has hung in the Landis Room of the Vineland Historical and Antiquarian Society for decades and is the only known image of Landis's sister. The choice of Matilda as subject remains a curious one, especially since their relationship at this point wasn't always agreeable. Tension between Richard and Matilda certainly existed within this timeframe as a letter from Landis to Richard, dated June 17, 1895, intimates: "be pleasant and kind to your aunt. She has done much for us, has been your savior and protector. Now do something for her. I shall not only thank you, but God will help you for it."

Landis continued to support his son's artistic endeavors. On the evening of September 19, 1895, he offered the use of his Vineland home for an exhibition of Richard's paintings on the eve of his son's departure for Rome. Landis, according to a newspaper report, opened his house to friends, giving them the "privilege of enjoying the paintings of his artist son, Richard W. M. Landis." Forty pieces of art were exhibited, some originals and some copies of other works of art, including a portrait of Richard's younger brother James.

The article covering the event proclaimed in its headline, "Charles K. Landis, Esq. Gives an Elegant Art Entertainment at his Residence [-] Throngs of Representative Vineland People Examine the Works of Richard W.M. Landis and Express Hearty Admiration." It's apparent the newspaper reporter recognized Richard's talents immediately, proclaiming, "There is in every detail unmistakable evidence of genius and genius of the highest order…Although barely a youth, our Vineland boy has applied himself with such earnestness that more than forty pictures, his own work, graced the walls of his father's handsome residence; and these pictures are not crude efforts, but have the inspiration and brush of a master. Probably, the best were the portraits; they were the most enthusiastically praised by the connoisseurs…"

The exhibit included original works such as the portraits commissioned by the State of New Jersey of Cattell and Dr. Parrish of Burlington, New Jersey, portraits of his brother James and relative Mary Lewis Landis, *View at Sea Isle*, *Meadow and Sand Dunes at Sea Isle*, *Morning Scene at Sea Isle*, *Fishing Boats in the Morning*, *A Young Bacchanal*, *Head of a Model in Paris* and several still life paintings and charcoal studies. Copies of works by other artists included Valazquez's *Philip IV, King of Spain* and *Portrait of Alonzo Cano*, and Cano's *The Virgin and Child* as well as American Rembrandt Peale's *General George Washington*.

The fact that Richard displayed an interest in the styles of Valazquez and Cano explain the look of some of his still life endeavors from the same period, particularly such paintings as *Still Life with Newspaper* and *Still Life with Pipe and Stein*, remarkable pieces that are almost photographic in style and that demonstrate a keen eye for detail. Richard's *Grist Mill of John Roberts III, Oak Lane, Gladwyne, Pennsylvania* is another example that suggests the promise witnessed by the reporter at the exhibit in the Landis home. Furthermore, Richard's study of Peale's portraits mirrors his own undertakings in that genre with his portraits of Matilda and his brother James. His accomplishments would guarantee that his artworks would continue to grace various exhibitions throughout the following century.

Richard sailed for Rome on September 25, 1895. In his journal, Landis petitioned God to "help him in his efforts! And that he may become a great artist." During Richard's second trip to Europe, he and his father exchanged correspondence regularly. Richard's letters reveal a genuine interest in the art he is seeing and studying and there is a sense of enjoyment in sharing it with his father. Landis's correspondence conveys a sense of pride over his son's development as well as contentment in knowing he made the right choice in allowing Richard a career in the arts. When Landis received a photograph of a Titian painting sent by his son, he encouraged him to paint his own version of the work, which Landis would later sell for him. Richard also sent a photograph of his copy of a portrait of Valasquez, which prompted his father to write, "He is doing well." But Landis also contacted the U.S. Ambassador to Rome to request that the diplomat assist his son while he was studying there.

While Richard's artistic accomplishments earned him the respect and support of his family, his love life was having an adverse effect. It would reach a boiling point when Richard, shortly after his return from Europe, secretly married Emma Frambes of Philadelphia on February 14 1899. Emma, the daughter of Lewis Frambes, had visited Vineland two months prior to the marriage and caught the attention and heart of Richard who began visiting the Frambes household in Philadelphia after Emma returned home. The relationship did not meet the approval of Landis.

On Valentine's Day, the couple, without telling the Frambes family or Landis, visited the Reverend J.F. Crouch, the pastor of a Methodist Church in Philadelphia, and were married. Stewart Campbell, Richard's friend, served as witness. The newlyweds then lived with the bride's parents, who accepted the secret wedding. In an unidentified newspaper article, dated March 2, 1899, it was reported, "All that now remains to be done is to secure the forgiveness of Mr. Landis Sr."

According to an article in the *New York Evening Telegram* the following year, "Richard Landis incurred his father's wrath by marrying against his wishes. Upon his return from abroad, having studied art in Paris and Rome, he startled Vineland society by suddenly marrying Miss Emma Frambes, of Philadelphia."

Landis was apparently unwilling to accept the marriage. Later court records reveal that "Mr. Landis made inquiries and obtained some information in regard to Richard's wife, which evidently further displeased him. He appears to have had some question about the character of Richard's associates prior to his marriage."

Despite his feelings, Landis seemingly attempted to help Richard's artistic career. In 1900, the *New York Times* reported that, "Mr. Landis, while seemingly implacable toward his sons, interested himself in Richard, who is an artist, and assisted him by arranging with friends, prominent business men in Philadelphia, where Richard was living with his bride, to have painted by the young artist portraits of themselves at the father's expense." Nonetheless, by 1900 Richard and Emma, possibly having tired of Landis's resistance to the marriage, left Philadelphia, relocating to Chicago where the former Mrs. Landis now resided. It has been reported that Richard never set foot again in the Landis Vineland residence until after his father's death.

While his older brothers were betrothed and settling into their respective careers, James Montevert Landis, or Monte, as he was called by his family, was still trying to find his place. Having spent his first seven years in the custody of his mother and his later childhood and adolescence in Vineland, Monte was just beginning a restless trek that would take him through a series of jobs and locations. A letter from Landis to Richard dated June 17, 1895 informs him that "Monte is working in Brooklyn..." The job was not specified but, by the end of summer, Monte was back in Vineland and assisting and accompanying his father. On September 27, he departed for New York again to seek a position with the electric company Gourley and Co., writing to his father two days later that he had been awarded the job. Landis was pleased with the news, but it wasn't long before Monte would return and take a job locally with the Western Union Telegraph Company as an operator.

Of the Landis siblings, Monte would soon have the rockiest relationship with his father, resenting the intrusiveness and demands that he should return immediately after work to spend his evenings at home. Having already demonstrated a tendency to keep a close watch on Richard's activities earlier in the decade, Landis now continued the practice with Monte, believing that his youngest son was keeping company with questionable individuals and hiring someone to follow him. Monte, however, was less tolerant of the surveillance than his older brother, and the mistrust soon soured and strained the relationship.

Chapter 11
Consequences

When Landis passed away on June 12, 1900, it was the end of an accomplished life as an entrepreneur and a year-long bout with personal turmoil in the form of private suffering that largely centered on his relationship with his two younger sons. The estrangement that resulted from these matters would soon capture the interest of Vinelanders and the country alike as Landis reached from beyond his grave and, for a final time, created an allure the national media couldn't resist.

The wheels had been set in motion by a monumental decision several months prior to Landis's death. It would result in a painful division of the family that hadn't been witnessed since Clara's departure and subsequent victory in her custody battle. It would also set the stage for the final time the surviving members of Landis's immediate family would gather together in one place.

The domestic unrest had been precipitated through an action taken by Landis on the afternoon of April 16, 1900. He had made a decision about a matter he undoubtedly had been deliberating for some time and proceeded to attach a codicil to the will he had executed March 15, 1898. According to court records, "The codicil changes the bequests to Richard and to James and provides that the one shall go to the Vineland Historical Society, and the other to the children of... son Charles [K. Landis, Jr.]." The change in the will was followed that evening by a heated argument with his youngest son, after which Landis ordered Monte to leave and not return.

In 1957, Landis employee George G. Walker admitted he had been witness to the incident that estranged his employer from his son and the details he provided are illuminating. Monte chose to visit a young woman in Millville on the evening of April 16 and missed the 10 o'clock train back to Vineland. When he arrived home, it was late and Landis banished him. According to Walker, Monte sought his father's forgiveness, which was not forthcoming.

Walker offered another instance which demonstrated how steadfast Landis remained in resisting forgiveness. "I was in the office alone," said Walker who, along with William McKillip, a barber, had been witnesses to the codicil of the Landis will, "and saw Landis coming from his house across the street toward the office. Monte met his father at the intersection and spoke to him, but Landis wouldn't recognize him." The son followed his father into the office where Landis took his seat on a rocking chair.

Monte approached his father, Walker recalled, and said "Good afternoon, pa," but his greeting went unacknowledged. The son was visibly upset and offered to shake hands with Landis who finally spoke, stating, "I have nothing to say to you."

On June 15, 1900, the same day Landis was buried at Siloam Cemetery, the reading of his will took place. The details of the will were limited when initially announced in a carefully worded release presented by Fry and omitted any information about how the inheritance had been divided among family members other than the amount accorded Matilda, who had been appointed executrix of the will. "After bequeathing to his sister Miss Matilda Landis $500 a year from 1875 with interest for taking care of himself and children," the June 16, 1900 edition of the *Evening Journal* reported Fry as saying, "and a further sum of $1,800 and interest from 1877, Mr. Landis made some minor bequests and directed that after all debts are paid and bequests made, one-fourth of his estate, when converted into money, go to the Historical Society of Vineland together with a valuable portrait [sic] of himself by Turini of New York; also other paintings, books, statuary and historical notes of Vineland." Fry said that he spoke only about this portion of the will "because it related to the public welfare of Vineland."

The *Evening Journal*, however, deduced the unstated. "From the little points gathered here," it reported, "and these mixed with a good deal of guesswork, it is concluded that Miss Landis, Charles K. Landis, Jr. and his children are to be the beneficiaries of the will after the fourth is given to the Historical Society. It is pretty well understood the two sons, Richard and Monetvert, are disinherited by the document which was written by Mr. Landis himself." The newspaper also acknowledged lots bequeathed to Katherine Gittone, Landis's bookkeeper and interpreter for Italian-speaking clients who was now charged to continue in her capacity "for a period," and Marcus Fry, his chief clerk. It was also reported that residents "owing [Landis] for homes shall not be distressed."

Newspapers, both local and national were soon reporting the disinheritance of Richard and Monte. Articles clarified that the will divided the Landis fortune equally between Matilda, Charles Jr., the Vineland Historical and Antiquarian Society and the children of Charles Jr. It also reported that Gittone was bequeathed twenty-five building lots in Vineland and Fry twenty-five building lots in Sea Isle City "in gratitude for good and faithful service."

An examination of Landis's will, dated March 15, 1898, and the codicil, dated April 16, 1900, reveals some specifics not mentioned in the newspaper reports. In the original will, Landis mentions that there was railroad stock Matilda "loaned me in the time of much distress in 1877" that he had never repaid. Matilda was bequeathed her pay for caring not only for Landis and the children but also for serving as caretaker for her and Landis's aged parents. Monte was bequeathed the book *Life of Franklin*, Landis's gold watch and the encyclopedia presented to Landis by the residents of Vineland. Richard received art books owned by his father. It was also stipulated that Matilda was allowed to live in the house and Monte in his rooms until the homestead was sold.

In the codicil, Landis states that all that was originally bequeathed to Richard is now given to the Vineland Historical and Antiquarian Society and what was originally bequeathed to James is now given to Philip Baker of Vineland in trust for the benefit of Charles Jr.'s children, particularly for their education but also their general benefit. An appraisal of Landis's property was soon undertaken by Fry, including Landis's Vineland office and his Vineland and Sea Isle residences.

In the June 19 edition of the *Evening Journal*, an article announced that "Messrs. Richard and Montevert Landis have made a settlement with their aunt, Miss Matilda Landis, and therefore the will of the late Charles K. Landis will not be contested." The newspaper explains that two lawyers, Howard Carrow and Herbert C. Bartlett, had been engaged by the founder's sons but were notified to cease work on the case. The brothers' decision was met with favorable response from the community which, the paper reports, had been sympathetic to their situation. But within six days the apparent settlement had ceased to exist.

The *Evening Journal*, in its June 25 edition, reported that "the settlement in the C.K. Landis will case has not materialized as was hoped. J. Montevert Landis has given his lawyers orders to go ahead and contest the will. He said he could get nothing definite in the way of an agreement and feeling that he had some right in the estate of his father he had instructed his lawyers to make an effort to obtain that right for him."

Richard, at first, was reluctant to enter into the legal fray but, over the course of the next few months, changed his mind. As the *New York Evening Telegram* reported in December, "Richard, who at first hesitated to contest the will, owing toward friendliness with his aunt, lately associated himself with his brother Montevert against the will."

A trial date was set for December 6 at the Cumberland County Orphans' Court. As the final days of November passed in anticipation of what would be revealed in the testimony, newspapers carried an air of curiosity. By now, the media understood the financial import of the codicil with publications like *The North American*, in an article headlined "Disinherited Sons to Unveil a Dark Past," reporting that, with property included, more than two-thirds of Landis's fortune had been granted to Matilda. The newspaper also featured a photograph of Richard, exquisitely attired with a flower in his lapel and piercing eyes staring at the reader.

By the start of the trial, it became clear that the angle Carrow and Bartlett would pursue would make use of the verdict in the 1876 trial in which Landis was acquitted of the murder of newspaper editor Uri Carruth on the grounds of temporary insanity, asserting that Landis had been insane ever since. An unidentified newspaper, dated December 6, 1900, reported that "witnesses were unimportant and the testimony accounted tame by those who had intimation of coming family secrets." But as the trial proceeded, both Richard and Monte "charged that their remarkable father had in his late years but the mind of a child, being peevish, suspicious and not responsible. [But] it seemed as if filial respect restrained them from exposing the skeletons of the family..." Still, the most vivid contributions came from Landis's three sons whose allegiances and rivalries were clearly on view in the Bridgeton courtroom that December.

Taking the stand first, the twenty-five-year-old Monte presented a dysfunctional portrait of his father, claiming that

Landis altered his will after their April 16 confrontation. The youngest of the Landis brothers recounted his youth, recalling a trip to Europe with his mother before he was delivered into his father's custody at the age of seven. He testified that Landis was never violent with him but that they did not get along well. Monte stated that his father had demanded that his son return home immediately after work at 8 p.m., calling it "one of his hobbies." He explained that Landis had the Vineland marshal follow him, believing that his son was hanging around with "evil persons" that included prostitutes. In later testimony, a Constable Nickerson admitted he had been hired by Landis to shadow Monte. He told the court that, after trailing him, he witnessed nothing detrimental about Monte's character.

Monte felt that his father, just before his death, "was seemingly in a state of nervous exhaustion. He thought he was on the verge of ruin, and solemnly prophesized that his future home was the poorhouse." But Monte admitted to feeling resentful that he had to work as a Western Union Telegraph operator while Landis was rich. The *New York Evening Telegram* reported that Monte had claimed "since the Carruth tragedy his father always had an insane fear of being murdered, and even went to the extent of fearing he would be killed by some of his own children; that he actually at times became greatly excited over this haunting fear."

The most condemning testimony, however, was reserved for Matilda, who was in attendance at the courthouse. "She said that I was not the son of my father," Monte is reported as saying, "and called me a number of ugly names. Until I was twenty years old she used to whip me, using a cowhide and sometimes a yardstick. She told my father that I was a hostler, which I regarded as an unwarranted imputation against my mother, the daughter of Commodore Meade." Mrs. O.D. Graves, confirming Monte's account, claimed Matilda had repeatedly called him illegitimate in her presence. He also accused his aunt of controlling his father and continually nagging and prejudicing him against his youngest son. Monte also testified that he had been made to sleep in the bathroom, a charge corroborated by another witness in the trial.

Like his younger brother, Richard had issues with his aunt and conveyed them with the same frankness. Citing his marriage to Emma Frambes as the circumstances that had "brought on differences with his father," Richard accused Matilda of not liking his wife and speaking disparagingly of her with Landis. Another witness corroborated his testimony, saying that Richard was forced to leave the household because he had married a "common woman."

Additional newspapers reported that Richard also referred to an incident he witnessed whereby his father encouraged Monte and Charles Jr. to fight with knives, the veracity of which was not corroborated by any other witnesses, including Monte and Charles Jr., whose attendance was in triple capacity as witness, defendant and chief counsel in the case against his brothers. By now, Charles Jr. had a successful law practice in Sea Isle City, where he lived with his wife Mary and their four children, but there is no evidence he had maintained contact with his siblings. The fact that he had received an inheritance and that his children had been bequeathed what had originally been reserved for Monte could not help but intensify an already adversarial situation.

Addie Judd, seamstress for the Landis family, testified that she "noticed no unpleasant relations between father and son," a claim supported by testimony from house servant Henrietta Thomas, "but thought Miss Landis did not treat James as well as the other sons." Judd also testified that Monte was "obliged to sleep in the bathroom while his brothers occupied beds." However, Charles Jr. told the court that his father was "kind to all his sons and showed no preference."

While much of the testimony focused on family relationships, the lawyers for the Landis brothers produced witnesses to confirm their claim that their father was insane. Philip Baker recounted an incident at a Sea Isle City dinner at which Landis was speaking. He said that after a comment was made by another attendee, Landis attacked the man with a knife and had to be stopped from "going any farther." Charles Jr. countered that his father had no knife, had used no force and simply had come to his aid when the man had accosted the younger Landis, saying his father was "no good." John Ring spoke of meeting Landis, who gave evidence of "vivid hallucinations." T.J. Ware claimed that Landis had told him he hadn't seen Ring for a year, even though he had witnessed them talking together recently.

Determining the validity of the trial testimony is impossible. It was reported that Vinelanders were sympathetic with the Landis brothers and some may have been attempting to help Richard and Monte secure an inheritance that was rightfully theirs. But various documentation indicates that there were other residents who had harbored grudges against Landis or who had disagreed with his decisions. The trial may have been used as an opportunity to discredit Vineland's founder with impunity.

One such report that remains unsubstantiated concerns Landis's private habits to which only the closest family members would have been privy. On December 8, the *Evening Journal* reported: "It was in evidence that Landis would never go into a lighted room at night until the curtains were drawn for fear someone would shoot him. He never retired without a revolver under his pillow and always carried one." Such a report was certainly contradictory to Landis's reluctance to accept a pistol offered him for protection while in Egypt in 1890.

The trial heated up considerably when Matilda, the recipient of the largest amount of the family fortune, took the stand on December 7. She had been in attendance on the opening day of the hearing, one newspaper commenting that "her clean-cut face and her modish style of dressing would at any rate make her an unusual figure anywhere…During the trial, she toyed with a lorgnette and a massive black chain to which it was attached. She appeared bored with everything until the Landis boys took the stand. Then she dropped the lorgnette, leaned eagerly forward so as not to miss a word." The paper reported that she also frequently whispered into the ears of the lawyers.

The following day, the *Evening Journal* reported that Matilda told the court she handled her brother's business "to a certain extent" when he was away, in addition to her role as housekeeper. She also claimed the role of peacemaker between her brother and Monte, hiding a revolver "in fear of tragedy." She, like others who testified, reported that Landis, on the night he evicted his youngest son, had claimed Monte had threatened his life, but no one actually heard the threat.

Matilda denied calling Monte names but felt that he was a bad influence on Richard. As for her accusations about Monte's illegitimacy, she stated, "I might have questioned Monte's legitimacy. I don't know whether I said he was not his son." She did claim that her brother "charged Monte with running around with prostitutes," an accusation the youngest Landis son denied.

She briefly rendered her nephew in a positive light when she recounted that she lent him $100 and he paid it back with interest. Mostly, however, her testimony was negative, calling Monte "unfilial." She said Landis had told her not to let his youngest son into the house again
and denied refusing to allow Richard's wife to enter the house, explaining that she had advised him to leave his wife in Philadelphia because she disapproved of her visiting.

She did not discuss her brother's mental state or offer any testimony to refute statements made by others about the behavior of Landis over the previous year. Instead, her testimony largely concerned Monte and her late brother's relationship with him. In the end, Matilda's testimony would play no part in the decision of the ruling. The ruling would be delivered approximately two weeks after the conclusion of the trial and would reference correspondence that had not been reported during the hearing.

On December 27, 1900, the codicil of Landis's will was upheld by Judge Trenchard, and heightened the drama that surrounded the Landis family. Trenchard's decision, as recorded in the *New Jersey Law Journal*, examines every angle used by the brothers' attorneys in an attempt to prove that Landis was insane when he removed Richard and Monte from the will and that the town founder had been wrongly influenced by his sister Matilda.

Beginning with the testimony of friends and employees who spoke of how Landis exhibited strange behavior during his final year, Trenchard concludes that "witnesses produced by the appellant testify to slight mistakes as to matters, which, in my opinion, tend to show nothing more than a misunderstanding or momentary forgetfulness, as likely to result from inattention or indifference to matters spoken about. It will be noticed that none of these alleged mistakes relate to the testator's family or property."

Addressing Monte's accusation that Landis had altered the will following the heated confrontation he had with his father on April 16, the judge acknowledged the town founder's temper and disregard for reason, citing the 1875 incident when Landis shot Uri Carruth. "It may be true that, when aroused in anger, his better judgment was disturbed," Trenchard writes, "but there is no proof that he was excited or in a passion at the time of the execution of either the will or codicil. The proof is to the contrary thereof. The quarrel with James could not have influenced him in making the codicil, because the codicil was made and executed at three o'clock in the afternoon and the quarrel did not occur until the evening of that day."

As for Richard and Monte's conduct, Trenchard relied upon evidence that Landis himself provided. If there was anything the siblings had overlooked, it was the fact that their father was a lawyer and saw fit to submit evidence pertaining to their exclusion from the will. This was in the form of two letters, one "written to Richard by a young lady," dated June 1, 1897, and the other "written by James to Richard" from Jersey City on May 29, 1898. While he doesn't reveal the specifics of each letter, Trenchard does indicate that their placement meant Landis "indicated premises from which it was possible for him to draw his conclusion."

The judge writes that "Mr. Landis made inquiries and obtained some information in regard to Richard's wife, which evidently further displeased him. He appears to have had some question about the character of Richard's associates prior to his marriage. He was greatly incensed because of James' absence from home evenings. He was displeased with his associates and with his failure to render an account in certain business transactions…He seems to have believed the conduct of both Richard and James to have been undignified and a reflection on the honor of the family, and to have been deeply offended thereby… It may be that the testator's belief as to the conduct of Richard and James was a mistake; it certainly was not a delusion because it had basis on (a) what [he had been told] about Richard's wife, and (b) James' suspicious unwillingness to say where he had been upon returning home late at night and to render an account, which circumstances bear a natural relation to the letters found with the will. In this connection the two letters are significant."

When it came to Matilda, Trenchard offered that "there is no direct proof that Miss Landis procured, or was instrumental in making, either the will or codicil… Whatever may have been her feelings towards [James] in the early days, I think she had no ill feeling in the more recent years, as her letters to James and those to his father

494

concerning him show much depth of affection and solicitude...Whatever the truth may be, the proofs strongly indicate that Mr. Landis never doubted the legitimacy of James."

After the announcement of Judge Trenchard's decision, the *Evening Journal* reported that Monte would appeal. This would result in another loss for the youngest Landis sibling, whose
involvement with the telegraph industry did not provide a career in the way Charles Jr.'s legal work and Richard's artistic endeavors became a profession. His work for Western Union seems to have lasted a few years into the 1900s and would not be his last attempt to find an occupation.

The year after his father's death, Monte married Grace Hoover Kincaid, a Bridgeton resident and daughter of John Chatten and Phoebe (Mann) Kincaid, in a ceremony in her hometown on May 2, 1901. The following year, their only child, James Montevert Meade Landis, was born October 25, 1902.

By the middle of the decade, Monte took an interest in the world of Vineland journalism. *The Vineland Daily News* had been established by Walter E. Cansdell on February 4, 1889, becoming successful only after it began publishing as a weekly called *The News* on July 5, 1890. Cansdell sold the paper in 1892 to buyers identified as the Miller Brothers, and the new owners changed the political allegiance of the publication from Republican to "Staunchly Democratic." The newspaper employed a series of different editors, including Mary C. Hutchens, before it was sold to the Vineland News Company in 1901. In October of that year,

W. D. Wilson was both editor and publisher until Garfield Pancoast succeeded him in December when the periodical reverted back to its Republican support. On May 5, 1905, the business was purchased by Frank Mortimer whose ownership lasted only four months.

On September 8, 1905, Monte and a *Philadelphia Inquirer* journalist by the name of James Cooper would acquire the newspaper and convert it into an afternoon daily. Maintaining the Republican allegiance, they issued the first installment on September 11 as *The Vineland Evening News*. The co-owners were intent on capturing an immediate readership by offering the first week of issues free. The publication featured interviews with prominent Vineland citizens discussing the town's greatest needs. The marketing ideas, while clever and admirable, overlooked the one obstacle to the young publishers' success. The dedicated following of the town's rival newspaper, *The Evening Journal*, could not be challenged, and on March 17, 1906, *The Vineland Evening News* would end its run, although it was briefly reincarnated the following year as *The Weekly News* under the ownership of George S. McGinley.

During autumn 1906, Monte moved to Chicago, leaving behind his hometown of Vineland and the acrid memory of his disinheritance and joining his mother and Richard. His wife and son remained with Grace's family in Bridgeton for several months before joining him. Monte began work with the railroad and would be employed by several of the Midwest rail systems. For most of 1907, the couple remained in the Midwest raising their son.

Around September of that year, Grace traveled back to Bridgeton with their child on what appeared to be a brief visit. The vacation, however, extended to several weeks and during that time she met professionally with attorney J. Ogden Burt. Statements by Grace in a later interview seem to indicate she was initiating divorce proceedings but had second thoughts about finalizing the matter. Apparently, her husband was informed of her intent and, concluding that an affair with the Bridgeton attorney was the cause of her actions, traveled back to Cumberland County to confront his presumed rival. His brief visit would garner the attention of the press before he had departed.

On Wednesday, October 16, 1907, Monte began an eighteen-hour journey from Chicago to Bridgeton on what would be his last visit to Cumberland County. Upon disembarking in Bridgeton, he obtained transportation to Burt's offices. Around 9:30 on the morning of October 17, 1907, he climbed the stairs to the lawyer's rear office above Walter E. Ware's clothing store. His arrival summoned Burt from his front office and interrupted a consultation with Captain Sanford Bacon. Stepping through the folding doors that separated his offices, the attorney stared at the man and asked who he was and what he wanted. The visitor from Chicago never identified himself. Instead he proclaimed, "You have been familiar with my wife."

Monte then produced a written agreement, the contents of which remain undisclosed, and demanded Burt sign it. The lawyer refused to put his signature on the document. It was at this point that Landis aimed a 32-caliber Iver-Johnson revolver at Burt's head. The attorney, aware of the open doors from which he had entered the room, accepted the risk and ran into his front office, attempting to pull the doors shut as Monte squeezed the trigger. But instead of a lead ball striking its target, a spray of bird shot, commonly referred to as "mustard ball," issued from the gun, leaving Burt unharmed. When Monte tried to open the doors, presumably to launch a second assault, he discovered they were being held shut by Captain Bacon. With his prey inaccessible, Landis retreated to the Bridgeton streets.

Dr. E. T. Davis, who occupied the adjacent office and had heard the shot, ran into the Burt offices and learned of what had transpired. Out on the street, he spotted Landis. The *Bridgeton Evening News* reported that Davis engaged another resident to keep an eye on Monte while he ran to City Hall to report the shooting to the mayor. The citizen entrusted with the task had no problem maintaining his surveillance. Monte did not attempt to run.

At City Hall, Officer Aaron Smith was apprised of the situation and left for the sheriff's office to report the incident, while at Burt's law offices, the attorney assured those who arrived to lend support that he was fine, but it was obvious he was considerably shaken by the assault.

Meanwhile, Monte walked over to Broad Street and followed the pathway to the same location at which Smith had arrived moments earlier. He had decided to turn himself in and, upon entering the sheriff's office, was apprehended and jailed, spending the remainder of the morning and most of the afternoon in a cell awaiting what would happen next.

According to the *Evening News,* Mayor George Hampton arrived at the sheriff's office between 3 and 4 o'clock to meet with Monte, who was summoned from his cell and brought to the third floor where Hampton was waiting. A report in the *Los Angeles Herald,* explains that Monte "was given a hearing by Mayor George Hampton and was recommitted to jail in default of $500 bail to await the action of the grand jury. 'Assault with intent to kill' is the specific charge against the prisoner." As the news reports of the time explained, even though the cartridges Landis used were filled with bird shot, at close range the damage would be the same as that of a lead ball. Because the shot fired at Burt was at a distance, it scattered, causing no harm.

The charge posed a serious problem and the accused man wasted no time contacting his older brother, Charles, who agreed to come to his aid. Then in a curious move, instead of returning Monte to his cell, the authorities instead confined him to the third floor of the building which contained several empty cells and a corridor. But an *Evening News* reporter, granted an interview with the prisoner, described Monte freely pacing the hallway. The local press even joked about the third floor being Monte's suite.

Monte exhibited a mix of responses concerning his actions. Although he made no effort to escape after voluntarily turning himself in, his initial explanation was that his confrontation was an attempt to "show Burt up" in front of the citizens of Bridgeton. During his time in jail, he inquired of a reporter from the *Evening News* if Burt had died yet. When he was notified that the attorney had survived the attack, he asked if the lawyer had been seriously hurt. The newspaper reported that Monte displayed no evidence of relief over Burt's survival.

Monte explained to the reporter that he never lost his nerve when confronting the attorney, claiming that his aim wasn't accurate. When asked how he had procured the cartridges for the revolver, the former Vinelander said that individuals could obtain anything as long as they had money.

And when confronted with the fact that the cartridges contained bird shot, Monte simply laughed. Burt announced that he would not be pressing charges against his attacker because he believed his assailant "is mentally unbalanced." Still, the son of Vineland's founder spent Thursday and Friday in jail while discussions were no doubt conducted behind closed doors. By Saturday, Monte was released on $500 bail. According to news accounts, he was on the first train to Chicago and "it is believed nothing more will be heard of the case." The accuracy of that statement would be confirmed with the passage of time.

In 1907, Monte's name would appear once again in the *Evening News*. In late December, he initiated proceedings for a divorce on grounds of cruelty. When interviewed by the press, his wife said she had not yet been notified on the matter but admitted that she felt that her husband was crazy and had feared for her life when she was with him. Her interview was frank and candid and was conducted at what appeared to be the start of a new life in Bridgeton.

There is no evidence that Monte ever returned to South Jersey, but surviving correspondence with Cumberland County Judge Royal P. Tuller reveals that he remained somewhat informed about Vineland. A January 11, 1908 handwritten letter Monte sent to the judge, reveals he is still residing in Chicago at the Great Northern Hotel on Jackson Boulevard and that he had focused his attention on the divorce.

> In regard to my case it is not my desire that it should be put over this term unless it is impossible to give us a stay. There are two depositions to be taken here

in Chicago which is my entire… defense. Therefore may I beg and implore you just to give me sufficient stay to obtain these that [my] case may come in this term as I wish to settle the matter up. Bartlett will appear before you Monday the 13th.

Monte's divorce was soon finalized, guaranteeing that his son Meade would grow up in Bridgeton. He would remain in Chicago with his mother and, at some point, he and Clara decided to move to California and settle in Los Angeles.

Monte seems to have lost touch with Tuller for a period of time but reached out to the judge in 1920. By now he had remarried and was still living in Los Angeles, where he had established a company with Frank Romo and Orion D. Belt, Romo, Landis & Belt, Real Estate Investments that was located at No. 17 Merchants Trust Building at 207 South Broadway.

In a letter typed on his company's stationery and dated September 13, 1920, Monte informs Tuller he is curious about his family in South Jersey and relays belated information concerning his mother.

> Not having for a long time heard from any of my folk curiosity prompts me to write. Do you see Aunt Tilly and how is she? What has become of Charlie and what is he doing. In short whats [sic] new? Confidentially, my old mother died last August a year ago, bless her soul, she thought a great deal of you and showed me a picture she had of yourself. Are you still Aunt Tilly's attorney? Whatever you write me will be absolutely confidential. This is a lovely

country and am doing well. Kindest personal regards from us both.

The former Clara Meade Landis, the Brooklyn girl whose father, brothers and uncle had earned noteworthy military careers and whose relationship with Landis had been problematic, had died in Long Beach, California on August 8, 1919, ironically the fifty-eighth anniversary of Vineland's founding. According to information uncovered by the Vineland Historical and Antiquarian Society, Clara passed away at Seaside Hospital at the age of 70.

Her third husband, T. J. McAfee, had apparently died years earlier, and it was reported that, at the time of her death, she was survived by Monte and two daughters by McAffee, Mrs. H.A. Bryant of Milwaukee, Wisconsin and Mrs. Violet Miller of Long Beach, California. There was no mention of her oldest living son Charles. Clara was buried at Sunnyside Cemetery in Long Beach.

Monte wrote Tuller again on December 3, 1920, and his inquiries and accounts are more revealing than his previous letter:

> Am in receipt of your letter for which I wish to thank you. It seemed good to receive some news from Vineland which was comprehensive. The correspondence from there is as a rule very vague guarded and in the abstract. I mean from anyone whom fate has made me a relative. What you say about California is all true. It is indeed a lovely place and gorgous [sic].

There is [sic] quite a bunch of Vinelanders out here. Andrew Erickson is here he told me he saw you on his visit back there last summer. Doubtless there are so many changes back in the old town I would hardly know it. Do you ever see or hear anything of my little boy back in Bridgeton? I used to correspond with him and send him presents but his mother in a rash moment of temper sent me an insulting telegram so from that time on I thought it imprudent to hold any more communication with him, but when he gets older all the difficulty will be regulated. Any news you may have of him will be appreciated. The present Mrs. Landis thinks the world of him and feels for me in his regard very greatly. Business out here is on the boom, though they tell me back east the reaction has set in and there is lots of employment.

My dear brother Charlie we never hear from, but he is as you say "efficient unto himself." Mrs. Landis never forgot that remark of yours and often laughs over it.

Let us hear from you Judge anytime. We are both pleased to get your letters
and Mrs. L. joins us in wishing you a most Merry Xmas with a healthful, prosperous and Happy New Year following. Remember me kindly to anyone who may by chance ask about me. With sincere personal regards from us both, I am very truly yours, J.M. Landis

There is no further surviving correspondence from Landis's youngest son. Monte remained in Los Angeles where he would die, at the age of fifty, on February 26, 1926.

In 1917, the Landis will, attended to by attorneys since it had been contested in 1900, suddenly became the source of a new controversy that again earned the Landis family some media attention. On November 17 of that year, according to newspaper reports, complaints were made against "the intermediary accounts filed by Matilda." Once again, her nephew Charles was called upon to represent her.

The decision, rendered in 1921, explains that the controversy concerned Matilda's reported misappropriation of funds involving the annual $500 salary plus interest bequeathed by Landis for her services since 1875. According to a 1921 article in the *North American*, "It was alleged she paid herself the principal of the legacy and then claimed and paid to herself interest upon the legacy from the year 1875, which interest amounted to $19,356." The amount would have affected the sums willed to other heirs of the Landis fortune, including the Vineland Historical and Antiquarian Society, who were represented in the hearing by Leverett Newcomb. The ruling by the court, reported June 30, 1921, ordered Matilda to return the $19,356. The will and its distribution of Landis's holdings have remained undisturbed since.

A resident of Chicago at the time of his father's death, Richard and his wife Emma eventually relocated to Philadelphia, where he continued his artistic career. The couple had a daughter named Emily. But Richard's life and career were cut short on July 11, 1912, when he died of Bright's Disease, a kidney disorder more commonly referred to today by its official designation of glomerulonephritis. He was thirty-nine years old.

Charles Jr. had been living with his wife Mary in Sea Isle and still practicing law. He also had served as solicitor for Sea Isle City and for three building and loan associations in Cape May County. Around 1908, he organized the Sea Isle City Realty Company, which developed the Venicean Park Section of the town.

It appears that, around 1903, Charles Jr. and Mary had become guardians of a child, the identity of whom is unknown. Extant correspondence between Charles Jr. and Judge Royal P. Tuller in 1911 discusses the eight-year-old guardianship. In a February 18 letter to Tuller, Charles Jr. writes that he is

> entitled to all the monies received by the orders if the ward were adequately maintained, educated and supported. The express provision of the law is in aid of the pecuniary means of the parent. It seems to me that I should file a voucher made by myself personally to myself as guardian for the entire amount received as expended for the support, maintenance and education of the ward. This would save the expense of a formal certification of eight years of petty receipts. My wife and self will appear at any appointed time for examination and produce receipts &c. so that you can verify the general voucher accordingly.

On February 20, Tuller responded, saying he agreed with Charles Jr. that the ward was entitled to the full amount of the voucher, that it wouldn't be necessary for Charles and his wife to testify and that he would look further into it.

Charles Jr.'s legal career would last fifty-seven years but his ties to Vineland dissipated over time and it is reported that, after Matilda's death, he seldom visited his birthplace. He died at his home in Sea Isle City at the age of 78 on September 17, 1949. He and his wife are buried in the Landis plot at Siloam Cemetery. The grave marker includes the word "tolerance." Their son Charles 3rd had died at the age of fourteen on December 20, 1910, while Robert had passed away at a nursing cottage in Browns Mill, New Jersey on April 15, 1943. Gordon had relocated to the Pennsylvania territory where the Landis clan first settled upon arriving in the United States from Europe. He apparently lived out the remainder of his life in Chester. Daughter Mary remained close to home, marrying Alfred Hampson. They are both buried in Siloam Cemetery

Matilda lived out the rest of her years in Vineland. Shortly after midnight on Saturday, April 23, 1932, she died suddenly at the age of 84 at her home of the previous twenty years at 200 North East Avenue. It was reported that she had been seriously ill on two occasions over the previous month, but her doctor had not labeled her condition as dangerous the night before her death. Her obituary explained that, just after midnight, Matilda had asked her nurse for a glass of water. Upon the attendant's return, she discovered Matilda had passed away.

In her will, Matilda bequeathed $1,000 to the Society for the Prevention of Cruelty to Animals, $1,000 to the Siloam Cemetery Association for perpetual care of the Landis plot, $1,000 to her nurse and $4,000 to Mrs. Catherine G.

Montegelfe. The Vineland Historical and Antiquarian Society was given a painting of her brother, his archives having already been donated to the society. Other paintings, furniture and household objects were left to Charles Jr. except for jewelry and furs that were divided between her nephew and his daughter Mary. Charles Jr. and Mary served as executors of the estate.

Funeral services for Matilda were held three days later at Trinity Episcopal Church, of which Matilda had been a member. Vineland Mayor Samuel L. Gassel ordered "that all public-spirited citizens as well as the schools take such proper action as is deemed best" and were "requested to cease their activities for the moment at the tolling of church bells to honor the outstanding citizen and sister of the founder of Vineland." The Board of Commissioners of the Borough of Vineland passed a resolution that "sincere regret is expressed at her demise." That Tuesday, Matilda joined her brother in the Landis gravesite at Siloam Cemetery. She was buried in the plot next to her brother, a spot no doubt meant originally for Clara. Matilda's death signaled the end of the first generation of Vineland Landises.

Epilogue

Charles Kline Landis's death in June 1900 prevented him from witnessing Vineland's big step into the 20th century. The town was about to open new plants for sewer, water and electricity, progress of which Landis would have approved. But the advancements signaled a new age, one in which the principles upon which Vineland was founded no longer existed. Progress and commerce, as had already been demonstrated, had no room for the visions of novice entrepreneurs looking to establish utopias. Fittingly, the latter half of the 19th century was interred with Landis.

On June 15, 1900 businesses in Vineland closed for an hour as Charles K. Landis was laid to rest at Siloam Cemetery. Decades earlier, stores and factories might have remained closed for a longer period. Only several days prior to the funeral, the story of Landis's death had not merited the *Vineland Evening Journal* altering its tradition of reserving the front page for national news. Landis's brief obituary appeared on the third page amidst the usual sundry happenings about the town.

If Vineland displayed a certain lack of interest, it did not prevent friends and mourners in Vineland, Hammonton, Sea Isle City, Landisville, New Italy, Camden and Philadelphia from attending the funeral ceremony and burial. An Episcopal burial service, conducted by Rev. C.A. Brewster, was held at Trinity Church after a procession down Landis Avenue. Afterward, the Vineland Lodge of Free Masons conducted the funeral service of its order at the gravesite.

Pall bearers were former Senators Philip Baker and S.R. Fowler, Judge Nixon, former Sea Isle City Mayor Thomas

Ludlam, Judge Moore of Clayton and W.V. Prince, as well as honorary pall bearers Richard J. Byrnes, Landis's former business partner in founding Hammonton, and G. Gittone, a close friend of the deceased.

The Landis burial site tells its own story of the family history. The interment of some and the absence of others is an eerie reflection of the relationships that had existed in life. It's impossible, however, to witness in the grave markers resting a few yards away from Valley Avenue all the accomplishments, defeats, victories and scandals that contributed to the legacy of the man who founded Vineland.

A week before his death, Landis dictated a letter he wished to be printed in a local newspaper. It would turn out to be his final communication to the public of Vineland. In it, his faith in the town's recent accomplishments is clear, and he saw in these achievements its continued development. While the town's interest in its founding father had waned over the decades and its life had been reshaped by politics, Landis remained steadfast in his belief in Vineland. His parting words were nothing less than encouragement:

> To appreciate the bright prospects of Vineland's future, it is only necessary to consider the new improvements now on hand. The list published last year has all been completed and now the following are additional.
> The New Town Hall $10,000
> New Building for Woman's Home for Gymnasium and Recreation Hall $10,000
> Peoples Water Works, West Ave. and Pear St.

Sewage Plant, West Ave. and Pear St.

Mr. Jonas this summer builds an additional glass tank at his factory which is equivalent to another factory and will require the employment of 44 more men. He also starts immediately 5 more double houses to rent his men. Mr. Jonas is what is called a successful man, and his good taste evidently, by the beauty of his place, equals his success.

Electric Light

Paving on Landis Ave. as voted

Trolley between Millville and Vineland now in progress.

New Glass Tank at the Old Whitney Factory, which will nearly double present capacity, now building.

Last but not least, the improvement of the Public Squares which will be a beautiful ornament.

Well may it be said "beautiful & progressive Vineland."

Let the work be kept up.

C.K. Landis

Appendix 1: A Word About Sources

The sources used in the research for this book cover a wide array, from the writings of Charles K. Landis, to historic documents, newspaper accounts and editorials. Their inclusion has been evaluated and weighed, yet it is necessary to discuss the merit of key sources.

Since this is largely a biography of Landis, his words comprise a good portion of the quoted sources in order to place his voice at the center of the book and to illuminate the interior landscape of the subject. Of the materials quoted, his journals are utilized the most. They were erratically maintained, sometimes ceasing for years before they were resumed for another brief period. Unlike most of Landis's other writings, the journals chronicle his life, a fact which provokes a question as to whether the information within them is accurate or significantly skewed by perspective. Any diary will be slanted to some degree, but Landis was as meticulous in his written endeavors as he was in his business dealings. That they are emotional and intimately reflective only on rare occasions seems to indicate that his intent in recording his daily activities was to create a historical account of his actions and opinions, however intermittent they may be. The absence of journal accounts during two crucial periods in Landis's life, the early years of his marriage and the shooting of Uri Carruth and its aftermath, as well as the lack of any later writings that revisit these or any other missing periods, seems to indicate that Landis was not interested in compiling a complete description of his life; whether he intended his journals to survive for future generations to examine is impossible to know for certain.

It is my belief, after extensive reading and evaluation, that Landis's journals offer, for the most part, an accurate historical record of the portions of his life he chose to chronicle and that the perspective they offer provides viable insight into the thoughts and emotions of its author. However, it is also evident in cases in which a comparison can be made between a journal entry and another information source that the journals do suffer from moments of omission when a topic seems to be withheld or skirted for personal reasons. This is best illustrated in the 1874 European journals in which Landis discusses situations regarding his family in America. Surviving correspondence reveals there was much more occurring than entries reveal, but the absence of these details does not render the journal inaccurate, only willfully incomplete.

Another issue that arises with the journals is the discovery that certain entries, particularly those of 1875, had portions excised when published in the *Vineland Historical Magazine* decades later. The missing sections all deal with Landis's comments on the dissolution of his marriage to Clara and the attempts made to rectify it. The only rational explanation for such editing is that, at the time the journals were published, Landis's sister Matilda was still alive and in possession of the remainder of his archives earmarked for the Vineland Historical and Antiquarian Society, which published the magazine. Since the omitted portions portray Landis at one of his most vulnerable stages, it may have been deemed wise to remove the less-than-flattering segments.

If Clara had maintained a journal at any point in her life, no such record has surfaced. Therefore, her only direct commentary on her years with Landis is derived from testimony and interviews that were quoted extensively in newspaper accounts during two later periods in her life, and it becomes necessary to place her comments within the proper context in which they occurred. On the occasion of her 1877 child custody battle with Landis, her account of her husband's actions toward her and the children during the early 1870s paints a harsh picture of her spouse that other existing sources neither deny nor corroborate. When it comes to the events of February 1875, the time separation papers were signed and Clara left the family home for a short period, her account differs from the details contained in Landis's journal and omits information about her departure and return. It must be remembered that the circumstances in which her statements had been made were crucial to her winning custody of the Landis children and, without corroboration from other parties who would not have been privy to the most private matters discussed, there remains a question about whether her depictions might be, to some degree, embellished in order to achieve her goal.

In a set of interviews following the arrest and incarceration of her third husband on charges of bigamy in the 1880s, Clara discussed her background, her marriage to Landis and her current situation. The most surprising of her statements erroneously declared that Landis had stood trial a second time for a crime that never occurred. During the time the interviews were conducted, Clara found herself destitute and fighting for the release of her then husband and it appears she earned the sympathy and support of readers once her story was carried by a number of national newspapers. However, the blatant falsehood of assigning Landis a second crime for which he faced legal consequences remains an accusation that brings its own set of questions.

Nevertheless, I have included in the book a number of pertinent statements by Clara from both periods in order to represent her side in the various issues and accusations and to provide her with a significant voice in this biography. I will leave it to the reader to decide on the veracity of the comments, but I will also remind everyone that only two people had the most intimate knowledge of the Landis marriage, and ultimately their words are merely a hint toward understanding the complexity that comprised their short relationship.

Landis's letters, essays, editorials and reflective pieces covering a variety of topics, represent his opinions and personal views and remain largely outside the historical account of his life as portrayed in his journals. Correspondence and testimony by others contain personal and opinionated material but, in certain cases, provide historical context and information.

As for the role of Vineland newspapers during Landis's years, it is important to note that political agendas governed many such publications of that era. Democrat and Republican newspapers were used as mouthpieces for the preferred politics and as a weapon against opposing ideology. The *Vineland Weekly* was a Republican publication and Landis's paper of choice. He used it as a forum for many articles about the town and its development and later as a means of defending himself against an onslaught of published attacks. The *Independent*, on the other hand, was founded as an alternative press, one that stood opposed to Landis's plans for Vineland and that voiced its opposition loudly and aggressively once Uri Carruth assumed editorship. The bias of Carruth's writings, as evidenced in the examples used in this book, speak for themselves, but it must be noted that *The Independent*, despite its extreme methods, was an exception when it came to reporting anything controversial about Landis and his family. Most Vineland newspapers chose to minimize or overlook such coverage, which is why it was necessary to rely on outside newspapers for such matters since they were not bound by conscience or allegiance when it came to Vineland's founder.

When it comes to the several chronicles written about Vineland, it should be noted that both chroniclers, A.G. Warner and B.F. Ladd, found themselves in opposition to Landis. However, I have chosen to rely on A.G. Warner's 1869 account of the town as a more objective rendering of the settlement's history over B.F. Ladd's continuation of the town's story. Whatever differences he may have had with Landis, Warner was more accommodating in incorporating the town's founder into his narrative, whereas Ladd reduces Landis's role to a minimum of acknowledgements, a decision which may be explained by his involvement with *The Independent* and his role in filing the murder charge against Landis at the time of Carruth's death.

Sources carry with them their own agenda that can shape a work of research. I have attempted to approach those used in this book with a discriminating eye. Any information I have rejected is because it appeared dubious and unsubstantiated. For material that could not be verified yet was worthy or essential in some way, the information was qualified as such in the text.

Appendix 2: A Selection of Landis Writings

Despite his forays into fiction writing, which include *A Trip to Mars*, *Autobiographical Sketch of a Tree*, *Carabajal*, and *The Information Bureau*, Landis spent much of his life producing mostly non-fictional and promotional material, in the form of speeches, articles and pamphlets on topics ranging from farming, railroads and temperance to porcelain, china and travel. The following is a selected list of works by Landis that survive in either published or manuscript form:

Calender (sic) for the Farm: a manuscript.

China: a manuscript concerned with "the form and decoration of china and porcelain in the style of art" as it originated in Italy.

Cinque Centi: a Landis manuscript which, according to a slip of paper included with it, "is the first of a series of articles upon Art to be illustrated by examples of work by well-known Masters."

Counting House Almanac for 1863" an almanac with only Vineland information, ads and articles; ads offer tracts available from $15 and $20 per acre payable within four years.

Facts About Vineland, New Jersey: an undated promotional piece that was probably was written in the late 1870s.

Farm Management: a piece, published as an article, that is "...a study of careful study and well-maintained discipline. Farm operation should be regulated in order to be successful."

"Flower-Bed Stipulations:" a response to a letter in the *Cape May County Times* in 1899.

Fruit: a thirty-seven-page manuscript about the planting and cultivating of fruit.

General Railroad Law: a speech by Landis before the Railroad Committee of the House Assembly of New Jersey delivered February 6, 1878.

How to Build Up a Town: a manuscript of Landis's essay on "the earning of good wages by the working people" in which he declares, "the worst slavery on earth is when a working man is held down to low and unjust wages with a starving family staring him in the face and he cannot help himself...America was settled...by the oppressed working people of Great Britain and the rest of Europe to get away from this so that they should be free and equal and have their just rights, the greatest of which was their honest earnings. This is what has made America great like a lighted torch in the eyes of nations and when these traditions are ignored and forgotten, she will go down as quickly from her high position as a flaming torch thrown into the sea."

Lecture Upon Agriculture and Other Suggestions Upon the Same Subject: a twenty-two-page speech printed at the office of the *Vineland Weekly* in 1866 and delivered before the Vineland Agricultural and Horticultural Society, March 3, 1865.

Manuscript of The Ideas of an American about Italy: a speech delivered in Vineland upon his return from Europe in 1874.

Shade Trees and Planting: a manuscript of a 44-page manual on farming and fruit growing in Vineland's extremely favorable soil; 40 pages are devoted to highly detailed chapters that include "Size of Farm," "Houses," "The Farm" and "Farm Crops," which features an extensive list and explanations for a variety of options. There are also 2 pages about poultry and 2 pages about shade trees.

Speech by Charles K. Landis Before the Judiciary Committee on Local Opinion: Landis's speech on temperance.

The Social Science of Vineland: article published in *Fraser's Magazine*, 1875. Published in the U.S. as The *Settlement of Vineland in New Jersey*.

Travel in Europe: an account of life in England, France Germany as witnessed by Landis in 1874. The last portion is about how America could better itself by emulating the Europeans.

Untitled manuscript of speech by Landis at Plum Street Hall defending himself against accusations from Carruth about railroad improprieties.

Vineland: a statement presented to the Jury of the Paris Exposition, 1867 and published by E.C. Markley & Son, 422 Library St., Philadelphia, PA. The statement is about Landis's accomplishments in creating Vineland and the text is a promotion of Vineland's accomplishments – the front of the book has Landis's official application statement for the Grand Prize of 100,000 francs.

Vineland – General Information: an undated promotional piece.

Vineland, New Jersey & Its Attractions: an 1880 promotional piece.

Vineland, The New Settlement: a manuscript.

Bibliography

While much of the research involving Landis's life and outlook is derived from the preserved correspondence, documents and notes contained in the Vineland Historical and Antiquarian Society (VHAS) archives, several key primary sources used in the writing of this book have been officially published. Except where otherwise noted, Landis's journals are sourced from the *Vineland Historical Magazine*, which printed all extant entries from 1920 to 1964, and are included in the bibliography only when not identified within the text. Landis's account of establishing Vineland is derived primarily from two published sources: *The Founder's Own Story*, released by the VHAS in 1903, and the highly informative "The Social Science of Vineland," originally published in *Frazier's Magazine* in England in 1875. Two works of fiction, *Carabajal* and *Autobiographical Sketch of a Tree*, were also published, the former by its author in 1894 and the latter posthumously. The typescript of the novel *A Trip to Mars* was the source consulted for this biography.

Two chronicles about the early decades of Vineland that provided significant information about those years and the development of the town are A. G. Warner's *Sketches, Incidents, and History: Vineland and the Vinelanders* and B.F. Ladd's *History of Vineland*. Warner's text was sourced from issues of *South Jersey Magazine* spanning Winter 1994 to Winter 1996. Ladd's chronicle, along with an expanded edition completed after his death, was sourced from the Spring/Fall 1974 issue of *The Vineland Historical Magazine*. Complete information on the Warner and Ladd sources can be found in the bibliographies for Chapters 2 and 3 respectively.

I have chosen to exercise authorial preference in select instances when presenting quoted material from journals, letters, documents, etc. Punctuation and, in certain cases, what modern readership would consider indiscriminate capitalization of common nouns, have been adjusted to conform with modern-day grammar to facilitate the flow of passages and to eliminate ambiguous or unclear syntax. In addition, most abbreviations in the quoted material, including the ampersand, have been rendered as complete words to maintain textual continuity throughout the book. I do apologize to purists who insist that historical writings should not be modified in any fashion but assert that the minimal alterations made here, from a practical consideration, provide a more readable rendering for 21st century audiences without, in any way, varying or subverting the meaning or context intended by Landis or others and, from an aesthetic consideration, remove the dividing line that exists between Landis's 19th century and our own era.

Prologue

Details of Landis's final days, presumably recorded by clerk Marcus Fry, are sourced from the Landis office daybook dated August 22, 1899-November 1, 1900 and contained in the Landis Archives of the Vineland Historical and Antiquated Society. General information about Landis's condition in his final days is sourced from clippings of newspaper accounts of Landis's death contained in the archives of the Vineland Historical and Antiquarian Society. Information about Landis's Jamaican trip is taken from his final journal entries.

Chapter 1: Early Years

Landis's surviving novel fragments, "Description of a Steam Hydrant," Ridgeway promotional pamphlet and certificate of indenture for the Colville project are sourced from the Vineland Historical and Antiquarian Society archives.

"Addis, J.B." *American Drama Bibliography*, retrieved from www.collections.chadwyck.com/html/ amdram/bibliography/a.htm.

Addis, J.B. *Vanity or A Lord of Philadelphia*. Philadelphia: T.K. and P.G. Collins, Printers, 1854.

Brown, T. Allston. *Story of the American Stage*. New York: Dick and Fitzgerald Publishers, 1870.

"City Affairs." *American and Gazette*, 10 August 1858: photocopy, n.p.

Eshleman, Henry Frank. *Historic Background and Annals of the Swiss and German Pioneer Settlers of Southeastern Pennsylvania*. Lancaster, PA: No publisher listed, 1917.

The Federal Reporter: Cases Argued and Determined in the Circuit and District Courts of the United States, Volumes 111-112. St. Paul: West Publishing Company, 1902.

Gans, Emmett William. *A Pennsylvania Pioneer: Biographical Sketch with Report of the Executive Committee of the Bell Estate Association*. Mansfield, OH: R.J. Kuhl Printer, 1900.

Koedel, R. Craig. *South Jersey Heritage: A Social, Economic and Cultural History.* Washington, D.C.: University Press of America, Inc., 1979.

Landi, Florindo. *Casa Landi* website, 2010. www.casalandi.net.

"Landis, Charles K." *Biographical Review.* Boston: Biographical Review Publishing Company, 1896.

Landis, David Bachman. *Landis Family of Lancaster County, A Comprehensive History of the Landis Folk from the Martyr's Era to the Arrival of the First Swiss Settlers.* Lancaster, Pennsylvania: Published and Printed by the author, 1888.

Lee, Francis Bazley. *Genealogical and Memorial History of the State of New Jersey, 1869-1914.* New York: Lewis Historical Publishing Company, 1910.

Loper, George G. "The Landis Family Papers." *South Jersey Magazine*, Winter 1985: 6-9.

McMahon, William. *The Story of Hammonton.* Egg Harbor City, New Jersey: Laureate Press, Inc., 1966.

Smith, C. Henry. *The Mennonites: A Brief History of Their Origin and Later Development in Both Europe and America.* Berne, Indiana: Mennonite Book Concern, 1920.

van Braght, Thieleman J. *Martyrs Mirror.* Scottdale, Pennsylvania: Herald Press, 1938.

Wentzel, Don. "Hammonton's Railroads." *South Jersey Magazine*, Fall 1988: 2-5.

Wilbur, H.W. and W.B. Hand. *Illustrated History of the Town of Hammonton with an Account of Its Soil, Climate and Industries.* Hammonton, New Jersey: The Mirror Steam Printing House, 1889.

Chapter 2 The Birth of Vineland

Landis's deed to his first Vineland property, certificate of indenture with Richard Wood, correspondence, manuscript of "The Social Science of Vineland," document detailing House's arrangement in land sales and letter on expatriation of former slaves as well as the John Gage land sale advertisement and correspondence/select journal entries by Richard Wood are sourced from the Vineland Historical and Antiquarian Society archives.

Ankenbrand, Frank, Jr. (ed.). "Richard Davis Wood: Extracts from his Journals" *Vineland Historical Magazine*, January 1939: 167-174.

_____ "Richard Davis Wood: Extracts from his Journals" *Vineland Historical Magazine*, April 1939: 207-213.

_____ "Richard Davis Wood: Extracts from his Journals" *Vineland Historical Magazine*, July 1939: 239-245.

Brandt, Del. "Vinelander Recalls Working for Landis." *Vineland Times Journal*, August 1962: photocopy, n.p.

Demitroff, Mark. "Sugar Sand Opportunity: Landscape and People of the Pine Barrens." *Down Jersey: From Bayshore to Seashore.* Harrisonburg, Virginia: Vernacular Architecture Forum, 2014: 30-36.

Flood, Loren D. "Vineland's First Post Office." *Vineland Historical Magazine*, Centennial Number, 1961: 38-40.

Goodheart, Adam. *1861: The Civil War Awakening*. New York: Alfred A. Knopf, 2011.

Landis, Charles K. "Vineland, Fruit and Farm Lands" *The Country Gentleman, A Journal for the Farm, the Garden and the Fireside Devoted to the Practice and Science of Agriculture and Horticulture at Large*, 28 September 1865.

Landis, Charles K. "Washington in 1861." *Vineland Historical Magazine*, January 1918: 5-8.

"Local Miscellany," *Hammonton Item*. 3 February 1872: 5.

McMahon, William. *South Jersey Towns: History and Legend*. New Brunswick: Rutgers University Press, 1973.

Nordhoff, Charles. *The Communistic Societies of the United States*. New York: Harper & Brothers, 1875, retrieved from www.sacred-texts.com/ texts.com/ utopia/csus/csus29.htm

"A Novel Enterprise." *American Agriculturalist*. April 1865. Reprinted in *South Jersey Magazine*, Spring 1974: 14-17.

Petway, Pauline J. "History of Negroes in Vineland." *Vineland Historical Magazine*, Centennial Number, 1961: 61-64.

"Social Ideas Aroused Hate for Landis, Grandson Says."
Vineland Times Journal, 9 August 1961: 1, 12.

Treese, Lorette. *Railroads of New Jersey: Fragments of the
Past in the Garden State Landscape*. Mechanicsburg,
Pennsylvania: Stackpole Books, 2006.

Warner, A.G. "Sketches, Incidents, and History: Vineland
and the Vinelanders." *South Jersey Magazine*, Winter
1994: 25-30.

_____ "Sketches, Incidents and History: Vineland
and the Vinelanders." *South Jersey Magazine*, Spring
1994: 34-37.

_____ "Sketches, Incidents and History: Vineland
and the Vinelanders." *South Jersey Magazine*, Summer
1994: 18-21.

_____ "Sketches, Incidents and History: Vineland
and the Vinelanders." *South Jersey Magazine*, Fall
1994: 35-38.

_____ "Sketches, Incidents and History: Vineland
and the Vinelanders." *South Jersey Magazine*, Winter
1995: 45-48.

_____ "Sketches, Incidents and History: Vineland
and the Vinelanders." *South Jersey Magazine*, Spring
1995: 46-49.

_____ "Sketches, Incidents and History: Vineland
and the Vinelanders." *South Jersey Magazine*, Summer
1995: 33-37.

_____"Sketches, Incidents and History: Vineland and the Vinelanders." *South Jersey Magazine*, Fall 1995: 35-38.

_____"Sketches, Incidents and History: Vineland and the Vinelanders." *South Jersey Magazine*, Winter 1996: 7-13.

Wentzel, Don. "Vineland's Second Railroad." *South Jersey Magazine*, Fall 1983: 2-6.

_____ "The Millville & Glassboro Railroad", *South Jersey Magazine*, Summer 1991: 2 - 5.

_____ "Vineland's First Railroad." *South Jersey Magazine*, Summer 1983: 2-5.

_____ "Millville's Railroads", *South Jersey Magazine*, Winter 1996: 2 –6.

Wilentz, Sean. *The Rise of American Democracy*. New York: W.W. Norton and Company, 2005.

Chapter 3: Early Vineland

Information on Vineland's shoe industry is sourced from the *Vineland Historical Magazine* 2003 article "Vineland's Leading Industries, 1888" which reproduces sections of the 1888 *Vineland. Its Products, Soil, Manufacturing Industries and Commercial Interests* by Wanser and Osgood. The itinerary of events held at Cosmopolitan Hall in 1886 is selected from Frank D. Andrews's weekly column in the *Vineland Evening Journal*, "History of Cosmopolitan Hall, which ran from 1915 to 1916. Landis's manuscript of "The

Social Science of Vineland" is sourced from the Vineland Historical and Antiquarian Society archives.

Ankenbrand, Frank Jr. "Frank DeWette Andrews."*Vineland Historical Magazine*, Centennial Number, 1961: 56-59.

Bennett, Eileen."Wild Vineland Livestock Cause Great Bovine War." *The Press of Atlantic City*, 28 June 1998, retrieved from www.pressofatlanticcity.com.

"The Bovine Wars, An Episode During the Settlement of Vineland." *Vineland Historical Magazine*, July 1924: 192.

Bridges. "Christmas Reception Given by Mr. Landis in 1863." *Vineland Historical Magazine*, October 1920: 208-209.

"Council Proceedings." *Vineland Evening Journal*, 14 November 1900: 3.

Dillingham, William Paul. *Reports of the Immigration Commission*. Washington: Government Printing Office, 1911.

"Early Educational Developments in Vineland." *Vineland Historical Magazine*, April 1924: 173-177.

"The First Vineland Schools." *Vineland Historical Magazine*, July 1924: 191.

Koedel, R. Craig. *South Jersey Heritage: A Social, Economic and Cultural History.* Washington, D.C.: University Press of America, Inc., 1979.

Ladd, B.F., Wanser and Osgood. "History of Vineland." *Vineland Historical Magazine*, Spring & Fall 1974: 1-64.

"The Male and Female Industrial College at Vineland, N.J." *Vineland Historical Magazine*, July-October 1950: 120-127.

"New Jersey." *New York Times*, 28 November 1868, retrieved from newyorktimes.com.

Pryor, George. "Report on the Bovine War in Vineland." *Vineland Historical Magazine*, July 1924: 193.

Stanton, Elizabeth Cady, Susan B. Anthony and Matilda Joslyn Gage. *The History of Woman Suffrage, Volume 3*. Rochester, New York: Charles Mann Printing Co., 1886.

Taylor, Thelma H. "A History of Cosmopolitan Hall."*Vineland Historical Magazine*, Centennial Number, 1961: 29-37.

Vineland, N.J. Centennial 1861-1961. Vineland Centennial, Inc., 1961.

"Vineland's Civil War Record." *Vineland Historical Magazine*, April 1922: 24-25.

Winslow, Theresa. "A History of the Vineland Historical and Antiquarian Society." *Vineland Historical Magazine*, January-October 1969, 633-671.

"Woman Suffrage." *New York Times*, 4 December 1868, retrieved from www.nytimes.com.

Zislin, Phyllis *A. History of the Vineland Free Public Library*. A Project for Seminar in Current Issues in Libraries in the Graduate Division of Glassboro State College, 1970.

Chapter 4: Controversy, Clara and Carruth

Landis and Clara's marriage certificate, the Clara-Elmer papers, correspondence and expense accounts of the Landises and Edward Wood's correspondence are sourced from the Vineland Historical and Antiquarian Society (VHAS) archives. Select articles by Carruth about Landis are sourced from a scrapbook collection that is part of the VHAS archives. Information about *The Vineland Weekly* and *The Independent* are sourced from Frank D. Andrews lengthy series "History of Vineland Newspapers" in the *Vineland Historical Magazine* 1925-1927.

Acts of the Ninety-Third Legislature of the State of New Jersey. New Brunswick, New Jersey: A.R. Speer, 1869.

Andrews, Frank D. "Panic of 1873." *Vineland Historical Magazine*. photocopy.

Carr, Ezra S. *The Patrons of Husbandry on the Pacific Coast*. San Francisco: A.L. Bancroft and Company, 1875.

"The Case of Commodore Meade." *New York Times*, 5 December 1868, retrieved from www.nytimes.com.

"The Case of Commodore Meade." *New York Times*, 6 December 1868, retrieved from www.nytimes.com.

"The Commodore Meade Case." *New York Times*, 8 December 1868, retrieved from www.nytimes.com.

Forty-Eighth Report to the Legislature of Massachusetts Relating to the Registry and Return of Births, Marriages and Deaths in the Commonwealth for the Year ending December 1889 Together with the Reports Relating to the Returns of Libels and Divorce and to the Returns of Deaths Investigated by the Medical Examiners for the Year 1889. Prepared by the Secretary of the Commonwealth with Editorial Remarks by Samuel W. Abbott, M.D. Boston: Wright & Potter Printing Co., 1890, pg. 371.

Gershenowitz, Harry. "Landis County." *South Jersey Magazine*, Winter 1984:39-40.

Landis, Charles, K. Letter to the Editor. *The Vineland Weekly*, 12 December 1868.

Lee, Jennifer."New York and the Panic of 1873." *New York Times*, 14 October 2008, retrieved from www.nytimes.com.

"Local Intelligence: Case of Commodore Meade." *New York Times*, 9 December 1868: 4, retrieved from www.nytimes.com.

Nealis, William T. "Letter from the Physician of the City Prison." *New York Times*, 5 December 1868, retrieved from www.nytimes.com.

The North American Journal of Homeopathy, Volume 17. New York: William Radde, 1869.

"Social Ideas Aroused Hate for Landis, Grandson Says."
Vineland Times Journal, 9 August 1961: 1, 12.

"Terrible Murder in Vineland." *New York Times*, 20 March
1875, retrieved from www.nytimes.com.

"A Triple Romance. "*St. Louis Globe-Democrat*, 31
December1884, reproduced in an unidentified
Minnesota newspaper 4 January 1885.

Vroom, Garret D.W. *Reports of Cases Argued and
Determined in the Supreme Court and, at Law, in the
Court of Errors and Appeals*. Trenton, NJ: Sharp
Printing Company, 1887.

Chapter 5: Homecoming

Transcriptions of the letters by John and Portia Gage are
provided courtesy of the Wilmette Historical Museum,
Wilmette, Illinois, Patrick Leary, curator. The originals of
the letters can be found in the Museum's collection.
Testimony by various individuals about Landis and Clara are
sourced from a notebook in the possession of the Vineland
Historical and Antiquarian Society (VHAS). These
handwritten accounts, which might be depositions or
transcription of court records, correspond to the accounts
reported in various newspaper during the trial. A document
of costs accrued by Landis for his arrest and Bassett's
correspondence are also contained in the VHAS archives.
Landis's unedited handwritten journals, preserved by the
VHAS, are the source of the January-March 1875 entries
quoted in this chapter.

"Carruth's Valedictory." *The Daily Phoenix*, 1 June 1875: 3, retrieved from chroniclingamerica.loc.gov/lccn/sn8402700.

"City and Suburban News: New Jersey." *New York Times*, 18 April 1875, retrieved from www.nytimes.com.

Dowling, Francis. "Some Remarks on Gun Shot Wounds of the Brain, in Connection with the Late Carruth Murder" in *The Cincinnati Lancet & Observer, Volume 19*, J.D. Culbertson, editor. Cincinnati: J.D. Culbertson, 1876, 65-72.

Landis, Charles K. "An Interview with President Grant." *Vineland Historical Magazine*, October 1918: 68-69.

Nashville Union and American, 17 June 1875: 2, retrieved from www.newspapers.com/newspage/80786858.

"Terrible Murder in Vineland." *New York Times*, 20 March 1875, retrieved from www.nytimes.com.

Thomas, A.R. (ed.). "Death of Uri Carruth – Post-Mortem Examination." *American Journal of Homeopathic Materia Medica and Record of Medical Science*. 1 November 1875: 111-113.

"The Tragedy," *The Independent*, 25 March 1875: 1.

Vroom, Garret D.W. *Reports of Cases Argued and Determined in the Supreme Court and, at Law, in the Court of Errors and Appeals*. Trenton, NJ: Sharp Printing Company, 1887.

Chapter 6: Trial

On February 8, 9 and 11, 1876, the *Bridgeton Daily* reprinted editorials from the *West Jersey Press, New York Tribune* and *Philadelphia Ledger* on the aftermath of the Landis trial in 1876. The *Bridgeton Daily* articles were reproduced in *South Jersey Magazine*, Winter 2001, pages 38-42, from which the relevant quotes in this chapter are sourced. Articles from the *New York Times* coverage of the Landis trial, which were published from January 12 to February 4, 1876, were also sources for this chapter and were retrieved from www.nytimes.com. The manuscript of Judge Reed's address to the jury at the Landis trial, Carruth's outstanding bills, Isaac N. Wilson's letter to Landis about Carruth's motives and *The Independent*'s February 12, 1876 editorial on the verdict of Landis's trial are sourced from the archives of the Vineland Historical and Antiquarian Society.

"The Acquittal of Mr. Landis." *Brooklyn Daily Eagle*, 7 February 1876: 2, retrieved from www.newspapers.com/newspage/50428315.

"The Carruth Tragedy Shooting." *Philadelphia Times*, 12 January 1876: 1, retrieved from www.newspapers.com/newspage/52210586.

Thomas, A.R. (ed.). "The Landis Verdict." *American Journal of Homeopathic Materia Medica and Record of Medical Science*. 1 March 1876: 229-230.

"The Trial of Charles Landis." *South Jersey Magazine*, Spring 2000: 39-44.

_____ *South Jersey Magazine*, Summer 2000: 29-35.

_____ *South Jersey Magazine*, Fall 2000: 21-25.

_____ *South Jersey Magazine*, Winter 2001: 38-42.

"Murder Trial." *Reading Times*, 14, January 1876: 1, retrieved from www.newspapers.com/newspage/ 46331978.

Chapter 7: A New Normal

A Trip to Mars is sourced from the typescript of the novel contained in the Vineland Historical and Antiquarian Society (VHAS) archives. "Life at Vineland" article clipping is from an unidentified newspaper from February 1877. Landis's unedited handwritten journals, preserved by the VHAS, are the source of the July 1878 entries quoted in this chapter.

"Another Vineland Mystery Uncovered at Museum."*Vineland Historical and Antiquarian Society Newsletter*, Winter 2014.

"Not Wisely But Too Well." *Buffalo Courier*, 9 November 1884: photocopy, n.p.

Republic of Industry or First Guise Association of America. A Concise Plan for the Reconstruction of Society. Vineland, New Jersey: no printer listed, 20 October 1876.

Sanders, Elizabeth. *Roots of Reform: Farmers, Workers and the American State, 1877-1917*. Chicago: University of Chicago Press, 1999.

"The Vineland Tragedy" *The Independent Hour*, 1 March 1877: 5.

Vroom, Garret D.W. *Reports of Cases Argued and Determined in the Supreme Court and, at Law, in the Court of Errors and Appeals*. Trenton, NJ: Sharp Printing Company, 1887.

Chapter 8: Temperance

An unidentified and undated news clipping about Landis's 1880s endorsement to maintain Vineland's temperance status is sourced from the Vineland Historical and Antiquarian Society archives.

Andrews, Frank D. "Early History of the Temperance Movement in Vineland." *Vineland Historical Magazine*, April 1923: 97-102.

"Ardent Spirits." The Library Company of Philadelphia, retrieved from www.librarycompany.org/ArdentSpirits.

"Beer Supply in S.J. Increases." *Vineland Evening Times*, 8 April 1933: 1.

"Boro Lowers Fee for Liquor Sale." *Vineland Evening Times*, 27 December 1933: 1-2.

"Boro, Township Defer Rum Action." *Vineland Evening Times*, 9 December 1933: 1.

"Borough [Election Results]" *Vineland Evening Journal*, 7 November 1906: n.p.

"Boycotting the Saloons." *New York Times* 16 October 1891, retrieved from www.nytimes.com.

Coffey, Thomas M. *The Long Thirst: Prohibition in America: 1920-1933*. New York: W.W. Norton & Company, 1975.

"Consolidation Brings Retirement of Stevens After 40-Year Career of Service to Public." *Vineland Times Journal*, 1 July 1952: 6.

"Drys Will Celebrate." *Vineland Evening Journal*, 15 January 1920: 1.

Franklin, Benjamin. *The Autobiography of Benjamin Franklin*. Mineola, New York: Dover Publications, Inc., 2012.

Nordhoff, Charles. *The Communistic Societies of the United States*. New York: Harper & Brothers, 1875, retrieved from www.sacred-texts.com/utopia/csus/csus29.htm.

"Real Beer Flows Freely; Greeted by Orderly Crowd." *Vineland Evening Times*, 7 April 1933: 1.

"Pulpit Editorial on 'Passing of Booze.'" *Vineland Evening Journal*, 12 January 1920: 1.

"Question Legality of Boro's Liquor License Resolution." *Vineland Evening Times*, 21 December 1933: 1, 3.

Tower, W. F. "Personal Reflections of the Temperance Men and Women in Vineland's Early History." *Vineland Historical Magazine*, April 1930, 229-233.

"Township Adopts Its Liquor Act." *Vineland Evening Times*, 30 December 1933: 1-2.

"Township's Charter of 1864 Bans Rum Sale Without Vote." *Vineland Evening Times*, 5 December 1933: 1.

"Township Comm. Plans Liquor Law." *Vineland Evening Times*, 20 December 1933: 1.

"Township Defers Beer Licensing." *Vineland Evening Times*, 6 April 1933: 1-2.

"Township Orders $20 License Fee for Selling Beer." *Vineland Evening Times*, 11 April 1933: 1.

United States is Dry Nation Today." *Vineland Evening Journal*, 17 January 1920: 1.

"Vineland Borough to Grant Liquor Licenses; Place Ban on Saloons." *Vineland Evening Times*, 20 December 1933: 1.

"Voting Machines." *Vineland Evening Journal*, 16 May 1907: n.p.

"Voting Machine Instructions." *Vineland Evening Journal*, 5 November 1906: n.p.

Chapter 9: Exile

The journals of Richard and Michael Landis, information concerning the legal battle between Landis and Whelan, correspondence by Charles K. Landis Jr. to his father, by Hosea Allen about Mrs. Carruth's pursuit of damages and by Philadelphia businessmen Morton, Showaker, Capp,

Harrison and Strawbridge regarding the parkway project are sourced from the Vineland Historical and Antiquarian Society archives. Clara Meade's activities from 1879 to 1886 are derived largely from newspaper accounts relating to her situation at the time of her third husband's arrest and incarceration on charges of bigamy.

Andrescavage, Michael. "West Jersey and Seashore Railroad (WJ & S) and Its Predecessors." *sjrail.com*. Railroad IncrediProductions, 2000.

Atwater, Richard M. "The Origin of Our Summer Home at Sea Isle City, 1881." *South Jersey Magazine*, Summer 1991: 19-23.

Baer, Christopher T. *PRR Chronology* website. Pennsylvania Technical and Historical Society, 2004, retrieved from www.prrths.com/newprr_files/ Hagley/PRR_hagley_intro.htm.

"Behind the Bars." Unidentified Kentucky newspaper, 1884: photocopy, n.p.

Burr, Philip W. III. "Ludlam's Beach Light: Sea Isle City, NJ 1885-1924." *South Jersey Magazine*, Fall 1999: 27-35.

Dilworth, Richard (ed.). *Cities in American Political History*. Thousand Oaks, CA: CQ Press, 2011.

Dorwart, Jeffrey M. *Cape May County, New Jersey: The Making of an American Resort Community*. New Brunswick: Rutgers University Press, 1993.

"A History and Description of Vineland's Activities at the Sesqui-Centennial." *Vineland Historical Magazine*,

April 1927.

"Matilda Landis." *Central Reporter: Cases, Courts of Last Resort, New York, New Jersey, Pennsylvania, Delaware, Maryland, District of Columbia, Vol. III.* Rochester, NY: The Lawyer's Cooperative Publishing Company, 1886.

McCaffery, Peter. *When Bosses Ruled Philadelphia: The Emergence of the Republican Machine 1867-1933.* University Park, Pennsylvania: Pennsylvania State University Press, 1993.

Moss, Roger W. *Historic Landmarks of Philadelphia.* Philadelphia: University of Pennsylvania Press, 2008.

"Not Wisely But Too Well." *Buffalo Courier*, 9 November 1884: photocopy, n.p.

"Remarrying His Second Wife." *New York Times*, 29 May 1886, retrieved from www.nytimes.com.

"Sea Isle City," *South Jersey Magazine.* Summer 1990: 30-35.

"Social Ideas Aroused Hate for Landis, Grandson Says." *Vineland Times Journal*, 9 August 1961: 1, 12.

"A Triple Romance." *St. Louis Globe-Democrat*, 31 December 1884. Reproduced in an unidentified Minnesota newspaper 4 January 1885: photocopy, n.p.

Wentzel, Don. "The Rails come to Seven Mile Beach." *South Jersey Magazine*, Summer 1987: 2-7.

Unidentified article title, *New York Tribune*. 31 December 1885: photocopy, n.p.

Chapter 10: The Final Decade

Dr. Wiley's bill for services to Landis in the 1890s, Maurice River Water and Electric Power Company records, Landis correspondence and manuscripts for the fictional "How Mayors Do In Japan," and *The Information Bureau*, Charles Landis Jr.'s correspondence, "Our Marriage Vows" booklet and collected news clippings about his wedding are sourced from the Vineland Historical and Antiquarian Society archives.

"At Sea Isle City." *Philadelphia Times*, 30 June 1895:14, retrieved from www.newspapers.com/newspage/55566395.

"Biological Investigation*." Forest and Stream: A Weekly Journal of the Rod and Gun*, 20 August 1891: 3.

Bolton, Herbert Eugene (ed.) *Spanish Exploration in the Southwest, 1542-1706, Volume 17* New York: Charles Scribner's and Sons, 1916.

Brandt, Del. "Vinelander Recalls Working for Landis." *Vineland Times Journal*, 7 August 1962: photocopy, n.p.

Collins, Paul. "You and Your Dumb Friends." *The Believer*, March 2004, retrieved from www. believermag.com/issues/200403/?read=article_collins.

Gershenowitz, Harry. "John Muirhead MacFarlane (1855-1943), Eminent Neo-Lamarckist." *Vineland Historical*

Magazine, 1985: 53-56.

Gershenowitz, Harry. "Mr. Landis and the Laboratory of Marine Biology at Sea Isle City." *Vineland Historical Magazine*, 1982: 7-10.

Harap, Louis. *The Image of the Jew in American Literature: From Early Republic to Mass Immigration*, Syracuse, New York: Syracuse University Press, 2003.

Lieberman, Maggie. "Ex-Office Boy Recollects Landis as 'Kindly but Set.'" *Atlantic City Press* 3 August 1957: photocopy, n.p.

"Local News." *Vineland Evening Journal*, 14 February 1896. n.p.

"Local News." *Vineland Evening Journal*, 15 February 1896. n.p.

MacFarlane, John M. "New Year Memories of Summer Days in New Jersey." *Cape May County Magazine of History and Genealogy*, June 1958.

"School of Biology." *University of Pennsylvania Bulletin*, February 1893.

Thorpe, Francis Newton (ed.). *Benjamin Franklin and the University of Pennsylvania: Bureau of Education Circular of Information No. 2, 1892*. Washington: Government Printing Office, 1893.

Thorpe, Francis Newton. *William Pepper, M. D., LL. D. (1843-1898): Provost of the University of Pennsylvania*. Philadelphia: John P. Lipincott Company, 1904.

"University of Pennsylvania." *New York Times,* 4 October 1891, retrieved from www.nytimes.com.

van Braght, Thieleman J. *Martyrs Mirror.* Scottdale, Pennsylvania: Herald Press, 1938.

Chapter 11: Consequences

Matilda's obituary and related articles, correspondence from Charles K. Landis Jr. and James Montevert Landis to Judge Royal P. Tuller and news clippings concerning James Montevert's 1907 assault on J. Ogden Burt are sourced from the Vineland Historical and Antiquarian Society archives. Legal information concerning the ruling in the case of Landis's will was sourced from the *New Jersey Law Journal, Volume 24,* credited to Abraham Van Doren Honeyman, Charles Louis Borgmeyer and William Ernest Holmwood.

Brandt, Del. "Vinelander Recalls Working for Landis." *Vineland Times Journal* 7 August 1962: photocopy, n.p.

"Disinherited Sons to Unveil a Dark Past." *The North American*, 1900: clipping, n.p.

"Famous Will Case Closed." *Swayzee Press*, 20 February 1902: n.p.

"Fight for Fortune of Famed Founder." *New York Evening Telegram*, 6 December 1900: 6.

"Fighting for a Fortune." *New York Daily Tribune*, 30 November 1900: n.p.

"Fight for Landis Fortune Now Ended." *North American*, 11 February 1901: clipping, n.p.

"Fired on Lawyer in his Office." *Bridgeton Evening News*, 17 October 1907: clipping, n.p.

"Landis Case Before Courts Again." *North American*, 17 November 1917: clipping, n.p.

"Landis's Sons Disinherited." *New York Times*, 17 June 1900, retrieved from www.nytimes.com.

"Landis Will Case Decision." *New York Times*, 24 July 1901, retrieved from www.nytimes.com.

"Landis Will Contest." *New York Times*, 7 December 1900, retrieved from www.nytimes.com.

"Landis Will Contest." *New York Times*, 8 December 1900, retrieved from www.nytimes.com.

"Landis Will Sustained." *New York Times*, 28 December 1900, retrieved from www.nytimes.com.

Lieberman, Maggie. "Ex-Office Boy Recollects Landis as 'Kindly but Set.'" *Atlantic City Press* 3 August 1957: photocopy, n.p.

Los Angeles Herald 4 November 1907: 8, retrieved from chroniclingamerica.loc.gov/lccn/sn85042462/1907-11-04/ed-1/seq-8.

Stevens, Benjamin. "Memorial Address: Charles K. Landis Jr." *Vineland Historical Magazine*, January-April 1950: 83-86.

Unidentified article title, *Bridgeton Evening News*, 25 October 1907: clipping, n.p.

Unidentified article title, *Bridgeton Evening News*, 27 December 1907: clipping, n.p.

Unidentified article title, *Vineland Evening Journal*, 7 December 1907: clipping, n.p.

Unidentified article title, *Vineland Evening Journal*, 8 December 1907: clipping, n.p.

Unidentified newspaper clipping, 6 December 1900 from the VHAS archive.

Unidentified newspaper clipping, 30 June 1921 from the VHAS archive.

"Vineland's Founder Dead." *New York Times*, 13 June 1900, retrieved from www.nytimes.com.

Epilogue

Landis's last letter and clippings of newspaper accounts of Landis's death and burial are sourced from the archives of the Vineland Historical and Antiquarian Society.